Creating the
John Brown Legend

Creating the John Brown Legend

Emerson, Thoreau, Douglass, Child and Higginson in Defense of the Raid on Harpers Ferry

JANET KEMPER BECK

Foreword by RICHARD T. GILLESPIE

McFarland & Company, Inc., Publishers
Jefferson, North Carolina, and London

LIBRARY OF CONGRESS CATALOGUING-IN-PUBLICATION DATA

Beck, Janet Kemper, 1951–
Creating the John Brown legend : Emerson, Thoreau, Douglass, Child and Higginson in defense of the raid on Harpers Ferry / Janet Kemper Beck ; foreword by Richard T. Gillespie.
p. cm.

Includes bibliographical references and index.

ISBN 978-0-7864-3345-2
softcover : 50# alkaline paper ∞

1. Brown, John, 1800–1859—Public opinion. 2. Brown, John, 1800–1859—Influence. 3. Harpers Ferry (W. Va.)—History—John Brown's Raid, 1859—Public opinion. 4. Public opinion—United States—History—19th century. I. Title.
E451.B39 2009 973.7'116—dc22 2009009456

British Library cataloguing data are available

©2009 Janet Kemper Beck. All rights reserved

No part of this book may be reproduced or transmitted in any form or by any means, electronic or mechanical, including photocopying or recording, or by any information storage and retrieval system, without permission in writing from the publisher.

On the cover: Inset: detail of painting of John Brown by J.W. Dodge, ca. 1865, from the original picture taken from life; illustration of the Harpers Ferry insurrection, Captain Alberts' party attacking the insurgents, *Frank Leslie's Illustrated Newspaper*, 1859 (both images from the Library of Congress).

Manufactured in the United States of America

McFarland & Company, Inc., Publishers
Box 611, Jefferson, North Carolina 28640
www.mcfarlandpub.com

*To my underground railroad, Skip and James Beck, with love.
In you, I've found my North Star.
And
to my students in the Student Support Services program
at Appalachian State University.
Not a day goes by that you don't make me want
to be a better teacher, scholar and friend.*

When the sword glitters o'er the judge's head
And fear has coward churchmen silencèd,
Then is the poet's time, 'tis then he draws,
And single fights forsaken virtue's cause.
He, when the wheel of empire whirleth back,
And though the world's disjointed axle crack,
Sings still of ancient rights and better times,
Seeks suffering good, arraigns successful crimes.
— *Thoreau, quoting Andrew Marvell,*
John Brown's Memorial Service,
Concord, Massachusetts
2 December 1859

Contents

Foreword by Richard T. Gillespie — 1
Preface — 3

PART I: THE CATALYST: JOHN BROWN AND THE ASSAULT ON HARPERS FERRY

One: History's Version — 9
Two: John Brown — 19

PART II: THE PLAYERS

Three: Ralph Waldo Emerson — 29
Four: Henry David Thoreau — 42
Five: Frederick Douglass — 52
Six: Lydia Maria Child — 63
Seven: Thomas Wentworth Higginson — 81

PART III: THE VERBAL ASSAULT ON HARPERS FERRY

Eight: Literature's Version — 111
Nine: Epilogue — 151

Timeline — 165
Chapter Notes — 173
Bibliography — 191
Index — 203

Foreword by Richard T. Gillespie

Some twenty-five years ago, a well-meaning letter was sent to the *Martinsburg Journal*, the daily paper serving Harpers Ferry, West Virginia. Written by someone who lived away, the letter suggested that John Brown should be moved from his resting place at his farm near Lake Placid, New York, to a more suitable place at Harpers Ferry, where he had come to fame and martyrdom. Perhaps the writer meant to boost tourism in that nook of West Virginia, or perhaps just admired Brown. But Old Brown, Old *Man* Brown, Old *Devil* Brown, just cannot be laid to rest that easily, even in modern times. A veritable firestorm of letters descended on the editor of the Martinsburg paper. For days it went on, pro and con, but mostly vehemently against. As a seasonal National Park Ranger at Harpers Ferry National Park at the time, along with my colleagues I watched with intense interest. From all my experiences interpreting John Brown with visitors from around the land, I was not at all surprised at the response. John Brown was then, and is now still, one of the most controversial Americans ever to enter the nation's consciousness.

For in a very intense way, Brown represents something—he is an icon for *direct* action even to the point of focused, directed *violence*. In a day of national bombings, kidnappings, and other terrorist actions, this tack can only be controversial, however laudable the goal. Certainly, in the time of post-civil rights, post–9/11 consciousness, an armed attack on slavery will be seen more in light of its violent nature than its goal of unsettling the complacent majority in their acceptance of slavery.

It has been noted that, while the idea of America may be liberal or even radical, most Americans, busy with capitalistic endeavor, are conservatively focused on the need for a stable, level playing field. Those like Brown who would throw the understood stability out the window with radical action would seldom be acceptable, then or now. It is interesting to consider the moral dilemma Brown presents us; it is even more intriguing to see how those we most admire have responded to John Brown. Teddy Kennedy says that his brother, the president, had one book above all others from his studies of history that he loved—Stephen Vincent Benét's epic historical poem, *John Brown's Body*. Perhaps John F. Kennedy was taken with the famous passage that suggests Brown's inevitability—"*Sometimes there comes a crack in time*," writes Benét—but perhaps it was the provocation Benét provides us as those who would see positive change come. *Is* change just something that comes when its time has come? Or is it something that can be brought on by the actions of man?

Politicians, clergymen, writers, and reformers all wrestled with the idea of slavery in 19th century America. It was a long road to the Civil War and a long road to the emancipation that came with it. It took a sizable evolution in the thought patterns of Main Street America—Benét would certainly add something about a good dose of inevitability—for slavery to end. But in 1859, at just the moment that public attention was cast elsewhere, to the worst economic depression of the 19th century by that year, John Brown ignored the economy and took action against the moral ill of slavery. Such a resulting conundrum for those trying to come to terms with what would be best for the American "city on a hill!"

Philosopher-lecturer Ralph Waldo Emerson, philosopher-naturalist Henry David Thoreau, activist-reformer and former slave Frederick Douglass, children's author Lydia Maria Child and Unitarian minister Thomas Wentworth Higginson all had struggled with how to combat the ills and growth of the "peculiar institution" of slavery. Over the years, as slavery grew and grew and the patience of the South with Northern ideas of reform evolved to utter intransigence, Emerson, Thoreau, Douglass, Child and Higginson intensified in their hatred of slavery, and themselves became less patient and more willing to seek more effective means of action. We focus on these writers more for literary reasons. Yet with the exquisite moral compass each possessed, to view the moral dilemma presented by John Brown's actions in Kansas and his raid on Harpers Ferry through *their* eyes allows us a fascinating insight into changing thought in the North as the Great Rebellion neared. Too, how these veritable heroes of American literature grapple with Brown's action and its implications provides a back window into their own thinking.

Janet Beck has juxtaposed the moral struggle of Emerson, Thoreau, Douglass, Child and Higginson in a manner that allows empathy and the ability to contrast their responses. Seeing each in the light of Brown puts them in sharp focus—something that few of us want done to ourselves. Yet Brown *does* that—he confronts us, still, as he confronted antebellum America, and leaves us fascinated in our armchairs, but uncomfortable in our actions.

Richard T. Gillespie
Skye House
Taylorstown, Loudon County, Virginia

Historian Richard T. Gillespie is director of education for the Mosby Heritage Area Association of Northern Virginia and a former park ranger at Harpers Ferry National Park.

Preface

On 16 October 1859, John Brown and twenty-one followers seized the federal arsenal at Harpers Ferry, Virginia, and held it for thirty-six hours. The event stunned a nation already wearied from the Dred Scott decision, the passage of the Fugitive Slave Law and the border skirmishes in "Bloody Kansas." Early reaction to the raid ranged from indignant horror in the South to stunned disbelief in the North. Initially, almost no one defended Brown. Even William Lloyd Garrison's antislavery newspaper, *Liberator*, was surprisingly reticent on the subject. The defense of Brown was left largely to four men of letters: Ralph Waldo Emerson, Henry David Thoreau, Frederick Douglass and Thomas Wentworth Higginson. Galvanized by events in Virginia, they strongly defended Brown, a man they had come to regard, for varying reasons, as a friend. They were aided in this endeavor by Lydia Maria Child, who had never met Brown but whose antislavery sentiments led her to sympathize with the "brave old man" nonetheless. Prior to October 1859, each had supported Brown with their dollars. After the raid, they would provide influential support with their actions and words. This is the story of how the staid Unitarian Emerson, the gentle naturalist Thoreau, the articulate ex-slave Douglass, the earnest young minister Higginson, and the matronly children's author Child, came to defend John Brown and his historic act of violence against the United States government.

An examination of press reports immediately after the raid, those appearing while Thoreau, Emerson, Douglass, Child and Higginson mounted their spirited defense as well as materials published after their intervention, illustrates the full extent of their public relations campaign on Brown's behalf and the profound effect his literary friends had on public opinion. If one could characterize Brown in twenty-first century terms as a domestic terrorist, then one could certainly describe these writers as incredibly effective "spin doctors." Nowhere in modern times, the availability of widespread media notwithstanding, can one find a more effective campaign than theirs. The events at Harpers Ferry, as interpreted by these litterateurs over the course of several months, provide a glimpse into a time when literature and history collided and literature rewrote history.

I confess that, years ago, when I began this project, I did not set out to write about John Brown's raid at Harpers Ferry. I wanted to leave *that* story—summed up in the first part of this book—primarily to the historians, "the tools to those who can use them." In principle, I agreed with Child, who said, "Others may spend their time in debating whether John Brown did wrong or not; whether he was sane or not...." And Brown's story *has* been ably told—from the earliest biographers, James Redpath, Franklin Sanborn, and Osborne Anderson, all friends of Brown, all with a decided point of view, through Oswald Villard's more objective, comprehensive biography in 1910 and historian Stephen B. Oates' Brown biographies of the 1970s (*To Purge This Land with Blood: A Biography of John Brown* and *Our Fiery Trial: Abraham Lincoln, John Brown and the Civil War Era*), to the latest well-researched effort by David Reynolds, *John Brown: Abolitionist*—historians have attempted to understand, analyze, or explain the most famous homegrown terrorist in American history. But while I find Brown fascinating (who could not?), my primary interest lies with the *second* draft of the events at Harpers Ferry—the revised story of the raid orchestrated and crafted not by Brown or his raiders, but by a small group of similarly brave (or equally foolish, depending on your point of view) men and women. Were it not for *their* interpretation of events, Brown might very well have been lost to history—a footnote at best, a period at worst. As it is, we continue to discuss Brown, we *debate* Brown—in spite of the fact that the 19th century American press was initially quite willing to dismiss him out of hand as a "lunatic"—largely because his literary friends redeemed, restored, *rewrote* his reputation. They recast Brown's acts at the ferry in terms of noble goals, high aims and sanctified purpose. Brown wasn't "insane," his five defenders scoffed; rather, he was a martyr for a holy cause whose execution "will make the gallows glorious like the cross." Slowly and steadily, a new Brown emerged from the ashes, and it was a resurrected, almost unrecognizable Brown who rose from the debacle of the engine house through the words of these American writers.

One of my trusted mentors, Grace McEntee, told me once that a preface defines the emotional reason for the book. To explain the *why* of this book, you need to understand another character—not Brown, but an equally slender, impassioned, bearded prophet-of-sorts who from an early age captured my affections—Henry. I first met Henry in high school, perhaps passed him in the hall with a nodding glance; but it wasn't until I took an undergraduate summer seminar in Concord, Massachusetts, with the esteemed Thoreau scholar Walter Harding that I really came to know him. Slightly awed (a *lot* awed), I and my fellow students read Harding's seminal biography, *The Days of Henry Thoreau* (although we chuckled at Harding's preferred title, *The Daze of Henry Thoreau*). We read the variorum *Walden* edited (of course) by Harding, a dog-eared copy of which still sits on my bookcase. Soon, I was immersed in all things Thoreau, as absorbed in his writings as I had been by the chilly waters of Walden Pond on a skinny dipping field trip under the blanket of the starless night sky.

Several years later, in graduate school, over pizza and beer (as all ridiculously impractical plans are born), I decided to leave my eastern North Carolina university, and briefly "sojourn" in Concord to research a textual problem on Thoreau in the singular collection of Thoreau's writings at the Concord Free Public Library. I would (I thought) write the paper of my career. Instead, I returned from my excursion to find a department chair (who would later become a dean) less than impressed. "You have shirked your assistantship duties," he informed me shortly before he had me tossed out of the graduate program. But that debacle did little to quell my relationship with Henry. In the curious and contrary ways of the young, it only served to stoke my passion. I continued my occasional jaunts to Concord and before long I had journeyed down Cambridge Turnpike to meet Waldo. Initially, I enjoyed him as you would any friend of an acquaintance (any friend of Henry's...), and I eagerly read through his journals seeking entries on my first love. Ah, I marveled, Henry visited Waldo on such and such a date, Henry house-sat while Emerson traveled, Henry built a cabin on Waldo's land, etc. Soon, however, and largely through the work of Len Gougeon, who illuminated Emerson's antislavery efforts, I became personally acquainted with, as Louisa May Alcott called him, "the great man of the town." Before long, I had devoured most of Gougeon's work on Emerson: "Abolition, the Emersons and 1837," *Virtue's Hero*, "Emerson and Abolition," *Emerson's Antislavery Writings*. Through Gougeon's eyes, I discovered Emerson, a man of substance, a man with considerable financial obligations, and a man who was willing to risk his substantial reputation to right a wrong. And yes, I now had someone vying with Henry for my affections, a second entry into my pantheon of heroes.

It was not until I returned for a more successful stint in graduate school many years later that I was introduced to the third member of what would one day become a quintet—Frederick Douglass. Through a series of classes taught by Bruce Dick, a professor at Appalachian State University, whose enthusiasm for African American literature equaled or surpassed mine for the transcendentalists, I devoured the slave narratives of Douglass, stunned by the stark stories told by one for whom reading was against the law. At this point, at Bruce's encouragement and under his direction, I paused to write a thesis on the heroic and adventurous public relations campaign of Emerson, Thoreau and Douglass in their defense of Brown. The world needed, I thought, more people like these three who would stand up for what they believed to be right, people of principle who would have subscribed to the words on a bumper sticker in my office: SPEAK YOUR MIND, EVEN IF YOUR VOICE SHAKES. That thesis became an early draft of the book you hold in your hands.

By the time I finished graduate school, I had met not only Frederick but also Lydia Maria Child, who tartly informed her southern correspondent Mrs. Mason (wife of Senator Mason of Virginia, no less) that "here in the North, after we have helped the mothers in childbirth, we do not *sell* the babies." I was enchanted. A suggestion by John Higby in the English Department at Appalachian State University led me to Thomas Wentworth Higginson, whose passion for writing was overshadowed only by his absolute fearlessness in defending a cause, a man who spent his life waiting for "one occasion worth bursting the door for" and found it in Brown.

I am grateful to a number of scholars whose work preceded mine and who furthered my friendship with my characters, people who made it a joy for me to be stuck so much of the time in the nineteenth century. A particular thanks is due Richard Gillespie, who took a group of Thoreau Society members in the chill of the March night air from the Kennedy farmhouse to the damp, dark engine house several years ago at Harpers Ferry. By the flickering candlelight, as I glanced at the faces of my fellow "raiders," John Brown became more than an enigma to me.

Other scholars deserve special mention as well:

On Thoreau: thanks to Sandy Petrulionus, whose article "'Swelling That Great Tide of Humanity: The Concord, Massachusetts, Female Anti-Slavery Society" introduced me to the fascinating women of Concord and their antislavery activities. She has, I understand, a new book, *To Set This World Right: The Antislavery Movement in Thoreau's Concord*, which expands upon her earlier research and which fellow Thoreauvians are finding fascinating. On Frederick Douglass: I gleaned a great deal from the work of Benjamin

Quarles, including *Blacks on John Brown, Allies for Freedom, Black Abolitionists*, etc. I also learned a considerable amount from William McFeely's biography, *Frederick Douglass*. On Child: I am grateful to Carolyn Karcher "down the road apiece" at Duke University for her scholarship and to Deborah Clifford for her biography, *Crusader for Freedom: A Life of Lydia Maria Child*. On Higginson: Tilden Edelstein, Anna Wells and Mary Thacher Higginson provided valuable biographical insights. A special thanks is due Wentworth for conscientiously writing his mother and thereby preserving details of many of his adventures for future generations. (There is a moral here, James.) Always, of course, I am indebted to Henry, Waldo, Frederick, Maria and Wentworth for leading such extraordinary lives, folks who, unlike many of their fellow travelers then or now, did not "when [they] came to die, discover that [they] had not lived." My greatest challenge in telling their stories was simply to, as much as possible, step aside and let them speak.

I am immensely grateful and hugely indebted to the literary alpha and omega of this project, Bruce Dick and Grace McEntee. Bruce launched this endeavor and helped from the outset to chart my course, while Grace, with her tireless, exceptional editing through many final drafts, steered it safely home. Without them, there would be no book.

To the following librarians and libraries without whom I would have been lost: Sean Casey and the staff at the Boston Public Library Rare Books and Manuscripts Room (with a particular thanks to Barbara Davis, who helped me over the span of several years with unflagging good humor and patience), the Massachusetts Historical Society, the American Antiquarian Society in Worcester, Leslie Perrin Wilson of the Concord Free Public Library, and Jack Love, at Appalachian State University's Belk Library and Information Commons, who jokingly told me there would be a seismic shift in the building once I completed my research and returned all of my overdue books. In addition, I would like to thank the following collections and curators for the visual images in the book: Jeff Cramer at the Thoreau Institute in Walden Woods, Richard Raymond, museum curator at Harpers Ferry National Park, the Library of Congress Prints and Photographs Division, Nancy Sherbert at the Kansas State Historical Society, Leslie Perrin Wilson and Constance Manoli-Skocay of the Concord Free Public Library, Elaine Grublin at the Massachusetts Historical Society, John P. Maranto, curator of Archives and Small Objects at the B&O Railroad Museum, Lori Hanssen Davis at the Wayland Historical Society, Leianne Neff Heppner, curator of the Summit County Historical Society, and Sean Casey and the Boston Public Library/Rare Books Department. This book is richer for their efforts.

On a personal note, I have many folks to thank. Len Gougeon graciously read and commented upon an earlier draft of this work, as did Bruce Dick, Grace McEntee, Emory Maiden, Philip Stark (at the Emerson house), Richard Gillespie, Don Jewler, Adam Griffey, Jim Kemper, Nancy Rattan, Skip Beck, James Beck, Cathia Silver and Cama Duke. Thanks largely to your encouragement, I kept writing. There are two graduate students whose research and editing talents made a difference, as did their friendship: Adam Griffey and Suzanne Ingram—I owe you. A thank you is due as well to my friends and family, whose personal support sustained me through countless drafts: Skip Beck, James Beck, Jim Kemper, Susan Perry, Harriette Buchanan, Eugenia Kaledin, Traci Royster, Virginia Munroe, Ed Gaither, Gary Nemcosky and Nancy Rattan. I am also grateful to my two Barbaras (Finan and Anthony) for graciously opening their homes to me during my research trips to Massachusetts. To my mom and dad, Jo and Warren Kemper, who sent me to that summer seminar in Concord so many years ago (although they could ill afford it) and ignited my life's work—I wish so much that you could be here to read this book.

Without the financial support of the following individuals and organizations at Appalachian State University my research trips would not have been possible. I am deeply grateful to the Office of International Programs, the English Department, the Learning Assistance Program, the Student Support Services Program, the Office of Academic Affairs, the Hubbard Center for Faculty and Staff Development, and the Cratis D. Williams Graduate School. Particularly, I would like to thank Edelma Huntley and the graduate school for a University Research Council grant, a graduate student research grant, and monies from the Cratis D. Williams Thesis Award. Kathy Isaacs at the Hubbard Center graciously shared her knowledge about copyrights and permissions and thereby helped me navigate an alien world—my deepest thanks. I also greatly appreciate the support (both financial and moral) of Dr. Jeanne Dubino in the English Department and Dr. Dave Haney in the Office of Academic Affairs (although Dave's own research interests are right century, wrong continent—just kidding). Finally, for their editorial assistance, a special thanks to Sandy Ballard, Harriette Buchanan, Heather Wright and Skip Beck.

And so, as Walter Harding once introduced me to a friend of his and changed my life, I invite you to step into my world peopled with characters of intrigue, courage, passion and, above all, principle. As Wendell Phillips cabled Higginson upon the arrest of fugitive slave Anthony Burns, "You'll *come*, of course...."

Part I

The Catalyst: John Brown and the Assault on Harpers Ferry

One

HISTORY'S VERSION

> The committee find[s] ... that the armory and other public works of the United States were in the possession and under the control of this hostile party for more than thirty hours; that ... they resisted by force the lawful authority of the United States sent there to dispossess them, killing one, and wounding another of the troops of the United States.... They killed in the streets three of the citizens of Virginia who were alone and not even in military array, beside the negro who was killed by them on their first arrival.[1]
>
> *Report of the Select Committee of the U.S. Senate on the Events at Harpers Ferry, Virginia*

On the morning of Sunday, 16 October 1859, there was little reason to suppose that the day would be different from any other for residents of Harpers Ferry. Citizens of the small town nestled between the Shenandoah and Potomac rivers would be getting ready for church services and prayers. It would not surprise these residents that the farmer they knew as Isaac Smith, new to the area since July, also began the day with prayers. As Smith's small group of twenty-one followers worshipped, they heard selections from the Bible on the evils of slavery and concluded their service with an impassioned prayer for God's assistance in the liberation of slaves closer to home. After breakfast, they quietly began preparations to move revolvers, rifles and pikes to a nearby schoolhouse in preparation for their evening raid on the federal arsenal at Harpers Ferry.[2] The man leading the worship service was in fact not Isaac Smith but John Brown. Before the day was out, Brown's name and that of the quiet village would become a part of history.

The rest of the October day passed quietly. At eight o'clock that evening a horse and wagon were driven to the door and the wagon was loaded with pikes, a sledgehammer and a crowbar. Leaving his son Owen with F.J. Merriam and Barclay Coppoc to guard the schoolhouse and its contents, Brown signaled the others to follow him.[3] Somberly, those leaving shook hands with those who remained in what nearly all believed to be a final farewell.[4] In the chill damp air, by the light of the moon, with weapons hidden so as not to attract attention, the men began walking the six mile journey to the federal arsenal "solemnly as a funeral procession."[5] Charles Tidd and John Cook went first, disabling telegraph wires as they went.[6] As the group stepped onto the bridge over the Potomac at half past ten, a watchman, peering into the night by the light of his lantern, approached and was taken prisoner. At first thinking it a joke, and later pleading for his life, he was told not to fear, that the group had come only to free the slaves. Another of Brown's sons, Watson, was left with Stewart Taylor to guard the bridge. They were given instructions to stop any visitors with their wooden pikes, a quieter solution to the problem of intruders than the rifles the group also had in their possession. The remainder of the men proceeded to the engine house, where they encountered a second watchman. Trembling with fear, the watchman refused them entrance, even with a gun pointed to his head, so they opened the gates forcibly with their crowbar and took their second prisoner of the evening. Shortly, the group encountered a third watchman, who accompanied them, either in sympathy or fear, "without hesitation."[7]

Brown's trusted lieutenant, John Kagi, an unbrushed, unshaven and disheveled man, was stationed with John Copeland at the armory while the prisoners were secured in the engine house. Brown's son Oliver, with the help of William Thompson, took possession of the main bridge leading out of town over the Shenandoah River.[8] Thus, in the dark of night, without a single shot fired, and with no alarm having been raised, John Brown and his twenty-one men quietly took possession of the federal arsenal at Harpers Ferry.

This photograph, circa 1862, shows the Harpers Ferry Armory with the engine house on the left. During the raid, the small structure would be crammed with existing equipment, the raiders and up to forty of their prisoners (Historic Photo Collection, Harpers Ferry National Historic Park).

With the arsenal secure, attention turned to procuring hostages from the town. Not one to overlook a symbolic gesture, Brown directed A.D. Stevens, Osborne Anderson, Charles Tidd and Shields Green, along with John Cook and Lewis Sherrard Leary, to take Colonel Lewis W. Washington, a descendant of founding father George, as the first captive and bring him to the ferry.[9] A.D. Stevens and Osborne Anderson were told to retrieve from Colonel Washington a sword previously owned by Frederick the Great and a pair of horse pistols once belonging to General Lafayette, which had been presented to him by George Washington. Dutifully, with lighted torches, the armed men knocked on Washington's door at midnight. When no one answered, they entered and searched his house. Taking the speechless Washington prisoner, Stevens asked the black Anderson to step forward and receive the precious sword into his hands, in accordance with Brown's specific instruction. Then, with the wails of the women echoing throughout the house, they secured Washington, placed him in his own wagon along with several male slaves, and proceeded to the home of a neighbor.[10]

John Allstadt awoke to sounds of a fence rail battering his front door and cries of "murder" from the women of the house. After learning he was to be taken prisoner, Allstadt "hesitated, puttered around, fumbled and meditated"[11] for as long as possible before being gathered with his son and six of his male slaves into the wagon with Colonel Washington.[12] Washington and Allstadt were then taken into the engine room at the ferry, where they remained under guard. Upon meeting Brown, Washington was told that perhaps he could be released in exchange for a "Negro man as a ransom."[13] Around this time, an armed contingent of insurrectionists, including five or six recently appropriated slaves, returned to the farmhouse to move additional arms to the school located less than a mile from the ferry. On the way, they seized a man named Byrne, who was added to the growing number of prisoners. As the night progressed, a total of between thirty and forty prisoners would join Washington and Allstadt in the engine house.[14]

The first shot of the evening was fired when Patrick Higgins, a watchman coming to work, was wounded for refusing to surrender. At this point, around 1:25 A.M., the Baltimore & Ohio mail train steamed into Harpers Ferry on its usual run and approached the bridge. As it attempted to cross, Higgins climbed on board and told the story of his attack. The engineer and the baggage handler tried to investigate, but they were deterred by four rifles pointed in their direction. Haywood Shepherd, a black baggage master, came out of the station looking for the missing watchman. He, too, was ordered to halt but kept going and was shot, receiving a mortal wound in the back. It is probable that he was much like Higgins, who claimed, "I didn't know what 'halt' mint [sic] then any more than a hog knows about a holiday."[15] Thus, in one of the great ironies of the raid, the first man to be killed was a free black man.

At three A.M. Brown gave permission for the train to proceed. The engineer, however, would not take the train across the bridge in the dark. It was daylight before the train continued its journey and 7:05 A.M. when it stopped at Monocacy and there sounded the alarm. Conductor Phelps telegraphed Baltimore that 150 insurrectionists had "come to free the slaves and intend to do it at all hazards." Further, he reported, "The leader of those men requested me to say ... that this is the last train that shall pass the bridge either East or West ... [and] you had better notify the Secretary of War at once." The message seemed so extraordinary that the reply read "Your dispatch is evidently exaggerated and written under excitement" and posed the question "Why should our trains be stopped by Abolitionists?" Nonetheless, by ten-thirty that morning U.S. President James Buchanan, Governor Henry A. Wise of Virginia, and Major General George H. Stewart of the First Light Division, Maryland, had all been notified of the insurrection.[16]

Two or three miles distant, as the sun rose on the largely unsuspecting village, the men of Harpers Ferry began their trek to work. As the men arrived for work, Brown's party began seizing them until, by their own count, there were close to forty prisoners. The townsmen "were gobbled up ... and marched to prison, lost in astonishment at the strange doings and many, perhaps, doubting if they were not yet asleep and dreaming."[17] The previously captured slaves were given pikes and told to guard the incredulous prisoners, which they did. Brown ordered Lewis Sherrard Leary, four slaves, and a free black to join Kagi at the rifle factory. George Mauzy wrote his daughter in England of events, saying, "This has been one of the saddest days that Harper's Ferry ever experienced. This morning when the armorers went to the shops to go to work, lo and behold, the shops had been taken possession of by a set of abolitionists and the doors were guarded by Negroes with rifles."[18]

It was late morning before the public became aware of the trouble in their midst. At eleven o'clock Brown sent word to his men at the farmhouse that he had peacefully taken the town and instructed them to continue with their moving. By the time the messengers could return to the ferry, however, word of the insurrection had spread. With it, so did panic, and "men, women and children could be seen leaving their homes in every direction...."[19] The growing sense of dread was not confined to the spectators. Brown announced to prisoners Whelan and Williams his plans, saying, "I came here from Kansas, and this is a slave state; I want to free all the Negroes in this state...."[20] The hostages were terribly frightened and asked permission to go home to see their families, for final farewells. Permission was granted and armed guards escorted the captives home and back again. During one of these expeditions, citizens fired upon Edwin Coppoc, an insurgent, but missed. Fire was returned and the sniper was shot.[21] Shortly, the townspeople received help from neighboring Charlestown, eight miles away, and Martinsburg, twenty miles distant. Men from these communities, bearing whatever weapons they could command had formed "military bands" and hurried to Harpers Ferry. As the day progressed, much drink was consumed and rifle shots could be heard ringing through the air.[22]

Brown, white beard flowing, with Colonel Washington's famous sword at his side, commanded his men. "The troops will look for us to retreat on their first appearance; be careful to shoot first," Brown urged. Although there was a surfeit of rifles about, Brown clung stubbornly to the famous sword as his lone weapon. Pikes, taken out of the wagon, were placed into the hands of the recruited slaves. As the troops came across the bridge within firing range, Brown cried, "Let go upon them!" Once the firing began, the militias retreated to await federal reinforcements. In the fire, Dangerfield Newby, a black insurrectionist, was shot through the head from a nearby house. Shields Green, another black raider, returned fire and killed the "cowardly murderer" before the latter could get his gun back through the sash.[23] Newby, whose motivation for joining the raid was to free his slave wife and seven children, became the first of Brown's men to die. Lying in the street for several hours, he would become fodder for a group of hogs that happened upon an unexpected meal.[24] Nearly as brutal was his treatment by the local citizenry who

As word of the raid spread, angry citizens in Virginia and Maryland rushed to Harpers Ferry to protect their neighbors. This wood engraving by "Porte Crayon" (David Hunter Strother) appeared in *Harper's Weekly*, 26 November 1859 (Library of Congress, Prints and Photographs Division).

An unknown artist captured the scene at Harpers Ferry as citizens took potshots at raiders Leeman and Thompson as they attempted to swim to safety. Leeman made it to an islet, at which time a citizen waded out and shot him in the head. Thompson was shot and thrown into the river, where some of the drunken citizens used his body as target practice until, full of lead, he sank (Kansas State Historical Society).

cut off bits of his ears for souvenirs and then kicked and beat his lifeless corpse.[25] Shortly, William Thompson, returning from the farm, was surrounded and captured. Later in the day, he was shot and thrown into the river, where some of the drunken citizens used his body for target practice until eventually, full of lead, he would sink.[26]

Late morning came and with it increased hunger among the prisoners. Brown sent out for food from the nearby Fouke's Hotel. "In exchange for 45 breakfasts," Brown released bartender Walter Kemp.[27] Once the food arrived, neither Washington, Allstadt, or Brown would touch it, fearing foul play.[28]

Around two or three that afternoon, Kagi realized the situation was fast becoming hopeless and sent word to Brown that they must all leave at once. Brown insisted that they hold on a few moments longer. Those few minutes that Brown chose to delay were extraordinarily costly, however, as during this time federal troops under the command of Colonel Robert E. Lee and Lieutenant J.E.B. Stuart arrived, blocking any hope of escape. After another hour of fierce fighting, Brown sent his son Watson outside with a truce flag. The flag was ignored and Watson was mortally wounded. He was able to get back inside where he lingered until the next day, his moans echoing throughout the arsenal. Edwin Coppoc later wrote, "I pulled off my coat and put it under him and placed his head in my lap, and in that position he died."[29] William Leeman made a dash into the cold waters of the Potomac in an attempt to swim to the Maryland shore. A sea of bullets followed and he was forced to take shelter on an islet. A local citizen waded

The scene in the Engine House shortly before Marines stormed the building: On the left are the hostages, including Col. Washington, descendant of founding father George. The picture accurately depicts the well-stocked weaponry of the raiders. The illustration appeared in *Frank Leslie's Illustrated Newspaper* 5 Nov. 1859 (Library of Congress, Prints and Photographs Division).

through the water and shot him in the head at point blank range. Leeman's body, like Thompson's, became a "target for the undisciplined militia and townspeople."[30]

An hour and a half later, A.D. Stevens went out with a flag, at which time he was wounded and captured. Jeremiah Anderson fell next on his way to deliver a message to Kagi.[31] Shortly Kagi and Lewis Leary ran out of the back of the rifle works, wading into the river, where they were shot to death by local townspeople. John Copeland attempted to flee with them, but was hauled ashore where the excited mob was so determined to lynch him that "some of his captors [had] already knotted their handkerchiefs."[32] He was saved by Starry, a local doctor, who prevailed upon his townsmen to jail him instead.[33] The wounded Leary lingered until the next day, but lived long enough to give an interview to newspaper reporters in which he begged them to write to his wife.[34]

With his ranks shriveling, Brown attempted to negotiate his release and that of his men in exchange for the release of the prisoners, an offer that was rejected. Instead, the Virginia militia demanded the immediate release of the prisoners in exchange for a judicial resolution to the event rather than a military one. Brown stubbornly refused and the cold, damp and altogether dismal night in the engine house began. Throughout the

A Porte Crayon rendering of John Brown lying injured on the floor of the engine house beside his son. Hostage Col. Washington would later report that John Brown "was the coolest and firmest man I ever saw in defying death and danger. With one son dead by his side, and another shot through, he felt the pulse of his dying son with one hand and held his rifle with the other, and commanded his men with the utmost composure" (Library of Congress, Prints and Photographs Division).

long night, Brown remained awake, calling out to his men to keep them alert. In the city streets, by contrast, many of the townspeople used the night as an occasion for celebration. The Wager House bar and Gault House Saloon reported record business.[35]

By early Tuesday, only Brown and four of his men were left to defend the engine house; the others lay dead or dying, including two of Brown's sons. The men who had remained at the farm fled. Shields Green was captured and would later be executed. Oliver Brown escaped as did F.J. Merriam and John E. Cook.

At sunrise, Lieutenant Israel Green ordered his men to break down the door to the armory. Later, Colonel Washington described events inside as troops battered the heavy wooden door, saying John Brown "was the coolest and firmest man I ever saw in defying death and danger. With one son dead by his side, and another shot through, he felt the pulse of his dying son with one hand and held his rifle with the other, and commanded his men with the utmost composure ... to sell their lives as dearly as they could."[36] Shortly, the door burst open and Lieutenant Green repeatedly struck at Brown's head with his sword. Insurrectionists Jeremiah Anderson and Dauphin Thompson were killed. One Marine was fatally shot and another severely wounded. Brown was carried outside where he lay on the ground bleeding.[37]

After his capture, an additional 200 Sharps rifled carbines, 200 revolver pistols still in boxes, 1,000 pikes, thousands of percussion caps, ammunition, and a large supply of gunpowder were confiscated. When the troops entered the building, they found the sword of Frederick the Great, formerly belonging to George Washington, lying on a fire engine.[38]

And thus it was that, by the time Thoreau raised his voice to defend Brown as "an angel of light," the blood of ten men lay on his hands.[39]

Two

JOHN BROWN

There was no inkling of the terrible violence yet to come when, in 1812, forty-seven years before the raid on Harpers Ferry, an adolescent John Brown drove a herd of cattle one hundred miles from his Hudson home in the Ohio country on a trip that would profoundly change his life. Arriving at his destination, he stayed with a family who had a slave his own age. The two boys became friends but, as young Brown was quick to notice, they were treated quite differently. While Brown enjoyed a great deal of freedom, his friend was "badly clothed, poorly fed; & *lodged in cold weather*: & beaten before his eyes with Iron Shovels or any other thing that came first to hand." It was a lesson that would make John Brown a "most determined abolitionist" and one that would help drive him to the desperate acts at Harpers Ferry, Virginia.[1]

The man who would raid the federal arsenal was, by most people's standards, a failure. At various times he had attempted "tanning, surveying, and farming; ... he was shepherd, cattleman, wool merchant, and postmaster; for a while he bred race horses and speculated in real estate."[2] He succeeded at none of those things. Yet, Brown was, by all accounts, a man of principle and faith, a man who loved his family, and a man who abhorred slavery. So passionate was Brown on the subject that he deeply inculcated that belief in his children as well, leading biographer David Reynolds to maintain that "[t]he clan raised by John Brown was the only white family in pre–Civil War America willing both to live with black people and to die for them."[3] Frederick Douglass viewed Brown with similar lens. "I have talked with many men, but I remember none, who seemed so deeply excited upon the subject of slavery as he," he wrote.[4] In fact, over time, Brown would come to believe slavery an "egregious 'sin against God,' a sin that violated the commandments of an all-wise, all-powerful Providence...."[5] It was, perhaps, this passion for justice rooted in his deep religious faith, coupled with a propensity for ill-advised ventures, that would lead Brown to the raid on Harpers Ferry. Ironically, it was there that he would find his most noteworthy success, embedded in the ruins of his most spectacular failure.

Brown's early efforts to help slaves were modest in scope. One unrealized plan involved getting "at least one Negro boy or youth, and bring[ing] him up as we do our own."[6] Fifteen years later, Brown moved his family to North Elba, New York, on acreage purchased from Gerritt Smith, who provided 120,000 acres of land for settlement by black families. In a letter to his father, Brown wrote, "There are a number of good colored families on the ground; most of whom I have visited." He concluded, "I can think of no place I would sooner go ... than to live with those poor despised Africans to try, & encourage them...."[7] The family did in fact live happily for two years as the only white people in the region.

PART I: THE CATALYST

By the time he met Frederick Douglass in 1848 Brown believed that slaveholders were unworthy to live, although outwardly he projected only an image of calm concern for those less fortunate than himself.[8] Douglass was immediately impressed by Brown, who was a determined and imposing figure. Samuel Lawrence, a business acquaintance, would later say Brown was "rather above medium height—thin, gaunt and withy; his hair cut short all 'round; face marked with will, compressed lips, looking like one of Oliver Cromwell's best captains."[9] Brown's stern countenance was no doubt enhanced by his increasing disgust with, and concern over, slavery. Determined to do all he could to abolish the institution, Brown sought a location in the slave states from which he might rescue slaves through a series of guerilla-like raids and set them quickly on their way to Canada. He settled on the mountains, believing that "throughout history" their natural geographic advantages had "enabled the few to defend themselves against the many...."[10] Before long he had confided to Douglass his plans for a "black state in the Appalachian Mountains."[11] Brown also apprised others of his plans, including Thomas Wentworth Higginson, who would one day write, "I never shall forget the quiet way ... [Brown] once told me that 'God had established the Alleghany Mountains from the foundation of the world that they might one day be a refuge for fugitive slaves.'"[12]

By 1855, Brown was apparently unable to subdue his feelings on the slavery question, telling an acquaintance that he "would prefer a dissolution of the Union to a continuance of slavery." His friend was so shocked by this radical pronouncement that he "requested him to leave, and ... never saw him again."[13] Around this same time Brown's interest was captured by events in Kansas, where a struggle for the state's sympathies was being fiercely fought. With the enactment of the Kansas-Nebraska Act in May 1854, the territory opened to settlement, and persons on both sides of the slavery question came intent on calling it their own. Not surprisingly, Kansas soon became a literal battleground. Northern newspapers were replete with "glowing accounts of the extraordinary fertility, healthfulness and beauty of the Territory," as well as "urgent appeals to all lovers of freedom who desired homes in a new region to go there as settlers, and by their votes save Kansas from the curse of slavery."[14] It was an offer that

John Brown is beardless in this portrait, much as he appeared when Henry David Thoreau and Ralph Waldo Emerson met him during his first visit to Concord in 1857. The photograph was taken between 1840 and 1850 (Kansas State Historical Society).

ultimately Brown couldn't resist—a new opportunity full of promise, far from the scenes of his numerous business failures that simultaneously provided a venue in which to fight slavery.

Brown, however, initially hesitated about making the move, perhaps reluctant to leave his wife and daughters and his home in the Adirondacks. As he pondered what his course of action should be regarding Kansas, he told his children that he had written Frederick Douglass asking his advice.[15] Meanwhile, Brown's sons Owen, Frederick and Salmon moved into Kansas Territory, arriving in the fall of 1854. Brothers Jason and John Jr. followed in the spring. For the Browns, it was a costly decision. On the trip west, cholera claimed Jason's four-year-old son, Austin.

Once in Kansas, Brown's sons lived in tents until they could construct shelter. "[N]early all our number were prostrate with fever and ague that would not stay cured," John Brown Jr. later wrote, adding, "The grass we cut for hay, mouldered in the wet for want of the care we could not bestow...."[16] Notwithstanding their noble suffering, the antislavery settlers were having little success in keeping Kansas a free state. On 30 March 1855, an election was held for the territorial legislature. Missourians crossed the border in great numbers "in wagons and on horseback, well armed with rifles, pistols and bowie knives, and two pieces of cannon loaded with musket balls" to cast their votes illegally.[17] The result was the election of a pro-slavery legislature which shortly enacted a series of laws against antislavery activists. The new legislation made it a felony to speak or write against slavery, and anyone guilty of running off slaves would be found guilty of "grand larceny." Furthermore, no antislavery person could sit on a jury. Throughout the spring and summer of 1855, local settlers "repudiated this fraudulently chosen legislature and refused to obey its enactments." Increasingly, it appeared to the Brown brothers that war was "inevitable."[18]

As they often did in times of trouble, the boys turned to their father for aid. On 6 October 1855, after receiving a letter from John Jr. describing the desperate need for arms to fend off pro-slavery forces in the area, Brown, with son Oliver and son-in-law Henry Thompson, joined his struggling sons in Kansas.[19] Once there, he quietly set about helping to make their homestead livable and began tending to their animals.

It was not long, however, before Brown participated in much darker acts in the interests of antislavery. If his raid on Harpers Ferry would come as a surprise to local townspeople and federal troops, it was less so to those who had known Brown in Kansas. John Brown moved to the territory intent on defending the interests of those wishing to see Kansas remain free, but that freedom came with a price. It was there he participated in the murders of five men at Pottawatomie, an incident that would forever tarnish his reputation.

On 22 May 1856, John Brown, his sons, and a group of like-minded citizens headed towards Lawrence in Kansas Territory to defend the town from the ongoing general unrest in the area. They were stopped en route with news that "two newspaper offices [had been] destroyed; their presses, books and papers thrown into the river; the Free State Hotel bombarded by cannon and set afire; and the home of Charles Robinson [a Free State leader] razed."[20] After months of unrest, Lawrence had been sacked by what historian James Ford Rhodes called a "swearing, whiskey-drinking, ruffianly horde" whose stated purpose was to serve "arrest writs against Free-State men who had been indicted for 'contructive treason' by a pro-slavery grand jury."[21]

James Townsley, a friend of Brown's, anticipated further trouble in the region, saying, "We expect to be butchered, every Free State settler...." Brown responded: "Now something *must* be done. We have got to defend our families and our neighbors as best we can." Increasingly agitated, he continued: "Something *is going to be done now.*" Theodore Weiner chimed in with news that pro-slavery men had ordered him to leave the area twice over the course of the last several days, adding that he did not intend to "stand such treatment much longer." Talk then turned to "some radical retaliatory measure—some killing...." As the morning wore on, Brown's sons John Jr. and Jason proceeded to sharpen some "odd-shaped cutlasses" Brown had brought west with him. At least one man, worried that things might be getting out of hand, went to Brown and urged caution. Brown replied, "I am eternally tired of hearing that word caution. It is nothing but the word of cowardice."[22]

Around two o'clock that afternoon Brown, four of his sons (Owen, Frederick, Salmon and Oliver), and son-in-law Henry Thompson, along with Theodore Weiner and James Townsley, armed with rifles, revolvers, knives and broadswords, departed for Pottawatomie. As they rounded the crest of a hill, a man approached on horseback with delayed word of the assault on Senator Charles Sumner by pro-slavery congressman Preston Brooks of South Carolina. With that, Jason Brown remembered, "the men went crazy—*crazy*. It seemed to be the finishing, decisive touch."[23]

That night the men camped about a mile above Dutch Creek. The next day the band rested upon their arms in the open air waiting for the cover of darkness. Around eleven P.M., armed with pistols and knives, the men approached the Doyle cabin. Once inside, they informed the family that they were from the army and that Mr. Doyle and his sons must surrender. The husband was led outside followed shortly by the two boys, William and Drury, aged twenty and twenty-two. Mrs. Doyle pleaded tearfully for the life of her youngest son, John, and he was spared. Meanwhile, outside, Brown shot Doyle in the forehead while John Jr. and Salmon Brown began hacking the sons with their swords. John Jr., Salmon and Henry Thompson afterwards swore that Brown did not kill Doyle, but shot him after he was already dead. Townsley, also a witness, disagreed. In any event, three men lay dead. Mahala Doyle testified that the next morning she went in search of her family and found her husband with a bullet wound in the head. Nearby was her dead son William with his head cut open, a knife wound in his jaw and a hole in his side. Drury was found by his surviving brother near a ravine with his fingers and arms cut off, his head cut open and a hole in his breast.[24]

The band's next stop was the home of Allen Wilkinson, a member of the state's pro-slavery legislature. Brown's men asked, "Are you a northern armist?" When Wilkinson replied, "I am," he was told, "You are our prisoner ... open the door."[25] He stalled, saying he needed to get a light. At this point the marauders threatened to break down the door and Wilkinson, relenting, let them inside. Four men entered and told him to dress. Mrs. Wilkinson unsuccessfully pleaded with the men to let her husband stay. Unwilling to wait until Wilkinson put on his boots, the armed band took him out into the night. The next morning he was found 150 yards from his home, his throat cut twice.[26]

With four men dead in the grass, Brown, not yet finished, proceeded to the home of James Harris. Around 2:00 A.M. the unsuspecting Harris was asleep with his wife and child when a knock came at the door. Upon opening it, he looked into the face of John

Brown and his son Owen, whom he recognized. Both men were armed with sabers and revolvers. Brown and his men, announcing that the northern army had arrived, took Harris outside to question him. Peppered with questions about his political inclinations and slavery leanings, Harris finally convinced the men he came to Kansas for the high wages rather than for any political purpose. Escorting Harris back inside, Brown next took out William Sherman, who was spending the night at the Harris homestead after having purchased a cow earlier in the day. After fifteen minutes the nighttime visitors left. The next morning Harris found Sherman near his house with his left hand cut off, his skull split open in two places and his brains washed out into the water.[27]

Their work finally finished, Brown's party proceeded back to camp, their swords, "unmannerly breached with gore," rinsed in the waters of Pottawatomie Creek.[28] For the rest of his life, Pottawatomie would be problematic for Brown who, for many years, chose simply to deny to friends and followers his involvement in the brutal murders. Years later, John Brown, Jr., would attempt a defense, saying that up until this time antislavery settlers had chosen to turn the other cheek to the violence perpetrated by their pro-slavery counterparts. But ultimately the Brown family came to the conclusion that Kansas would not be saved until "her relentless foes came to realize that they were to receive death for death." "It was ... resolved," therefore, "that they, their aiders and abettors, who sought to kill our suffering people, should themselves be killed, and in such a manner as should be most likely to cause a restraining fear," John Jr. explained.[29] Certainly, the brutal murders elicited fear, but they also resulted in widespread condemnation. For while it is accurate that the majority of the violence was committed by pro-slavery settlers, it is also true that only eight pro-slavery settlers were murdered outside of battle during this period and that five of those were killed during Brown's raid at Pottawatomie.[30]

Mahala Doyle, whose husband and two sons were slain, later maintained that her family moved to Kansas "where there would be no Slave labor to hinder white men from making a fair days wages...." Further, she asserted that the family had "never owned any Slaves, never expected to, nor did not want any...."[31] In spite of Mahala's implication that the Browns had killed innocent men, John Brown, Jr., insisted that "The men my Father caused to be put to death were of the sort ... who would be found on their farms quietly at work during the day, but at night would mount their horses, and ride twenty miles to saw the timbers of a rail-road bridge, thus letting down to destruction not only our troops, but women and children who perished by a common death...."[32] Regardless of whose story is believed, the horrific murders without a doubt shocked the community, and the events at Pottawatomie drove all of Brown's men, other than Jason and John Jr., who had not participated, underground.

While in hiding, Brown gained a reputation for guerilla warfare.[33] During the summer following the events at Pottawatomie, Brown committed a series of "bloody guerrilla attacks" along the Missouri-Kansas border.[34] On 2 June, he attacked and defeated two dozen Missourians under the command of a deputy U.S. marshal. This time, Brown had no taste for violence, instead choosing to hold the Missourians captive in exchange for an equivalent number of Free Soil prisoners.[35] Two of his sons, John Jr. and Jason, previously taken prisoner, were released by this agreement.[36]

On 30 August 1856, Brown again encountered pro-slavery forces, this time at

Osawatomie. After learning one of his sons had been killed in an attack on the small settlement, Brown and his band of thirty-five fought fiercely against "decidedly superior numbers," but eventually had to retreat. The settlement was then torched by the victors.[37] Brown wrote his wife of the tragedy:

> On the morning of the 30th Aug. an attack was made by the ruffians on Osawatomie numbering some 400 by whose scouts our dear Fredk. was shot dead without warning he supposing them to be Free State men as near as we can learn.... I was about 3 miles off where I had some 14 or 15 men ... that I had just enlisted to serve under me as regulars. These I collected as well as I could with some 12 or 15 more & in about ¾ of an hour attacked them from a wood with thick undergrowth. With this force we threw them into confusion for about 15 or 20 minutes during which time we killed & wounded from 70 to 80 of the enemy *as they say it* then we escaped as well as we could with one killed while escaping; two or three wounded; & as many more missing. Four or five Free State men were butchered during the day in all. Jason fought brave by my side....[38]

By fall, a new governor, John W. Geary, restored a measure of peace in the battle-ravaged state and Brown decided to leave Kansas. Henry Thompson, Salmon and Oliver,

This image shows Free-State prisoners including George W. Brown, John Brown, Jr., Jedge Smith, Charles Robinson, Gaius Jenkins, Mr. Williams and George W. Deitzler. The men were arrested by Pro-Slavery forces in "Bloody Kansas" during the fierce fighting over Kansas' admission to the union as a free or slave state (Kansas State Historical Society).

tired of the fighting, had left in August. By October, Brown, John Jr., Owen and Jason had moved into Iowa.[39] "[Brown] leaves the States, *with a feeling of deepest sadness,*" Brown wrote, "after having exhausted *his own small means*, and with his *family and his brave men*; suffered hunger, cold, nakedness, and some of them sickness, wounds, imprisonment *in irons ... and others death*...."[40] Brown's party, "after lying on the ground for months in the most sickly, unwholesome, and uncomfortable places; *some of the time with sick and wounded* destitute of any shelter; and hunted like wolves; sustained in part by Indians" suffered substantially for a cause that "every citizen of this '*glorious Republic*' is under equal moral obligation to do...."[41]

It was a powerful appeal, designed no doubt to evoke guilt and open the purses of the armchair abolitionists in New England, and, in fact, in early 1857 Brown made his way to Boston where he persuaded a number of influential men to provide resources for the aid of Kansas while asking very few questions. Through most of the summer months, the guerilla warrior now found himself immersed in fund-raising in the East. It was during one such trip that he met Ralph Waldo Emerson and Henry David Thoreau. By November Brown had returned to Kansas for a brief stay. Realizing a calm had settled on the region and there was not much work to be done, he began formalizing plans for a raid on Harpers Ferry. Heading East, he stopped once again in Concord.[42] He also spent several weeks with Frederick Douglass in Rochester and apprised him of his plans.[43] When Hugh Forbes, a British mercenary hired by Brown to train recruits, leaked word of his impending Harpers Ferry plans, Brown was forced to delay the insurrection for a year. In the meantime, he led a raid in Missouri, liberating a dozen slaves and escorting them to Canada. For this act, President James Buchanan put a price of $250 on his head. Brown, with uncharacteristic humor, responded that he would give $2.50 for Buchanan's.[44]

By 1859, it was clear that Brown no longer considered a political resolution to the slavery question viable. Slavery, he felt, would not be crushed except through violent means.[45] Feeling secure that no one had taken Forbes' warnings seriously, Brown was ready to attack the federal arsenal. He would be assisted, in part, by ten men he had recruited for the task while in Kansas, including his son Owen.[46]

Brown instigated his plan by moving his tiny band to the Kennedy farmhouse outside the town of Harpers Ferry. In the guise of a farmer, he "bought a horse that turned out to be blind, a small wagon, a cow, a mule and some pigs. These, with a mongrel dog, presented to the Captain by a neighbor's boy ... constituted the live stock of the place."[47] Day after day during the long summer months, the men hid out at the farm, often in the tiny, hot attic. Brown's daughter would later state, "We were in constant fear that people would become suspicious ... and we were all so self-conscious that we feared danger when no man pursued or even thought about it."[48] The bane of their existence was Mrs. Huffmaster, a nosy neighbor and "veritable thorn in the side of the band" who would frequently stop by for an unannounced visit, on more than one occasion coming close to unraveling their plans.[49] As the weeks rolled by, tedium was often the men's worst enemy and Brown attempted to keep his recruits occupied "reading magazines, telling stories, arguing politics and religion, and playing checkers and cards."[50] In addition, they practiced frequent drills and studied military manuals in preparation for the raid.[51] As the long days passed, the men grew increasingly frustrated and Brown realized that he could not wait forever. The time had come for the culmination of his life's work.

Part II

The Players

Three

RALPH WALDO EMERSON

Unlike Thoreau, Douglass, Child, or Higginson, Ralph Waldo Emerson was not, by temperament or philosophy, a reformer. A quiet and gentle man, he saw himself as a scholar and poet, roles to which he felt well suited. "The office of the scholar is to cheer, to raise and to guide men," he wrote: "It becomes him ... to defer never to the popular cry."[1] Thus, he was loath to give his support to reformers, whom he saw as "[m]admen, madwomen, men with beards, Dunkers, Muggletonians, Come-outers, Groaners, Agrarians, Seventh-day-Baptists, Quakers, Abolitionists, Calvinists, Unitarians and Philosophers...."[2] Certainly, the early days of the abolitionist movement did seem to attract an array of lively personalities—Charles Burleigh with his "long curls on his shoulders [and] ... rather ill-trimmed beard,—in a beardless period," and "Father Lamson [with his] white habiliments and white beard."[3]

Indeed, as Thomas Wentworth Higginson wryly observed, "To the occasional policeman present, for whom the abolitionists themselves seemed as much lunatics as their allies, the petty discrimination of putting out only the craziest must have appeared an absurdity...."[4] Emerson concurred with this sentiment, noting in his journal that abolitionists are "an altogether odious set of people, whom one would be sure to shun as the worst of bores & canters."[5] But, however reluctant Emerson may have been to associate himself with a reform movement or reformers in general, he keenly felt pressure from friends and family who embraced the abolitionist cause. Also, like many in his time, he felt propelled by historic events beyond his control. From the murder of abolitionist publisher Elijah Lovejoy to the passage of the despised Fugitive Slave Law, Emerson was profoundly influenced by the unsettling events around him. The combination of social pressure from those closest to him, his growing influence as a prominent American writer and speaker and the correspondent sense of duty this position engendered, and his belief that historical events compelled a response from moral men finally propelled Emerson into the abolitionist crusade and, ultimately, to the defense of Captain John Brown.

While Emerson may have been slow to embrace abolition as a cause, he was the product of a family with strong sympathy for the oppressed. As early as 1798, Emerson's father, William, helped maintain the Smith School in Boston that offered free education for "colored children of both sexes."[6] His aunt, Mary Moody Emerson, of whom he was quite fond, was active in the early antislavery crusade of the 1830s and 1840s, as was his step-grandfather, the Reverend Ezra Ripley.[7]

Emerson's early views of slavery would be shaped by these familial influences as well as by William Ellery Channing, a well-known Unitarian minister of great reputation and a teacher while Emerson was at Harvard. As early as 1835, in *Slavery*, Channing condemned the practice, saying, "The first question to be proposed by a rational being is, not what is profitable, but what is Right."[8] While the work would bring searing criticism from other Unitarian clergy, Emerson praised it in his journal as one of the "perfectly genuine works of the times."[9] Undeniably, however, Channing advocated a conciliatory approach to the slavery question: "How slavery shall be removed, is a question for the slave-holder, and one which he alone can fully answer."[10] Further, Channing cautioned, "[o]ur danger is that we shall substitute the consciences of others for our own," advice that Emerson would assimilate.[11] In spite of Channing's moderate views on the question, he was one of very few ministers to publicly acknowledge the slavery issue. At the time, the churches, along with almost every other organization, closed their doors to the abolitionist movement. "Not a minister—excepting Dr. Channing, and the one in Pine Street Church—would even venture to read a notice of an anti-slavery meeting."[12]

Emerson's earliest personal involvement in the antislavery cause can be traced to his pulpit at the Second Church in Boston. In his first sermon, entitled "Pray Without Ceasing," Emerson mentioned the blight of slavery. Further, at a time "when all the pulpits were silent on the subject of slavery," Emerson courageously invited abolitionists, including Samuel May and Arnold Buffum to share his pulpit.[13]

As the young Emerson began the slow progression from Unitarian minister to transcendental lecturer, he came to a number of conclusions which profoundly influenced his thinking and which he would hold for the rest of his life. These included the importance of the individual, the human's capacity for achievement, and the notion of self-reliance and moral responsibility. These same beliefs, however, would also make it increasingly difficult to join a single-issue reform movement that relied on the power of group protest to achieve its aims. Throughout the 1830s these themes were developed in his public addresses, published essays (*Nature* in particular), and private journals.[14] In 1837, Emerson was asked to deliver an address at the Phi Beta Kappa club at Harvard. In it, he advocated aca-

Ralph Waldo Emerson was not, by temperament or philosophy, a reformer. Yet, increasingly, he felt himself "heart-sick" over the plight of the slave. In an 1844 address, he described "men's backs flayed with cowhides, [and] runaways hunted with bloodhounds." He concluded: "The blood is anti-slavery: it runs cold in the veins: the stomach rises with disgust, and curses slavery." Of all Brown's defenders, Emerson's wealth and position of influence made him a formidable and hugely influential spokesman on Brown's behalf (Library of Congress, Prints and Photographs Division).

demics leaving their studies to make themselves useful to the world. It was good advice during the tumultuous times, but counsel that Emerson himself would find difficult to embrace.

In 1835, Emerson married Lidian Jackson and moved to Concord, Massachusetts. With both the marriage and the move, Emerson placed himself in closer proximity to abolitionist sentiment. Concord was a hotbed of abolitionist activity and a well-known stop on the Underground Railroad. The two local newspapers, the *Yeoman's Gazette* and the *Concord Freeman*, were both pro-abolitionist and inundated the local citizenry with over 125 articles on the slavery question between 1835 and 1837.[15] Throughout the 1830s, William Lloyd Garrison's *Liberator* was regular reading in Emerson's household.[16] Emerson noted in his journal that while Concord hosted the likes of Webster, Garrison and Phillips it also had "shows and processions, conjurors and bear-gardens, and even Herr Driesbach with cats and snakes."[17] It was this mixture of absurd and gravitas that allowed one older resident of Concord to conclude that outsiders tended to view Concord's residents as "very queer."[18] For all that, Emerson would soon come to be "recognized by all as the chief pride and ornament of that little town...."[19]

That Emerson was feeling abolitionist pressure in his new environment is evidenced by a wry journal comment in which he complained that in Concord "every third man lectures on Slavery."[20] In fact, one of those lecturers was his younger brother Charles, who delivered a speech in Concord on 29 April 1835 denouncing slavery and calling for the immediate emancipation of the slaves.[21] Even while Charles was preparing the public address, Emerson was wrestling privately with the issue in his journal. He noted on 16 April 1835 that the slavery question is "one on which he may exhaust his whole love of truth,—his heart & his mind. This is one of those causes which will make a man."[22] And, when he was invited in 1837 to lecture at the Salem Lyceum the following winter with the stipulation that "The subject is of course discretionary with yourself [as long as] no allusions are made to religious controversy or other exciting topics upon which the public mind is honestly divided," he declined. "I am really sorry that any person in Salem should think me capable of accepting an invitation so encumbered," he wrote.[23] Later, Emerson resolved his differences with the Lyceum and lectured there, on *his* terms, for forty consecutive seasons.[24]

While Emerson obviously realized the importance of the slavery question, and passionately supported free speech, he would remain ambivalent about pouring his energies into a social movement. During an 1838–1840 lecture series entitled "The Present Age," Emerson adhered to his developing sentiment that "the movements of the early nineteenth century can be explained as the awakening of the individual."[25] In these lectures one sees the tension between the individual and society, conflicting ideas that would haunt Emerson's efforts to move toward reform. Further complicating Emerson's position was his conviction, common in his day, of the inferiority of the African race, a belief in stark contrast with the transcendental notion that one could rise above circumstances by individual effort. The extent to which this caused Emerson conflict can be seen in a journal passage dated 2 December 1836: "I think it cannot be maintained by any candid person that the African race have ever occupied or do promise ever to occupy any very high place in the human family." Yet, even while he harbored questions concerning racial differences, he continued to be tormented by his inaction on the slavery question. In a 24 November 1837 passage, he wrote, "When a zealot comes to me & represents the importance of this Temperance Reform my hands drop—I have no excuse—I honor him with shame at my own inaction. Then a friend of the slave shows me the horrors of Southern slavery—I cry guilty guilty!"[26]

The passage is interesting in that Emerson uses the language of religion to describe a social movement. The reference to "zealots" is indicative of Emerson's continued sense of discomfort with the emotionality of reform. Intertwined with the unease, however, is the clear sense of guilt. Further compounding Emerson's problem was the fact that, increasingly, friends of the slave were friends of his as well.

Lidian harbored no such ambivalence about the slavery question. When the abolitionist sisters Angelina and Sarah Grimke spent a week in Concord in the fall of 1837, Lidian entertained them and from that point forward she dedicated herself to antislavery, saying, "I think I shall not turn away my attention from the abolition cause till I have found whether there is not something for me personally to do and bear to forward it."[27] She was true to her promise. Over time, she became a "zealous member" of the Anti-Slavery Society, hosting meetings, taking an active role in Concord reform activities, and entertaining numerous abolitionists, including the prominent Wendell Phillips.[28] The abolitionist fit was a good one for Lidian, who throughout her life held great sympathy for the less fortunate.

It was not as comfortable a match for her husband, who wrote in a 2 February 1835 journal entry: "Though the voice of society should demand a defence of slavery from all its organs that service can never be expected from me." Yet, even while resisting a public stand, he admitted, "I do not wish to live in a nation where slavery exists."[29] Again, Emerson distances himself from the communal "voice of society." However, his guilt, his growing belief in the black man's essential humanity, or his simple fury over the murder of the Reverend Elijah P. Lovejoy, the abolitionist publisher, drove Emerson in November of 1837 to break his long silence and address the slavery question publicly for the first time.

Emerson was particularly vexed and unsettled by Lovejoy's murder, an attack that he viewed as an assault on free speech. In his journal, he described Lovejoy as heroic, a man who would willingly "die for humanity & the rights of free speech & opinion."[30] Emerson's concern over the muzzling of open debate is apparent in an address he delivered in the Second Church in Concord. "I regret to hear that all the churches but one, and almost all the public halls in Boston, are closed against the discussion of this question. Even the platform of the lyceum, hitherto the freest of all organs, is so bandaged and muffled that it threatens to be silent," he said.[31]

While advocates of free speech could not help but be pleased, his comments that day concerning slavery were more problematic. "When we have distinctly settled for ourselves the right and wrong of this question, and have covenanted with ourselves to keep the channels of opinion open, each man for himself, I think we have done all that is incumbent on most of us to do," he maintained. "Sorely as we may feel the wrongs of the poor slave in Carolina or in Cuba, we have each of us our hands full of much nearer duties."[32]

Abolitionists, expecting a fiery outburst after the simmering of so many years, were sorely disappointed. The speech reflected much of the ambivalence Emerson still felt on the slavery question, focusing primarily on the abolitionists' rights to free speech. In much the manner Channing recommended, Emerson expressed sympathy for both the slaveholder and the slave.[33] "Let our own evils check the bitterness of our condemnation of our brother, and, whilst we insist on calling things by their right names, let us not reproach the planter, but own that his misfortune is at least as great as his sin."[34] If the address was a disappointment to the antislavery community, it also clearly was not satisfying to Emerson, who would not address the slavery issue again for another seven years.

And yet, his fury over Lovejoy's murder smoldered. In Boston during the winter of 1838 he gave a stock speech on Heroism and had his "cultivated Boston hearers [in] full sympathy," when, near the end, he suddenly stopped, looked out at the audience and added, "It is but the other day that the brave Lovejoy gave his breast to the bullets of the mob for the rights of free speech and opinion and died when it was better not to live." At this point, Emerson's son Edward later noted, a "cold shudder ran through the audience at the calm braving of public opinion...."[35]

Presumably in response to his wife's urging, Emerson made another public statement about oppression in 1838, when in an open letter to President Martin Van Buren he expressed outrage at the forced relocation of the Cherokees.[36] Lidian felt strongly about this issue. In a letter to her friend Lucy Jackson Brown dated 23 April 1838, she wrote, "[O]ne month from to-day the Cherokees old & young—sick and well—are to be forcibly dragged from their homes by *harpy* government contractors...." Lidian then described a meeting held in Concord at which "Mr. Emerson made the first address; stating the case and reading to the assembly the 'Appeal of the Cherokees.'" She added, lest there be any mistake, "He also expressed his sentiments on the subject very decidedly." In concluding, she referred Lucy to "the 'Liberator' or some other paper which contains the 'Appeal.'"[37] Yet while Lidian took great joy in her husband's public pronouncement, Emerson did not, as he indicated in his journal:

> Yesterday went the letter to V[an] B[uren] a letter hated of me. A deliverance that does not deliver the soul.... this stirring in the philanthropic mud, gives me no peace.... I fully sympathise, be sure, with the sentiment I write, but I accept it rather from my friends than dictate it. It is not my impulse to say it & therefore my genius deserts me, no muse befriends, no music of thought or of word accompanies. Bah![38]

Regardless of Emerson's personal feelings, the "Appeal on Behalf of the Cherokees" is considered a significant milestone in Emerson's reform consciousness. It is his first public response to an injustice occurring outside his immediate sphere.[39] Lidian was aware of the significance of this event. In her letter to Lucy Brown, she writes with obvious pride: "Did you hear that Mr. E's letter came out in the Intelligencer (National) the very day or the day before it was published here?" She also notes that "Dr. [W.E.] Channing and Mr. [Wendell] Phillips honoured us with a long call last Wednesday."[40]

In spite of Emerson's defense of the Cherokees, throughout the late 1830s and early 1840s he refused to be drawn into the slavery controversy. Nonetheless, aware of his growing reputation and the significance attached to his public appearances, Emerson attended abolitionist gatherings in Concord and elsewhere and was apparently generally impressed.[41] "To all meetings held in Concord for the cause of Freedom, spiritual or corporal, he felt bound to give the sanction of his presence whether the speakers were good or bad," his son wrote.[42] Regardless of that, Emerson refused to become a member of a reform group. Unlike his wife, he would never join an abolitionist society, although several organizations urged him to do so.[43] Part of his reluctance might be explained in an 1842 journal entry in which he wrote that he preferred persons like his friend Judge Hoar, "strong & worthy persons ... who support the social order without hesitation or misgiving. I like these: they never incommode us by exciting grief, pity, or perturbation of any sort." But having said that, in a further indication of his internal conflict, he added, "my conscience[,] my unhappy conscience respects that hapless class who see the faults & stains of our social order and who pray & strive incessantly to right the wrong...."[44]

Notwithstanding his personal ambivalence, he supported Lidian in her continued discussions concerning abolition and women's rights.[45] She, in turn, continued to exert an influence on Emerson's developing social consciousness. In Concord, "abolitionism was predominantly women's work" and it was "largely through these outspoken women sharing their homes that Concord's famous men came to accept leading roles in the fight against slavery."[46] The *Concord Freeman* went so far so to say, "The truth is, *men* have faltered and have failed in their duty touching this matter of slavery," concluding therefore, that the movement needed greater numbers of women.[47]

In March of 1844, Emerson gave a speech at Armory Hall in Boston in which he acknowledged the growth of reform movements. In his remarks, he conceded that most reforms empower the individual, providing a "growing trust in the private self-supplied powers of the individual."[48] But he reminded his audience that "no society can ever be so large as one man" and he urged an "inward" union, to be accomplished by the "reverse of the methods" most reforms use. He also could not resist having a bit of fun at the expense of reform, citing "a society for the protection of ground-worms, slugs and mosquitos...."[49]

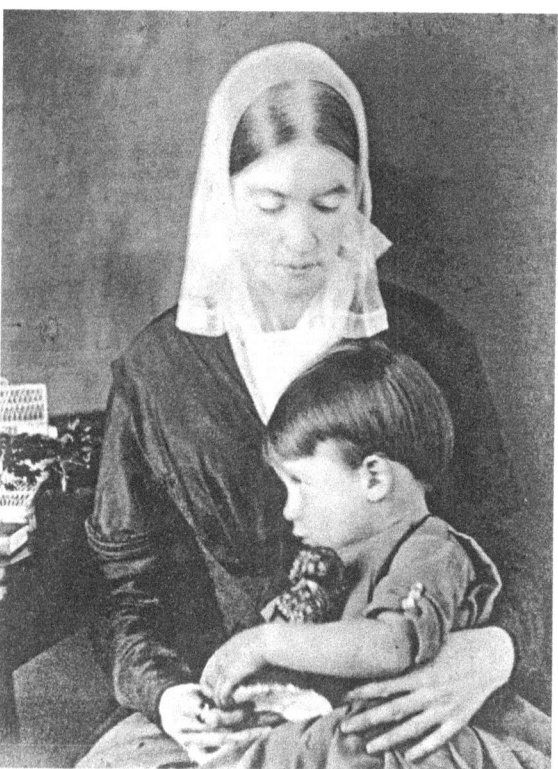

As Emerson struggled with the communal nature of social movements and attempted to reconcile that with his transcendental views concerning the power of the individual, Lidian continued to nudge her husband in the direction of reform. Most scholars accept that she likely played a role in Emerson's return to the antislavery stage in his 1844 speech "Address on the Emancipation of the

Emerson's wife, Lidian, may look motherly in this 1847 photograph taken with son Edward, but she was a powerful influence in bringing Emerson into the abolitionist fold. Always less ambivalent than her husband about antislavery, on 4 July 1855, she draped her home in black to protest the state of the union (courtesy Concord Free Public Library).

Negroes in the British West Indies." Each year in Concord the Female Anti-Slavery Society (to which Lidian and the Thoreau women belonged) celebrated the anniversary of the British abolition of West Indian slavery. In 1844, Emerson was invited to speak at the event and gave the keynote address, sharing the platform with Samuel Joseph May and Frederick Douglass.[50] The day was rainy and tables had to be arranged in the courthouse to accommodate the participants. Permission to use the churches had been denied as had the use of "Sleepy Hollow" cemetery. Nathaniel Hawthorne offered the beautiful, tree lined grove of the Old Manse, but rain prevented an outdoor gathering. "Notwithstanding the unpropitious aspect of the morning," wrote one attendee, "thirteen towns were represented among the audience that assembled to hear the address from Mr. Ralph Waldo Emerson."[51]

In preparation for the speech, Emerson privately and extensively studied the history of slavery, reading firsthand of the injustices against the slave.[52] In the address, Emerson argued that the emancipation of Jamaica's slaves was the result of a series of legal battles dating back to the 18th century.[53] Perhaps more important than the argument itself, however, was the tone of the piece. The speech was eloquent and put to rest forever the image of a faltering Emerson engendered seven years before. In the 1 August speech, Emerson describes himself as "heart-sick" over the plight of slaves. He depicts "the slave-ship ... in whose filthy hold [the slave] sat in irons, unable to lie down; bad food, and insufficiency of that; disfranchisement; no property in the rags that covered him; no marriage, no right in the poor black woman that cherished him in her bosom,—no right to the children of his body...." While Emerson's research is apparent in his detailed description of the plight of the slave, so is an empathy heretofore missing in his comments on the subject. After describing the whipping of "old men ... tender women; and, undeniably, though I shrink to say so,—pregnant women" and describing "men's backs flayed with cowhides, [and] ... runaways hunted with blood-hounds," Emerson railed: "The blood is moral: the blood is anti-slavery: it runs cold in the veins: the stomach rises with disgust, and curses slavery."[54]

The speech was an overwhelming success both in terms of attendance and reception. In the audience, both men and women were moved to tears as Emerson described the plight of the slaves. The abolitionist community, who viewed the address as Emerson's entry into their movement, was overjoyed. Abolitionist journals, including the *Liberator*, *Herald of Freedom*, and *Emancipator*, praised the speech.[55] Emerson himself was more ambivalent about its significance. Although he worked long hours composing it and chose it as one of the few antislavery speeches to be published in his lifetime, he was still uncomfortable with this foray into the world of social reform. Shortly after the address he wrote his friend Thomas Carlyle: "Though I sometimes accept a popular call, & preach on Temperance or the Abolition of slavery, as lately on the First of August, I am sure to feel before I have done with it, what an intrusion it is into another sphere & so much loss of virtue in my own."[56]

Thus, while social pressure continued to force Emerson into the public eye, he persisted in viewing these efforts as diversions from his central role as a scholar and a poet. As with the 1837 address, Emerson was quick to point out the nature of the speech as a "popular call," somehow a diversion from his primary mission. Further, he refers to the talk not as a lecture, but as the result of a call to "preach." Prior to the speech, Emerson had written John Greenleaf Whittier, an active abolitionist: "I am almost ready to promise you as soon as I am free of this present coil of writing, my thought on the best way of befriending the slave & ending slavery."[57] Again, the expectation was that the real work, the "present coil of writing," would come first and then, as time permitted, Emerson would attend to the discussion of slavery. Edward Emerson explained: "As the agitation went on, the calls were more frequent, and often against all his instincts and desires he left his study and his pine grove to attend meetings where was little to console him."[58]

Perhaps the elder Emerson might have continued to take refuge in his pines, but in November of 1844, his friend Judge Hoar traveled to South Carolina with his daughter Elizabeth at the request of the governor of Massachusetts. Their official mission was to protest the seizure and imprisonment of free blacks from northern ships entering southern harbors. Emerson was very close not only to Judge Hoar, but to his daughter as well—Elizabeth had been engaged to Emerson's brother Charles and after his death continued to remain in the Emerson family fold. The trip south was a disaster and ended with the Hoars fleeing South Carolina in fear for their safety. Emerson was infuriated by their expulsion. Taking up his pen on 17 December, he wrote a letter to Horace Greeley of the *New York Daily Tribune* describing details of the incident and expressing his admiration for Hoar's bravery. In January, Emerson took part in a protest concerning the treatment of the family at the hands of the citizens of South Carolina. In his remarks, he castigated South Carolina for excluding "every gentleman, every man of honour, every man of humanity, every freeman from its territory."[59] In addition, he signed a petition in opposition to the annexation of Texas.[60]

The new year found Emerson once again forcefully defending free speech, this time in his native Concord. In 1845, members of the Concord Lyceum resigned to protest a speaking invitation to the famous abolitionist orator Wendell Phillips. Emerson, along with Thoreau, forcefully defended Phillips's right to speak.[61] Earlier, Emerson had made a similar stand against inequality when he refused to speak at the New Bedford Lyceum because blacks were refused membership, an act for which Frederick Douglass later praised him.[62] The fact that Emerson aligned himself with Charles Sumner on this issue strengthened public perception that he was willing to be associated with "reformers and firebrands."[63] The Massachusetts Anti-Slavery Society passed a formal resolution on 29 January praising this act of courage which read, in part, "Charles Sumner and Ralph Waldo Emerson ... deserve the warmest thanks ... and we rejoice that [their action] comes from a quarter, which must strike a strong blow against the prejudice of color...."[64] The resolution in full would be printed in the 6 February edition of the *Liberator*.

Nonetheless, philosophically Emerson continued to struggle with the notion of social reform. Scholar Len Gougeon notes that Emerson, even after trading in the pulpit for the lectern, continued to view slavery as an issue of individual morality rather than as the province of a collective social movement.[65] However, in spite of his philosophical disengagement, historical events and social pressure continued to influence Emerson. In the 1840s, throughout New England support for the abolitionist movement grew. In Concord, Emerson's friends Henry Thoreau, Bronson Alcott and Frank Sanborn held antislavery sentiments. By mid-decade, with the annexation of Texas, concern increased about the power of the slave states. The advent of the Mexican War in 1846 and the resulting acquisition of new potentially pro-slavery territories intensified these concerns.

Slowly Emerson inched towards the abolitionist fold. When in August of 1845 Emerson was invited to give a speech once again at the anniversary of West Indian emancipation, he agreed. It was the second of Emerson's major antislavery addresses, and he would give it to a large audience in Waltham, Massachusetts, comprised of citizens from Boston, Concord and surrounding areas. The following year, he gave a third speech at the 1 August 1846 anniversary, as well as an address on 4 July in Dedham to help raise money for antislavery lectures throughout the state.[66]

In July, Thoreau refused to pay his poll tax to support the war, culminating in his night in the Concord jail. Emerson's reaction to the episode is revealing. He confided to Alcott that he viewed Thoreau's action as "mean and skulking and in bad taste."[67] In his journal Emerson commented, "Don't run amuck against the world.... As long as the state means you well, do not refuse your pistareen."[68] Further, Emerson noted, "it is worth considering that refusing payment of the state tax does not reach the evil so nearly as many other methods within your reach. The state tax does not pay the Mexican War. Your coat, your sugar, your Latin & French & German book, your watch does. Yet these you do not stick at buying."[69]

A legend would grow out of Emerson's encounter with Thoreau over this incident. Supposedly, Emerson asked his friend why he went to jail. Thoreau is said to have replied, "Why did you not?"[70] Whether or not the event occurred, the story aptly illustrates the positions of the two friends on the slavery question. Emerson thought, while his transcendental pupil Thoreau acted. Emerson's continued inaction in the face of his friend's growing abolitionist activity must have been uncomfortable. Emerson later amended his opinion of Thoreau's protest, conceding that Thoreau's position was stronger than that of abolitionists who opposed the war but did nothing.[71] "My friend Mr. Thoreau has gone to jail rather than pay his tax," he wrote. "On him they could not calculate." He then concluded: "The abolitionists denounce the war & give much time to it, but they pay the tax."[72] Emerson might have been including himself in that assessment.

September of 1846 would see Massachusetts return an unidentified slave to the South. In response, a citizens' meeting of protest was called. Emerson did not attend the meeting at Faneuil Hall presided over by John Quincy Adams.[73] However, indignant at the treatment of Sims, and furious over the encroachment of southern slavery into his beloved Massachusetts, Emerson wrote the committee. "If I could do or say anything useful or equal to the occasion, I would not fail to attend the meeting on Thursday. I feel the irreparable shame to Boston of this abduction," he began. "If it shall turn out, as desponding men say, that our people do not really care whether Boston is a slave-port or not, provided our trade thrives, then we may, at least, cease to dread hard times and ruin," he averred. "It is high time our bad wealth came to an end. I am sure, I shall very cheerfully take my share of suffering ... and shall very willingly turn to the mountains to chop wood, and seek to find for myself and my children labors compatible with freedom and honor."[74] While this might be a facile declaration for some, it was a courageous threat for someone of Emerson's resources, who by 1850 was one of the wealthiest men in Massachusetts. Shortly, defending the rights of fugitive slaves to freedom in Massachusetts would become less an academic exercise and more a personal imperative as Emerson's neighbor and close friend Bronson Alcott harbored a fugitive slave in his home from December 1846 through mid–January 1847 and most likely again in February 1847.[75]

With the new decade came the passage of the Fugitive Slave Law as part of the Compromise of 1850, in which California was admitted to the union as a free state. The bitter underside of the compromise demanded that fugitive slaves, when captured, be returned to their owners, even those from the free states. This provision infuriated many Massachusetts citizens, who felt they were being asked to enforce a law in which they did not believe. Also abhorrent to many was the fact that the law denied the testimony of runaways, assumed guilt rather than innocence, and impacted fugitives who had been living as free men and women for years.[76] In his journal Emerson called the law a "filthy enactment ... in the 19th Century, by people who could read & write" and vowed, "I will not obey it, by God."[77] Emerson was angry not only over the law itself, but infuriated and heartsick over Massachusetts senator Daniel Webster's support of it. He was also aware that a number of New Englanders approved of the compromise.[78] Perceiving a dearth of men of courage willing to speak eloquently for the abolitionists' side, he resolved to fill the vacuum. In his first Fugitive Slave Law speech of 3 May 1851, "Address to the Citizens of Concord," Emerson charged that "[t]he last year has forced us all into politics, and made it a paramount duty to seek what it is often a duty to shun. We do not breathe well. There is infamy in the air."[79]

The episode was a particularly painful one for Emerson as Webster had been "an idol of his youth." But once Webster "turned his back on anti-slavery principles," Emerson began to publicly admonish him in speeches, although Webster was still so beloved that attacking him publicly carried a risk. While giving one such speech in Cambridge, Emerson was "interrupted by the outcries and groans of young Boston Southern sympathizers...."[80] Nevertheless, he continued, saying, "Nobody doubts that Daniel Webster could make a good speech. Nobody doubts that there were good and plausible things to be said on the part of the south." But, he concluded, "this is not a question of ingenuity, not a question of syllogisms, but of sides. How came he there?"[81]

With the passage of the detested Fugitive Slave Law, Emerson seemed to find a niche for the educator he saw himself to be. With Webster's defection, with men of perceived intellect enacting these laws, Emerson envisioned a need for someone who could argue convincingly for the slave from both the head and the heart. The law continued to profoundly disturb Emerson, who "woke in the mornings with a weight upon him." His son would later write of it: "For a time [the new law] darkened the face of day, even to this apostle of Hope." Around this time, Emerson's school-aged children were assigned an essay on "The Building of a House." Emerson admonished them: "You must be sure to say that no house nowadays is perfect without having a nook where a fugitive slave can be safely hidden away."[82] From this point forward, Emerson, convinced that the "government itself is a treason," became a committed abolitionist.[83]

His entry into the movement, while taking longer than some would have liked, was offset by the power of his influence, which cannot be overestimated. By the 1850s Emerson was widely respected throughout the country. In Rochester, he was upheld as a cultural minister;[84] as far west as Cincinnati and Chicago, the press hailed him as "the poet and philosopher ... universally recognized as one of the great thinkers of the age."[85] Frank Preston Stearns labeled Emerson "the most famous American of his time," who internationally was "looked upon as the best representative of our Western Hemisphere...."[86] In fact, one British guest at a Harvard Phi Beta Kappa dinner commented that upon his return home he would be asked two things: "if he had seen Niagara Falls, and if he had met Emerson."[87] Ardent abolitionist Thomas Wentworth Higginson probably described public sentiment about Emerson best when he quoted a western agent who said Emerson's reputation rested "not on the ground that the people understand him," but that "'they think such men ought to be encouraged.'"[88] The abolitionist community could not be happier to finally call the influential Ralph Waldo Emerson one of their own.

As evidence of his growing commitment to the abolitionist cause, Emerson began lecturing in western New York in February 1851. Rochester was an area of great social activism at the time, a haven for both the women's suffrage movement and the antislavery community, which centered around Frederick Douglass.[89] In May of that year, Emerson's newfound activism led him to campaign for John G. Palfrey, a Free Soil candidate for Congress. While campaigning, Emerson repeated his Fugitive Slave Law speech in Lexington, Fitchburg, Cambridge and Waltham. Palfrey would lose the election, but he would carry Concord by a sixty-eight vote margin.[90] By November of 1852 Emerson would support his words with dollars and contribute funds to the Boston Vigilance Committee.[91]

In 1854, on the seventh anniversary of Webster's 7 March speech endorsing the Compromise of 1850, Emerson wrote and delivered a new speech about the Fugitive Slave Law in which he conceded, "It is not possible to extricate oneself from the questions in which your age is involved." In the talk, delivered at the New York Tabernacle, he said, "Now it is a law of our nature that great thoughts come from the heart." The speech was indeed heartfelt and concluded with Emerson's call to "every noble and generous spirit in the land; to every poetic; to every heroic; to every religious heart...."[92] Again, in speaking of a crusade, Emerson uses the vocabulary of religion. His conclusion, however, unites the poetic and religious into a heroic heart.

Emerson had now found his calling as a poet reformer, a resolution that pushed him to further activism. In an extraordinary departure from his usual practice, he eschewed his usual stock in trade lectures during the 1854–1855 lecture series and spoke primarily from two lectures on slavery.[93] And in July 1854, both Emerson and Lidian attended a public protest in Concord over the return of fugitive Anthony Burns to slavery.[94]

Still, Emerson continued to feel out of his element in his newfound role as reformer. On 17 January 1855 he wrote his brother William: "I am trying hard in these days to see some light in the dark Slavery question to which I am to speak next week in Boston." He added, "to me as to many tis like Hamlet's task imposed on so unfit an agent as Hamlet." He continues in self-deprecating terms: "Howbeit, if we only drum, we must drum well."[95] Lidian, always less ambivalent than her husband about the antislavery movement, draped her home in black on 4 July to protest the current state of the union.[96]

In the spring of 1856, events in Kansas deteriorated into border warfare as pro-slavery and antislavery forces battled for the state. Emerson wrote his brother William: "But what times are these, & how they make our studies impertinent, & even ourselves the same!"[97] In response to the crisis, he began exploring other ways to make a difference. In June, Emerson donated $50 to the Free State cause. A month later, he joined others in sending a letter to the governor asking that citizens of Massachusetts be protected while in Kansas.[98]

In September, Emerson spoke at a Kansas relief meeting in Cambridge. His friend

Franklin Sanborn saved the broadside announcing the speech, which read in part "RALPH WALDO EMERSON will address the meeting. E.B. Whitman, Esq., our fellow citizen, is expected from Lawrence, [Kansas Territory], with late and reliable news...."[99] The emotionality that gripped those present at the event is reflected in a letter written by fellow Unitarian Theodore Parker, who heard Emerson speak: "The accounts are awful for Kansas. Five persons were shot after they had surrendered. Scalping is ... common.... We are now in a civil war"[100] In his speech, Emerson urged listeners to "give largely, lavishly" to donate funds towards the purchase of, among other things, Sharps rifles for the freedom fighters in Kansas.[101] In soliciting funds for the purchase of rifles, Emerson moved from philosophic and moral argument to a tacit acceptance of violence as a necessary tool to achieve abolitionist ends.

Thus, by the time John Brown came to Boston in January of 1857 to meet with Franklin Sanborn, who ran a small school in Concord under Emerson's guidance, Emerson was well acquainted with events in Kansas. Brown wanted money and supplies for his mission there, in particular, "guns, ammunition, and at least $30,000 in cash or pledges, preferably cash...."[102] But Emerson would not meet Captain John Brown for the first time until several months later. In March, returning from a lecture tour, Emerson dropped in on Thoreau one afternoon to find him deep in conversation with Brown. Thoreau introduced the two men, and Emerson invited Brown to spend the next night in Concord as his guest. Emerson was impressed by the speech Brown gave at the Concord town hall. "Captain John Brown of Kansas gave a good account of himself," he wrote in his journal. "One of his good points was, the folly of the peace party in Kansas...."[103]

Brown, in addition to demonstrating the bowie knife and chains which he said had been used by federal troops to bind his son, spoke forcefully, giving an account of the battle of Black Jack, with no mention of events at Pottawatomie. By the time he left Concord, Brown had received contributions from Sanborn and Emerson as well as from Thoreau's father.[104] In addition, Brown was cultivating powerful friends throughout the state. Samuel Gridley Howe's wife, Julia, wrote, "In [his Kansas] effort [Brown] had the hearty support of most of the anti-slavery men of Massachusetts. The year before, the people of the Bay State had sent $100,000 in money, arms and clothing ... and [the state] was ready ... to do still more."[105]

When Brown returned to Concord in 1859, Emerson was a firm supporter. On 8 May of that year, Brown gave another lecture in the town hall. As in 1857, Sanborn, Emerson and Thoreau were all present.[106] Bronson Alcott attended and later wrote in his journal: "[Brown] tells his story with surpassing simplicity and sense, impressing us all deeply by his courage and religious earnestness." He continued: "Our best people listen to his words—Emerson, Thoreau, Judge Hoar, my wife—and some of them contribute something in aid of his plans without asking particulars, such confidence does he inspire with his integrity and abilities." Alcott also made clear that his audience was aware of Brown's potential for violence in defense of his cause. Describing Brown and his compatriot Anderson, Alcott writes, "They go armed ... and will defend themselves if necessary." In regard to a specific plan, Brown was vague and left them "much in the dark concerning his destination and designs." But while his specific strategy might have been unknown, Brown did not conceal "his hatred of slavery nor his readiness to strike a blow for freedom at the proper moment."[107]

The extent to which the Concord group supported such efforts with their somewhat limited means is revealed in a letter from Emerson to James Russell Lowell dated 13 July 1859. In it, Emerson, who is attempting to raise money for the struggling Alcott family, laments, "But the Kansas claim drained some of our friends, & others failed us...."[108]

Several months later, Brown and his men would attack Harpers Ferry, aided by the resources of his Concord friends, including Emerson, the gentle man of letters.

Four

HENRY DAVID THOREAU

Literary scholars have seen Henry David Thoreau's defense of John Brown as an extraordinary departure from what is generally viewed as the pacifism of "Civil Disobedience." A careful study of Thoreau's antislavery and reform writings, as well as an understanding of Thoreau's temperament, negates this view. Unlike Emerson, Thoreau was comfortable with and active in the abolitionist community early on. His finely tuned sense of moral outrage coupled with his understanding of symbolic gesture made him well suited to be a friend of the slave. At the same time, however, Thoreau never thought of himself as an Abolitionist, or for that matter, a member of any organized reform effort. For Henry was above all an individual, telling the Temperance Society that "he was too Transcendental to join societies for reforming other men."[1] Upon learning that his acquaintance Thomas Wentworth Higginson had gone to Mount Ktaadn, Thoreau wryly observed that he was "glad to hear" it, thinking a mountain "so much better to go to than a Woman's Rights or Abolition Convention."[2]

Yet Thoreau, like Emerson, was surrounded by family members with strong abolitionist leanings. His mother, Cynthia, sisters Sophia and Helen, Aunts Maria and Jane Thoreau and Louisa Dunbar were all founding members of the Concord Female Anti-Slavery Society.[3] Additionally, his mother and sisters regularly subscribed to antislavery periodicals, and his mother's boardinghouse was a haven for antislavery agitators who regularly visited Concord.[4] Franklin Sanborn asserted that Lidian Emerson and the "ladies of the Thoreau and Dunbar ... families" were among the most active members of the Concord Anti-Slavery Society nearly from its inception.[5] Ann Bigelow, an active member of that organization, insisted that hiding runaway slaves in Concord was a frequent activity and one largely undertaken by one of three people, herself, Mary Rice or Cynthia Thoreau.[6] Thoreau himself alludes to having entertained escaped slaves in his Walden cabin, "runaway slaves with plantation manners, who listened from time to time, like the fox in the fable, as if they heard the hounds a-baying on their track...." In particular, he describes "One real runaway slave ... whom I helped to forward toward the northstar." Biographer Walter Harding generally dismisses this claim, as the cabin was too small for overnight guests. Yet elsewhere Thoreau refers to his "'best' room ... on whose carpet the sun rarely fell ... the pine wood behind my house," thus leaving the question unresolved.[7]

Whether slaves actually stayed at the Walden cabin or not, Thoreau was involved in a very concrete way in the antislavery movement. Harding acknowledged that Thoreau routinely assisted slaves who arrived on his mother's doorstep and steered them safely toward Canada.[8] In addition to the practical rescue of slaves, Thoreau also understood the power of the written word and symbolic gesture to effect change. He once wrote that the "art of composition is as simple as the discharge of a bullet from a rifle, and its masterpieces imply an infinitely greater force behind them."[9] Thoreau missed very few opportunities to make a political statement with an act or a word. Even his move to the Walden woods was largely a symbolic one since he was only a mile or two from the center of Concord village. And while Thoreau shared some nineteenth-century prejudices against blacks, he was almost unmatched in the intensity of his passion for justice and what scholar Michael Meyer refers to as his belief in the "absolute moral necessity of ending slavery in the United States."[10]

While Emerson was slow to embrace social issues, Thoreau as early as July 1840 was discussing the relationship of the individual to society. In an unpublished piece, "The Service," Thoreau wrote that "A man's life should be a stately march to an unheard music, and when to his fellows it seems irregular and inharmonious, he will be stepping to a livelier measure, which only his nicer ear can detect."[11] Thoreau would later revise

Before the decade was out, Thoreau would be the first to speak on Brown's behalf. Later, he became what one historian later described as "an accessory after the fact" to Harpers Ferry, when he put escaped raider Francis Merriam on the train towards Canada. A crayon portrait of Henry David Thoreau by Samuel Worcester Rowse done in 1854 (courtesy the Thoreau Institute at Walden Woods).

the statement to the more memorable (and better written) "If a man does not keep pace with his companions, perhaps it is because he hears a different drummer. Let him step to the music which he hears, however measured or far away."[12] In spite of the awkward wording, the original passage illustrates that from his earliest writings, Thoreau was focused upon the individual's relationship to society. In his 1843 "Paradise to be Regained," Thoreau reiterates the view that reform comes from individual change and that political systems limit individual freedom.[13] Like Emerson, Thoreau felt individual change was a step on the continuum of societal transformation, a theme reiterated in a lecture given in Boston in the spring of 1844 in which he encouraged his audience to focus on the interior landscape to effect reform.[14]

About this time, Thoreau wrote a review of Nathaniel P. Rogers' abolitionist paper, *Herald of Freedom*. Rogers was one of only three men to receive Thoreau's unqualified praise, the others being Wendell Phillips, the noted abolitionist, and, later, John Brown. Rogers responded to Thoreau's praise with an article in the *Herald of Freedom* on 10 May 1844. In it, Rogers acknowledges how rarely such praise occurred: "I had been praised before ... but it was by my own outcast fellow-laborers in the forlorn service of Anti-Slavery." He continues: "But this was not an abolitionist ... nor a personal friend—but a stranger ... to take notice, and such notice, of the most odious and despised publication of the time...." Astonished at this praise from so unexpected a quarter, Rogers surmises Thoreau must be "a German," because "if he had any reputation, he wouldn't be likely to hazard it, by a notice of our poor, 'infidel' ... sheet." Seemingly unaware of the irony in defending one group of Americans while dismissing another, Rogers concludes with the hope that "the writer will let Anti-Slavery have the benefit of his beautiful pen."[15]

Thoreau's courageous defense of Rogers was soon to be followed by one of his earliest acts of personal protest. In January of 1844, in what would prove to be a controversial decision, Wendell Phillips, a well-known abolitionist lecturer, was invited to speak on the subject of slavery at the Concord Lyceum. In a letter to the *Liberator* dated 11 February 1844, H.M. described the tension surrounding the invitation: "The week before he was to come, a gentleman introduced a resolution to the Lyceum, that Mr. P. be invited to lecture on some other subject than slavery; that the sentiments Mr. P. uttered, when he lectured here the last winter, on the same subject, were vile, pernicious and abominable."[16]

Those anticipating a controversy were not disappointed. A local citizen, Mr. Robinson, described the evening of the speech, saying, "To-night all our folks have gone to the Lyceum to hear Wendell Phillips lecture on slavery. We expect a small row...."[17] In spite of the unease, Phillips came and "spoke an hour and a half, receiving the most fixed attention," even as he pronounced "treason against Church and State." His speech, while worrisome to some, delighted his supporters, with the anonymous H.M. pronouncing it "a most magnificent burst of eloquence from beginning to end."[18]

Opponents of Phillips, however, were still outraged several days later when they assembled in the First Church to censure the speaker. Unbeknownst to them, Phillips was present, albeit hidden in the rear of the building. At nine o'clock, Mr. Phillips arose, came forward and asked permission to respond to those present.[19] He then exhorted the young people in the audience to action, in a charge which no doubt resonated with Thoreau: "I would say to you, my young friends, who have been cautioned against excitement, and advised to fold your hands in selfish ease, throw yourselves upon the altar of some noble cause. To rise in the morning, to eat, and drink, and gather gold, is a life not worth having. Enthusiasm is the life of the soul."[20]

Henry, Sophia and Helen, were so impressed with Phillips that they voted to have him return to speak once more on the subject of slavery. The sentiment carried, and in the spring of 1845 the famed abolitionist was invited again to the Concord Lyceum. This time, no longer content to simply voice their opposition, the conservative members of the committee chose instead to resign in protest over the controversial choice of speaker. Thoreau, along with Emerson, vigorously defended Phillips, and Thoreau received an appointment as a replacement member on the lyceum committee. The next day, he wrote to the *Liberator* defending Phillips's right to speak.[21] The letter, written 12 March, was published anonymously, but in it, Thoreau left little doubt as to his opinion of both the controversy and the speaker.

He began by offering Phillips "both our thanks and our sympathy." Acknowledging that the "admission of this gentleman into the Lyceum has been strenuously opposed by a respectable portion of our fellow-citizens," Thoreau asserted that "the speaker's aim [was] to show what the State, and above all the Church, had to do ... with Texas and slavery" and contended that "[t]hese were fair themes, and not mistimed...." He continued his defense of Phillips, saying, "He at least is not responsible for slavery, nor for American Independence; for the hypocrisy and superstition of the Church, nor the timidity and selfishness of the State; nor for the indifference and willing ignorance of any." The young Concordian was impressed, too, by Phillips's discussion of Frederick Douglass. In the letter, Thoreau praised Douglass as "a fugitive slave in one more sense than we; who has proved himself the possessor of a *fair* intellect, and [who] has won a colorless reputation in these parts...." He then dismissed as cowardly the New Bedford citizens who, according to Phillips, did not want Douglass to pen his autobiography, and who had anxiously cautioned, "He had better not!" Thoreau adds with disbelief and no small amount of disdain that this hesitation "was echoed under the shadow of Concord monument...."[22] Thoreau's admiration of Phillips led to what is, for him, unusual high praise: "We would fain express our appreciation of the freedom and steady wisdom, so rare in the reformer, with which he declared that he was not born to abolish slavery, but to do right. We have heard a few, a very few, good political speakers, who afforded us the pleasure of great intellectual power and acuteness, of soldier-like steadiness, and of a graceful and natural oratory; but in this man the audience might detect a sort of moral principle and integrity...."[23]

Perhaps the most personally significant and lasting lesson Thoreau took from Phillips's experience at the lyceum was "the readiness of the people at large, of whatever sect or party, to entertain, with good will and hospitality, the most revolutionary and heretical opinions, when frankly and adequately ... expressed."[24] It was something Thoreau, no doubt, would remember when he took to the lecture platform himself to espouse a political cause. In the meantime, his eloquent defense of Phillips stood as his first letter to the editor and was published in the *Liberator* on 28 March 1845. For her part, Helen Thoreau described the incident in a letter to a friend: "Aunt Maria has, I suppose, kept you informed of our controversy with the Lyceum, a Hard battle but Victory at last." Probably thinking of her brother's appointment to the lyceum committee, she concluded: "Next winter we shall have undoubtedly a free Lyceum."[25]

The summer of 1846 was a pivotal time in Thoreau's antislavery activity. On the first of August, he was host for the annual West Indian emancipation celebration. The gathering, perhaps, took place at the pond and may be what he refers to in the following passage in *Walden*: "I have had twenty-five or thirty souls, with their bodies, at once under my roof."[26]

As the year came to a close, Texas entered the union as a slave state. By 11 May 1846 Mexico had declared war. Thoreau was vehemently opposed to a war he saw as an excuse to extend the slavery territories. His response was to refuse to pay his poll tax, thereby initiating his famous night in the Concord jail. In actuality, Thoreau had stopped paying his tax perhaps as early as 1842 to protest slavery, but the gesture had been ignored for several years.[27] On the July night in question, Staples, the local jailer, offered to pay Thoreau's tax if he was "hard up" for funds, in addition to offering to persuade the town selectmen to reduce the tax if Thoreau felt overburdened. Instead, Thoreau insisted he be jailed. Thoreau's individual protest might have ended there—since an undetermined benefactor paid his tax before nightfall—had an unwilling Staples not declared that he wasn't going to put his boots back on to release his prisoner. Thus, Thoreau spent the night in jail, a night that would reverberate through literary history for the next 150 or so years.[28]

Local interest in Thoreau's overnight incarceration was intense. In response to the deluge of questions, Thoreau spoke to the Concord Lyceum 26 January 1848 on "The Relation of the Individual to the State." In 1849 Elizabeth Peabody published the lecture as "Resistance to Civil Government" in the first and only edition of *Aesthetic Papers*. Neither then, nor throughout Thoreau's life, would the lecture attract much attention.[29] In 1866, four years after his death, it would be published as "Civil Disobedience" and profoundly influence men a century later, including Martin Luther King, Jr., and Mahatma Gandhi.

Throughout the lecture, Thoreau emphasized the importance of individual conscience over blind adherence to the state. While not necessarily advocating violence as a means of achieving reform, he nevertheless strongly asserted the right of the individual to follow the higher law of individual conscience, even when the result is at odds with the state. He asked, "Must the citizen ever for a moment, or in the least degree, resign his conscience to the legislator?" posing the rhetorical question, "Why has every man a conscience, then?" It is obvious that Thoreau's sympathies lie with "heroes, patriots, martyrs, reformers in the great sense, and *men*—[who] serve the state with their consciences also, and so necessarily resist it for the most part...." The penalty for those who adhere to conscience is to be "commonly treated as enemies" of the state. Yet, it is clear that, from Thoreau's perspective, they are the true heroes of reform.[30]

Thoreau specifically addressed the issue of revolution in the essay, saying, "[W]hen a sixth of the population of a nation which has undertaken to be the refuge of liberty are slaves ... I think that it is not too soon for honest men to rebel and revolutionize." Further, he calls upon abolitionists to "at once effectually withdraw their support, both in person and property, from the government of Massachusetts...."[31]

Nancy Rosenblum, in her introduction to *Thoreau: Political Writings*, concludes that Thoreau's greatest challenge in the essay was to reverse the common view of good citizenship as conformity and replace it with the notion that individual conscience is paramount to principled democratic government.[32] Given this view, Thoreau's move from the passive resistance of "Civil Disobedience" to his later tacit approval of violence in "A Plea for Captain John Brown" is less revolutionary than one might imagine.

The passage of the Fugitive Slave Law in 1850, forcing northerners to actively participate in the return of southern slaves, pushed Thoreau, already at the limits of his patience with the government, to the breaking point. When Thomas Sims, a young black man was arrested in Boston under the auspices of the new law, Thoreau experienced what he described as a "moral earthquake." "About a week ago," he wrote in his *Journal*, "the authorities of Boston, having the sympathy of many of the inhabitants of Concord, assembled in the gray of the dawn, assisted by a still larger armed force, to send back a perfectly innocent man, and one whom they knew to be innocent, into a slavery as complete as the world ever knew." In a series of entries dated April 1851, Thoreau speaks directly to his neighbors: "I wish my townsmen to consider that ... neither an individual nor a nation can ever deliberately commit the least act of injustice without having to pay the penalty for it."[33]

As he was increasingly wont to do, he then attacked the Fourth Estate and advised abolitionists "to make as earnest and vigorous and persevering an assault on the press" as they had made on the church with some effect. "I repeat the testimony of many an intelligent traveller, as well as my own convictions, when I say that probably no country was ever ruled by so mean a class of tyrants as are the editors of the periodical press in *this* country" he fumed. Specifically, Thoreau was annoyed with the tenor of the reports. "Almost without exception the tone of the press is mercenary and servile," he wrote, adding: "The *Commonwealth,* and the *Liberator,* are the only papers, as far as I know, which make themselves heard in condemnation of the cowardice and meanness of the authorities of Boston as lately exhibited. The other journals ... by their manner of referring to and speaking of the Fugitive Slave Law or the carrying back of the slave, insult the common sense of the country."[34]

He then turned his attention to the Democratic *Herald*. "Has not the Boston *Herald* acted its part well, served its master faithfully?" he asked. "How could it have gone lower on its belly?" His anger rising to fever pitch, Thoreau concluded his tirade: "When I have taken up this paper [*Boston Herald*] or the Boston *Times*, with my cuffs turned up, I have heard the gurgling of the sewer through every column; I have felt that I was handling a paper picked out of the public sewers, a leaf from the gospel of the gambling-house, the groggery, and the brothel...."[35]

Thus, it is not at all surprising that when a second fugitive slave, Anthony Burns, was returned to slavery in March of 1854, Thoreau could no longer simply confine his ire within the pages of his journal. On 4 July 1854, when William Lloyd Garrison called a meeting in Framingham to protest the Fugitive Slave Law, Thoreau was present to deliver a scathing address entitled "Slavery in Massachusetts." The speech, biographer Henry Canby notes, "is not on slavery, of which Thoreau knew little or nothing in its historical and economical aspects, nor on the South and Southerners, of which he knew less."[36] Instead, Thoreau spoke passionately to his fellow citizens of the North, and in particular to his neighbors in Massachusetts. "My thoughts are murder to the State, and involuntarily go plotting against her," he declared.[37]

Many of the issues Thoreau addresses in the essay are similar to those in the earlier "Civil Disobedience." Again, Thoreau's message is that man must obey the higher law of his conscience, which would necessarily hold slavery to be immoral and even obscene.[38] Thoreau writes: "What is wanted is men, not of policy, but of probity,—who recognize a higher law than the Constitution, or the decision of the majority." What is strikingly different from his earlier public address, however, is the tone of the piece, the sense of urgency that now the evil is on the very doorstep of Massachusetts. Thoreau laments, "I feel that my investment in life here is worth many percent less since Massachusetts last deliberately sent back an innocent man, Anthony Burns, to slavery." While "Civil Disobedience" advocates man making a principled stand against an unjust law, in this address, paradoxically, Thoreau sees the government as breaking the law and man as upholding it. "The law will never make men free; it is men who have got to make the law free," Thoreau asserts, adding that men are "lovers of law and order who observe the law when the government breaks it."[39]

Also significant in the address is the internal conflict between reformer and artist, so prominent in Emerson's considerations. Like Emerson, Thoreau struggled with the

NO SLAVERY!

FOURTH OF JULY!

The Managers of the

Mass. ANTI-SLAVERY SOC'Y

Invite, without distinction of party or sect, ALL who are ready and mean to be known as on LIBERTY'S side, in the great struggle which is now upon us, to meet in convention at the

GROVE IN FRAMINGHAM,

On the approaching FOURTH OF JULY, there to pass the day in no idle glorying in our country's liberties, but in deep humiliation for her Disgrace and Shame, and in resolute purpose---God being our leader---to rescue old Massachusetts at least from being bound forever to the car of Slavery.

SPECIAL TRAINS

Will be run on that day, TO THE GROVE, from Boston, Worcester, and Milford, leaving each place at 9 25 A. M.

RETURNING---Leave the Grove about 5 1-2 P. M. FARE, by all these Trains, to the Grove and back,

FIFTY CENTS.

The beauty of the Grove, and the completeness and excellence of its accommodations, are well known.

EMINENT SPEAKERS,

From different quarters of the State, will be present.

Earle & Drew, Printers, 212 Main Street, Worcester.

This 1854 broadside announces a Fourth of July gathering at Framingham, MA. Thoreau shared the platform with famed abolitionists William Lloyd Garrison and Sojourner Truth. In a dramatic gesture, Garrison burned copies of both the Fugitive Slave Law and the United States Constitution. An equally incendiary Thoreau proclaimed, "My thoughts are murder to the State, and involuntarily go plotting against her" (courtesy the Massachusetts Historical Society).

role of a literary man in a time of revolution. Here, he acknowledged that "Art is as long as ever" but concluded that "life is more interrupted and less available for a man's proper pursuits." Much less conflicted than his friend about his dual role as writer and reformer, Thoreau saw a clear choice, choosing action over reflection: "It is not an era of repose. We have used up all our inherited freedom. If we would save our lives, we must fight for them."[40]

As with the Sims episode, Thoreau turns his fury on the newspapers, which he views as standing silently by while Massachusetts returned Anthony Burns to the South. First, he acknowledges the enormous influence of the press, elevating it to a place above the Bible in the public consciousness. "We [as a society] do not care for the Bible, but we do care for the newspaper," he writes. His ire is not confined to the publishing world, but is also directed at the citizens who regularly read the newspapers, people whom he feels are "in the condition of the dog that returns to his vomit." It is interesting that Thoreau so virulently and publicly condemns the "corrupt press" which he himself will manipulate in a few short years in his defense of John Brown.[41]

Although Thoreau, by all accounts, was not much of a speaker, this speech was a success. Walter Harding asserts that only when "aroused in the fight for justice [was Thoreau] sufficiently dynamic to excite his audience."[42] The speech at Framingham was one such occasion; a second, years later, would be his pleas for John Brown.[43] "Slavery in Massachusetts" received widespread press coverage and was published, in whole or in part, in the *New York Tribune*, the *National Slavery Standard* and the *Liberator*.[44]

Not surprisingly, then, Thoreau was receptive to the words of the incendiary John Brown when he met him for the first time in March 1857. Brown, having spoken at a hearing of the Massachusetts legislature, proceeded to Concord to call on his friend Franklin Sanborn. Sanborn, then a teacher at the school he and Emerson had begun, visited with Brown a short while but soon had to return to his students. Looking for a solution to the dilemma of how to entertain Brown during the rest of the school day, Sanborn took Brown across the street to the Thoreau home and left him deep in conversation with Thoreau about affairs in Kansas. Sanborn later recalled,

When Brown returned to Concord in 1859, he had added the long, flowing beard seen in this photograph. Louisa May Alcott's father, Bronson, felt it gave Brown "the soldierly air, and port of an apostle" and concluded, "Though sixty years of age, he is agile and alert, resolute, and ready for ... any crisis. I think him about the manliest man I have ever seen." The photograph, by Black and Bachelder, was taken in May of 1859 (Library of Congress, Prints and Photographs Division).

"Brown narrated in detail to Thoreau his most noted battle in Kansas—that of Black Jack, the June before, where, with nine men, he captured twenty-odd men."[45]

Later in the day, Emerson dropped by to visit Thoreau and was introduced to Brown. That night, both men listened as Brown gave an address in the Concord Town Hall during which he dramatically displayed a bowie knife he had taken from a border ruffian as well as a chain he claimed had been used to bind his son in Kansas. All of the men gave funds to Brown: $100 from Sanborn, $50 from Emerson and $10 from Thoreau's father. Thoreau, annoyed because Brown would not outline his plans for the money, contributed only a "trifle."[46] "I had so much confidence in the man,—that he would do right,—but it would seem that he had not confidence enough in me, nor in anybody else that I know, to communicate his plans to us," Thoreau confided in his journal.[47]

Thoreau was correct in his assessment that Brown did not fully convey his intentions to his Concord audience. According to historian Paul Finkelman, Brown was already planning the raid on Harpers Ferry, although he did not inform his New England supporters of this fact. Neither did he choose to acknowledge his role in the Pottawatomie massacres. The Massachusetts press had not reported widely on events at Pottawatomie, instead giving extensive coverage at the time to stories concerning the caning of Massachusetts senator Charles Sumner on the Senate floor by proslavery representative Preston Brooks.[48] Apparently, while his Massachusetts friends believed their funds would go to support the antislavery war in Kansas, they did not know the specifics.[49] Michael Meyer concurs that Thoreau's knowledge of Brown's activities was most likely limited to what Brown wanted him to know, with Brown's activities often described as "heroic" in the northeastern press where he was seen as a "champion of free soil forces."[50]

Several years would pass before Brown's next visit to Concord in the spring of 1859. In the meantime, with Walden frozen over, Thoreau and Emerson went skating with George Luther Stearns, a supporter of Brown from Medford, Massachusetts. During the cold winter afternoon, Stearns praised Brown with great conviction. On a second visit to Concord on 8 May, Brown was more forthcoming about his plans, giving details and again asking for funds. Thoreau was more favorably disposed to Brown on this second visit, with many of his concerns seemingly put to rest.[51] Bronson Alcott was also impressed and wrote of Brown in his journal: "Since here last he has added a flowing beard, which gives the soldierly air, and port of an apostle. Though sixty years of age, he is agile and alert, resolute, and ready for ... any crisis. I think him about the manliest man I have ever seen...."[52]

Alcott also offers in a journal entry a revealing suggestion about Brown's plans: "I infer it is his intention to run off as many slaves as he can, and so render that property insecure to the master."[53] The use of the verb "infer," coupled with the vague assessment of Brown's objectives, supports the notion that even with the additional details, few in Concord grasped the full import of Brown's activities. They were, to a man, however, confident of his ability to execute his objectives. Alcott enthused, "I think him equal to anything he dares, the man to do the deed if it must be done, and with the martyr's temper and purpose."[54] There is no evidence that Thoreau or Emerson differed from their friend's assessment. It is interesting to note that Alcott describes Brown as both a "martyr" and an "apostle," eerily prescient of the language the same group would use to defend their friend several months hence after the raid on Harpers Ferry.

As the summer wore on, the men of Concord visited with one another on lazy afternoons. On one such June evening, Thoreau joined Sanborn for tea at the Alcott home. Talk turned to Brown, with Alcott noting in his journal that Sanborn was "revolutionary in a quiet way" and suggesting that he perhaps was involved in "abetting Captain Brown and the Emigrant Aid measures." Alcott added, "I think [Sanborn] is brave, and likely to do good service for freedom if necessary."[55] The men of letters who passed these quiet summer evenings together were entranced by Brown and intrigued by his tales of border warfare in Kansas. They did not object when he suggested it was "'better that a whole generation of men, women and children pass away by violent death' rather than that a violation of the Holy Gospel or the Declaration of Independence be further tolerated."[56] Thoreau, initially a skeptic, was now firmly in Brown's camp. He saw in Brown a man much like himself—a man of principle, courage and action; a man who fought slavery not only by word but by deed; a man who understood both symbolism and history. Therefore, when the events at Harpers Ferry came to his door, Thoreau was ready with a "composition ... as simple as the discharge of a bullet from a rifle" and equally as effective.[57]

The young, dashing Franklin Benjamin Sanborn was a neighbor of both Thoreau and Emerson. He helped to fund Brown's raid, but perhaps even more important, he introduced Brown to his friends Emerson and Thoreau, who would become among the strongest of his literary defenders (courtesy Concord Free Public Library).

Five

FREDERICK DOUGLASS

While Emerson and Thoreau would gradually move toward the acceptance of violence as a necessary precondition to the abolition of slavery, Frederick Douglass for many years would be encouraged by the white abolitionist community to be less confrontational in his philosophy. From the violence implicit in his quarrel with Covey, the cruel overseer, as described in his *Narrative of the Life of Frederick Douglass*, Douglass would be asked to move toward the moral suasion advocated by William Lloyd Garrison, his mentor in the abolitionist movement. Douglass's effectiveness as an abolitionist depended upon a complex image, incorporating the manly daring of an escape from slavery with the refined skills of an orator and a writer. While audiences had to be willing to accept Douglass as an escaped slave, he also had to be intellectual enough to offset preconceived nineteenth-century notions of black inferiority. In addition, he had to be a slave who was not only worthy of escape but also worthy of a place in the white hierarchy of the often racist antebellum abolitionist movement.

The fact that Douglass was not only able to meet but also to transcend the almost impossible demands placed upon him by the abolitionist community is astonishing. But the endless balancing act he had to perform also explains a great deal about why he was drawn to John Brown. Brown offered an easy friendship and familiarity with blacks largely absent elsewhere in the abolitionist movement. Additionally, Brown viewed violence as a natural response to the imprisonment of a people and understood Douglass's growing frustration not only with the lack of national progress on the slavery question but also with the unreasonable constraints placed upon him by the abolitionist community. Somewhat surprisingly, given Douglass's intense admiration of Brown, their shared belief in the equality of the races, and an increasing mutual frustration with the ineffectiveness of moral appeal as an instrument of change, Douglass would refuse Brown's request to join him at Harpers Ferry. Brown, who felt betrayed by Douglass, would die and become a martyr. Douglass, who felt guilty about his refusal to participate, would live to help make him one.

By the time Douglass escaped from slavery and settled in New Bedford, Massachusetts, in 1838, the abolitionist movement had been active for nearly a decade. During the 1830s, a small number of working blacks had donated what money they could to antislavery periodicals and had attended, when possible, antislavery meetings.[1] Throughout the decade, black abolitionists continued to be influenced by their white counterparts who were, for the most part, the leaders of the movement. And yet, advocating moral reform as a resolution to the slavery question, white abolitionists often seemed, to their black counterparts, much more interested in ethics than concrete progress.[2] Nonetheless, blacks gave their support in increasing numbers to these white abolitionists, including

Five. Frederick Douglass

For many years, Frederick Douglass would advocate a peaceful resolution to the antislavery crisis. But after meeting Brown, he conceded that "While I continued to write and speak against slavery, I became all the same less hopeful of its peaceful abolition. My utterances became more and more tinged by the color of this man's strong impressions." Brown visited Douglass often and during one such visit completed plans for his raid on Harpers Ferry. Date of photograph unknown (Library of Congress, Prints and Photographs Division).

William Lloyd Garrison, whom they held in high regard. Garrison, for his part, continued appeals "to our free colored brethren," assuring them "[w]e know that you are now struggling against wind and tide."[3] His appeals to the black community for help were answered. In 1831, on the day before the initial run of Garrison's *Liberator* went to press, James Forten, a black abolitionist, sent in $54 to cover twenty-seven subscriptions. It was these funds that enabled Garrison to buy the paper necessary to print the first issue. During the first three critical years of the paper, blacks comprised three-fourths of the 2,300 subscribers.[4] Garrison recognized the crucial role people of color played in the *Liberator*'s success. In addition to financial support, blacks contributed greatly to the content of the paper, writing letters and essays for its columns. Garrison acknowledged that "the paper ... belongs especially to the people of color—it is their organ."[5] From his days in New Bedford, Douglass subscribed to the paper.

The early hope blacks felt about the abolitionist movement, however, faded and by the late 1830s black disillusionment prevailed. Prior optimism was replaced with the sense that the cause was "tainted with racism, a loss of mission, and senseless infighting."[6] Blacks were frustrated not only with the internal strife so prevalent among white abolitionists, but with the lack of racial integration within the movement itself. Additionally, for all the abolitionists' claims of enlightenment, even Massachusetts continued to be a less than welcoming place for persons of color. Thomas Wentworth Higginson recalled this was a time of "negro pews, negro cars, and even negro stages." In particular, he remembered the ejection of a colored woman from a stage on Massachusetts Avenue. If a black chose to ride on a train, they were forced to sit in a separate car while whites who attempted to sit with blacks were physically ejected.[7]

The rampant racism and widespread lack of sympathy for the antislavery community impaired the fledgling antislavery societies from having their message heard. "All the public halls ... of any tolerable size, were one after the other refused us," Samuel May would later write. "Even Faneuil Hall, the so-called cradle of American liberty, was denied to our use, though asked for in a respectful petition signed by the names of a hundred and twenty-five gentlemen of Boston...." However, several weeks later, Faneuil Hall, "in which had been cradled the independence of the United States, was turned into the Refuge of Slavery" when "fifteen hundred of the 'gentlemen of property and standing'" were granted use of it.[8]

Further compounding the abolitionists' problems, scandal haunted the fledging movement when it was discovered that two slave narratives were not what they were purported to be. The 1836 *Memoirs of Archy Moore* was found a year later to have been created by white historian Richard Hildreth and falsely presented as a fugitive slave autobiography. The *Narrative of James Williams*, published by the Massachusetts Anti-Slavery Society, came under attack in 1838. After an investigation, the society published a retraction that stated "the statements of the narrative ... are wholly false" and "withdrew the book from sale."[9] By 1839, even William Whipple, a firm supporter of moral suasion, concluded that it was "not lack of elevation, but complexion that deprived the man of color equal treatment."[10] The thirties, while trying, nonetheless prepared a new generation of more militant black leaders to take the stage in the coming decade.[11] Among them was the young Frederick Douglass.

Douglass's first public antislavery comments were delivered sometime around 1841 to black churches in New Bedford.[12] However, the remarks that would change his life were delivered 16 August 1841 in an abolitionist meeting in Nantucket. Called upon to speak and unaccustomed to the limelight, Douglass initially spoke haltingly. Garrison followed Douglass to the platform and used Douglass's remarks as the foundation of a stirring speech during which he asked the audience, "Shall such a man ever be sent back to bondage from the free soil of old Massachusetts?" With a roar the crowd rose to its feet shouting, "No! No! No!"[13] The "rescue" of the black Douglass by the white Garrison, the spontaneous collaboration of the two men at the lecture platform, and the profound effect of their partnership on those present foreshadowed the uneasy relationship between the two reformers that would last for many years. In the audience that day was John A. Collins, an agent of the Massachusetts Anti-Slavery Society, who believed the public was intensely interested in hearing slaves' stories. He approached Douglass, asking him to become an abolitionist speaker, thereby initiating an arrangement that would prove hugely successful for both parties.[14]

Rapidly overcoming his initial hesitation, Douglass quickly became a powerful orator with an implicit understanding of dramatic appeal. In January 1842, at a gathering of the Massachusetts Anti-Slavery Society, he began by saying, "I appear before the immense assembly this evening as a thief and a robber. I stole this head, these limbs, this body from my master, and ran off with them."[15] Douglass's undercurrent of illegality as a result of his status as an escaped slave titillated his listeners, whose own lives held no opportunity for drama of this magnitude.

Yet the greater Douglass's oratorical progress and the more like his mentors in thought and word he became, the more uneasy white abolitionists grew, at one point urging him to retain "a little of the plantation speech" and to defer from an analysis of slavery. "Give us the facts," they insisted, "we will take care of the philosophy."[16] They urged Douglass to describe his escape from slavery, nothing more. This would leave white abolitionists to spell out the political implications of the act as they saw it. Additionally, the more philosophical Douglass became, the more difficult it would be for audiences to believe his status as escaped slave. Nonetheless, the advice must have been galling to Douglass, who having escaped the literal bonds of slavery now found himself in another, more subtle but equally confining, bondage.

But if the white establishment of the abolitionist movement sometimes had concerns with the unconstrained speaker, the press did not. When Douglass spoke at the annual 1842 meeting of the New England Society, an editorial writer enthused that he had rarely heard a better speech, noting "the appropriateness of his elocution and gesticulation, and the grammatical accuracy of his sentences."[17] Unfortunately, the racism inherent in the reviewer's words offset his praise. The notion that Douglass's appropriate speech and good grammar deserved comment is symptomatic of the widely held nineteenth-century prejudice that blacks were incapable of high levels of thought, a notion the articulate Douglass continually belied

Between 1838 and 1844 Douglass voraciously read antislavery periodicals, including the *Liberator*, *National Anti-Slavery Standard*, *Liberty Bell*, *Emancipator*, *Anti-Slavery Almanac*, and *American and Foreign Anti-Slavery Reporter*, all of which gave him exposure to speeches and autobiographical accounts of the lives of fugitive slaves. Additionally, these publications published reviews of both black and white autobiographies, providing Douglass with valuable advice on what made a successful narrative. He was also influenced by his association with Quaker Isaac T. Hopper, an early participant in the Underground Railroad who published a successful column of slave narratives entitled "Tales of Oppression" in the *National Anti-Slavery Standard*.[18]

Ironically, as the increasingly learned Douglass gained proficiency as a speaker, his audience responded to him with growing skepticism. After a speech in 1844, the *Liberator* reported that the audience refused to believe he had been a slave: "How a man, only six years out of bondage, and who had never gone to school could speak with such eloquence—with such precision of language and power of thought—they were utterly at a loss to devise."[19] In response to such criticism, Douglass determined to write an autobiography authenticating details of his life in bondage.

The result was the *Narrative of the Life of Frederick Douglass* published by the American Anti-Slavery Society in May 1845. By fall, the autobiography had sold five thousand copies at 50 cents apiece. Four additional printings of two thousand copies each were introduced within a year.[20] Subsequent editions were later published by commercial printing houses.[21] As the growing literary public read personal accounts of "shipwrecks, slavery, and Indian captivities" with great interest,[22] the *Narrative* was everything its readers desired—intriguing and mysterious yet educational and moral in tone. Aside from being great entertainment, the account served another purpose: verifying the details of Douglass's life as a slave as well as confirming his intellectual capability. The *National Anti-Slavery Standard* reviewed the autobiography on 12 June 1845, saying, "This book ought to be read by all before whose mental blindness visions of happy slaves continually dance. It is the story of the life of a man of great intellectual power...."[23]

Once Douglass found his literary voice, it is not surprising that he wanted an independent organ for the expression of his antislavery sentiments. Thus, two months after a call at the black national antislavery convention for an independent black press, Douglass responded with the first edition of his privately owned newspaper, *North Star*. The publication (which began in a church basement) would last thirteen years and in 1851 would be renamed the *Frederick Douglass' Paper*. In addition to giving him autonomy, Douglass hoped the paper would be "a *telling* fact against the American doctrine of natural inferiority, and the inveterate prejudice which so universally prevails in this country against the colored race...."[24] So important was this vehicle to Douglass that he would pour $12,000 of his own resources into his newspapers over the course of eight years.[25] Both papers were also important to John Brown, who was a subscriber to the *North Star* as well as to the later *Frederick Douglass' Paper*. In January of 1852, Brown wrote his family that he hoped they could pay for the paper because he had exercised "some liberty in ordering it continued."[26] Years later, in Osawatomie, he would write them again of his joy in finding "here last night one of Frederick Douglass's papers."[27] John Brown, Jr., would add his praise to that of his father's, saying he was gratified that at least one newspaper was determined to teach people the truth about the Fugitive Slave Law, writing to Douglass "that paper is your own."[28] In spite of his often limited resources, between December of 1851 and April of 1858, Brown sent Douglass payments ranging from 75 cents to $5.00 to ensure his continued subscription to the newspaper.[29]

Yet, even with an independent vehicle at his command, Douglass had to measure his response to the antislavery question, approaching the subject of violence in his speeches and writings with caution. In the *Narrative* he seems to tacitly accept violence as a necessary response to the brutality perpetrated upon him as a slave. In describing the famous encounter between himself as a sixteen year old slave and Covey, the cruel overseer, Douglass writes: "[H]e had drawn no blood from me, but I had from him.... The white man who expected to succeed in whipping, must also succeed in killing me."[30] The threat is clear—Douglass will kill rather than be a passive victim. Yet, as Raymond Hedin notes, Douglass's description of the fight follows an "extended, unsuccessful plea with his owner, Thomas Auld, for relief from Covey's brutality." The fight therefore becomes a "last, *rational* recourse rather than a sign of [Douglass's] bestiality."[31]

Perhaps emboldened by the *Narrative*'s success and his growing reputation as an abolitionist leader, or perhaps simply frustrated with the lack of progress on the slavery question, Douglass resorted to an uncharacteristic endorsement of violence in a 31 May 1849 address at Faneuil Hall. In the speech he acknowledged, "I should welcome the intelligence tomorrow ... that the slaves had risen in the South, and that the sable arms which had been engaged in beautifying and adorning the South, were engaged in spreading death and devastation there."[32]

On 5 July 1852 in Rochester, Douglass gave possibly the most famous antislavery speech of his life, entitled "What to the Slave Is the Fourth of July?" In the address Douglass, while not advocating a violent overthrow of slavery, in a clever rhetorical device equates the slaves' position with that of the revolutionary fathers. He cautions his audience: "Oppression makes a wise man mad," and warns, "With brave men there is always a remedy for oppression." Aware that he is on the threshold of advocating revolution himself, he disingenuously concedes: "The timid and the prudent (as has been intimated) of that day, were, of course, shocked and alarmed by [this philosophy]." Describing the "fathers of the country" as "peace men," he reminds his listeners that they nonetheless "preferred revolution to peaceful submission to bondage."[33] By equating the hesitancy of those who feared colonial rebellion with those who currently opposed the violent abolition of slavery, he was able to indirectly accuse his audience of cowardice should they hesitate to endorse any available means to eradicate the evil institution. The speech showcases Douglass at his oratorical best. It also illustrates his increasing frustration with the policy of moral suasion advocated by the Garrisonians.

In 1853, Douglass published a novella, *The Heroic Slave*. The main character of the piece is Madison Washington, the hero of the 1841 mutiny aboard the slave ship *Creole*. For years, Douglass had mentioned Washington, who would have been a familiar figure to his audiences, in speeches. It was not until after the passage of the Fugitive Slave Law, however, that an angry and emboldened Douglass would cast the preeminent figure of a violent slave uprising as a sympathetic literary hero.[34] In Douglass's account, slaves use their broken fetters to kill the captain of the slave ship, a symbolical acknowledgement of a moral justification for violence. In a similar vein, in an address entitled "We Are in the Midst of a Moral Revolution" delivered to a large audience at the Broadway Tabernacle in New York on 10 May 1854, Douglass declared "Liberty and Slavery are eternally forbidden to be at peace," and concluded, "There is no middle ground; the choice it leaves to liberty is, KILL OR BE KILLED."[35] However, as late as 1856, during the dark days of "bleeding Kansas," Douglass would continue efforts to advocate a peaceful resolution to the slavery question. In an editorial in his paper in September of that year, he wrote, "[T]he strife we are called upon is not a war-like one.... With us the only hardship is, the industry and persistence with which our efforts must be made." He then called upon the "right of petition, the right of the press, and free speech [which] are left to us," and concluded that "the use of these is all that is required for the acquisition of our rights in the northern States."[36]

While Douglass grappled with how to approach the subject of violence in his speeches and writings, he was not averse to resorting to a violent act when necessary in his private life. In September 1841, while traveling on the Eastern Railroad, Douglass was asked to leave the first class section. He refused and was forcibly removed. Three weeks later he returned with John A. Collins and again attempted to sit in first class. Once again the railroad employees removed him. This time, however, Douglass grasped his seat so firmly that it was torn from the floor.[37] Another incident, which would leave a lasting impression on Douglass, involved an 1843 speech in Pendleton, Indiana. After an anti-abolitionist mob attacked his speaking partner at the rostrum, Douglass grabbed a piece of lumber and began swinging. He would often cite this episode as a turning point in his views on antislavery violence. A reporter covering an 1854 speech in which Douglass referred to the incident, wrote, "'[Douglass] stated he was once a believer in nonresistance...' but 'he dropped the idea on seeing a dear friend assaulted and beaten in a cruel and inhuman manner....'" The reporter then revealed that Douglass confessed he took a club and "went at 'em' with all his strength," concluding that Douglass felt he had done no wrong.[38] From 1841 through 1850 Douglass was involved in at least six violent physical altercations, none of them in the presence of Garrison.[39]

Violence also touched Douglass in an episode he would later describe in his *Life and Times of Frederick Douglass* (1881). Three black men, being pursued under the auspices of the Fugitive Slave Law, killed one of their pursuers and wounded another. The fugitives then made their way to Douglass's home, a well-known stop on the Underground

Railroad. In a lens similar to the one with which he viewed Brown's activities, Douglass wrote, "I could not look at them as murderers. To me, they were heroic defenders of the just rights of man against manstealers and murderers." Douglass sheltered them in his house and helped them on their way to Canada. For his efforts, he was given as a souvenir the revolver which had been taken from the dead man.[40]

Douglass's flirtation with violence as a solution to the slavery question found a kindred spirit in John Brown. While Brown may have kept his white supporters intentionally in the dark concerning his more militant plans, from the outset he felt comfortable discussing them with blacks. In fact, the first person outside of his family in whom he confided his master plan was Thomas Thomas, a black porter. Thomas was largely unimpressed with the idea; but undeterred, Brown sought and received approval from black abolitionists, among them the Rev. J.W. Loguen of Syracuse and the Rev. Henry Highland Garnet of Troy. It is not surprising that Garnet approved, for he was quite a revolutionary in his own right. In an 1843 speech entitled "Address to the Slaves of the United States of America," he declared, "Strike for your lives. Now is the day and the hour.... Let your motto be resistance! *resistance!* RESISTANCE!"[41] Brown was so impressed by these remarks that he purportedly attempted to have them printed in a pamphlet with David Walker's incendiary *Appeal*.[42] Loguen and Garnet, for their part, shared their positive impressions of Brown with Douglass who, in turn, traveled to Brown's New York home in November of 1847.

From their first meeting, the revolutionary Brown made a good impression. Douglass wrote in the *North Star* that he had enjoyed meeting Brown, who "though a white gentleman, is in sympathy, a black man, and as deeply interested in our cause, as though his own soul had been pierced with the iron of slavery"[43] Brown, for his part, continued cultivating the support of blacks and sought out at one time or another Martin R. Delany, Stephen Smith, William Still, and Charles H. Langston in

This photograph by John H. Tarbell of Asheville, NC, shows an African American man reading Joseph Barry's *The Strange Story of Harper's Ferry*. African Americans evidenced a brave and strong support for Brown without the hesitation apparent throughout much of the white community. Barry was a local resident and eyewitness to the raid (Library of Congress, Prints and Photographs Division).

addition to Douglass, Loguen and Garnet. But it was clear that it was the well-known and highly regarded Douglass whose aid he particularly wished to enlist.[44] Indeed, it attests to Brown's ties in the black community that the suggestion Douglass meet Brown came from the two black men rather than from the white abolitionist organization.[45] The respect Brown received from the black community was mutual. Apparently no black who knew Brown ever criticized his behavior toward their race. Unlike most white abolitionists, Brown's ties to the black community were both strong and close.[46]

Douglass' first meeting with Brown coincided with Douglass' lecture tour. Brown invited Douglass to stop by Springfield, Massachusetts, on his way to Rochester. During this overnight visit, Brown earnestly confided in Douglass his conviction that slavery constituted a "state of war and the slave had a right to anything necessary to his freedom." He also relayed his belief that "No people ... could have self-respect, or be respected, who would not fight for their freedom."[47] Douglass would incorporate this second point in many of his lectures of the 1850s. From the time of his meeting with Brown forward, Douglass began to doubt slavery could be abolished by nonviolent means, believing instead that it "could only be destroyed by bloodshed."[48]

In *The Life and Times of Frederick Douglass*, he detailed his initial meeting with Brown: "I chanced to spend a night and a day under the roof of a man whose character and conversation, and whose objects and aims in life, made a very deep impression upon my mind and heart," he wrote. Douglass was ready for Brown's message that slaveholders had forfeited their right to live, that the slaves had the right to gain their liberty in any way they could, and agreed with Brown, who "did not believe that moral suasion would ever liberate the slave, or that political action would abolish the system."[49] One night during the visit, in a conversation beginning after supper and lasting until 3:00 A.M., Brown unveiled his plans for an invasion.[50] The news must have astonished Douglass, who later admitted that he "ventured at some points" to oppose Brown's ideas. However, Brown "seemed to convince all" and Douglass found many of his fears allayed. The plan the two men discussed that evening involved establishing a black state in the Allegheny Mountains, but "did not, as some suppose, contemplate a general rising among slaves, and a general slaughter of the slave-masters." Rather, the proposal involved the creation of "an armed force which should act in the very heart of the South," for Brown was "not averse to the shedding of blood...."[51]

Like Emerson and Thoreau, Douglass was deeply impressed with Brown. He would never again pass through Springfield without calling on him. Brown, in turn, never went through Rochester without visiting Douglass. A correspondence ensued between the two men in which Brown often turned to Douglass for advice and direction. The relationship had a profound influence on Douglass, as well, who conceded that "while I continued to write and speak against slavery, I became all the same less hopeful of its peaceful abolition. My utterances became more and more tinged by the color of this man's strong impressions."[52]

In 1851, it was Brown who advocated violence. While in Springfield, Massachusetts, he formed the League of Gileadites, an organization designed to help blacks defend themselves against slave catchers. In his advice to the group, Brown encouraged, "Nothing so charms the American people as personal bravery."[53] In response to the Fugitive Slave Law, Brown urged the Gileadites to use force when necessary.[54]

By the mid–1850s, both Douglass and Brown had turned their attention to Kansas. Douglass used his *Frederick Douglass' Paper* to support the efforts of the antislavery settlers. In one article, referring to Kansas as a "hell-bent scheme for extending human bondage," he encouraged that emigrants be "sent out to possess the goodly land."[55] On 4 July 1856, he ran a letter from a Free State settler to his parents describing conditions in Kansas Territory: "Dear Parents;—To-day I write you under circumstances more painful than have ever been witnessed before in Kansas. The war has actually begun...." The young man then proceeded to describe a raid in which "a body of 100 horsemen" rode through town firing into homes, breaking windows, smashing belongings and plundering personal possessions. "In this manner they treated nearly every house in town" he concluded.[56]

Among those informing Douglass of the events on the ground in Kansas was John Brown, Jr., In mid-August 1855, he wrote a long letter to Douglass in which he expressed his fear that a free Kansas would mean freedom for white men only. "Shall Kansas be a free *White* state only, or a state in which *all* shall have their rights protected irrespective of color?" he asked. He worried openly of the "most outrageous restrictions [being placed] upon the colored man" by Kansas settlers.[57]

Six weeks prior to the massacre at Pottawatomie, John Brown, Jr., again wrote Douglass describing the deteriorating events in Kansas. "Our enemies are determined to drive us into forcible resistance," he wrote. "Hourly are we moving in the midst of inflammable material which it needs but a spark to ignite."[58] That spark would come in the form of the series of brutal murders at Pottawatomie. Nevertheless, the friendship between the Browns and Douglass continued to grow, and in September of 1856, when Douglass realized that the purported death of Brown in Missouri was false, he was very much relieved, as evidenced by his report to his readers that Brown "deserved a better fate 'than to perish in an obscure fight with the ruffian hordes of Missouri.'" Further, Douglass expressed the hope that Brown would live to "succeed in planting in Kansas a free and prosperous community."[59]

Shortly after the raid at Pottawatomie, Brown came to Rochester to visit Douglass for several weeks. During that time, he began work on a constitution to govern his followers.[60] Douglass, for his part, took the opportunity to defend Brown against the Kansas charges. In a departure from his public utterances advocating nonviolence, Douglass fumed in a *North Star* editorial: "[Brown] has been charged with murder! What could be more absurd! If he has sinned in anything, it is in that he has spared lives of murderers, when he had the power to take vengeance upon them."[61] In a May 1857 address, Douglass decried the notion that blacks did not care "enough for liberty to fight for it." The converse was true, insisted Douglass, as indicated by every Southern slave insurrection.[62]

Throughout the decade, the Browns kept in touch with Douglass. In October of 1856, Watson Brown visited Douglass at his home in Rochester, as did Brown himself two months later. The following spring, Brown was a guest at an antislavery gathering in Worcester, Massachusetts, and heard Douglass give an address which he pronounced "powerful indeed." By January of 1858, Brown had returned from Kansas and was back at Douglass's home. Not only did Douglass promise him $50, but, more important to Brown, he seemed "to appreciate my theories & my labours."[63] Over the course of several weeks in February, Brown shared Douglass's roof as he began to finalize his plans for an invasion. Although occasionally making references to the government arsenal at Harpers Ferry, he seemed much more interested in writing a constitution to form "a regularly-constituted government" for a slave state in the Alleghenies.[64] Later Douglass denied he discussed specific plans for the raid: "Once in a while he would say he could, with a few resolute men, capture Harpers Ferry, and supply himself with arms belonging to the government." Yet, Douglass averred, "he never announced his intention to do so."[65]

From Douglass's home, Brown wrote letters to a number of black leaders, hoping to enlist their attendance at a planned meeting in Philadelphia. He advised that return correspondence be addressed to N. (Nelson) Hawkins and posted in care of Frederick Douglass. Brown then enlisted Douglass's thirteen year old son, Charles, to pick up and deliver his mail from the post office. The meeting that Brown desired was postponed to accommodate Douglass's plans, and eventually took place on March 16. While overall attendance was not what Brown had hoped, the meeting drew four of the most prominent African American abolitionists of the time, including Douglass and the militant Reverend Henry Highland Garnet. William Still and Stephen Smith, both well known for

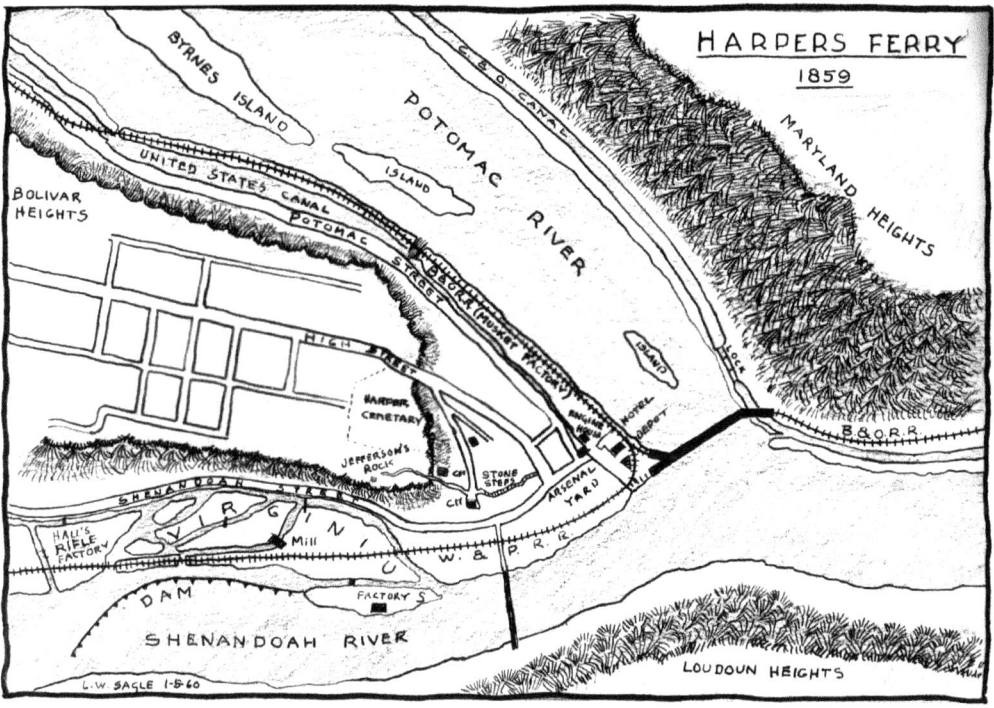

A close look at this hand-drawn map of Harpers Ferry dated 1859 illustrates the futility in Brown's choice of location. Locked in by rivers on both sides, there was little chance for escape, a fact that perhaps led Frederick Douglass to refuse Brown's offer to accompany him on the raid. Douglass warned Brown that he was "going into a perfect steel-trap, and that once in he would never get out alive" (from the collections of the B&O Railroad Museum).

their Underground Railroad operations, also attended. Brown was pleased and reported to his wife, Mary, that he was impressed by the earnestness of the people of color in the crusade.[66]

However, even as Brown continued his plans for the raid, an acquaintance, Colonel Forbes, determined to expose him. It was Douglass who came to Brown's rescue. "I think I was the first to be informed of [Forbes's] tactics, and I promptly communicated them to Captain Brown," Douglass wrote. Learning that Forbes had betrayed Brown by revealing his plans to the government, Douglass informed Brown, thus leading "to the postponement of the enterprise another year." While at Douglass's home, Brown made the acquaintance of Shields Green, a fugitive slave, to whom Brown "confided ... his plans and purposes." Green easily believed in Brown, and promised to go with him "whenever he should be ready to move."[67]

In the fall of 1859, three weeks before the attack on Harpers Ferry, Brown contacted Douglass, asking him to come with Shields Green to a quarry in Chambersburg, Pennsylvania, where he was making imminent plans for the raid. Douglass did so, stopping on the way to receive money for Brown from the Reverend and Mrs. James Gloucester. To shield the true purpose of his visit, Douglass gave a speech the evening of the 20th in the town hall.[68] But, once arriving in Chambersburg, Douglass "sat down among the rocks" with "Mr. Kagi, Captain Brown, [and] Shields Green" and "talked over the enterprise which was about to be undertaken." This time, Brown clearly delineated his plans for the "taking of Harper's Ferry," and asked Douglass's opinion on the matter. Douglass claimed to have adamantly opposed the idea, telling Brown he was "going into a perfect steel-trap, and that once in he would never get out alive...." Realizing Brown "was not to be shaken," Douglass nonetheless told him that "Virginia would blow him and his hostages sky-high, rather than that he should hold Harper's Ferry an hour." Brown desperately wanted Douglass to accompany him on the raid and pleaded, "Come with me, Douglass; I will defend you with my life. I want you for a special purpose. When I strike, the bees will begin to swarm, and I shall want you to help hive them." But no plea could entice Douglass, who had already made up his mind: "My discretion or my cowardice made me proof against the dear old man's eloquence—perhaps it was something of both which determined my course."[69] Shields Green would accompany Brown to Harpers Ferry, from which neither would return alive. Soon after, Douglass would leave for England, a wanted man.

Six

LYDIA MARIA CHILD

Unlike her male counterparts, Lydia Maria Child would never meet John Brown, nor would she entirely come to accept violence as a necessary condition for the eradication of slavery. A pacifist and a woman of self-described "peace principles," she would speak against violence until her death. Yet, she would become one of John Brown's most ardent, influential and effective supporters. This apparent contradiction is one of many in her character, for Maria, as she preferred to be called, was a philanthropist of limited means, a childless author of children's books, a wage earning woman who dispensed advice for housewives, a pragmatist married to a dreamer, an independent woman in a time of bondage, and, underneath her matronly exterior, a revolutionary.

Although today she is perhaps best remembered for her Thanksgiving verse "Over the river and through the woods to grandmother's house we go," her literary accomplishments reflect a divergent group of interests and abilities. At one time or another she penned historical fiction, children's stories, poetry, essays, and political tracts. She edited the *National Anti-Slavery Standard* and pioneered the art form of the letter with her successful *Letters from New York* series. She crafted one of the first novels by an American woman, *Hobomok*, and is said to have been one of the creators of the children's literature genre. She gave housewives advice with the best-selling *The Frugal Housewife*, the first of its kind for American women, and gave birth to the "genre of antislavery fiction that Harriet Beecher Stowe would later popularize."[1] As scholar Carolyn Karcher marveled, "Merely to total up her output—forty-seven books and tracts, enough uncollected fiction and journalism to fill up one or two more volumes, and more than two thousand surviving letters—is to recognize the magnitude of her achievement."[2] How Child evolved from children's writer to her position at the epicenter of one of the greatest political controversies of all time, Harpers Ferry, and the price she paid for that journey, is one of the most fascinating and heroic stories in American literature.

Lydia Maria Francis was born on 11 February 1802. She would change her name at age 19 to Maria, not being fond of the name Lydia.[3] Like most women of her generation, Maria's schooling was limited to public education, with the exception of a single year in private school. One of Francis's early teachers, "marm Betty," was most notable not for her teaching prowess but for having been caught by Governor Brooks "drinking out of the nose of her tea-kettle."[4] On the other hand, Maria's brother, Convers, would be encouraged to attend Harvard, where he would remain as a professor of theology. For many years, it was Convers, a friend of Emerson's and a transcendentalist himself, who would encourage Maria in her reading and intellectual pursuits. Yet, even while her brother served as a foil for her scholarly interests, he was more conventional than his impassioned sister, often urging caution when Child espoused abolitionist positions.

Personally, he would wait until the antislavery cause gained a modicum of respectability before endorsing it.⁵

Maria's literary career began on a quiet Sunday in 1824 between services at Convers's church. Having read an article in the *North American Review* suggesting the rich fodder of American history for historical novels, she determined to write one herself. Before the day was out, she began *Hobomok*, a startling tale of miscegenation. In six weeks, the story of a white woman who marries an Indian was completed and it was published in May 1824. *Hobomok* would later be termed "the first New England historical novel...."⁶ Thomas Wentworth Higginson, a contemporary and friend of Maria's, claimed it "marked the very dawn of American imaginative literature."⁷ The novel was in many ways a precursor of Maria's entire career—a courageous tale of equality of the races told within a new genre in American literature, written by a woman in a hitherto predominantly male sphere.

The slender brown volume was published, like those of other female writers of the time, anonymously and at Maria's own expense. Before long, however, word was out that *Hobomok* was the work of Convers Francis's younger sister.⁸ The novel's plot revolves around the story of young Mary Conant, who, believing her white suitor to be dead, marries an Indian, Hobomok. When she realizes that fiancé Charles Brown is, in fact, alive, she divorces Hobomok to return happily to the arms of her well-bred first love. The story, a daring one for its time, deals not only with miscegenation but divorce. Deborah Clifford contends that "no other writer had had the nerve to speak approvingly of marriage between an Indian and a white woman," adding that "even the subject of divorce was taboo...."⁹ Sales of the novel were slow. The prestigious *North American Review*, in a review not altogether unfavorable, denounced Mary Conant's marriage to Hobomok as "not only unnatural, but revolting ... to every feeling of delicacy."¹⁰ Undaunted, Maria appealed to George Ticknor, an influential voice in literary circles. Soon, a new, more flattering review appeared in the *Review* and sales of the novel improved.¹¹

While Maria was exploring a literary career, her personal life was taking a dramatic turn. In December she was introduced to David Lee Child, a young lawyer. By 1828 they would wed,

Children's author Lydia Maria Child was a pacifist. Yet, she became one of Brown's most influential and ardent supporters. Few could guess that under her matronly exterior lay a revolutionary. Date of photograph unknown (Wayland Historical Society).

embarking on a marriage in which almost from the beginning she was the sole support. David, by all accounts a good man, was nonetheless an impractical one, choosing to invest in various enterprises and charitable causes which left the young couple virtually penniless. Maria, in addition to caring for David and at times her aging father, also became the family's chief breadwinner.

Perhaps it was this newfound responsibility, or a recognition of the subscribed role of female writers, but Maria's literary interests soon took a dramatic turn. Higginson observed, "In those days it seemed to be held necessary for American women to work their passage into literature by first compiling some kind of cookery book," or in the words of Charlotte Hawes, "First this steak and then that stake."[12] Thus, in 1824, Maria published her first children's book, entitled *Evenings in New England*, in which she reveals some of her earliest thoughts on the slavery question. The book takes the form of a conversation between a young man, Robert, and his Aunt Maria. Robert observes that Southerners must be quite cruel if they keep slaves. Aunt Maria disagrees, saying, "I regard slavery rather as their misfortune than their fault," echoing Emerson's early views on the subject. "Many of their best men would gladly be rid of it," she wrote, "and some time or other, I have no doubt they will."[13] In a story entitled "The Little Master and His Slave," Maria advocates educating slaves and relocating them to Haiti, where they can be free.[14] While neither position could be termed radical, the very fact that Maria tackled the vexing question of slavery as early as 1824 when others were silent on the subject can be viewed as courageous.

In 1826, Maria began editing the first children's magazine in the United States, *The Juvenile Miscellany*, a decision that was not only lucrative but one that also increased her burgeoning popularity. The timing was fortuitous, as the number of literate American women had doubled between 1790 and 1840, providing Maria with a new, eager market of readers.[15] Once again, Maria would use the magazine as a vehicle for her antislavery sentiments. Nearly every issue of the new magazine beginning in September 1830 refutes black prejudice in some form.[16]

Meanwhile, like the Emersons, Maria and David worked together to protest the removal of the Cherokees from their homeland. Maria chose the moment to publish anonymously a children's book entitled *The First Settlers of New England*, educating the public by detailing various stories about Indians while choosing not directly to discuss the Cherokee question. She learned early the art of indirect influence, deemed necessary by her gender, and used it to great advantage throughout her life. Her husband, David, not so constrained, led a forceful editorial campaign against the relocation, for which he received thanks from Chief John Ross in 1831.[17]

By 1829, Maria and David's financial situation was dire. While editor of the *Massachusetts Journal*, David had been a defendant in two losing libel lawsuits and Maria fast realized that it would be up to her to tackle the family's growing debts. She rose to the challenge with the publication of *The Frugal Housewife*, sharing her cost saving ideas with a generation of American women. While there were other such manuals, this was the first designed solely for an American audience. In it, Maria offered suggestions for dealing with everything from bedbugs to cockroaches. The book was an indisputable bestseller, selling 6,000 copies the first year.[18] By 1855, the book was in its thirty-third American edition, in addition to twelve editions in the British Isles.[19] In 1831, Maria took advantage of her growing popularity to publish *The Mother's Book*, aimed at the same audience. Once again, the book proved to be a resounding success, reaching eight American and twelve English editions by 1845. It was also translated into German.[20]

At long last it seemed as if Maria's literary popularity was assured. John Greenleaf Whittier, a poet and friend, later claimed that at this point in her life Maria was "the most popular literary woman in the United States."[21] The Boston Athenaeum, the only public library at the time, acknowledged Maria's success with the almost unheard of gift of a free membership. It seemed that little could stand in the way of her continued success, little except perhaps her growing antislavery consciousness. In January of 1831, with the publication of *Jumbo and Zairee*, Child reflected her growing concerns about the slavery controversy. Unlike the temperate *Evenings in New England*, here Child decries slavery as "wrong in the site [sic] of God." Since it "cannot be made right by the laws of man," she urges masters to free their slaves.[22] Although in the end of the work she returns slaves to their African homeland, her position is clearly edging towards a far more radical one than many of her contemporaries.

This growing preoccupation with slavery was, perhaps, an outgrowth of her continued association with William Lloyd Garrison and his band of antislavery reformers. David joined Garrison and "a dozen or so others" on a brutally cold January day in 1832 in the basement of an African American church to discuss formation of the New England Anti-Slavery Society.[23] Both Maria's published antislavery sentiments, and her husband's obvious association with the reform movement, were daring. At the time, southern riots against African Americans were commonplace, with "people merely suspected of abolitionist tendencies ... hounded out of town and sometimes publicly whipped."[24] Abolitionist literature was seized from southern post offices by gangs who then burned the offending documents. Things were no better in New England where merchants, who derived a living, albeit indirectly, from slavery, were determined to quash the public debate. They were aided in this endeavor by ministers who barred abolitionist speakers from their pulpits. Throughout the North, "rioters led by 'gentlemen of property and standing' disrupted abolitionist meetings, threatened abolitionist leaders with lynching, [and] destroyed abolitionist printing presses...." Even the United States Congress refused to discuss slavery and enacted a gag rule forbidding discussion of the issue.[25]

Thus, it was particularly brave when Maria, using her free library privileges at the Boston Athenaeum, quietly began research on the most extensive study of slavery to appear to that date. Possibly she was inspired to do so by Garrison's 1833 statement that "the destiny of the slaves is in the hands of the American women, and complete emancipation can never take place without their co-operation."[26] His words were indeed prophetic: by 1838 over six thousand American women were enrolled in the membership ranks of antislavery societies.[27] In addition to their primary role as fund-raisers and organizers of antislavery events, women were also wielding a profound influence on the men in their lives, who were perhaps increasingly embarrassed by their own inaction in regard to the slavery question. The Emerson and Thoreau households were only two of many where the women took a lead in social reform. With Garrison's call to women, Maria must have found herself in something of a predicament. Like Emerson, she understood the struggle between writer and reformer. "My natural inclinations drew me much more strongly towards literature and the arts than towards reform, and the weight of

$200 Reward!

Ranaway from the sub-scriber, living in Saline county, on the 4th inst., two Negro men, named Jim and Jack---each aged about 25 years.

Jim is dish-faced; has sore eyes and bad teeth; is of a light black or brown color; speaks quick, is about 5 feet 7 inches high; had on when last seen, blue cotton pants, white shirt, white fulled coat and new custom-made boots.

Jack had on the same kind of clothing with shoes, has a very small foot, wears perhaps a No. 6 shoe, and has heavy tacks in the heels; is about the same height and color of Jim. They are doubtless aiming for K. T.

A reward of $100 each will be given if taken outside of the State, or $50 each if taken in the State, outside of Saline county. **G. D. WILLIAMS,**
Spring Garden, P. O., Pettis county, Missouri.
Harrisonville, Mo., June 7th, 1860.

A two hundred dollar reward was offered for escaped slaves from Saline County, Missouri, described in this poster dated 7 June 1860. Lydia Maria Child effectively quoted similar sources to decry slavery in her famous letter to Mrs. Mason of Virginia. Child claimed she might have quoted from "hundreds of such advertisements, offering rewards for runaways, 'dead or alive' ... with 'ears cut off,' 'jaws broken,' 'scarred by rifle-balls,' &c." The correspondence with Mason would be published, bringing Maria the largest readership of her career—300,000 in an era when a typical best-seller might run to 8,000 (Kansas State Historical Society).

conscience was needed to turn the scale," she later conceded.[28] But her association with Garrison and early reformers, coupled with her innate sense of justice and fair play, soon turned the tide in ways she could not have imagined.

The year 1833 would be remarkable both for the country and for the Childs. The American Anti-Slavery Society was formed at a Philadelphia convention and was "everywhere spoken against."[29] At the same time, Maria's literary career was flourishing. In July, the *North American Review*, which had once found *Hobomok* offensive, published a twenty-five page overview of her work, concluding with "[W]e are not sure that any woman in our country would outrank Mrs. Child," and deeming her "just the woman we want for the mothers and daughters of the present generation."[30] The *Review* would change its opinion dramatically a month later when Maria "startled the country" with a slim volume entitled *Appeal in Behalf of That Class of Americans Called Africans*.[31] In the volume, Maria condemned both southern and northern prejudice against blacks, urged racial equality and detailed the proud history of the African race. Ethiopia, she argued by example, was a distinguished culture. Throughout the heavily researched work, she employed a clever technique which she would later use to great effect in defense of Brown—the reliance on southern sources to detail the abuses of slavery. To what extent her critics actually read the work is difficult to ascertain as the incendiary title alone was enough to provoke fear and outrage. For most southerners, the notion of any appeal in the context of slavery echoed David Walker's 1823 *Appeal*, which was said to have incited Nat Turner's bloody rebellion.[32]

Bravely, she denounced the widely held notion of black inferiority, blaming the institution of slavery rather than the slave for any perceived inferiority. "With our firm belief in the natural inferiority of negroes, it is strange we should be so much afraid that knowledge will elevate them quite too high for our convenience," she wrote. Dismissing the question as a "most absurd apology, for personal prejudice," she avowed, "I shall take some pains to prove that the present degraded condition of that unfortunate race is produced by artificial causes, not by the laws of nature."[33]

In a chapter entitled "Prejudices Against People of Color, and Our Duties in Relation to this Subject," she decried the racial prejudice of not only the South, but also of the North. "Will any candid person tell me why respectable colored people should not be allowed to make use of public conveyances, open to all who are able and willing to pay for the privilege?" she asked, adding, "If they can afford to take a carriage or boat for themselves, then, and then only, they have a right to be exclusive."[34]

Yet, while Maria went to great lengths to dispute the inferiority of the Negro race, and vehemently condemned racial prejudice, she stopped short of suggesting revolution as a solution to the nation's woes. "I do not wish to promote insurrections," she affirmed. "I would, on the contrary, do all I could to prevent them." Acknowledging that "If insurrections do occur, they will no doubt be attributed to the Anti-Slavery Society," Maria warned that it was not the abolitionists but rather "the increased severity of the laws" which was "very likely to goad an oppressed people to madness."[35]

Maria was at least partially aware that her "mite into the treasury" might displease "all classes," and yet, she avowed it was her "duty to fulfil this task; and earthly considerations should never stifle the voice of conscience."[36]

The effect of the volume's appearance was immediate and extraordinary. Samuel May would later marvel that Child "was extensively known in the Southern as well as the Northern States, and her books commanded a ready sale there...." However, he had no idea that "she possessed the power, if she had the courage, to strike so heavy a blow [against slavery]."[37] The influence of the *Appeal* lay not only in its words, but also in its timing. It was only two years previously that Garrison had begun the *Liberator*, and two years hence that he would be dragged through the streets of Boston and almost lynched by "gentlemen of property and standing."[38] For "such an author—ay, such an *authority*—[to] espouse our cause just at that crisis ... was a matter of no small joy, yes, exultation."[39]

Yet, while the small band of abolitionists rejoiced, Maria's reading public reacted with almost universal outrage and condemnation. Those who had loved her and held her to be an icon for American women, now excoriated her. From this point forward, "her life was a battle; a constant rowing hard against the stream of popular prejudice and hatred."[40] Wendell Phillips concurred: "Hardly ever was there a costlier sacrifice. Few of us can appreciate it to-day. Narrow means just changing to ease; after a weary struggle, fame and social position in her grasp; every door opening before her; the sweetness of having her genius recognized." All of this was destroyed in the aftermath of a public statement of conscience. "No one had supposed that independence of opinion on a moral question would wreck all this"[41]

The financial impact on the Childs was immediate. Whittier observed that "[s]ocial and literary circles, which had been proud of her presence, closed their doors against her" while "sale[s] of her books, [and] the subscriptions to her magazine, fell off to a ruinous extent."[42] Harriet Martineau commented, "Her works were bought with avidity before, but fell into sudden oblivion as soon as she had done a greater deed than writing any or all of them."[43] Sales further deteriorated when ministers urged their congregations to steer clear of the young reformer, warning "evil and ruin to our country, if the women generally should follow Mrs. Child's bad example, and neglect their domestic duties to attend to the affairs of state."[44]

The Boston Athenaeum, once her proud patron, immediately withdrew Maria's library privileges, while a future attorney general of Massachusetts supposedly employed tongs to toss the odious work out of his window.[45] Edward Everett Hale, an adolescent at the time, later claimed when he saw the volume in a bookstore window that he considered throwing a stone at it.[46]

As if the scorn of strangers was not bad enough, Maria's friendships suffered as well. When Child approached Catherine Sedgwick asking her to contribute to her next antislavery volume, *The Oasis*, Sedgwick delayed her response. Finally, she agreed on the condition that she could espouse a moderate antislavery position calling for colonization, a position not terribly far from Maria's earlier pronouncements on the subject. In an eloquent response, Child refused, saying, "To the last hour of my life my voice and my pen shall be given to ... [antislavery] work—by the way-side and by the fire-side—at the corners of streets, in the recesses of the counting room—in the publicity of the stage-coach, and the solitude of prayer." She then concluded: "For this cause I wish to live—for this cause I am willing to die."[47]

In spite of her bravery in publishing and then defending her work, Maria must have been devastated by the fury swirling around her. At the same time, she was prepared for it. In the preface to the *Appeal* she wrote, "I am fully aware of the unpopularity of the task I have undertaken; but though I *expect* ridicule and censure, I cannot *fear* them." She added, "Should it be the means of advancing, even one single hour, the inevitable progress of truth and justice, I would not exchange the consciousness for all Rothchild's wealth, or Sir Walter's fame."[48] At the same time, it is hard to believe that the courageous young writer was prepared for "how entirely [she] cut herself off from the favor and sympathy of a large number of those who had previously delighted to do her honor."[49] Before the end of 1834, so many subscriptions had been cancelled to the *Juvenile Miscellany* that she was forced to resign as editor.[50] Southern bookstores previously anxious to have her works now shipped them back to the publisher citing lack of demand.[51]

Maria, true to her character, never complained about the reaction to her *Appeal*, choosing instead to rededicate herself to the antislavery cause. One clue, however, to the personal cost she paid can be found in a poem she wrote which appeared in the *Liberator* shortly after the publication of the *Appeal*. Maria cited the poem's subject as a contemporary painting, "Maro seated amid the ruins of Carthage," but one does not have to look hard to see the lonely young author behind the lines:

> Pillars are fallen at thy feet,
> Fanes quiver in the air,
> A prostrate city is thy seat,—
> And thou alone art there.
> No change comes o'er thy noble brow,
> Though ruin is around thee;
> Thine eye beam burns as proudly now,
> As when the laurel crowned thee.
> It cannot bend thy lofty soul
> Though friends and fame depart;
> The car of fate may o'er thee roll,
> Nor crush thy Roman heart.
> And Genius hath electric power,
> Which earth can never tame;
> Bright suns may scorch, and dark clouds lower,
> Its flush is still the same.
> The dreams we loved in early life,
> May melt like mist away;
> High thoughts may seem, 'mid passion's strife,
> Like Carthage in decay.
> And proud hopes in the human heart
> May be to ruin hurled,
> Like mouldering monuments of art
> Heaped on a sleeping world.
> Yet there is something will not die,
> Where life hath once been fair;
> Some towering thoughts still rear on high,
> Some Roman lingers there![52]

With the publication of the *Appeal*, Child's literary career, the primary source of the couple's income, was decimated. Both the *Juvenile Miscellany* and *The Mother's Book* went out of print. *The Frugal Housewife* held on, although sales dropped precipitously.[53]

But while Maria lost friends and resources as a result of her moral position, she also gained a reputation of prominence within the abolitionist movement almost unparalleled for a woman. In New York, the Reverend Ludlow publicly proclaimed that "Mrs. Child had done more to wake up the people to effort in this cause of God and humanity than all the men that went before her in this country."[54] Her influence propelled many into the abolitionist ranks, including Thomas Wentworth Higginson, who financially backed John Brown and later became Emily Dickinson's editor, and future senator Charles Sumner, who would be remembered for the brutal beating he sustained on the floor of Congress at the hands of southern congressman Preston Brooks.[55] Maria admitted that William Ellery Channing, the prominent Unitarian minister whose *Slavery* influenced the young Waldo Emerson, "thought I went too far."[56] Nevertheless, Channing acknowledged that the *Appeal* had awakened his conscience, leading him to ponder "whether [or not] I ought to remain silent on the subject [of slavery]."[57]

In the black community, Child's *Appeal* engendered admiration and respect. Maria herself later maintained modestly that her book "produced a sensation disproportioned to its merits."[58] But James Forten, a black abolitionist, would have disagreed with that assessment, declaring the work one of the best of its kind.[59] Maria's close relationship with the black community, which would last throughout her life, was a result of her decided lack of personal racial prejudice. Even in the ranks of the abolition movement, socializing between blacks and whites was extremely rare. While black women were permitted to join female antislavery societies, this openness was not always present in the male organizations. Maria, however, had little use for racially based social constraints and when a black couple came by her house to seek legal advice from David, she invited them to stay to tea. Fearing social repercussions for the Childs, they refused, yet the story of the invitation spread, causing, according to Harriet Martineau, "loud laughter" among aristocratic ladies as "Boston ... rang with the report that Mr. and Mrs. Child had given entertainment to colored people."[60]

All the frenzy surrounding Maria as a result of the publication of the *Appeal* did not deter her reform activities, rather it seemed to solidify her devotion to the antislavery cause. The next four books she published were antislavery, beginning with *The Oasis*, published in 1834. Inside the book's cover, in a statement entitled TO THE PUBLIC, Maria wrote, "I assure you I do not take pleasure in bidding defiance to public prejudice." Yet, she reiterated that while she respected the "opinion of the meanest individual in the community," she did not "fear the censure of the highest."[61] In the preface, she added, "[T]here are doubtless many who still think the writing [of] such a book as this requires apology; but to such I have no excuse to offer. Their God is not my God."[62]

As she and David pursued their antislavery course, events propelled them into ever more dangerous territory. In August of 1835, British abolitionist George Thompson gave an address in Boston honoring the first anniversary of the British emancipation of the West Indies. Maria was in the audience and anxiously noted a number of southerners standing in the rear as well as "a dozen or more stout truckmen, in shirt sleeves, with faces red enough to make a rain-drop sizzle...." Shaken, with heart pounding, Maria feared a violent eruption. Thompson mounted the platform and began his address to a tension filled audience. As Maria scanned the crowd, she noticed that the front and rear entrances were barred by "desperate-looking fellows, brandishing clubs and cart-whips." At the conclusion of the address, Maria rose, and with a group of other women, surrounded the speaker, peppering him with conversation as they slowly edged toward the rear of the platform. Reaching a door, the circle of women parted and Thompson dashed safely to a waiting car followed by "a volley of oaths from the truckmen, and a deafening rush down the front stairs...."[63]

When it was determined that she and David would accompany Thompson to England as antislavery lecturers, Maria was decidedly thrilled. Accordingly, they auctioned off their furniture on 6 August in preparation for the move. Because of the fierce antislavery sentiment, Thompson and the Childs were hustled out of Boston on 10 August and taken to Brooklyn where they would await their departure.[64] But anti-abolitionist feelings ran high in New York as well. On the steamboat journey to New York, they were surrounded by "polished gentlemen" with "fierce manifestations of hatred" on their faces. Once having landed, these men were "suddenly transformed into demons ... follow[ing] close behind us, as we walked the deck, with clenched fists ... uttering the most fearful imprecations."[65] After arriving at the home of an antislavery supporter, Maria wrote a friend: "I have not ventured into the city, nor does one of us dare to go to church today, so great is the excitement here. You can form no conception of it. 'Tis like the times of the French Revolution, when no man dared trust his neighbors." Fearing that "[p]rivate assassins from New Orleans are lurking at the corners of the streets," Maria confided that she feared for Thompson's safety, admitting "I tremble for him...."[66]

Her fears were not unfounded. The next morning their host returned with a placard which had been posted throughout the city alerting residents that the "notorious English swindler and vagabond, George Thompson, is now in the city" and providing an address where he could be located. The sign continued: "'I hereby order my trusty followers to bring him before me, without delay.'" The edict was signed "JUDGE LYNCH," in effect issuing a public call for a lynching. Throughout the long nights in New York, Maria "started at every sound...." In the midst of the turmoil, although feeling she was "not of sufficient consequence to endanger anybody," Maria nonetheless feared her presence in the house would lead the way to Thompson, so she journeyed to a hotel in Bath and "staid there alone." She would later write, "Never, before or since, have I experienced such utter desolation, as I did the few days I remained there," adding, "It seemed to me as if anti-slavery had cut me off from all the sympathies of my kind."[67]

But, terrible as this was, it was not nearly as painful for Maria as what lay ahead. As she and David waited on the dock to board the ship for their trip to England, David was arrested for nonpayment of a debt owed to his former law partner. Uncharacteristically, the stoic Maria, nerves frayed, "was, for once, seen to sit down and weep...."[68]

Although the great promise of a perhaps easier and less troubled life in England now seemed cruelly out of reach, Maria did not mourn long. By late September, her equilibrium seemingly restored, she wrote Convers: "Sometimes we may be tempted to think it would have been better for us not to have been cast on these evil times; but this is a selfish consideration; we ought rather to rejoice that we have much to do as mediums in the regeneration of the world...." Responding to his admonition that she "be prudent," she contended, "I will be so, as far as is consistent with a sense of duty; but this will not be what the world calls prudent." Citing the importance of "great principles," she reminded him, "I have examined the history of the slave too thoroughly, and felt his wrongs too deeply, to be prudent in the worldly sense of the term."[69]

In spite of her brave words to Convers, her next work was, in fact, free of any antislavery sentiments. *Philothea*, a novel that is both transcendentalism and romance, appeared in bookstores two weeks before Emerson's seminal volume *Nature*. Critics praised Child's work, which explored the connection between the material and spiritual worlds while not mentioning slavery. In what could be viewed as both apology and explanation, Maria defended her apparent change in direction saying, "The hope of extended usefulness has hitherto induced a strong effort to throw myself into the spirit of the times...," but she concedes, "there have been seasons when my soul felt restless in this bondage ... so I, for awhile, bid adieu to the substantial fields of utility, to float on clouds of romance."[70] In the preface of the 1848 edition, she wrote, "This volume is purely romance; and most readers will consider it romance of the wildest kind adding "For such I have written it. To minds of different mould, who may think an apology necessary for what they will deem so utterly useless, I have nothing better to offer than the simple fact that I found delight in doing it."[71]

Philothea was greeted with critical acclaim. Edgar Allan Poe deemed it "an honor to our country, and a signal triumph for our country-women."[72] In Concord, it was a favorite of the young Louisa May Alcott, who acted out the story on her lawn, and college student Henry Thoreau, who copied various excerpts from the work into his journal. Sales of the work, however, were disappointing. A fellow writer, S.J. Hale, who had chastised Maria for "doing incalculable injury to humanity" through her reform activities, attributed the sluggish sales somewhat gleefully to "the bitter feelings engendered" by the antislavery controversy.[73] Regardless of that possibility, the work survived three editions. Maria's response to the novel's reception was predictable. In a letter to Convers, she wrote that while she was happy he liked *Philothea*, she cared "far less about literary success than I could easily make people believe...." At the same time, she confessed to being gratified by the critical acclaim because "it will help to increase my influence in the anti-slavery cause."[74]

Maria's brief sojourn into the world of imagination and romance ended in early August when slavery was brought back to the forefront of her thoughts and energies. Upon learning a young slave girl, Med, was soon to be returned from Boston to the South, Maria was galvanized into action. With a group of women she boldly visited Thompson Aves, who was holding the slave until his daughter could return with him to New Orleans. Aves later claimed the women gained access to his home by pretending to be Sunday school teachers, an accusation that does not seem entirely outside the realm of possibility for the ingenious Mrs. Child, whose own version of events simply says, "Suffice it to say, the way was opened for us."[75] Regardless of how they gained access to the unhappy Aves, the women were unsuccessful in their attempt to persuade him to release Med. However, shortly a writ of habeas corpus was issued prohibiting Med's return until a trial could decide the issue. Maria sat rapt with anxiety in the courtroom as the trial progressed and rejoiced when the judge announced a landmark ruling that if temporarily in a free state, a slave had the right to remain.[76] It was a huge legal victory and one in which Maria no doubt took a great deal of satisfaction. In a letter to a friend, she reported on both the result and the negative reaction to it by the *Commercial Gazette* which, the day after the ruling, said, "such cases cannot but injure the custom of our hotels, now so liberally patronized by gentlemen from the South."[77]

But as gratifying as Med's victory was, soon Maria would suffer a profound personal disappointment. David, once again in financial difficulty as a result of a lost lawsuit, was urged by friends to go to England to study beet production, a fad of the 1830s. Maria stood on the dock and waved good-bye "while one I loved so much was going where I so much wished to go."[78] While it was not in Maria's nature to complain, the stinging injustice of David traveling alone to England was, in biographer Deborah Clifford's words, "a bitter blow from which she never entirely recovered." Further compounding her disappointment must have been the continued negative reaction to her work. While Maria realized the need to increase the family's struggling finances through her writing, she was not finding a ready audience. From 1836 to 1842 she only published two books, and by 1838 no one but the antislavery press seemed interested in her work.[79]

It was at this juncture, in 1837, that Maria was asked to be a delegate from the Boston

Female Anti-Slavery Society (BFASS) to the Woman's Anti-Slavery Convention in New York. This was no small undertaking in a time when "True Women (always capitalized) were required, on Biblical authority, to be silent and submissive...." In spite of these strictures, Maria and approximately two hundred like-minded women "came together 'in fear and trembling'" to establish "the first Anti-Slavery Convention of American Women." The gathering was held at New York's Third Free Church and lasted for three days. Afterwards, the event would gain historic significance for being the first public political gathering of American women as well as the first interracial meeting of any significance as black women from several organizations joined their white sisters in reform.[80] Before the convention's conclusion, the women had prepared statements for publication, created a drive to collect a million antislavery signatures on petitions to Congress, and raised the necessary funds to pay for the use of the church as well as the printing of their work. Reporters, kept out of the gathering, attempted to peek inside to discern the participants whom they later categorized as "misguided ladies" at a "very silly convention." In demeaning terms, the *New York Commercial Advertiser* disparaged the "'oratoresses' who put aside their frying pans to debate weighty matters of state."[81] Nonetheless, the women pursued their vision undeterred by the rebuke and cynicism of the press.

Maria was elected vice president of the gathering, and she offered a number of significant resolutions, among them the following:

> [That] the great question is not one of treatment, but of *principle*; hence, that no compromise can be made on the score of kind usage, while man is held as the property of man.[82]
>
> That we recommend to the women of those states where laws exist recognizing the legal right of the master to retain his slave within their jurisdiction, for a term of time, earnestly to petition their respective legislatures for the repeal of such laws; and that the right of trial by jury may be granted to all persons claimed as slaves.[83]
>
> That a Convention of Anti-Slavery Women be held annually (with the permission of Providence) in Boston, New-York, Philadelphia, or elsewhere, until slavery is abolished.[84]
>
> That we, as abolitionists, use all our influence in having our colored friends seated promiscuously in all our congregations; and that as long as our churches are disgraced with side-seats and corners set apart for them, we will, as much as possible, take our seats with them.[85]

In a further resolution, Maria exhorted her sisters to use their indirect influence on their husbands and fathers. Maria was an expert in this form of backdoor persuasion and remarkably she acknowledged the necessity for it in a resolution: "That we recommend to the wives and daughters of clergymen, throughout the land, to strengthen their husbands and fathers to declare the whole counsel of God on the subject of slavery, fearing no danger, or prejudice, or privation, being willing 'to suffer persecution with them for Christ's sake.'"[86] Another resolution chastised churches for their "death like apathy" and stated that "the Northern churches have their own garments stained with the blood of slavery, and are awfully guilty in the sight of God."[87]

It was lost upon no one that as the women strove for the rights of others, they were "freeing themselves" as well.[88] As a result, as Maria and her fellow female reformers gained prominence as abolitionist speakers, organizers and lecturers, they were increasingly the target of unsolicited and unwelcome advice. In June 1837, the Congregational General Association of Massachusetts wrote a stinging critique of women who chose to participate in the reform movement. "The appropriate duties and influence of women are clearly stated in the New Testament," the letter warned, expressing "regret [for] the mistaken conduct of those who encourage females to bear an obtrusive and ostentatious part in measures for reform."[89] David, however, continued to be a strong proponent of the right of Maria and others to publicly speak their minds, saying he would "feel ashamed now and forever after" should he be the cause of Maria's silence on an issue she felt needed attention.[90] Nathaniel Rogers, the editor Thoreau praised for his antislavery stance, concurred. In December, he exhorted women: "Slavery must be abolished at all sacrifices. You must see that it is done. You are as responsible for its being done, as men are. You are more responsible—for you have more moral influence."[91] Garrison's support for women's involvement in the antislavery cause also remained strong. His stance was not only just, it was self-serving, for the contributions of women financed half of his bills at any given time.[92]

Yet, even as Maria labored valiantly for the antislavery cause, she began to have deep reservations about whether or not moral suasion could successfully bring an end to American slavery. After moving to the conservative area of Northampton, her deepening despair was reflected in a letter to a friend, "I do not believe the South will voluntarily relinquish her slaves, so long as the world stands," she wrote, concluding that emancipation would come about only "through violence." A woman of peace, Maria lamented this state of affairs saying, "I would it might be averted; but I am convinced that it cannot be."[93]

Nineteen thirty-eight also brought Maria to the defense of Emerson, who was at the center of a whirlwind for his refusal to administer communion to his congregation. She wrote Convers: "How absurdly the Unitarians are behaving.... If Emerson's thoughts are not their thoughts, can they not reverence them, inasmuch as they are formed and spoken in freedom?"[94]

Yet, even while her efforts remained focused on others, the year brought grim prospects for the Childs. Maria's books were still not selling and while *The Frugal Housewife* held on, she could not find outlets for her new work.[95] By June 1839, so dire were their financial prospects that Maria returned to Boston, forced to stay for a time with friends. It would be October before she and David were reunited.[96] Before she could act on an impulse to take a job teaching school to increase their income, she and David were asked to edit the *National Anti-Slavery Standard* for $1,000 a year. Neither Maria nor David particularly wanted to live in New York, but by 1841 they had decided to accept the offer with the understanding that David would continue to attend to his now failing beet business and spend as little time as possible in the city while Maria would assume the majority of editorial responsibilities.[97] Higginson would later claim that "Mr. Child's health being impaired, his wife undertook the task alone" for the first two years of their joint editorship.[98]

Regardless of her initial reluctance, Maria plunged into her editorial responsibilities with the same passion which imbued all of her antislavery work, using her new position to foster a mutual respect with people of color. She broke ranks with earlier editors of the *Standard* "who had editorialized against colored conventions and other forms of black separatist action." She chose instead to establish a dialogue with the African American community. Whenever possible, she published articles and speeches by Frederick Douglass and others who increasingly criticized the pervasive racism of the abolitionists.[99] Financially, the paper thrived under her leadership. After merging with the *Philadelphia Freeman*, subscriptions to the paper increased dramatically. From January of 1841 to May of 1842, subscriptions doubled to 4,000. At the same time, Maria received plaudits from a variety of quarters. Lucretia Mott praised Maria for aiding women in addition to espousing antislavery.[100] Samuel May, Louisa May's uncle and a leader in the antislavery movement, later declared that Maria not only "elevated [the *Standard*'s] literary character, [but] extended its circulation, and increased its efficiency."[101]

Never one to be reticent about expressing her opinion, in one editorial Maria called for a repeal of the Union, believing that this was the only way the free states could alleviate their own guilt over slavery. At the same time, she admonished residents of northern states that they did not have the right to interfere in "the institutions or customs of the southern states ... except with ... weapons of argument and wit," once again echoing her peace principles.[102] Yet, while Child increased the paper's circulation, expanded her own literary horizons and editorialized with impunity, the balancing act her position called for was difficult, if not impossible, with advice coming from so many quarters. In 1842, she resigned her position, saying, "He who turns from the light of his *own* judgment, and the convictions of his *own* conscience, has neither rudder nor pilot in the storm," and adding that the "freedom of my own spirit makes it absolutely necessary for me to retire. I am too distinctly and decidedly an individual, to edit the organ of any association."[103] Once she was free from editorial responsibilities, she asked that her name be removed from the ranks of the AASS (the American Anti-Slavery Society).[104] Never again would Maria be a member of an organized reform movement.

While at the *Standard* seeking an outlet for her creative, less utilitarian, energies, Maria began writing a column detailing her adventures in the city of New York. These letters became increasingly popular and eventually resulted in her published *Letters from New York* series which was critically praised and which signaled her reemergence into literary circles. One might think, given the past reception to her antislavery work, Maria might hesitate to address social problems in these letters. Karcher contends, however, that Child used these letters as a vehicle to explore urban concerns about the poor, capital punishment, and prison reform, which were neglected by many of her male counterparts, Emerson and Thoreau among them.[105] Nevertheless, in 1843, in deciding to publish a collection of her letters in book form, she was uncharacteristically cautious in choosing the content of the letters to be included, choosing to eliminate a letter about capital punishment, two about women's rights, and two about slavery. Her editors convinced her to let the capital punishment and women's rights letters remain, but expressed worry about letters which might offend the South. Ultimately, Maria chose to publish the work at her own risk and under her own editorial control. This was particularly notable given that David, now $30,000 in debt, had filed for bankruptcy and by June of 1843 all of the Childs' personal property had been sold at auction to pay his debts. Their home, in Maria's father's name, remained, but Maria realized she had to take action to protect the couple's future. Therefore, in 1843 she filed a petition to separate her financial affairs from those of David. The decision was a good one as *Letters from New York* was so successful that by December, nearly all of the first edition of 1,500 were sold, and a second edition had been issued. With the coming of spring, Maria had offers for a series of children's books as well as a new edition of *Philothea*.[106] A second volume of *Letters from New York* was published in 1845, and like the first volume would go through at least seven editions.[107]

For the next decade, the now middle-aged Maria seemed content to retreat from a public antislavery persona. In 1843 she was gratified by a visit from Emerson, who provided tickets to his lecture series and then stopped by to chat. Maria attended the lectures, pronouncing them "a prodigious treat." Nonetheless, she was disappointed in Emerson's attitudes toward slavery. "He gave, in one of the lectures, such a glowing and graceful picture of Southern manners and character, that I might have supposed he considered arbitrary power one of the most beneficial influences on man," she wrote. "I should not have quarreled with this," she added, "had he made the least allusion to any *bad* effects." Nor, she fretted, did Emerson even "*allude* to slavery," leading her to conclude that "I cannot think that this is manly and true; for the subject *must* occur to him."[108]

Dr. Palfrey, whom Emerson supported during his 1847 run for Congress, called on Maria to help him find homes for five of his inherited slaves whom he had liberated, telling her he was influenced to do so by her *Appeal*. Charles Sumner, the Massachusetts senator, wrote Maria claiming that her early antislavery writing "had an important effect on his course in Congress...."[109] In 1846, Edgar Allan Poe again praised Child, this time for her "graceful and brilliant *imagination*," a trait he found "rarely noticed in our countrywomen." He concluded by saying "Her bearing needs excitement to impress it with life and dignity. She is of that order of beings who are themselves only on 'great occasions'"[110]

Thus, the years from 1845 to 1855 passed uneventfully for the Childs, largely untouched by the "great occasions" Poe thought stoked Maria's spirit. In 1853, Maria continued her quiet antislavery commitment with a biography entitled *Isaac T. Hopper; a True Life*. In the work, she not only recounted the adventures of "Friend Hopper," but she also rewrote many of the slave narratives he originally published in newspapers under the heading "Tales of Oppression."[111] In so doing, she tackled two commonly held 19th century prejudices: that slaves are lacking in morality, and that they are less intelligent than their white masters. "Who that reads the account here given of Daniel Benson, and William Anderson, can doubt that slaves are capable of as high moral excellence, as has ever been ascribed to them in any work of fiction? Who that reads Zeke, and the Quick Witted Slave, can pronounce them a stupid race, unfit for freedom?" she asks in the preface. "Verily, the slave-power is strong," Maria concludes, "but God and truth are stronger."[112]

By the late 1840s, Child had begun work on what would become a lengthy tome of three volumes entitled *The Progress of Religious Ideas through Successive Ages*. The effort took six years to complete and did no more than break even financially. In July of 1848 she wrote her brother: "My book gets slowly on. I am not sustained by the least hope that my mode of treating the subject will prove acceptable to any class of persons." Nonetheless, as was her habit, Maria promised, "No matter! I am going to tell the plain unvarnished truth, as clearly as I can understand it, and let [all religions] growl as they like."[113]

In spite of her brave words, the decade was a trying one for Maria as she kept house and felt far removed from the reform activity of her earlier years. "What are we here for? I wish I knew," she plaintively wrote Convers, adding, "[S]omehow or other, we *all* get fetters on us."[114] A sense of weariness seemed to pervade her soul as she told a friend that "never before [had she] suffered so much from discouragement and pecuniary anxiety." While Maria conceded that she and David were no worse off financially than they had been previously, it was harder because she was "older" and had "the remembrance of Northampton to terrify [her] perpetually."[115] And so, the years passed with Maria at turns taking care of David and her aging father as she quietly chafed at the chains of her own personal bondage.

All that changed, however, on 19 May 1856, with the beating of her hero, Senator Charles Sumner, by southern congressman Preston Brooks. Maria had admired and corresponded with Sumner previously, gratified by his insistence that she had influenced his antislavery sentiments. Thus, when word arrived that he had been severely beaten, Maria's "first impulse was to rush directly to Washington" to nurse him. Instead, she wrote a long, poignant letter, confiding in Sumner: "At times, my old heart swells almost to bursting ... for it is the heart of a man imprisoned within a woman's destiny."[116] It is obvious from the letter that in addition to thinking about the societal constraints imposed upon her as a woman, Maria was also carefully weighing her pacifism against the necessity of violence for ending the scourge of slavery: "I confess that my peace-principles are sorely tried; insomuch, that nothing suits my mood so well, as Jeanne d'Arc's floating banner and consecrated sword." Yet, she concludes, "I believe in a holiness much higher than heroism.... I can never call those men murderers, who ... suffer and ... die in the cause of freedom." Still, she did not abandon her peace principles entirely, reminding him that "there is a higher standard than theirs, to which the human soul will gradually rise, until there remains no trace of the old ideas of overcoming evil by brute force." Ultimately, Maria weighed in on the side of pacifism, saying, "I honor those who conscientiously fight for justice, truth, or freedom; but I revere those who will *die* to advance great principles, though they will not *kill*."[117] Two days after writing Sumner, in a letter to friends Lucy and Mary Osgood, war was still in her thoughts: "I have always dreaded civil war and prayed that it might be averted; but if there is no *other* alternative than the endurance of such insults and outrages, I am resigned to its approach."[118]

Throughout the fall, Maria was consumed with worry for Sumner. Writing her friend Sarah Shaw, she confided that Sumner's beating "brought on nervous headache and painful suffocations about the heart." Fretting that she was powerless to help, she conceded, "I never was one who knew how to serve the Lord by standing and waiting; and to stand and wait then! It almost drove me mad."[119] To a second friend, Lucy Osgood, she confessed, "At times my peace principles have shivered in the wind.... I begin to hope that either the slave power must yield to argument and the majesty of public sentiment or else that we shall see an army in the field...."[120]

Struggling to find a peaceful alternative to the growing sectional crisis, by the 20th of July Maria had begun to consider the ballot box. "For the first time in my life, I am a *little* infected with *political* excitement," she wrote. The act of voting, however, would be denied her because of her gender. It is not hard to see the frustration behind the humor as she wrote friends Lucy and Mary Osgood: "For the sake of suffering Kansas, and future freedom in peril, I *do* long to have Fremont elected. Don't *you*?" She mischievously added, "Let's *vote!*"[121] On August 3, politics was still very much on Maria's mind. "Because I would *avert* war, I desire to have Fremont victorious," she wrote Sarah Shaw. "If the Slave-Power is checked *now*, it will *never* regain its strength. If it is *not* checked, civil war is inevitable; and, with all my horror of bloodshed, I could be better resigned to that great calamity, than to endure the tyranny that has so long trampled on us." Although Maria here comes perilously close to advocating violence, she concludes her letter by once again offering a political solution to the impending crisis: "What a shame that *women* can't vote!" She then accurately predicts, "I shall not live to see women vote." Even so, she threatens to return in the afterlife, saying, "I'll come and *rap* at the ballot box. Won't *you*?"[122]

Thus, while events in Kansas coupled with Sumner's beating reawakened Maria's antislavery commitment, they also seemed to increase her frustration—chained to an ailing father and a financially inept husband, unable to cast a vote, fettered by her gender, Maria must have felt a keen appreciation of what it meant to live in bondage. On 26 October she expressed as much in a letter to her friend Lucy Loring: "Oh, what misery it is, to feel such a fever heat of anxiety as I do, and yet be shut up in a pen-fold, where I cannot act!"[123]

As she often did when her antislavery sentiments threatened to engulf her, Maria took up her pen, producing a short story entitled "The Kansas Emigrants." The piece was serialized in the *New York Tribune*, preempting the serialized feature, *Little Dorrit*, by Charles Dickens. In the important weeks prior to the hotly contested presidential election between James Buchanan and the antislavery John Fremont, it was Maria's story on Kansas that took center stage. In the piece, Maria exercised some of her newfound political awareness, calling for antislavery proponents to support both the Free State settlers in Kansas and the Republican candidate for president, John Fremont. The work also makes a statement about the role of women in the antislavery conflict, as the protagonist is a gutsy female heroine whose ingenuity, bravery and wit are far more indicative of a 21st century heroine than her 19th century counterpart.

With winter approaching, Maria found a practical outlet for her energies and busied herself by sewing garments for the free state settlers in Kansas. To obtain the cloth, she wrote Mr. Hovey, who agreed to donate cotton, but not before complaining that "money and energy had better be expended on the immediate abolition of slavery, and dissolution of the Union...." Maria's response was both humorous and pragmatic: "I did not think it best to wait for either of these events before I made up the cloth [as] [c]old weather was coming on...." In eight days, Maria, by staying up late and garnering help from her neighbors, had turned "sixty yards of cloth into garments" to protect the Free State settlers from the brutal Kansas winter.[124]

Yet, even while she busied herself sewing throughout the fall, the upcoming election and her inability to vote in it were never far from her thoughts. She wrote David: "Voting day will bring you, of course. If you don't come, I shall put on your old hat and coat, and vote for you." With the publication of "The Kansas Emigrants" and the completion of her sewing project, some of Maria's old sense of humor returned. "I have been told that the 'Boston Post' was down upon me for the verse about President Pierce," she told David. "I couldn't help it. His name would not rhyme to anything but curse!"[125]

In 1857, Maria worked on a volume entitled *Autumnal Leaves*, which contained various poems and sketches. Higginson opined the title was suggestive that Maria "regarded her career of action as drawing to a close."[126] Garrison positively reviewed the work in the pages of the *Liberator*, evoking the past and entailing Maria's early contributions to the antislavery movement. "It cost her friends, reputation, pecuniary support, and subjected her to hostile influences such as few have been called to encounter," he reminded his readers in asking them to purchase the volume.[127]

So, while Maria spent the year on the reflective *Autumnal Leaves*, frustrated by her domestic responsibilities and feeling impotent to change a world she increasingly viewed as hostile to antislavery, her husband, David, and nephew-in-law, George Stearns, would meet John Brown and hear graphic firsthand accounts of life in "bleeding Kansas." But as the decade drew to a close, it was the peace-loving, fifty-seven year old Maria, author of children's books, who had never met Brown, and who, armed only with a pen, would finish the charge John Brown began at Harpers Ferry.

Seven

THOMAS WENTWORTH HIGGINSON

Unfortunately, Thomas Wentworth Higginson is best remembered in literary circles today as Emily Dickinson's erstwhile editor, the man who confidently predicted she would never be famous, the man who by his own accounting "tried ... to lead her in the direction of rules and traditions" and who fretted over her "obscure, and sometimes inscrutable" writing.[1] Nor, one might suspect, is Wentworth, as he preferred to be called, highly regarded by Whitman scholars, as, by his reckoning, *Leaves of Grass* should have been "ploughed under." Higginson first read the latter work while on a sea voyage. "I perhaps felt a little prejudiced against him from having read his 'Leaves of Grass' on a voyage, in the early stages of seasickness,—a fact which doubtless increased for me the intrinsic unsavoriness of certain passages," he wrote.[2] While these assertions alone would certainly be enough to call into doubt his judgment (at least on literary matters), he went on to say, "[I]t inspires to this day a slight sense of nausea, which it might, after all, have inspired equally on land."[3]

For years it appeared that, try as he might, Wentworth would never measure up, in his own estimation or that of others, to those he so much admired—among them Emerson, Thoreau and Child. As he himself put it, he was like "a horse that had never won a race, but was prized as having gained second place more than any other."[4] One might say he was somewhat cursed by the greatness of his acquaintances. Still, his proximity to what Anna Wells called "the great and near-great" gave him a unique vantage point from which to view and record the events of the antebellum era. Perhaps in emulation of his heroes, at various times Higginson attempted nature writing, lecturing, and editing; but Thoreau was the better writer, Emerson the more successful lecturer and Child the more astute editor. And while Wentworth longed for a life of great adventure, much as Douglass lived, instead he remained valiantly tethered for many years to an invalid wife who kept him close to home and free of the adventure his spirit craved.

Here Wentworth's story might have ended in obscurity had it not been for a fortuitous confluence of events: his introduction to the antislavery movement in general and to fellow revolutionary John Brown in particular. Abolition provided Higginson a calling, one to which he brought a fierce determination, an unswerving commitment and a raw physical courage unmatched in the litterateurs he so admired. For while Higginson greatly esteemed Thoreau, Emerson and Child, the latter of whom he credited with his entry into the abolitionist movement, they each came to respect him and his singular contributions to antislavery, contributions they, for various reasons, could not emulate. A not easily impressed Thoreau would describe Higginson with awe as "the only Harvard Phi Beta Kappa, Unitarian minister, and master of seven languages who has led a storming party against a federal bastion with a battering ram in his hands."[5] And so it was, while Emerson, Thoreau, Douglass and Child might have rallied the faithful with the pen, it would be left to the Reverend Higginson to take up the sword.

As a young man, fame eluded the earnest Higginson. "As author, reformer, soldier, preacher, editor, traveler, politician, historian, naturalist, orator, teacher, and friend of the great and near-great, he had his hands on her a dozen times" only to see her slip away, according to biographer Anna Wells.[6] But Higginson would claim it was not praise, but rather a "boyish desire for a stirring experience" that moved him, a trait he credited to his "two soldier and sailor grandfathers," who bequeathed to him "an intrinsic love of adventure."[7] Wentworth delighted in the fact that he was born in Cambridge (22 December 1823) on the very street "down which the provincial troops marched to the battle of Bunker Hill...."[8] But if his grandfathers' adventures and physical proximity to former great battles contributed to his swashbuckling nature, no doubt his grandmother played a role as well. At age seventeen she married Thomas Storrow, a British prisoner during the Revolutionary war, and then determined to sail with him to England.

This portrait of minister Thomas Wentworth Higginson was taken in 1857, three years after he attempted a raid on the courthouse to rescue fugitive slave Anthony Burns and two years before he would subscribe to a plan to kidnap Governor Wise of Virginia and hold him captive in exchange for Brown's release (courtesy the Massachusetts Historical Society).

To these familial early influences must be added literary ones. As early as seven, Wentworth was reading Child's *The Juvenile Miscellany* as well as his mother's copy of *The Frugal Housewife*.[9] The early reading paid off and he entered Harvard at age fourteen, the youngest in his class. He dealt with this challenge as he approached much of life, as "a battle to be won."[10] While at Cambridge, he read Emerson, who would become "a lifelong source of influence," and pronounced his works a "revelation" made all the more significant at the time by the "comparative conventionalism of the ... literature of that period."[11] Upon graduation, he attended Emerson's lectures and throughout his life continued to read certain of his works "over and over."[12] When Emerson spoke to the need for a revitalized religion, it was an impressionable young Wentworth in the audience who speculated on whether he, too, would one day ascend the lecture platform.[13]

It was not Emerson, however, but Lydia Maria Child who ultimately helped propel

Wentworth into the abolitionist crusade.[14] Higginson was particularly impressed by Child's *Appeal*, a "little work, for all its cumbrous title ... so wonderfully clear, compact, and convincing ... so absolutely free from all unfairness or shrill invective" that it succeeded in helping to make him an abolitionist. Higginson yearned "to be counted worthy of such companionship" and worried that "nothing had been left" for him to do in the valiant antislavery crusade.[15] By early 1846, Higginson had become an ardent Disunionist, promising "to use whatever means may lie in my power to promote the Dissolution of the Union...." He undertook this association bravely, knowing full well that "a time is coming which may expose to obloquy and danger even the most insignificant of the adherents to such a cause."[16] Little could he realize the momentous role left for him in the movement, one which, seemingly, only he, rather than any of his heroes, could perform.

While in college, Higginson was exposed to another group that would one day play a role in his life that he could not have imagined: students from the South with their "charming manners, social aptitudes, imperious ways, abundant leisure, and plenty of money...." Even as he acknowledged the Southerners as "graceful dancers, often musical, and sometimes well taught," he also found them to be "often indolent, profligate, and quarrelsome...." [17] How "quarrelsome" they could, in fact, be he would not learn until much later.

Wentworth graduated from Harvard during a heady time. "We are all a little wild here with numberless projects of social reform. Not a reading man but has a draft of a new Community in his waistcoat pocket," Emerson wrote Thomas Carlyle.[18] Wentworth, citing the influence of Child's *Letters from New York*, desired to "put [himself] on more equal terms with that vast army of hand-workers who were ignorant of much that I knew, yet could do so much that I could not."[19] To that end, he determined to grow peaches, an enterprise which he envisioned would enable him to learn how another class lived while affording him ample time for reading and study.

He quickly abandoned peach farming, however, deciding instead to attend Harvard's divinity school. There he was taught by Child's brother, Convers Francis, whom he described as having "a noted library and as dangerous a love of miscellaneous reading as my own." Access to Convers's library was particularly appealing to Wentworth, who at the time "lived literally on bread and milk" in order to save for the "buying of books." Given his early admiration of Child, and his association with her brother, it is not surprising that his first published piece would be "an enthusiastic review of Mrs. Child's 'Letters from New York,'" which he noted was "then eagerly read by us young Transcendentalists."[20] Particularly, he was impressed by Child's ability to judge "with a single piercing glance the Rights and the Wrongs."[21] The impressionable young Wentworth was strongly influenced by these relationships, and would later write, "It must be borne in mind that during all this period I was growing more, not less radical," adding, "my alienation from the established order was almost as great as that of Thoreau, though as yet I knew nothing of him except through 'The Dial.'"[22]

Upon graduation, the newly ordained minister began visiting prospective congregations where, conforming to customary practice, he delivered trial sermons in search of employment. One of his talks, "The Clergy and Reform," advocated that clergy be leaders in reform, especially where abolition was concerned.[23] To his credit, the young Wentworth did not attempt to hide his increasingly radical proclivities from prospective congregations. Aware that his political positions could be problematic, the young man confessed, "I can't make up my mind whether my radicalism will be the ruin of me or not."[24] No doubt the young minister who presented himself must have been singularly striking to some prospective congregants—a man who by his own account would be "gradually drawn into the temperance agitation, including prohibition; the peace movement, for which, I dare say, I pummeled ... lustily ... the social reform debate ... and of course the woman's rights movement, for whose first national convention I signed the call in 1850."[25]

Somewhat surprisingly, one congregation visited by the young reverend was the Unitarian church in Newburyport, Massachusetts. After a visit there he confessed, "I have tried to show my worst colors to the Newburyport people ... theological and political.... At any rate I must show what I am."[26] It was a remarkable confession, since Newburyport had a distinctly less than favorable reputation among antislavery activists. Ten years prior to his visit, members of the Essex County Anti-Slavery Society had been unceremoniously driven from meetings by a "barrage of sticks and rotten eggs tossed to the dissonant sounds of fish horns, tin pans, and angry shouts," an event which led John Greenleaf Whittier to comment, "As for Newburyport we shall remember it. We shall place it ... under *taboo*, until it comes to its senses."[27] It would seem, then, that the city was a somewhat unlikely place for the prospective minister to deliver a scathing sermon attacking "Polk and the Democrats for involving the United States in the 'slaveholders war'" even as he sought employment.[28] But, somewhat surprisingly, given the conservative and well-heeled nature of the Newburyport congregation, two days after delivering the antiwar sermon, Higginson was offered the job as minister.

In one sense, Higginson was very much aware of the political realities of abolition, acknowledging that "the anti-slavery movement drew a line of cleavage through all Boston society, leaving most of the powerful or wealthy families on the conservative side."[29] But he seemed less willing to apply that reality to the citizens of Newburyport. Establishing a precedent which he would repeat throughout his tenure at the church, the new minister invited the controversial William Henry Channing to deliver his ordination sermon. If the congregation needed further validation of the politics of their new minister, they had only to look at Channing, a man who all no doubt recognized as "one of the most radical Unitarian ministers."[30]

A further harbinger of Higginson's potential divide with his congregation concerned a number of retired sea captains who had spent a lifetime in trade with Charleston and New Orleans, and who, when occasion demanded it, fulfilled their duty by returning runaway slaves to port.[31] While the crusty sea captains might have appreciated the plain talking, hard working Higginson, clearly they abhorred his politics. Wentworth, for his part, found himself "at once the associate of all that was most reputable in the town," owing to his position, while at the same time personally driven by "a fatality in temperament, of all that was most radical."[32]

Not simply content to share his own ever more activist views with his congregants, Higginson made it a practice of inviting fellow Unitarian preachers to exchange pulpits. The steady stream of lecturers who also visited the town was often entertained by Higginson and his young wife, Mary. "Mr. Emerson comes on Friday and will stop here," Higginson wrote his mother. "'Tis a nice way of seeing great people, for they can't well be otherwise than complaisant when you rescue them from a dirty tavern and give them hominy for breakfast."[33]

One visitor to whom Higginson turned over his church must have excited particular comment. In an unprecedented move, William Wells Brown, a fugitive slave, took the Newburyport pulpit. Higginson then followed Brown's remarks with his own assault on slavery.[34] But even Wells's visit must have paled in contrast with the visitor who undoubtedly elicited the greatest anxiety among church members. Before long, radical Unitarian Theodore Parker, the self-proclaimed "most hated man in America," would preach in Newburyport.[35] Parker had been forced to resign from the Boston Association of Ministers for his views on religion and was felt by even the most liberal theologians to be an atheist. No one had invited Parker to share their pulpit since James Freeman Clarke had raised a furor in his own church by attempting it in 1845. Realizing that seeking permission to invite the radical Parker would incite his congregation, Higginson had a better plan. He issued the invitation privately and let astonished church members simply show up one Sunday to find Parker in their pulpit, where he preached a fairly uncontroversial sermon. The absent Higginson spoke that morning at Parker's church in West Roxbury. Mary must have been less than thrilled that she was left alone to defend her husband's action once members realized what was happening.[36]

Further creating difficulties with the conservative elements of his church was Higginson's decision in 1848, prompted by John Greenleaf Whittier, to become increasingly active in politics. While his heart was ready, Higginson did worry about the anticipated reaction of his congregation, telling Whittier, "My position is rather a difficult one just now, for my good friends here, though ready to allow me any amount of liberty in the pulpit, have yet prejudices which make it a hard trial to them to have their minister take the stump at a Presidential election, particularly on what they think a very wrong side."[37] Still, by the eve of the election he was not only actively campaigning, but had been selected as a delegate to the Essex County Free Soil Convention.[38] Unfortunately, his newfound political activism served to further alienate some of the most powerful members of his congregation, who retaliated by announcing that the church was not to be used for antislavery meetings, a position he defied.[39] In another indication of the loneliness of Higginson's position, for all his campaigning, once the votes were tallied it became clear that his Free Soil party had captured only seventy-three votes, a mere three percent of the total votes cast in Newburyport.[40]

The election results, in which Zachary Taylor, a slaveholder, was elected president, incensed Higginson. Two weeks after the election, Wentworth preached a Thanksgiving sermon entitled "Man Shall Not Live by Bread Alone" in which he fervently castigated church members for their political views concerning slavery. Further compounding his ire was the fact that the election had been gloriously celebrated with fireworks purchased by some of the most influential members of his own congregation, with an ensuing parade financed in part by none other than his own Sunday school superintendent.[41] Several days after the festivities, a still-smarting Higginson attended a lecture by Frederick Douglass and the contrast between the elaborate election celebrations and the stark earnestness of the escaped slave's story left him profoundly troubled and clearly not in any mood to parse words.

On Sunday, 30 November 1848, he ascended the pulpit to preach an impassioned sermon. "Another presidential election has just passed," he railed. "The plans I spoke of long since (a year ago last August, you may remember) as being then made to place yet another slaveholding President at the head of this nominally free republic, have been developed, consummated and carried through; carried through, with the consent, the approbation, nay, the enthusiasm, of a majority of you."[42] Accusing Massachusetts citizens in general, and his congregation in particular, of viewing slavery as "a distant abstraction" as long as tariffs were protected, he exclaimed:

> Slavery a distant abstraction! I listened this week to Frederick Douglass: and as I sat and looked at that extraordinary man, and trembled before the volcanic words in which the accumulated wrongs of an outraged race burst their way through his soul—and heard the depth of fiery earnestness with which he depicted his own and his brother's bondage, and the withering sarcasm with which he denounced the hypocritical religion of this slaveholding nation—when I heard this and remembered that this man himself, body, soul, God-given genius and all, was himself once the victim of this terrible institution, (and that three millions were there still,—and more coming,) I felt, Good Heavens! as if I were a recreant to humanity; to let one Sunday pass in the professed preaching of Christianity, and leave the name of SLAVERY unmentioned![43]

Higginson vowed to never again to let a Sunday go by without a mention of slavery. "I felt it a base, selfish sluggishness in me ever to let that fearful institution so pass from my thoughts as to omit the mention of its *name*, at least, in prayer or in preaching: and, so help me God, I never will again," he vowed.[44] It was a promise he would keep.

Higginson then turned his attention to the lukewarm reception given Douglass: "I thought of the position of this man among us: coming to us with his genius, his virtues, his burning eloquence, his sacred cause,—coming and going without enthusiasm, without applause—almost without a friendly hand to grasp his in sympathy.... I felt how low, how base, our moral standard,—and how thankful I should be that God had placed me where even my weak voice might be a gain to the cause of the oppressed against the oppressor!"[45]

Higginson acknowledged that his words might not be well received: "You call this fanaticism. I do not wish to *be* a fanatic,—but I have no fear of being called so." While admitting that these issues were unpleasant, still he could not let them pass unpronounced. "I must speak what is in my soul or nothing. I cannot say, Peace, Peace, when there is no Peace," he contended.[46]

However, this time it would seem the young minister had misjudged the depth of his congregation's resentment. By sermon's end, even his closest friends were angry, and the following Sunday produced "some empty seats."[47] No doubt further annoying his membership was the fact that the sermon was printed both in the town newspaper and in pamphlet form, events which served to gain Higginson approbation from abolitionist quarters.

As if Higginson were not mired in controversy enough, less than a week later Emerson made a contentious appearance at the Newburyport lyceum, where Higginson was a board member. The *Herald* warned that Emerson was a "professed pantheist ... [with] the dividing line between Pantheism and Atheism ... so fine as to be visible only to the microscopic eye."[48] Rumors abounded that Emerson would be the first in a long line of radicals to trouble the town. Further, word had it that he had been invited in direct defiance of the vote of the lyceum committee. It was left to the beleaguered Higginson to defend the choice of speaker. "In print he suggested that his fellow clergymen and all self-appointed keepers of Newburyport morality could surely find more constructive ways of showing concern for the corruption of the town's youth."[49] He then vigorously defended the vote, which he claimed to have been (as a result of his own influence) three to one in favor of Emerson. He neglected to mention that of eight voting members, four (all of whom opposed the invitation) were not present to cast a ballot.[50] Nevertheless, it was a courageous stand at a time when Higginson needed no additional controversy. But for all his public bravado, his increasing isolation was taking a toll and he urged Emerson to establish a journal similar to *The Dial* "for the comfort and encouragement of young men, who, but for that paper, had felt themselves 'lonely and unsupported in the world.'"[51]

In spite of his congregation's growing sense of frustration, Higginson's job was saved, in part, by his love for children and his unswerving work ethic. The young minister had instituted children's sermons and took great delight in planning Sunday school picnics. His community work propelled him into civics projects, including a night school for factory workers, a lyceum lecture series, a literary society, and board work on the public library.[52] In his extracurricular activities, he was extraordinarily successful. His was the first children's sermon in the United States (a practice widely continued today) and his evening school, where he taught both males and females, served as a model soon to be implemented in other states.[53]

That summer, Wentworth and Mary took a break from their duties and traveled to Concord, where they met Thoreau. Higginson was enchanted with Henry's *A Week on the Concord and Merrimac Rivers*, pronouncing it "rich in thought, and beauty ... a rare and delicious thing."[54] Yet he was shy in his praise. Wentworth wrote his mother, telling her he found "nobody who enjoys his books as I do (this I did not tell him)...."[55] Higginson would return to *A Week*, as he did all of his favorite books, and reread it once a year.[56] But with this assessment, Higginson found himself once more against the tide of literary public opinion. Thoreau himself said of his book, "I have now a library of nearly nine hundred volumes, over seven hundred of which I wrote myself" when hundreds of unsold copies of *A Week* were returned to be stored in his attic.[57] More important than their literary discussions, however, the two talked of how a man could live without sustained employment.[58] It was advice of which Higginson could soon make use.

For even as the couple enjoyed their summer visit with Thoreau, a storm was brewing in Newburyport, one that Wentworth did not anticipate and one for which he had no remedy. Alarmed by the number of influential, moneyed church members taking their leave, the church felt the time had come to fire their outspoken minister. Higginson wrote his mother that "discontents ... created ... by the necessity ... of speaking my mind" led to his resignation.[59] Thus, a mere two years into his pastorate, the congregation had had enough of antislavery. Higginson was philosophical about his fate. Acknowledging that "this experiment has failed," he conceded, "[T]he only wonder is it failed no sooner, all things considered." One church member went a step further, saying Higginson was "too much of a reformer.... [I]t was always strange to me how a man so strongly imbued with antislavery sentiments and others of a similar kind, should be permitted to settle there at all."[60]

Refusing to move in with relatives, the young couple continued to make their home in Newburyport. The unemployed Higginson frequently traveled to Boston, excursions which only served to stoke his reform activities. Mary, however, was less than impressed with her husband's associations, exclaiming at one point, "Why do the insane always come to you!"[61] Further, she observed, "It would not be nearly as exciting to him to visit an insane asylum as to mingle freely with these half (or wholly) insane individuals."[62] For a time, Higginson sought support from the members of the Town and Country Club, a literary society in Boston of which Emerson was a part. But before long, controversy followed him there when he nominated a female for membership. "[I]t seemed a rare opportunity for asserting a valuable principle, viz., the union of the sexes in all intellectual aims," Higginson explained of the failed attempt.[63] Once it became apparent that the club had little desire to accept women or, for that matter, blacks into their ranks, Higginson soon lost interest.[64] At home he stayed busy, continuing his factory school for girls, serving on the school committee, and organizing evening classes.[65] In short, as he cheerfully reported, "I was as acceptable a citizen of the town as could be reasonably expected of one who had preached himself out of a pulpit." [66] As for his congregation, he concluded, "An empty pulpit has often preached louder than a living minister."[67]

The enactment of the Compromise of 1850 reenergized Higginson's commitment to antislavery, and his response to the Fugitive Slave Law was unequivocal. "DISOBEY IT ... and show our good citizenship by taking the legal penalties!" he urged. Pronouncing the duty "plain," he added, "I cannot bear this." He went on to say, "I cannot tell what may happen; but I can tell what is right.... [I]f Massachusetts is not free, I know at least of one house that shall be.... And when I close that door against a hunted and guiltless man, or open it to his pursuers, then may the door of God's infinite mercy be closed forever against me."[68] On 29 September he wrote former classmate Charles Devens, now a U.S. marshal, urging him to disobey the law. "For myself there is something in the thought of assisting to return to slavery a man guilty of no crime but a colored skin [at which] every thought of my nature rebels in ... horror," he wrote. "I almost feel as if the nation of which we have boasted were sunk in the dust forever, now that justice and humanity are gone...."[69]

Shortly, Higginson would be even more explicit in his denunciation of what he viewed as the unjust law. Acknowledging "terrible times when it becomes necessary to speak of bloodshed," Higginson questioned at what point "a man must stop in defending his inalienable rights."[70]

Soon he would have the opportunity to translate rhetoric into action when authorities in Boston attempted to return a series of fugitives to the South. Beginning with the capture of Shadrach in February of 1851, followed by the arrests of Thomas Sims in April of the same year and the imprisonment of Anthony Burns in the spring of 1854, Higginson's convictions were increasingly put to the test, until by the time of the Burns affair, he had ascended into full battle mode.

Fred Wilkins, who took the name Shadrach, had been quietly working at a coffee house when he became the first black man in Boston arrested under the auspices of the Fugitive Slave Law.[71] With Shadrach's arrest, Theodore Parker arranged a meeting at the Melodeon, where he gave a fiery address. Higginson was present and Julia Ward Howe would later report that it was here she first saw the young minister whose task that day was to read scriptures relevant to the occasion, something, she pronounced, "he did with excellent effect."[72] Higginson would later concede that his desire to become involved with the Shadrach affair "did not come wholly from moral conviction, but from an impulse perhaps hereditary in the blood ... an intrinsic love of adventure...."[73] Nevertheless, the fugitive's capture ultimately failed to provide Higginson with the opportunity for treason that he craved. As Shadrach left his preliminary hearing, he was approached by Lewis Hayden, a strong black man, and then surrounded by a number of black well-wishers. Before the marshals could ascertain what had happened, or Higginson could formulate a plan for rescue, Shadrach was spirited away. The prisoner had "his clothes half off, and [was] so stupefied by the sudden rescue and the violence of the dragging off that he sat almost dumb, and I thought had fainted; but the men seized him and being powerful fellows hurried him through the square ... where he found the use of his feet, and they went off to Cambridge, like a ... squall, the crowds driving along with them and cheering as they went."[74] Ultimately, the fugitive was safely steered to Canada.[75] Higginson's response was to join the Vigilance Committee in Boston, where he assiduously planned for the next capture of a fugitive slave.[76]

He didn't have long to wait. In April, Thomas Sims was arrested and Higginson sprang into action. This time, however, the authorities were also better prepared. Higginson was notified of Sims's arrest by messenger: "Another fugitive slave is arrested in Boston, and they wish you to come."[77] Higginson hastened to the city and arrived at the *Liberator* office to find a number of men already gathered, among them the peace-loving Garrison. Wentworth was prepared to throw himself into any rescue plan and the "meetings where everyone present had to be identified & every window closed" must have gratified his long dormant sense of adventure.[78] But as Higginson surveyed the room, he was dismayed to see so many nonresistants. "It is impossible," he wrote, "to conceive of a set of men, personally admirable, yet less fitted on the whole than this committee to undertake any positive action in the direction of forcible resistance to authorities."[79] Further standing in the way of Higginson's revolutionary zeal was the fact that the courthouse was a veritable fortress, surrounded by a couple of hundred armed policemen who barred entrance to the already chained courthouse door. The federal courtroom itself, two floors up a narrow staircase, was guarded by six men, while another seven inside surrounded the young, and no doubt terrified, seventeen-year-old prisoner.

As his fellow conspirators busied themselves with meetings, speeches and broadsides, Higginson stubbornly clung to the hope of physical rescue, confessing to "all sorts of fantastic and desperate projects ... [which had] crossed the minds of those few among us who really, so to speak, meant business."[80] One plan involved stealing the official record of the case, which "lay invitingly" in view on the table, in an effort to procure time for other, less innocent measures. But while plans of rescue swirled, Wentworth once again turned to his old schoolmate, Marshal Devens, and unsuccessfully pleaded with him to "resign rather than be the instrument of sending a man into bondage...."[81]

On Tuesday evening, crowds gathered at Tremont Temple for a meeting. Higginson continued to hope for rescue and ascended the podium where he unleashed a "vehement speech." Samuel Gridley Howe was in the audience that night and claimed Wentworth brought those present "to the verge of revolution."[82] Burlingame agreed, reporting that Higginson "held the audience spellbound" with "a fire in the eye" that made those present "tremble."[83] But Higginson was followed to the podium by the more moderate Charles Mayo Ellis, whose measured remarks Higginson complained "threw cold water upon all action." Unwilling to give up plans of rescue, Wentworth determined that "if anything was done, it must be done by a very few."[84]

Higginson did, in fact, have a rather ingenious rescue plan brewing. Upon determining that the window of the second story cell holding Sims had no bars, Higginson urged that Sims make a desperate leap from his window onto a waiting mattress below. The plan relied upon the Reverend Grimes, a black clergyman with unrestricted access to the prisoner, visiting Sims in his cell. At a "specified hour" the prisoner was to stroll to the window as if for a breath of fresh air.[85] Thus poised, Sims would leap for the mattress which Higginson and his company would have strategically placed below. Sims would then be spirited to safety in a waiting carriage. The mattress was purchased, and the carriage secured, when, on "the very day of the project," Higginson looked up with utter dismay to see masons "at work putting bars to the window" of Sims' cell, an event which aborted the planned attempt at rescue.[86]

An alternative plan considered by the conspirators involved chartering a vessel and from there storming the *Acorn*, a ship on which it was supposed Sims would be returned. But this plot was deemed "impracticable, not because it was piracy," Higginson was quick to point out, "but because there was no absolute certainty that the fugitive would be sent South in that precise way."[87]

When no other immediate idea presented itself, Higginson, his hopes for a brilliant rescue dashed, went home resigned to the fact that Sims was to be returned to slavery. In his journal Higginson rued the lack of preparation which led to the mission's failure:

> It left me with the strongest impressions of the great want of preparation, on our part, for this Revolutionary work. Brought up as we have all been, it takes the whole experience of one such case, to educate the mind to the attitude of revolution. It is so strange to find one's self outside of established institutions, to be obliged to lower one's voice & conceal one's purposes, to see law and order, police & military, on the wrong side, & find good citizenship a sin and bad citizenship a duty, that it takes time to prepare one to act coolly & wisely, as well as courageously, in such an emergency.[88]

Further compounding Higginson's unhappiness over the plight of Sims was the fact that one of the sea captains from his Newburyport congregation was called upon to return the young man to slavery.[89] Six days after he did so, the fugitive received a public whipping.[90]

Even as he grieved over the plight of Sims, Higginson came away from the venture assured that there was a place for him in the abolitionist movement. While previously he had worried that all of the great work in antislavery had been accomplished, he now believed "there was plenty left to be done" and "battles" still left to be fought.[91] In the months following the Sims affair, for all his newfound enthusiasm, little opportunity for action presented itself, so Higginson turned his attention to writing editorials for the *Commonwealth*, the recently established organ of the Free Soil party, as well as composing articles for the *Newburyport Union*, which he described as a "liberal Democratic paper."[92] Throughout the late 1850s, he was also a frequent contributor to the newly established *Atlantic Monthly*, work for which he received praise from both Emily Dickinson and Henry Thoreau. Higginson was particularly gratified by Thoreau's response: "He is the only critic I should regard as really formidable on such a subject."[93]

Seven. Thomas Wentworth Higginson

In 1852 came the call which would change Higginson's life. The Free Church in Worcester, Massachusetts, needed a new minister and it seemed that the brash young reformer was just the man they wanted. Unlike Newburyport, Worcester was, according to the delighted Higginson, "a seething centre of all the reforms." He was elated to find himself "almost in fashion, at least with the unfashionable...."[94] As Wells put it, "Most of the eccentrics in the city attended the Free Church...."[95] Being in Worcester also enabled Wentworth to maintain contact with both Emerson and Thoreau. Emerson often traveled there to lecture, while Higginson spoke in Concord from time to time. Occasionally, the young man stayed at Emerson's, where he delighted in having his "modest portmanteau carried upstairs by Plato himself."[96] In 1850, Higginson felt so comfortable at Emerson's that he entered the great man's study and borrowed a first edition of Tennyson he found "especially tempting," in spite of the fact that Emerson was not home. Higginson wrote Emerson to confess his transgression. "Alas, that the conscience should be so hardened by time, but I have kept it six weeks, and do not feel so guilty as when I first pocketed it," he admitted.[97]

Both Thoreau and Alcott also made their way to Worcester—Alcott to host his famous "conversations," and Thoreau for visits with good friends Harrison Blake and Theophilius Brown. Higginson sometimes joined these men on their walks and pronounced Thoreau not only "a dry humorist," but also "a good walker." Of Alcott, he was not so sure, proclaiming him always ready to head for the nearest "convenient log."[98]

Higginson's sustained associations with these men continued to inform his reform consciousness. About one such visit, he wrote, "Last Friday night I went to Concord to an Anti-Slavery tea-party, where I spoke, together with the Lieut. Governor. Mrs. Emerson was there with her fine daughters—(R.W.E. being at the West) ... [along with] Thoreau and his mother and sister...." During these Concord visits he also renewed an acquaintance with Frank Sanborn, whom he described as "a remarkable young poetic youth ... more than six feet high ... [who had] walked to Watertown when I preached there."[99] It was an association that would have profound ramifications not only for Higginson but for John Brown as well.

In 1852, Higginson again lectured in Concord, this time on the subject of "Mohammed." Both Ellery Channing and Thoreau were in the audience. The talk disappointed the discerning Thoreau, who wrote: "Heard Higginson lecture to-night on Mohammed. Why did I not like it better? Can I deny that it was good? Perhaps I am bound to account to *myself* at least for any lurking dislike for what others admire and I am not *prepared* to find fault with. Well, I did not like it, then, because it did not make me like it, it did not carry me away captive. He is not simple enough."[100]

But Thoreau's complaint aside—just as Higginson had once heard Emerson lecture and determined that he could do so as well—on this night both Ellery and Henry left the lecture convinced that they could supplement their own respective incomes through the speaker's platform. Soon, Thoreau began preparation on his "Beans" lecture and Ellery on one entitled "Reality." Higginson graciously helped both men obtain speaking engagements.[101]

When he was not writing, delivering sermons, or lecturing in nearby towns on anti-slavery, Higginson was busy with community affairs, helping to organize the Worcester Public Library and the Natural History Society. During his tenure as a member of the school board, he helped bring an end to segregated schools and to shepherd a raise in female teachers' salaries, in spite of a brief dismissal for defending the right of a Catholic father to determine which version of the Bible his child could read in school.[102]

Still, while gratified by his newfound acceptance in the more liberal Worcester, and buoyed by his occasional speeches and forays into reform, Higginson's spirit continued to crave great adventure. When fugitive slaves arrived in the city, Higginson drove them, sometimes in the middle of the night, to safety.[103] He was continually aware of an "untamable gipsy element" which gave him "instant sympathy with every desperate adventure.... Never did I hear of anything daredevil without wishing to leave all else and do it...." To his diary, he confided, "All I ask of fate is—Give me one occasion worth bursting the door for—an opportunity to get beyond this boy's play...."[104]

On 25 May 1854, that moment arrived with the arrest in Boston of another fugitive slave, Anthony Burns, "a stout, good-looking negro, [appearing] much dejected, though by no means morose or disposed to obstinacy."[105] At first, community interest in the slave's plight appeared modest, but abolitionists issued a placard which appeared throughout the city and then ran in local newspapers as well:

> A MAN KIDNAPPED.—A Public Meeting will be held at Faneuil Hall this (Friday) evening, May 26, at 7 o'clock, to secure justice for a man claimed as a slave by a Virginia kidnapper, and imprisoned in Boston Court House in defiance of the laws of Massachusetts. Shall he be plunged into the hell of Virginia slavery by a Massachusetts Judge of Probate?[106]

On Thursday evening Higginson received word that a meeting would be held in Faneuil Hall on Friday night, prior to Burns's scheduled court date Saturday morning. Wendell Phillips wrote to Higginson, advising of "another kidnapping case," adding "[Y]ou'll *come* of course." But, prospects for rescuing the slave seemed dim, and Phillips signed the note "in no hope."[107] When word arrived of the capture, Bronson Alcott was in Worcester, having delivered an address at the home of Thoreau's friend, H.G.O. Blake. The men stayed up late into the evening contemplating what Alcott termed "the matter of rescue."[108] Friday morning found both Higginson and Alcott on the early train to Boston. They arrived to find a Vigilance Committee meeting already in progress, much like the one of several years before. Higginson was determined "that something shld. be done first or last,"[109] and was dismayed to find only a determination to "go out and gaze at ... [slave catchers], 'pointing the finger of scorn' ..." as they passed by. Higginson snorted, "[A]s if Southern slave-catchers were to be combated by such weapons...." The plan did have one unintended consequence, however. Soon the room was emptied of those who were not "willing to act personally in forcible resistance."[110]

Higginson was chosen chairman of the remaining thirty or so men, Samuel Gridley Howe offered some "good and spirited" advice, and a list was compiled of "those willing to act." The newly formed executive committee included Higginson, Wendell Phillips, Theodore Parker, Samuel Gridley Howe, Kemp (whom Higginson described as "an energetic Irishman"), and Captain Bearse. Higginson requested that his Worcester friend Martin Stowell be added to the list and this was done. Still, he was frustrated by the lack of progress: "[I]t seemed to me, at least, that something must be done; better a failure than to acquiesce tamely as before, and see Massachusetts henceforward made a hunting-ground for fugitive slaves."[111]

For all its disorganization, the group did manage to place broadsides around the city intended to incite their fellow citizens:

> **MURDERERS, THIEVES AND BLACKLEGS**
> **Employed by Marshal Freeman!!**
> MARSHAL FREEMAN has been able to stoop low enough to *insult even the United States Marines*, by employing **MURDERERS, PRIZEfiGHTERS, THIEVES, THREE CARD MONTE MEN, AND GAMBLING HOUSE KEEPERS** to aid him in the rendition of Burns.
> Let the people understand that United States Marshal Freeman has not confidence enough in the courage of his Deputies, nor the valor, powder and ball of the United States Marines to assist him in disgracing Massachusetts, and therefore has engaged the services of LEWIS CLARK, who fought Jack Smith, who was arrested, charged with MURDERING HIS OWN MISTRESS! by throwing her overboard, and who *now keeps a brothel* in this city; of JACK STEWART and his brother, *two Three Card Monte Robbers*; of CHARLES SCOTT, known to the police as *"Thiefy Scott,"* who is "kept" by a *prostitute*, and escaped from Leveret Street Jail about two years since where he was incarcerated for robbery; of BILLY MEAD and his brothers, who are engaged in *keeping gambling saloons and houses of prostitution*; and of some fifty other similar characters, *all of whom are known as villains* in the Criminal Records of Massachusetts!!!—
> **Will you Submit Quietly to such Insults?**[112]

But in truth, Higginson despaired of action by the group. He was encouraged, however, by the arrival on the evening train of Stowell. His Worcester friend came armed with a plan which Higginson found altogether delightful, "a flood of light"[113] and adventurous enough for even his spirited soul:

> Could there not be an attack at the very height of the meeting, brought about in this way? Let all be in readiness; let a picked body be distributed near the Court House and Square; then send some loud-voiced speaker, who should appear in the gallery of Faneuil Hall and announce that there was a mob of negroes already attacking the Court-House; let a speaker, previously warned,—Phillips, if possible,—accept the opportunity promptly, and send the whole meeting pell-mell to Court Square, ready to fall in behind the leaders and bring out the slave.[114]

The plan struck Wentworth "as an inspiration," and he deemed it "one of the very best plots that ever—failed."[115] The failure, however, would not be for lack of effort on Higginson's part. Under the pseudonym Higgins, he found "just time" to purchase a dozen hand axes (for paying cash he received a five percent discount, obtaining the axes for a dollar apiece).[116] Higginson, Stowell and Kemp were each to secure five men willing to attack, while the black abolitionist Lewis Hayden was to "rally ten negroes."[117] The plan faltered when, in the fevered excitement at Faneuil Hall, not all the prospective conspirators could be contacted. Even those who were approached did not fully understand the plan's fundamentals. Higginson "was cut to the heart to find so few, so very few" at Faneuil ready to act.[118] Still, word of the plot reached most of the committee. Some concurred, others did not. Captain Bearse, "distrusting anything to be attempted on land, utterly [declined] all part in it." Higginson, undeterred, stood ready at the courthouse: "Planting myself near a door which stood ajar, on the east side of the building, I waited for the trap to be sprung, and for the mob of people to appear from inside Faneuil Hall. The moments seemed endless. Would our friends never arrive?"[119]

Meanwhile, Samuel Gridley Howe told the crowd inside Faneuil: "That nothing so well becomes Faneuil Hall as the most determined resistance to a bloody and overshadowing despotism. That it is the will of God that every man should be free; we will as God wills; God's will be done! That no man's freedom is safe unless all men are free."[120]

Theodore Parker spoke next, bringing the crowd to near hysteria. When he proposed adjourning the meeting until morning, a "hundred voices cried out, 'no, to-night,' 'let us take him out,' 'let us go now,' 'come on,' and one man rushed frantically from the platform, crying 'come on,' but none seemed disposed to follow him." One man described events as "tumultuous in the extreme." In the pandemonium, about half the audience wanted to move to the courthouse, but amidst the shouts and cheers of the crowd, the plan frayed. The outcome seemed poised on a precipice when a shout rang out from the rear of the hall claiming, "I am just informed that a mob of negroes is in Court square, attempting to rescue Burns."[121] With that, hundreds of men rushed out of the hall and towards the courthouse.

Higginson, still at his post, was relieved to see "a rush of running figures, like the sweep of a wave, [come] round the corner of Court Square.... [I] watched it with such breathless anxiety as I have experienced only twice or thrice in life." Eagerly searching the crowd for his fellow conspirators, he quickly came to a shocking realization. "We had the froth and scum of the meeting, the fringe of idlers on its edge." The men Higginson counted on were still trapped in the hall in the midst of the teeming crowd. Stowell dashed up to Higginson and whispered, "'Some of our men are bringing a beam up to the west door, the one that gives entrance to the upper stairway.'" Immediately, Higginson hastened to the entrance and with a dozen others, both black and white, grabbed a fourteen-foot beam. He positioned himself in front, with a "stout negro opposite," and the "real attack had begun."[122] As a couple of men beat on the door with axes, others threw bricks at the courthouse windows, while "glass rattled in all directions." At 9:30 the courthouse bell sounded an alarm which echoed through the night.[123] In the midst of the melee, all was plunged into darkness when a black conspirator climbed a lamppost and snuffed out the light.[124]

Members of a jury inside the courthouse poked their heads out of windows to see what was happening and were shot at from below. In the confusion, alarmed ladies from the disrupted performance at the museum fled into the streets, joining the thronging crowd.[125] Meanwhile, Higginson and the men battered the courthouse door until it gave way, allowing room for only one to pass inside. Higginson glanced quickly at his fellow conspirator, a black man who "did not even look at me, but sprang in first" with Higginson fast behind him. This act, Higginson henceforth would maintain, "removed once [and] for all every doubt of the intrinsic courage of the blacks."[126]

Inside, six to eight policemen beat at the intruders with clubs. Higginson and his black comrade responded with fists flying, while "all around" they "heard the pistol shots."[127] Batchelder, a marshal's deputy, exclaimed, "I'm stabbed" and fell, caught before he hit the ground by Isaac Jones, a watchman. Police spilled through the streets as the "most intense excitement prevailed."[128] In the confusion, Higginson did not realize until the next morning that Batchelder had not been stabbed but fatally shot. Nor was he aware that his own chin had been badly cut, although he would proudly carry the scar for the remainder of his life.[129] As for the beating, Higginson averred, "I had never before known just how it felt, and to my surprise it was not half so bad as I expected."[130]

At the time, however, the murder of Batchelder quickly brought the entire episode to a halt. "[W]hat should have been the signal of success," rued Higginson, resulted instead in "a cessation of hostilities."[131] Frightened and confused, the crowd retreated across the street. About this time, the Boston Artillery, marching through town in their routine practice drill, blundered onto the scene. The crowd, fearing that the United States Marines had arrived, "saluted with hisses, groans, and other marks of derision." Unaware of the evening's hostilities, the bewildered soldiers stared at the mob. As the crowd realized that the men were, in fact, not there to constrain their evening's activities, they "gave them three cheers, and the company departed."[132]

Gradually Higginson was forced back as his supporters withdrew. "You cowards, will you desert us now?" Higginson cried while maintaining his position at the top of the stairs. But the crowd could not be rallied. As they retreated, Higginson rested his eyes upon the solitary figure of Bronson Alcott slowly approaching the stairs. With cane in hand, Alcott slowly and steadily ascended the steps. "Why are we not within?" he asked. "Because," came Higginson's impatient reply, "these people will not stand by us." Saying nothing, Alcott "paused again at the top, the centre of all eyes, within and without; a revolver sounded from within, but hit nobody; and finding himself wholly unsupported, he turned and retreated, but without hastening a step."[133] Alcott's courageous, solitary walk from the courthouse door signaled the end of the attempted rescue of Anthony Burns. Nine men, both blacks and whites, were arrested for minor offenses ranging from disturbing the peace to breaking a gas lamp, and with the arrival of two artillery companies, the crowd was silenced altogether. Shortly after midnight, the square was largely deserted.[134]

On Saturday morning, Mayor Smith stood on the courthouse steps and, to applause, promised that "a sufficient force was in readiness to preserve the public peace; and that, at all hazards, the laws of the city, the laws of the State, and the laws of the United States SHALL be maintained."[135] The same day, the unlikely prospect emerged of a peaceful resolution to the Burns affair. It appeared that Burns's owner was willing to sell him for $1,200 and Wendell Phillips and Francis Jackson had raised the necessary amount.[136] However, in the rush to secure the appropriate paperwork, the offer could not be made by the agreed upon deadline of midnight. By Sunday morning, $400 of the pledged funds pledged had been withdrawn and the deal fell through.[137] Amidst the negotiations, rumors swirled. One story circulated that a large contingent of citizens unhappy with Burns's return to slavery had ascended on the town, another that 400 Negroes had arrived from New Bedford. But authorities insisted that Washington had "telegraphed to the United States Marshal here to have the law carried out, and to call the United States troops here, and even those at more distant stations, to their aid for that purpose" should it be necessary.[138]

By Sunday evening, 28 May, it was apparent that negotiations to purchase Burns had failed. An estimated crowd of 50,000 lined the streets to watch 2,000 armed men conduct the lone black prisoner to a waiting ship.[139] First to appear were the United States troops encompassing the Fourth Regiment Artillery as well as the United States Marines from Forts Independence and Constitution. A pause ensued while the men inspected their muskets. Following these troops, over a hundred special officers employed by the United States government, armed with both swords and revolvers, marched to

The Man is NOT BOUGHT!!

He is still in the SLAVE PEN in THE COURT HOUSE!!

The kidnapper agreed, both publicly and in writing, to sell him for $1200. The sum was raised by eminent Boston Citizens, and offered him. He then claimed more. The bargain was broken. The kidnapper breaks his agreement, though the United States Commissioner advised him to keep it.

Be on your guard against all Lies.

WATCH THE SLAVE PEN!!

☞ LET EVERY MAN ATTEND THE TRIAL!!

Higginson labored valiantly to formulate a rescue when Anthony Burns was arrested in Boston in May 1854 under the auspices of the Fugitive Slave Law, an event which led Thoreau to characterize Higginson as "the only Harvard Phi Beta Kappa, Unitarian minister, and master of seven languages who has led a storming party against a federal bastion with a battering ram in his hands." This broadside, issued in 1854, refers to the unsuccessful attempt by other, less incendiary abolitionists, to raise funds to purchase Burns from his owners (courtesy the Massachusetts Historical Society).

the east entrance of the courthouse. Their appearance was "greeted with cheers, groans, hisses and other manifestations of approval or detestation." As U.S. Marshal Freeman and his associates escorted Burns from the courthouse doors they were met with cries of "Shame! shame!" The prisoner, however, "did not seem in the least ... excite[d]...."

The boisterous crowd then followed the march of the captive through State Street, "the whole entire route with mingled groans, cheers, and hisses...." No attempt at rescue was made, but the men guarding Burns were "greeted with a shower of cayenne pepper, cowitch, or some other most noxious substance," as well as a "bottle, containing a liquid, believed to be vitriol," all of which were thrown from the *Commonwealth* building."[140] Samuel Gridley Howe continued to hope that Burns would make an escape attempt, or failing that, make a statement by plunging "a knife into his own heart" rather than be returned to slavery.[141] But it was not to be. Symbolic protest, attempted rescue and verbal vollies aside, at 3:20 P.M., the heavily armed ship returning Burns to slavery began its slow sail down the harbor.[142] In Worcester, church bells tolled, marking its passage.

Higginson did not witness the return of Burns. Discouraged and disheartened, he returned home where he spoke to a crowd of a thousand cheering supporters.[143] "If I wished it, Worcester would rise for me, as one man," he wrote his mother. "Saturday night there was a great public meeting & a committee of 12 was sent up to escort me down, & I was received with cheer on cheer," he recounted.[144] "There never was such a time in Masstts.," he assured her. "Of course I was in Boston on Friday night & had something to do with the demonstration in Court Square. That attack was a great thing for freedom, & will echo all over the country. It came within an inch of success, & has achieved *a* great success at any rate. Of course I was unarmed, hurt nobody but a *door* & was unhurt myself but for some knocks & a scratch." Expressing remorse for the death of Batchelder, he said, "I am sorry for the death of the man, but shld. hv. been far more so for any injury to those outside." He assured her that the man was most likely killed by "one of his own blundering comrades."

Preparing his mother for what he thought to be his imminent arrest, he advised, "[T]hey are arresting ... boys, right & left, & charging them with *murder*, (of all things!)." He added, "At any rate they are making arrests, & I think it more than probable that I may come in for a share;—but don't be troubled, any penalty cannot be very severe: & I shall consider it the highest honor ever attained by a Higginson, and such I assure you will the sentiment of Massachusetts be."[145] But even as he reassured his mother, that same day Higginson was concerned enough about his position to write a note to Richard Henry Dana, Jr., inquiring about legal counsel. "I am informed that I am to be arrested for participation in the affairs of Friday night," he wrote, adding, "[T]here are especial reasons why I desire your aid, at least in the Police Court Examination.... I know that yr. time is severely drawn upon, in these revolutionary days, & if I ask too much, you must say so."[146] Richard Henry Dana, who like Thoreau, stood in awe of the valiant minister, said, "I knew his ardor and courage, but I hardly expected a married man, a clergyman, and a man of education to lead the mob."[147]

A day after his letter to his mother, Higginson wrote his brother of the episode. "A Law of Massachusetts is trampled under foot by these dastardly man stealers and their human blood hounds who have turned a Public Building of Massachusetts the Courthouse into a United States Jail, A Slave Pen!" he fumed.[148] "Yes Boston Court house filled with the Dregs of these sinks of pollution—the Hells of Boston, armed to the teeth with revolvers and bowie knives to prevent the rescue of a man from endless slavery and (shame on them) Boston's Whiggery looks quietly on and says the laws must be faithfully! executed, that is, the Fugitive Slave Laws."[149] To a friend he claimed, "[T]wenty more men, in the right place, would have rescued the slave, that all acknowledge."[150] Years later, Higginson would compare the violent killing of Batchelder to the opening shots fired at Fort Sumter, as "a proof that war had really begun."[151]

Meanwhile, rumors continued to persist about Higginson's capture. He assured his mother and sister that he would not resist an arrest, saying, "I think that months & years in jail would be well spent as a protest against Slavery.... The men now arrested are obscure men; *their* sufferings will be of comparatively little service; but I h[a]ve a name, a profession, & a personal position wh. wd. make my bonds a lesson & a stimulus to the whole country. What better things could I do, at liberty? What so good?"[152]

Higginson "patiently waited for the officers" whom he assumed were coming, but they were slow to appear and, busy as he was, he feared he could not "stay at home for them much longer."[153] "All kinds of reports come ... but *no* police officers," he fretted. "[S]ome of our lawyers say they will not dare arrest any wellknown person, but I think they will. But it will only do good if they do."[154] On 1 June, Higginson wrote his mother with a seeming wistfulness, as if fearing he would never be arrested: "It is now rumored that there are to be no more arrests; if so it is because they fear the effect of imprisoning me; for I know that my participation in the affair is notorious."[155] Higginson hastened to reassure his family: "[E]ven if I should be convicted of anything and imprisoned a month or two (which is improbable) it would do so much good to the community, that I could bear it very patiently."[156] Meanwhile, his friend Stowell, who had been arrested shortly following the melee, continued to reside at the jail, more concerned with release than capture. When Thomas Drew, a former pacifist, visited him, Stowell enlisted his aid in smuggling a pistol out of his cell in a "hollowed-out Bible."[157]

In spite of his reassurances, Higginson's mother continued to worry about her brash son. Utilizing a not-so-subtle tactic that mothers have employed for centuries, she wrote expressing concern not about *him*, but about his friends: "The plot thickens! I have not been aware of the excitement till I read Louisa's letter.... That gives a truly alarming idea of the ferocious sentiments of your friends. I am more frightened at *their* attitude than at anything else.... I should seek ... at all events to have the peace kept and no resistance to lawful authority—do not let your friends knock down the policemen if they come to take you—that would do you no good." [158] One such friend, the unrepentant Theodore Parker, spoke at the Melodeon on Sunday and said of the deceased Batchelder, "He was a volunteer in this service. He liked the business of enslaving a man, and has gone to render an account to God for his gratuitous work."[159]

On 4 June 1854, Higginson ascended the pulpit of his Free Church to mark the week's events with a sermon entitled "Massachusetts in Mourning." "You have imagined my subject beforehand, for there is but one subject on which I could preach, or you could listen, to-day," he began. "Is there any disinterested love of Freedom left in Massachusetts?" he asked, noting "that, at least, Freedom did not die without a struggle ... [I]t took thousands of armed men to lay her in the grave at last." In defense of his blows to the courthouse door, he said, "The strokes on the door of that Court House that night ... went echoing from town to town ... like the first drum beat of the Revolution—and each reverberating throb was a blow upon the door of every Slave-prison of this guilty Republic." Further, he maintained, "Words are nothing—we have been surfeited with words for twenty years. I am thankful that this time there was action also.... Our souls and bodies are both God's, and resistance to tyrants is obedience to Him...." As to the lack of freedom he felt in his home state as a result of the Fugitive Slave Law, he said:

> If we are all Slaves indeed—if there is no law in Massachusetts except the telegraphic orders from Washington—if our own military are to be made Slave-catchers—if our Governor is a mere piece of State ceremony, permitted only to rise at a military dinner and thank his own soldiers for their readiness to shoot down his own constituents, without even the delay of a riot act—if Massachusetts is merely a conquered province and under martial law—*then I wish to know it*, and I am grateful for every additional gun and saber that forces the truth deeper into our hearts.[160]

Continuing his defense of the use of force, the Reverend Higginson left little doubt as to his position: "[I]f men array brute force against Freedom—pistols, clubs, drilled soldiers, and stone walls—then the body also has its part to do in resistance." He urged defiance, saying, "[C]alm, irresistible force, in a good cause, becomes sublime...." He then proclaimed, "For myself, existence looks worthless under such circumstances; and I can only make life worth living for, by becoming a revolutionist."[161] Asserting the need for an active response to current events, he advocated, "The way to make principles felt is to assert them—peaceably, if you can; forcibly, if you must." Higginson, while not averse to milder measures, feared the time for moderation had passed, saying, "I do not discourage more peaceable instrumentalities; would to God that no other were ever needful. Make laws, if you can.... Use politics, if you can make them worth using.... But the disease lies deeper than these remedies can reach. It is all idle to try to save men by law and order, merely, while the men themselves grow selfish and timid, and are only ready to talk of Liberty, and risk nothing for it." Finally, he put forth a call to "show the world that a community may be educated in brain without becoming cowardly in body...."[162]

On 9 June, Higginson heard once again from his mother: "Do you mean to publish your Sunday Sermon? I hope not—for I do not want you to be *more* conspicuous."[163] But, in spite of his mother's concern that the publication of the sermon would further bring attention to him at a time when it was least desired, Higginson consented to its publication. Nor, as he awaited possible arrest for his part in the Burns affair, did he discontinue his responsibilities as an Underground Railroad conductor.[164]

A full six days after delivery of the sermon, on 10 June, came the warrant for Higginson's arrest. When the charge came, the *Worcester Spy* reported that Higginson was accused of having gathered "with 500 or more persons ... to disturb the peace ... riotously beset and attack the Court House ... break the glass in the windows ... force in and break open one of the doors of said Court House ... fire and discharge sundry fire-arms ... and ... utter loud outcries and hurrahs."[165] To the relief of Higginson's family, the charge was "for riot only," putting to rest fears that he might be indicted for murder.[166] An unrepentant Higginson later confided to a friend: "[I]t is difficult to write history & to live history at the same time,"[167] and admonished his fellow abolitionists: "[M]en must risk something; not only risk danger, but even failure and the disapprobation of critics.... A few more such defeats as that before the Court House, and we shall have a victory."[168] At his court appearance, a Boston paper declared Higginson "a man of talent, a great enthusiast, and though he stands within the pale of Unitarianism, he is regarded as a suspicious character, theoretically speaking."[169]

For the remainder of his life, Higginson claimed ignorance about who fired the fatal shot during the courthouse raid. While acknowledging Lewis Hayden had discharged a gun, he maintained that it was fired only after Batchelder had been hit. Hayden's bullet, he claimed, passed harmlessly between "the arm and body of Marshal Freeman," a fact which caused an exasperated Theodore Parker to moan, "Why did he not hit him?"[170] For his part, Higginson was alone in the conspirators in thinking something should be done for the family of the deceased deputy.[171] Of his own role in the affair, he maintained, "I hv. used no deception, & no violence: did not even strike a blow. I simply went unarmed into a danger, where ... men behind me shrunk from following."[172]

With Higginson back in Worcester, it wasn't long before trouble again landed on his doorstep. On 29 October 1854, a Boston policeman, Asa Butman, arrived in town, ostensibly to seek information about the riot. Worcester, being "intensely anti-slavery" and "having a considerable colored population," seemed fully disposed "to lynch the man, or at least to frighten him thoroughly...."[173] A group of sixty men gathered outside Butman's hotel during a long night that was disrupted by continual chants of "Bring out the kidnapper" and "Kill the scoundrel!"[174] When the cries produced no effect, some threw stones at the building, while others rang the doorbell and demanded to speak to the deputy marshal. At 3:00 A.M. the policeman showed himself, emerging with gun in hand to say he would not be intimidated. But his bravado carried a price. Shortly, an arrest warrant was issued on Butman for carrying a concealed weapon.[175] The hapless marshal then spent the rest of the night in jail, an internment which might not have been an altogether bad thing in light of his personal safety.

With the coming of day, it became eminently clear to everyone that Butman needed to flee Worcester. In a moment of supreme irony, Higginson himself stepped into the fray to help protect his pursuer, and thus hunter and hunted, at least for the moment, exchanged places. That morning, Higginson linked arms with the frightened man and slowly edged him through the angry crowd towards the railroad station and safety. The mob continued to hurl not only threats but also stones at the two men. As they made their way, Higginson shouted to the crowd that Butman had been promised a safe exit from the city in exchange for his pledge not to return. The fight was over and the abolitionists had won, Higginson cried loudly as he continued to drag Butman out of danger. Soon Higginson was shouting "at the top of his lungs," assuring the crowd that the best thing that could happen was that Butman make it safely back to Boston where he could educate his colleagues about the terrors awaiting pro-slavery men in Worcester.[176] As Butman and Higginson inched their way through the crowd, Joseph Howland, a "non-resistant," "satisfied his sensitive conscience by this guarded appeal, made at intervals in a sonorous voice: 'Don't hurt him, mean as he is! Don't kill him, mean though he be!'" Another of Butman's protectors, journalist Thomas Drew, assuaged his conscience somewhat differently. Driving away those who would harm the victim, he would, "when the coast was clear, run up and administer a vigorous kick to the unhappy victim, and then fall back to repress the assailants once more."

This unlikely group of guards, forced to abandon the idea of making it to the train station, headed instead for a waiting carriage and Higginson jumped in to take the reins. The crowd, sensing that Butman was about to make a break for it, seized the horse's head and grabbed the wheels. Higginson and Butman were then quickly shepherded instead to a nearby hack where they "were whirled away before the mob fairly knew what had happened." During the ride, as occasional stones flew through the window, and with his prisoner crouched in abject terror on the floor of the vehicle, Higginson took the opportunity to lecture Butman "on the baseness of his whole career," a speech Higginson felt might have "made my reputation as a pulpit orator had my congregation consisted of more than one, or had any modern reporter been hidden under the cushions." Before long, the men were overtaken by the city marshal, who escorted the now thoroughly terrified Butman safely back to his home in Boston.[177]

An account of Butman's unfortunate visit to Worcester soon appeared in the *Liberator*. Higginson wrote Mrs. Chapman that there was a *"dramatic perfection"* about the event, with "the entire disappearance of Butman's own friends leaving him to be literally and absolutely *saved* by abolitionists; the fortunate presence of just the right persons—Messrs. Hoar, Foster, Stowell & myself—I mean the right persons dramatically speaking; this joined with the really narrow escape of the man & the thorough frightening of one who had frightened so many:—all these gave a tinge of romance to the whole thing, such as was perhaps never surpassed."[178] The Higginsons saved a newspaper article about the event which read in part: "[Mr. Butman] awards praise to those who defended him after the storm had been roused, especially Mr. Higginson.... Some of the crowd did not distinguish in their attacks between Mr. Butman and Mr. Higginson. The latter gentleman received a considerable share of the missiles, and one large stone was thrown into the carriage, narrowly missing his head."[179] The widespread publicity surrounding both the Burns and Butman affairs served to make Higginson a hero in antislavery circles. After the Butman incident, Higginson remained in Worcester where he continued to view "any life as rather incomplete which did not ... include some experience of imprisonment in a good cause."[180]

Higginson's brush with the law did not intimidate him. Rather, it seemed only to stoke his antislavery sentiments. In August he spoke at a meeting commemorating West Indian slave emancipation and declared, "I hate the Fugitive Slave Law, not because it is unconstitutional ... but because it is *infernal*." While not entirely ruling out a political remedy, he believed the time was edging nearer for more radical measures. "At this moment, all hopes of American freedom, all hopes of the future destiny of the nation, hang concentrated on this one point:—Can we conquer Slavery, or shall Slavery conquer us?" Cautioning against placing too much hope on politicians, he maintained, "I tell you the conflict with Slavery is not a reform[,] it is Revolution."[181]

Ultimately, Higginson was never brought to trial for his role in the Anthony Burns riot. The first grand jury simply refused to indict him. A second grand jury did indict, but the indictments were quelled since the case was based on the Fugitive Slave Law of 1793, which had only a provision about resisting a federal officer, a charge not brought against Higginson. Several years hence, he would receive a gift from a fellow conspirator. One of his black accomplices in the Burns affair sent him an axe with a note acknowledging that, more than anyone, Higginson deserved to have it.[182]

Events in the Burns affair augmented Higginson's credentials as a reformer and, by the mid 1850s, the ever more militant Higginson was increasingly sought after as a speaker. In January of 1855, he lectured in Concord and spoke with Thoreau, showing him a new translation of the Vishnu Sarma.[183] He preferred lecturing on antislavery to being a "mere Lyceum lecturer" because as an antislavery voice he was greeted with "an enthusiasm of the heart and not merely of the head...." While on one lecture engagement, he spotted a sign which pronounced him "leader of the forlorn-hope from Worcester," a title he no doubt relished. Still, being a lecturer had its less laudatory moments, and Higginson wrote from Toledo: "Here I am spending Sunday in a city of absolute strangers in a wild snowstorm, in a rather forlorn hotel from whose windows no house is visible, but only a few sheds with a dirty pig or two, then a frozen river and a bleak uninhabited shore behind.... I doubt not that here also there are Abolitionists and Women's Rights people who would welcome me, could I only get at them."[184]

In the fall of 1855, the Higginsons sailed for Fayal in an effort to improve the somewhat hypochondriacal Mrs. Higginson's health. They returned in June of 1856 to find a new antislavery crusade needing attention. Events in Kansas now dominated not only the news but also the hearts and minds of their neighbors in Worcester. Before the couple had even debarked from the ship, news arrived of the caning of Sumner. The church's gathering, designed to welcome the couple home, instead quickly turned into a recruiting effort to find volunteers willing to make the trip to Kansas. Not surprisingly, Higginson was named secretary of a committee which ultimately furnished three parties for this purpose—two convened in Worcester and a third comprised largely of Maine lumbermen. Recruits arrived from throughout New England and included William Thompson of Vermont, who would later become Brown's son-in-law and perish at Harpers Ferry. An orthodox minister complained to Higginson of the lumbermen's "total depravity," saying if Higginson doubted him that he should himself organize a second party of lumbermen and accompany them to Kansas, to which Higginson intoned, "I should have liked to try the experiment"[185]

As an agent of the National Kansas Committee, Higginson did leave for Kansas in September of 1856. He wrote of his adventures in a series of letters signed simply "Worcester," which were published in the *New York Tribune* and later in a pamphlet entitled "A Ride Through Kansas." At the time of his trip, the railroad ended at Iowa City and emigrants to Kansas had an additional 600 miles to navigate. Higginson rode through Iowa sitting atop a stagecoach, and it seemed "as if I had crossed the continent...." Shortly after his arrival, he traveled "over about twenty miles of debatable ground, absolutely alone" from Nebraska City to Tabor. "Never before in my life had I been, distinctively and unequivocally, outside of the world of human law," he wrote. The law "had been ready to protect me, even when I disobeyed it." Yet, "[h]ere it had ceased to exist; my Sharp's rifle, my revolvers,—or, these failing, my own ingenuity and ready wit,—were all the protection I had." Far from being fearful, Higginson pronounced this state of affairs "a delightful sensation." Departing from Nebraska City, he shepherded a party of approximately one hundred and sixty men, along with twenty women and children, towards Kansas.[186]

Upon his arrival in Kansas, Higginson preached to the citizens of Lawrence. He took as his biblical text the same employed by the Reverend John Martin the Sunday after he had fought at Bunker Hill: "Be not ye afraid of them; remember the Lord, which is great and terrible, and fight for your brethren, your sons, and your daughters, your wives, and your houses."[187] By the time of Higginson's arrival, many of the hostilities had ceased, but the people in the Kansas Free State effort remained, for the large part, both poor and hungry.[188] Higginson would later say that from the time of his Kansas visit, he became increasingly certain that a future conflict was inevitable: "The absolute and increasing difference between the two sections of the nation had been most deeply impressed upon me by my first and only visit to a slave-mart."[189]

On 24 September, Higginson wrote home describing his foray into Kansas Territory:

> We camped out five nights which I enjoyed on the whole, though only in the last night did we have wood enough for the Maine style of tent, open toward the fire. Imagine me also patrolling as one of the guard for an hour every night, in high boots amid the dewy grass, rifle in hand and revolver in belt. But nobody ever came and we never had any danger. Only once, in the day time, the whole company charged upon a band of extremely nude Indians, taking them for Missourians....[190]

On 9 October 1856, while on his return trip, he wrote from the "Steamboat Cataract, aground on a bank in the Missouri River" that "My best hope is that the contest may be at once transferred to more favorable soil, Nebraska or Iowa, and result in a disruption of the Union; for I am sure that the disease is too deep for cure without amputation."[191] Once home, Higginson mourned that "the tonic life of the last six weeks was ended...." It occurred to him that "thenceforward, if any danger impended, the proper thing would be to look meekly about for a policeman, [and with this realization] it seemed as if all the vigor had suddenly gone out of me...."[192]

At a meeting on 2 January 1857, celebrating the twenty-fifth anniversary of the Massachusetts Anti-Slavery Society, Higginson reflected upon his Kansas visit: "I found a great deal in Kansas.... But I did not go there even to see an underground railroad, for I had seen that in Massachusetts." Rather, he maintained:

> I wanted to see something above the ground. All my life I had been a citizen of a Republic where I had seen my fellow-citizens retreating, and retreating, and retreating, before the Slave Power, and I heard that away off, a thousand miles west, there was one town where men had made their stand, and said to Slavery, "Thus far, but no farther." I went the thousand miles to see it, and saw it. I saw there the American Revolution, and every great Revolution of bygone days in still living progress.[193]

He also gave a prescient warning about future hostilities, saying, "To-morrow may call us to some work so stern that the joys of this evening will seem years away. To-morrow may make this evening only the revelry by night before Waterloo."[194]

As to whether Higginson met Brown in Kansas, he would never be sure. Brown was in hiding during the time of Higginson's visit. Higginson did recall going to visit a slave who was being "sheltered by a white man." He was quite sure the white man's name was not Brown, but uncertain as to whether it could have been one of Brown's widely used aliases. But, whether or not Higginson met Brown at the time, it is clear that through his contacts with Kansas he did meet a number of men whose names would become closely linked with both Brown's and his own, including the "noble and self-devoted man" George Luther Stearns of Medford, "who gave, first and last, ten thousand dollars to maintain liberty in the new Territory," as well as Samuel Gridley Howe and Frank Sanborn, "then the leading men in the Massachusetts Kansas Committee."[195]

Upon his return home, Higginson spoke widely on affairs in Kansas, appearing before both the Massachusetts and Vermont legislatures.[196] Later, he would defend Brown's acts at what he termed "the so-called 'Pottawatomie massacre'" in light of the context of affairs in Kansas at the time, saying, "I can testify that in September of that year [1856] there appeared to be but one way of thinking among the Kansas Free State men.... I heard of no one who did not approve of the act [at Pottawatomie], and its beneficial effects were universally asserted...." As for Governor Robinson of Kansas, who first endorsed and then later repudiated the act, Higginson deemed the reversal "simply disgraceful, or else the product of a disordered mind." Regarding his own feelings on the matter, Higginson spoke indirectly, saying, "Personally, I have never fully reconciled myself" to Robinson's earlier justification of the events of Pottawatomie, but for Robinson to have reversed himself and to have later addressed "the punishment due Brown for his crimes in Kansas" was simply too much for the loyal Higginson to comprehend.[197]

But if not in Kansas, it seemed inevitable that Brown and Higginson, the two fearless antislavery warriors, would meet. On 2 February 1858, Higginson received his first letter from John Brown, who was writing from the home of Frederick Douglass in Rochester. It would seem that Brown knew his audience well—from the opening line Brown's letter hinted at both danger and intrigue while disdaining concern about personal safety. "I am here *concealing my whereabouts* for good reasons (as I think) not however from any anxiety about my personal safety," he began. "I have been told that you are both a true *man*: & a true *abolitionist*," Brown continued, '& I partly believe,' the whole story." The letter then appealed for funds, thus setting a precedent which would remain a constant in the correspondence between the two men—Brown somewhat apologetically appealing for money, Higginson attempting to provide it whenever possible. "Last Fall I undertook to raise from $500 to $1000, for *secret service*, & succeeded in getting $500," Brown wrote, adding, "I now want to get for the *perfecting* of *by far* the most *important* undertaking of my whole life: from $500, to $800, within the next sixty days." Thus, from the opening words of their acquaintance, Brown enticed Higginson into his plans for Harpers Ferry. "I have written Rev. Theodore Parker, George L. Stearns, & F.B. Sanborn Esqr., on the subject; but do not know as either Mr. Stearns, or Mr. Sanborn, are abolitionists. I suppose they are." Brown requested that Higginson help him obtain the funds and then closed (again with a hint of subterfuge and danger): "I wish to keep it entirely still about where I am: & will be *greatly obliged* if you will consider this communication *strictly confidential*: unless it may be with such as you are *sure* will *feel*, & *act*, and *keep very still.*" He added, "Should be most happy to meet you again; & talk matters more freely. Hope this is my last effort in the begging line." He then signed the letter "Very Respectfully Your Friend John Brown."[198]

Not long after, on 8 February, Higginson responded to Brown's letter and asked for additional information. "I am always ready to invest money in treason," Higginson maintained, "but at present have none to invest." He did promise, however, to "raise *something*, if only $5 & send it on."[199] On 12 February came Brown's quick response. "Rail Road business on a *somewhat extended* scale; is the *identical* object for which I am trying to get means," Brown wrote. "I have been connected with that business *as commonly conducted* from my boyhood: & *never* let an opportunity slip."[200] To Higginson's questions, Brown responded:

> I now have a measure on *foot* that I feel *sure* would awaken in you something more than a *common interest*; if you could understand it. I have just written my friends G.L. Stearns, & F.B. Sanborn, asking them to meet me for consultation at Gerrit Smith's, Peterboro' [N.Y.]. I am very anxious to have *you come along; certain as I feel*; that you will never regret having been one of the council. I would most gladly pay your expenses had I the means to spare. *Will you come on?*[201]

Higginson was unable to attend the meeting in Peterboro. Instead, the two made plans to meet at Brown's room in March at the American House, where Higginson was instructed to "enquire for Mr. Brown (*not Capt. Brown*)...."[202] From their first meeting, Higginson was impressed by Brown, and his close observation of the man provides a shrewd glimpse into Brown's character:

> I saw before me a man whose mere appearance and bearing refuted in advance some of the strange perversions which have found their way into many books, and which have often wholly missed the type to which he belonged. In his thin, worn, resolute face there were the signs of a fire which might wear him out, and practically did so, but nothing of pettiness or baseness; and his talk was calm, persuasive, and coherent. He was simply a high-minded, unselfish, belated Covenanter; a man whom Sir Walter Scott might have drawn, but whom such writers as Nicolay and Hay, for instance, have utterly failed to delineate. To describe him in their words as "clean but coarse" is curiously wide of the mark.... [H]e had, on the contrary, that religious elevation which is itself a kind of refinement,—the quality one may see expressed in many a venerable Quaker face at yearly meeting. Coarseness absolutely repelled him; he was ... strict ... had little humor, and none of the humorist's temptation towards questionable conversation.... I saw him afterwards deeply disappointed and thwarted, and this long before his final failure, but never could find in him a trace of mere ambition; he lived, as he finally died, absolutely absorbed in one idea; and it is as a pure enthusiast—fanatic, if you please—that he is to be judged.[203]

Of Brown's plans, Higginson would soon come to learn a great deal. The Allegheny Mountains, Brown contended, were the perfect place to conceal fugitive slaves. Brown knew the area, he maintained, having surveyed it as a young man, and he spoke of locations which "could be held by a hundred men against a thousand." He shared with Higginson rough sketches illustrating the areas which could be utilized for this purpose as well as his plans for a series of "connected mountain fortresses." While Brown himself might be unaware of battle strategy, he had read of guerilla warfare, engaging Hugh Forbes, "an Englishman who had been a ... soldier," in his enterprise. Higginson would later describe Brown's design as "utterly clear of all attempt to create slave insurrection." Rather, as Higginson saw it, Brown hoped to establish groups of fugitive slaves in permanent fortresses throughout the mountains "like the Maroons of Jamaica and Surinam...." Failing that, Brown himself would escort the fugitives to Canada through already familiar pathways.

None of this seemed unreasonable to Higginson, who later wrote, "All this he explained to me and others, plainly and calmly, and there was nothing in it that we considered objectionable or impracticable; so that his friends in Boston—Theodore Parker, Howe, Stearns, Sanborn and myself—were ready to cooperate in his plan as thus limited."[204] With this tacit acceptance of Brown's mission as they understood it, and with the continued support of Gerrit Smith on whose New York land Brown made his home, these half dozen supporters of Brown's—Higginson, Parker, Stearns, Howe, Smith and Sanborn—became what would later be termed the Secret Six. The Six would provide support, both monetary as well as moral, for Brown and his plans even as they led straight to the door of the engine house at Harpers Ferry.

Repeatedly, the group proved themselves to be apt fund-raisers. It was a deep well to which Brown would return often. On 8 March 1858 Sanborn wrote from Concord: "Hawkins [Brown's alias] has gone to Philadelphia today—leaving his friends to work for him. $1000 is the sum set to be raised here—of which yourself, Mr. Parker, Dr. Howe, Mr. Stearns and myself each are [illeg.] to raise $100—Some may do more—perhaps you cannot come up to that—nor I, possibly."[205] On 1 April, George Stearns wrote Higginson that $375 had been collected to date.[206] In May, Brown wrote Higginson, saying, "We also beg our friends to supply us with Two or Three Hundred Dollars without delay...."[207] Brown assured Higginson "that none of our friends need have any friends fears in relation to hasty or rash steps being taken by us."[208] Higginson would prove himself to be both a staunch supporter and an enthusiastic fund-raiser on Brown's behalf. His letters repeatedly reveal him to have been "among the most extreme of Brown's supporters during '58 and '59." Higginson, along with Sanborn, Parker, Howe and Stearns, met with Brown from 1858–1859 in Boston, Worcester, Concord and Peterboro, and "Higginson raised money for him throughout this period, giving him $500 in gold 'with some promises' in May, '58, and varying sums at other times."[209]

But shortly the Six would find an obstacle to their plans upon which they hadn't counted. They had willingly "helped [Brown] in raising the money, and he seemed drawing toward the consummation of his plans, when letters began to come to his Massachusetts supporters from Hugh Forbes ... threatening to make the whole matter public unless we could satisfy certain very unreasonable demands for money." In a word, the group suddenly found themselves being blackmailed. It was Forbes's threat and the corresponding delay in plans that Higginson forever would contend doomed the Harpers Ferry episode to failure. The men simply could not "foresee the imprudence which finally perverted the attack into a defeat."[210]

Forbes's threats resulted in an immediate cleft in the committee. While all concurred they would refuse to meet Forbes's "preposterous demands" for money, they differed on whether Brown's mission should be aborted. The majority of the group thought that the "threat of disclosure made necessary an indefinite postponement of the whole affair," but Higginson, Howe and Brown himself "thought otherwise."[211] Higginson told Brown, "H[owe] & myself have seen no reason to be discouraged; while P[arker] & S[tearns] have thought the whole project at an end for this year. FBS [Sanborn] inclines to the latter opinion, but not so strongly."[212] Higginson forcefully urged his comrades not to give in to Forbes. On 7 May 1858, he wrote Jason Brown: "Sanborn writes an alarming letter of a certain H F [Hugh Forbes] who wishes to veto our veteran friend's project entirely. Who the man is I hv. no conception—but I utterly protest against any postponement. *If the thing is postponed, it is postponed forever....*" In closing, he added, "I believe that we have gone too far to go back without certain failure, & I believe our friend the veteran will think so too."[213] On the 18th he maintained the same, writing to Brown: "The sum raised by me was all I can possibly provide, but I have written to the others, strongly urging them not to give up the ship."[214] In a letter to Parker he declared, "[P]ostponement is abandonment," and admonished, "The more I think of it the more amazed I am, at the view which you & the two S's [Sanborn and Stearns] have taken." Reporting that Forbes is "certainly a blundering blockhead," he added, "[I]t would be disgraceful for us to be outmaneuvered by such a fellow." He then concluded, "If I had the wherewithal I would buy out the other stockholders & tell our veteran to go on: As it is, I can only urge it to the extent of my investment."[215]

On 31 May 1858, Brown came to Boston where he and Higginson met alone to discuss the situation. Both men came to the conclusion that "Forbes could do ... no real harm...." Both were anxious for plans to continue, but Higginson was forced to acquiesce, saying, "[A]s I could not unaided, provide the means, I was obliged to yield, as he did." Brown, for his part, agreed to the postponement and returned to Kansas with $500 in gold and guns supplied to him by the State Kansas Committee, turned over to him specifically at the direction of Stearns.[216] On 1 June, Higginson reported, "Saw [John Brown] in Boston." Brown communicated the current plan—to "postpone till next winter or spring when they wd. raise $2000 or $3000; ... & to transfer the project so as to relieve them of responsibility—& they in future not to know his plans." Higginson contended that Brown "agreed entirely with me, considered delay very discouraging to his 13 men & to those in Canada,—is possible to begin in the autumn ... if he had $300—it wd. not cost $25 apiece to get his men fr. Ohio & that was all he needed." Brown, said Higginson, had assured him that "[i]f he had the means, he wd. not lose a day." When Higginson expressed wonder that the others did not agree with them, Brown responded, "[T]hey were not men of action...." Higginson was not fully taken in by Brown's assurances, calling Brown a "sly old veteran" and noting "he had not said this to them, & had appeared to acquiesce far more than he really did" so that they "not think him reckless."[217]

By fall, Brown was still in Kansas and Higginson was still raising funds for him. In mid–September, Brown wrote Higginson thanking him for $50, and assuring him that "all seems quiet now." In the letter, Brown complained of being "still weak" from a six week long illness. "I have but Fourteen regularly employed hands the most of whom are now at common work: and some are sick. Much sickness prevails," he wrote. The letter appealed to Higginson to keep faith: "Dear Friends do be in earnest: the harvest we shall reap, if we are only up, and doing."[218] But faith was in short supply in Higginson's camp and he chafed at the continued delay. In response to another request for funds, on 1 May 1859, he wrote Brown: "I trust you will be able to obtain money from others—from me, there is little to be obtained." Meager resources were not the sole reason for Higginson's reticence. "My own loss of confidence is also in the way," he admitted, "loss of confidence not in you, but in others who are concerned in the measure. Those who were so easily disheartened last spring, may be again deterred now." Expressing complete faith in Brown, he added, "If I could fit you out, myself, for the operation, it would be soon done; as it is I will provide an additional remittance when you are once launched. But it is hard for me to solicit money for another *retreat*, when I think retreat is not needed." Saying he would join Brown himself if circumstances permitted, he closed: "I long to see you, with adequate funds in your hands, set free from timid advisers & able to act in your own way."[219]

Sanborn, meanwhile, kept up appeals to Higginson on Brown's behalf, asking for money in October 1858, and again in March, April and September of 1859.[220] On 11 September 1857, Sanborn wrote Higginson: "You do not understand Brown's circumstances.... He is as ready for a revolution as any other man, and is now on the borders of Kansas safe from arrest but prepared for action, but he needs money for his present expenses, and *active* support."[221] On 29 October 1858, Higginson wrote Brown: "I am rejoiced to find that you are not yet discouraged, and are still looking forward to the enterprise which *ought* to have begun last spring. I have never ceased to regret its postponement...." Acknowledging Sanborn's appeal for funds, Higginson apologized, saying, "I am sorry I can do so little; had I had a full purse, perhaps some things would have gone differently." He concluded: "I trust that your enterprise may not be deferred longer than next spring & that I may yet be able to render it some service beside good wishes. *Those* you (& your friends) always have...."[222]

The year 1859 passed quietly with little word from Brown. Higginson began to fear that "perhaps his whole project had been abandoned." Fund-raising continued, however, in Boston that spring, but Higginson remained largely disengaged: "It had all begun to seem to me rather chimerical. The amount of $2000 was, nevertheless, raised for him at Boston, in June, 1859...."[223]

On 4 June 1859, Higginson received the word from Sanborn for which he had long awaited: "Brown has set out on his expedition having got some $800 from all sources except from Mr. Stearns, and from him the balance of $2000...." Brown had left Boston, Sanborn reported, and planned to begin operations soon, perhaps by 4 July.[224] Higginson mistakenly assumed Brown was headed for Ohio, maintaining that "Nobody mentioned Harpers Ferry."[225] On 6 October word came that Francis Merriam was leaving Boston en route to "the pastures," where he would "look into matters a little for the stockholders." Higginson should expect a call from him and could pass on a message "for the shepherd."[226]

Ten days later, Brown struck his blow at Harpers Ferry. Of his five disciples on the continent at the time (Stearns, Higginson, Smith, Howe and Sanborn), Higginson would be the only one not to deny him: "As for Mr. Higginson, he stood his ground in Worcester, where all the world might find him."[227]

Part III

The Verbal Assault on Harpers Ferry

Eight

LITERATURE'S VERSION

> I walked up the bridge ... saw from five hundred to six hundred negroes, all having arms; there were two or three hundred white men with them.... Insurgents are Government employes headed by one ANDERSON.... Everything had been plundered, and all appeared determined to fight.... It is believed to be an abolition movement to protect runaways.... A large number of negroes stampeded last evening from several localities ... making for Harpers Ferry. The report that negroes have taken possession of Harpers Ferry, and now hold the Government Armory, has created great excitement here.[1]

Initially, reports of the events at Harpers Ferry were as hysterical as they were erroneous, leading one New York paper, the antislavery *Tribune,* to refuse to believe an insurrection had even taken place. While admitting that "some sort of a disturbance" had occurred, the paper believed the "nature of the affair must be grossly misapprehended." Incredulous, the *Tribune* asserted that "negroes are not abundant in that part of Virginia, while no Abolitionists were even known to peep into that quarter...."[2] It was not long, however, before the press would garner the facts and pass judgment on the events at Harpers Ferry.

Once the truth of the raid became apparent, the press's condemnation of Brown was swift and unanimous. The "plot ... of a crazed fanatic," concluded *The New York Times,* "the work of a madman" echoed the *Tribune,* "Brown's crazy attempt," cried the *New York Post.*[3] The Republican *New York Courier* on 18 October described Brown as "a man half-crazed and made utterly desperate by the murder of his sons by the border ruffians in Kansas."[4] A special correspondent reporting on 20 October from Harpers Ferry concluded, in *The New York Times,* that "The excitement is subsiding into astonishment at the insane undertaking of the insurgents."[5] The *Baltimore Republican,* a Democratic organ, fumed, "There is no language adequate to express the madness and infamy of this act."[6]

In Boston, the *Journal* referred to the raid as a "mad attempt" by "insane fanatics," while the *Evening Transcript* of the same city described Brown's raid as "an insane and villainous scheme, from first to last," and predicted that Brown would receive "little sympathy in the North."[7] Further South, the *Republican Banner and Nashville Whig* agreed, expressing satisfaction in "the unanimity of the Republican Press in condemning the course of the abolitionists...."[8]

Perhaps no one in journalism was more conflicted over the events at Harpers Ferry than William Lloyd Garrison, editor of the *Liberator.* Long a pacifist, Garrison had difficulty endorsing the violent raid. At the same time, he seemed unable to wholly condemn it, leaving his paper strangely silent on the subject. On 21 October, in a small insert on page two, Garrison finally broke his silence, calling the raid a "misguided, wild, and apparently insane, though disinterested and well-intended effort." He continued, "Our views of war and bloodshed, even in the best of causes are too well known to need repeating here; but let no one who glories in the revolutionary struggle of 1776, deny the right of slaves to imitate the example of our fathers."[9]

Many in the press addressed what they viewed as the greater ramifications of the affair. The Democratic *Locomotive* of Indianapolis deemed the undertaking a "fiendish plot" and determined that the "object [was] plunder, violations of female chastity, and an indiscriminate slaughter of all [in the southern states] who should oppose its fearful march."[10] The *Mercury* of Charleston, South Carolina, called the attack a "pregnant sign of the times," and claimed "[The raid] is a warning profoundly symptomatic of the future of the Union...."[11] The *Cincinnati Enquirer* (Democrat) opined the assault was a "presage of the future storm, that shall desolate the whole land, if the people give this Abolition doctrine their approval."[12] A Republican organ, the *Chicago Press and Tribune*, also predicted doom, but blamed Democratic policies: "Permit the Democracy to rule, and this Harpers Ferry blood is but the few falling drops which presage the burst."[13] Regardless of their biases, most Democratic and Republican papers chose to see the raid as a harbinger of a greater catastrophe to come. In so doing, they elevated Brown's failed attempt to a position of preeminence to which it otherwise could never have aspired.

While some in the press correctly predicted that the chasm between North and South would only be broadened by the events at Harpers Ferry, a minority felt the raid provided an opportunity for reconciliation. On Friday, 11 November, the *Liberator* reprinted articles from the *New Orleans Bulletin* and Maryland's *Frederick Herald*, both of which saw the attack as a setback to antislavery. The *New Orleans Bulletin* confidently, but erroneously, forecast that the raid would "give a blow to abolition in the Northern and Western States from which it will not soon recover," while the *Herald* offered the following: "[T]his Harper's Ferry failure will strengthen and consolidate the national sentiment of the country, and weaken sectionalism."[14] But, it was the prediction of the *Richmond Enquirer* which unfortunately would be more accurate. The rebellion, they contended, "has advanced the cause of Disunion more than any other event that has happened since the formation of the Government."[15]

As the press railed, few people in the country read accounts of John Brown's exploits with greater interest than did Frederick Douglass. On 17 October, the *Philadelphia Evening Bulletin* carried an advertisement for a speech that night by Douglass at National Hall. In the same issue, the paper reported rumors of a slave rebellion at Harpers Ferry. Immediately, Douglass realized that his "old friend [Brown] had attempted what he had long ago resolved to do," leaving Douglass "certain that the result must be [Brown's] capture and destruction." The announcement of the raid "came upon us with the startling effect of an earthquake," Douglass contended; "[i]t was something to make the boldest hold his breath."[16] Aware that he, too, was implicated, and unwilling to call undue attention to himself, he gave his stock lecture that night with no mention of the raid until the end, when he "digressed to speak of Harper's Ferry, calling it the legitimate fruits of slavery."[17]

By 20 October, Douglass could no longer afford to be as sanguine. *The New York Times* revealed that authorities had found "letters from various individuals ... [including] one from FRED. DOUGLASS, containing $10 from a lady for the cause," adding "All these [letters] are in possession of Gov. Wise."[18] Soon the Virginia governor would be looking for "Frederick Douglass, a negro man ... charged with ... inciting servile insurrection."[19] When a telegram arrived warning "we were all to be arrested," friends urged Douglass to leave the country. Douglass wryly admitted he was "seized with a desire to reach a more northern latitude."[20]

Friends advised Douglass that the New York papers were full of angry stories about the raid and his complicity in it. One article reported that a hundred southerners had banded together to offer a $2,500 reward for the head of Frederick Douglass.[21] On 22 October, the Rochester paper printed a letter from Douglass to Brown, which seemingly implicated Douglass further. In actuality, the letter had been written two years before, but the paper had omitted the year, making it seem a recent correspondence. Fearing what a search of his home might reveal, Douglass had an unsigned telegram sent to a friend saying, "Tell Lewis to secure all the important papers in my high desk." It was a fortuitous decision, since among those papers was a copy of Brown's constitution. With each passing hour, delay seemed less wise and Douglass decided the time had come when he, in fact, must "quit the country...."[22] Taking the same route he had so often used while assisting fugitive slaves, Douglass left for Canada. Apprehensive that he might possibly be taken while on the ferry to Camden, he asked friends to accompany him, but "[u]pon one ground or another, they all thought it best not to be found in my company at such a time...." Largely deserted, Douglass made the trip with a single friend by his side. "The truth is," he confessed "that in the excitement which prevailed, my friends had reason to fear that the very fact that they were with me would be a sufficient reason for their arrest...." Douglass's timing was fortuitous. As he spent "an *anxious* night," plans were, in fact, being hatched for his capture.[23] In truth, he might very well have been arrested before he left the city had not a sympathetic telegraph operator delayed for three hours the message ordering his arrest while he ensured Douglass was warned of the imminent danger.[24] Shortly, U.S. marshals would be in Rochester, engaged in an unsuccessful search for the fugitive Douglass.

On 6 November, Wise asserted that if Douglass "incited, or aided & abetted insurrection," he had "violated our laws [the laws of Virginia]," and could, therefore, "be demanded of England or any of the states."[25] Governor Wise appointed a special prosecutor, Andrew Hunter, to "find out the *whereabouts* of the Negro Frederick Douglass and keep an eye on his movements and associates." A week later, Wise hired a detective for $100 a month whose charge was to "ascertain when and where a requisition of arrest could reach Frederick Douglass" and from there, "establish how he might be brought to Virginia."[26] By 13 November, Wise considered the capture of Douglass so paramount that he apprised President James Buchanan of his plans for "the delivery up of the person of Frederick Douglass, a negro man, supposed now to be in Michigan, charged with murder, robbery, and inciting servile insurrection in the State of Virginia." Naming agents he had secured for this purpose, he cautioned, "They need to be very secretive in this manner ... and [have] some protection against obtrusive, unruly, or lawless violence."[27]

Clearly Douglass's decision to leave the country saved him from capture. But, however justified Douglass may have been in fleeing to Canada, his flight created a public relations problem at home. John E. Cook, one of the imprisoned insurgents, denounced Douglass as a coward, contending he had promised to be present at Harpers Ferry. Douglass was in the unenviable position of having to defend both himself and Brown from Canada. He rose to the challenge with a thoughtful letter to the *Rochester Democrat and American*, published 31 October 1859 and reprinted in *Douglass' Monthly* November 1859. Writing from "Canada West," he unequivocally denied he promised to be at Harpers Ferry, saying, "I have never made a promise so rash and wild as this," and defying any man living or dead to say otherwise. "Mr. Cook may be perfectly right in denouncing me as a coward. I have not one word to say in defense or vindication of my character for courage. I have always been more distinguished for running than fighting," he maintained. Clarifying his role in the antislavery movement, he echoed what would become a lifelong refrain: "I am ever ready to write, speak, publish, organize, combine, and even to conspire against Slavery, when there is a reasonable hope for success." Apparently the events at Harpers Ferry did not meet this test, however, as Douglass admitted, "My field of labor for the abolition of Slavery has not extended to an attack upon the United States arsenal."[28]

As interesting for what it doesn't say as what it does, the letter is hardly a stirring endorsement or even defense of Brown. Rather, the focus of the piece is Douglass, with little direct mention of Brown. While he does call Brown the "noble old hero whose one right hand has shaken the foundation of the American Union," he concludes, "My position in regard to the Harper's Ferry insurrection, may be easily inferred from these remarks...."[29] Essentially, the reader is left to assume Douglass's unstated position on the raid.

Contrary to Douglass's rather muted response, support among blacks for Brown's raid was strong, unmarked by much of the hesitation of the white abolitionists. For the most part, blacks, while uneasy about the violence of Brown's act, nonetheless had no intention of turning their backs on a white man who was willing to give his life for their cause, and many did not appreciate what they perceived as Douglass's willingness to do so. The editors of the weekly *Anglo-African* expressed dismay, saying flight was not the response of a heroic man, while black abolitionist J. Sella Martin chastised Douglass for "writing from the broad latitude of Canada West."[30]

The black community was not alone in condemning Douglass's departure. White abolitionists also disapproved of his flight. In a 16 November letter, Samuel May, Jr., never a fan of Douglass, wrote a Dublin publisher: "F. Douglass leaves here [the United States] by a circuitous route. He is implicated in the Harpers Ferry business, and took refuge in Canada. We all agree with you—to give him a wide berth, & take no notice of him. He is wholly selfish and unworthy of our trust for a moment."[31] It is unclear whether May is angry because of Douglass's involvement with Brown, his escape to Canada, or a combination of the two, but clearly Douglass's support in the abolitionist community was, for the moment, waning. The same day, the *Valley Spirit* in Chambersburg, Pennsylvania, where Brown and his men prepared for the attack, printed an article about Frederick Douglass's part in the raid: "FRED denies that he encouraged the Harpers Ferry adventure. We do not believe him." It concluded by calling Douglass "as impudent a liar and as bold a political rascal as HORACE, and as great a coward too."[32]

Eight. Literature's Version

Even with Douglass, one of their most influential spokesmen, absent, the news of Brown was so paramount that a consistent message about the raid soon emerged in the black community. On 24 October, Martin, in a public eulogy of Nat Turner, praised Brown, exhorting his brethren in the audience to "rise and liberate John Brown," a suggestion that was met with "tremendous cheers" from the crowd of 800. In a courageous speech to an all-white audience in Brockett's Bridge, New York, black abolitionist William J. Watkins called Brown a hero as brave and as holy "as ever the sun flashed on."[33] On 18 November 1859, a letter from Charles H. Langston, who would become the grandfather of poet Langston Hughes, was published in the *Cleveland Plain Dealer*. In the letter, Langston defended a Christ-like Brown, saying, "[h]is aims and ends were lofty, noble, generous, benevolent, humane and Godlike." Brown, he said, was a man who "went into Virginia to aid the afflicted and the helpless, to assist the weak and to relieve the poor and needy. To undo the heavy burdens, to let the oppressed go free, to do to others as he would have them to do to him. And above all to put to death, as the papers tell us, those who steal men and sell them, and in whose hands stolen men are found. [Brown's] actions then are only the results of his faithfulness to the plain teaching of the word of God."[34]

By late November, Douglass published a second letter, "To My American Readers and Friends," in the *Douglass' Monthly*, in which he announced he would be leaving for England on a long-planned speaking tour.[35] In the piece, he defended his decision to go abroad. "In ordinary conditions, considering the rapidity, safety and certainty with which a journey is now made to Europe ... a simple voyage from America to Great Britain would not seem to warrant a very ceremonious and formal parting, or to require apology or explanation," he wrote. Yet, in light of public opinion, Douglass clearly felt that his exodus required comment. "At the present moment, Slavery seems to have gained an advantage," he noted, adding:

> The audacity of the attack made upon it by that stern old hero, who looks death full in the face with a steady eye and undaunted heart, while pierced with bayonet wounds and covered with sabre gashes, has created for the moment, perhaps, a more active resistance to the cause of freedom and its advocates; but this is transient. The moment of passion and revenge will pass away, and reason and righteousness will all the more, for this sudden shock, roll their thundering appeal to the ear and heart of this guilty nation.[36]

In the letter, Douglass refers to Brown as a "stern old hero," even as he condemns the attack on the arsenal as "deplorable." Terming the raid the "battle of Harper's Ferry," he predicts that "Men will soon begin to look away from the plot to the purpose—from the effect to the cause—Then will come the reaction—and the names now covered with execration will be mentioned with honor, as noble martyrs to a righteous cause." Douglass also responded to charges that the black slaves captured at the ferry refused to lift arms against their masters. "All the efforts to disparage the valor of the colored insurgents are grounded in the fears of the slaveholders, not in the facts of the action," he wrote. This point was critically important in combating the prevalent racial stereotype of black cowardice in the face of physical danger. Recognizing the irony of defending the courage of his race from a post well out of the country, he turned to a discussion of his own retreat:

Almost ever since the Harper's Ferry disturbance, I have been assured that U.S. Marshals, in strong force, have been in search of me at different points, but chiefly at Rochester. A government which refuses to acknowledge—nay, denies that I can be a citizen, or bring a suit into its courts of justice—in a word, brands me as an outlaw in virtue of my blood, now professes a wish to try me for being a traitor and an outlaw! To be a traitor, two conditions are necessary: First—one must have a government; secondly—he must be found in armed rebellion against that government. I am guilty of neither element of treason.[37]

No doubt feeling that he had acquitted himself as well as possible to friends and the public alike, Douglass arrived in England without incident. On 30 November he wrote his friend Maria Webb in Yorkshire: "You have of course heard of the circumstances under which I was left no alternative but to leave the states or be implicated with John Brown, and perhaps, share his fate." Wishing to clear up "some misapprehension as to my relation to that brave and I believe good man," he referred to his published letter, saying he felt it "did much to set me right before the American people...." Denying that he had "any part of the charges brought against me in connection with the Harpers Ferry affair," he nonetheless felt certain that had he stayed he would have been executed. "If they did not kill me for being concerned with Dear old Brown they would have done so—for my being Frederick Douglass," he maintained.[38]

On 7 December, Frederick Douglass, still a wanted man, shared a speaker's platform in England with old abolitionist friends. In an address "remarkably optimistic" and "more biblical ... than usual," he did not utter a single word about John Brown.[39] In fact, while events at Harpers Ferry spurred a number of black abolitionists to ever more fiery rhetoric, the incident seemed to have the reverse effect on Douglass, making him more subdued than usual. Part of Douglass's uncharacteristically cautious reaction was no doubt the continued fervor back home surrounding his involvement in the raid. In a speech to medical students in Richmond, on 21 December, Gov. Wise received thunderous applause when he vowed, "Oh if I had had one good ... well-armed steamer.... [Douglass] should have been taken ... with very particular instructions not to hang him before I had the privilege of seeing him well hanged."[40]

While Douglass and the black community wrestled with the ramifications of Harpers Ferry, others were also reading press accounts of the raid with great interest. Thoreau and Alcott were visiting Emerson when word of the raid reached Concord on 19 October.[41] Thoreau was terribly upset at the news and filled his journal with an uncharacteristically angry outpouring of 11,000 words over the next five days.[42] Emerson wrote his brother William of the "sad Harpers Ferry business, which interests us all who had Brown for our guest twice." Emerson's first judgment of Brown's act was reserved, echoing his initial response to Thoreau's night in jail. "[Brown] is a true hero, but lost his head there," he wrote. Later, he would follow Thoreau's lead in a strong defense of Brown.[43]

In Concord, Emerson and Thoreau's friend Sanborn, upon hearing the news of the attack, realized that, like Douglass, he was implicated. He headed out of the country, arriving in Canada on the twenty-first.[44] In a letter to Theodore Parker dated 22 October, Sanborn refers to news accounts of Harpers Ferry and concludes, "Our old friend has struck his blow in such a way ... that it has recoiled, and ruined him, and perhaps those who were his friends.... [His act is] likely to ruin my worldly prospects for years to come, besides estranging and shocking my friends...." Sanborn's chief fear was that "I shall be much blamed for it all, and that by many whose good opinion I value highly." Still, he contended, "I believe I did what was best." He then signed the letter "Frederick B. Stanley né F.B. Sanborn."[45] Emerson, one of the friends about whom Sanborn was no doubt concerned, believed Sanborn's flight a mistake and wrote to Quebec urging his return "at the first hour wheels or steam will permit."[46] Higginson, too, thought the departure imprudent and wrote Sanborn saying as much. Sanborn responded with a testy reply: "Yours of yesterday and of Monday have been received, and in answer to the last, I would say, that I have no intention of going to Canada to avoid arrest—*as a criminal*, nor for any cause, if I felt reasonably sure of being protected here."[47]

Sanborn's words reflect the initial widespread negative public opinion about Brown. In truth, it seemed even Brown's staunchest supporters viewed events as irredeemable and hesitated to come to his defense. The *Liberator* agreed, reporting on "rats ... leaving the sinking ship." Citing "those who have heretofore pleasantly fraternized ... [but now] cry out lustily that they have no knowledge of this 'insane' fanatic Brown, and cannot ... be held responsible for his deeds," the paper wryly concluded, "The unfortunate seldom have many friends."[48]

For his part, Thoreau followed accounts in the press about the raid with growing dismay, but harbored no such reservations. "I have read all the newspapers I could get within a week, and I do not remember in them a single expression of sympathy for these men," he noted. A journal entry dated 22 October provides an early clue to his intentions. He wrote, "I wish to correct the tone and some of the statements of the newspapers respecting the life and character and last action of John Brown," adding, "The newspapers seem to ignore, or perhaps they are really ignorant of the fact that there are at least as many as one or two individuals to a town throughout the North who think as much as I do about him or his enterprise." His journal entries make clear the intensity of his support. "You who pretend to care for Christ crucified, consider what you are about to do to him who offered himself to be the savior of four millions of men!" he implored. With an eye on history, Thoreau recognized that Brown was worth more to the cause dead than alive, martyred than acquitted. "I almost fear to hear of his deliverance, doubting if a prolonged life, if any life, can do as much good as his death," he admitted.[49]

The first to decide that someone must speak out in Brown's defense, Thoreau sat up most of one night organizing his journal entries into a coherent lecture. The next morning, he polled his family regarding his decision to publicly support the raid—two concurred, one did not. Sanborn urged caution, warning that giving such a speech could be "dangerous," and advising Thoreau "it would be better to wait until there was a better feeling among the people."[50] In another sign of Brown's early lack of support, the committee members, both Republicans, as well as local abolitionists sent word they, too, thought Thoreau's actions imprudent. Regardless of this circumstance, Thoreau notified the town committee of his intention to speak at the town hall on 30 October. "I did not send to you for advice but to announce that I am to speak," he informed them.[51] The council could not deny a citizen of Concord the right to use the town hall, but they did refuse to ring the bell to announce the meeting. A defiant Thoreau rang it himself.

The night of the talk, the hall was filled—some had come to jeer, while Brown's supporters came in warily, as if afraid to be seen. All agreed it was a passionate Thoreau who spoke on "The Character of John Brown, now in the clutches of the slaveholder." In the speech, Thoreau portrayed Brown as a transcendental hero, a man of New England, an American Christ figure and a man in concert with the higher laws of his conscience.[52] The speech was a success. Edward Emerson thought Thoreau read from his paper "as if it burned him" and noted that many who "came to scoff remained to pray."[53] Alcott, who could not attend the lecture because of the short notice, commented in his journal that Thoreau spoke "to the delight of his company ... among them Emerson."[54]

On 6 November, in a letter to Thoreau's friend Daniel Ricketson, Alcott referred to Thoreau's lecture as "revolutionary" and added that John Brown is "a hero and Martyr after [Thoreau's] own heart and style."[55] Minot Pratt, a local citizen, wrote his wife of the speech: "Henry spoke of [Brown] in terms of the most unqualified eulogy. I never heard him before speak so much in praise of any man...."[56] Another of Henry's townsmen concluded, "It was a bold, strong argument he made, but in a time of fear and doubt," adding, "Few other persons had a definite opinion or dared utter their thoughts openly."[57] Even Sanborn, who felt that most of Henry's lectures generally "would have been reckoned dull," agreed that Thoreau was "mightily stirred by the emotions that a life so heroic excited in his fearless heart."[58] The speech was, by anyone's standards, a courageous one, given at a time when most abolitionists "were denouncing Brown as demented."[59]

Encouraged by the response of his Concord neighbors, Thoreau offered to repeat the lecture in Worcester for only the cost of his expenses. "I should like to speak to any company at Worcester who may wish to hear me," he wrote, adding, "I think we should express ourselves at once, while Brown is alive. The sooner the better." Thoreau drew upon his Worcester connections, writing Harrison Blake that "Perhaps Higginson may like to have a meeting."[60] While awaiting a response from Worcester, an urgent telegram arrived addressed to "Henry Thoreau or Ralph Waldo Emerson, Concord" requesting that "Thoreau must lecture ... Tuesday Evening—Douglass fails."[61] The director of the Fraternity Lectures in Boston needed Thoreau to speak in Boston on 1 November for the absent Douglass. It was Emerson who responded to the telegram on 31 October. "I think you cannot do a greater public good than to send for Mr. Thoreau, who has read last night here a discourse on the history & character of Captain John Brown, which ought to be heard or read by every man in the Republic," Emerson noted. "He read it with great force & effect, & though the audience was of widely different parties, it was heard without a murmur of dissent."[62] Emerson's recommendation clearly prevailed. On 1 November, Thoreau wrote Slack: "I will come to Boston as desired."[63]

Whether due to public interest in the issue, or the widespread advertising, the auditorium, one of the largest in Boston, was filled with folks crowding the hall a half-hour before the lecture was to begin.[64] The night began with a dramatic focus on the absent Douglass. Charles Slack of the Lecture Committee reflected the anxiety of the times: "At a late hour on Monday the Lecture Committee had received a communication from Mr. Douglass, written at a point not necessary to state, and the letter contained information which he was not permitted to divulge. But the reason that the lecturer did not appear was that he, a free man by his original right as well as by purchase, would not be safe this night in Boston."[65] The actual correspondence from Douglass to Slack, not quoted for obvious security reasons, was equally dramatic:

Confidential as to Marshals and my whereabouts.
Confidential
My Dear Sir:
Seventeen marshals are on the look out for me in the States, and to avoid arrest I must avoid a journey to Boston—It is a real calamity that deprives me of the privilege of fulfilling my engagement—and speaking to such an audience as that you anticipate—I should have written before—but for the hope that the clouds that now overshadow me would pass away—Instead of this they grow darker every hour—In haste
Yours Truly,
Frederick Douglass[66]

Thoreau began his ninety-minute "A Plea for Captain John Brown" by also invoking the name of the missing Douglass, saying that the reason "Douglass is not here is the reason of my being here."[67] He continued with a strong defense of Brown, saying, "I am here to plead his cause with you. I plead not for his life, but for his character,—his immortal life...."[68] Canby asserts that "the 'Plea' was not a 'vain attempt' to save the life of Captain John Brown," but rather "an argument for the occasional necessity of civil disobedience, a defense of violence in a good cause, and a eulogy of courage, uprightness, and the will to achieve in a man of principle." In short, Thoreau the "Puritan in thought" was "defending [Brown] a Puritan in deed...."[69]

In a style similar to his "Slavery in Massachusetts" address, Thoreau again attacked the press in a scathing indictment, this time for their coverage of the raid. "Even the *Liberator* called it 'a misguided, wild, and apparently insane—effort,'" he fumed. "As for the herd of newspapers and magazines, I do not chance to know an editor in the country who will deliberately print anything which he knows will ultimately and permanently reduce the number of his subscribers." Addressing "ye *Liberators*, ye *Tribunes*, ye *Republicans*" directly, Thoreau admonished, "When a man stands up serenely against the condemnation and vengeance of mankind ... we become criminals in comparison. Do yourselves the honor to recognize him." Thoreau dismissed the Democratic press entirely, saying, "[T]hey are not human enough to affect me at all."[70]

In spite of Thoreau's ire at the press, all of the major Boston newspapers covered his address, with the *Traveler* printing the speech almost verbatim. The *Liberator* reported that "A very large audience listened to this lecture ... giving hearty applause to some of the most energetic expressions of the speaker," and the *Boston Journal* concluded that the hour and a half lecture was "well received."[71] However, not every paper was complimentary; the pro-slavery *Boston Atlas and Daily Bee*, while reprinting much of the talk, nonetheless condemned Thoreau as a fanatic.[72] The *Springfield Republican*, in a play on the northeastern pronunciation of Thoreau's name, asserted that "This Thoreau seems to be a thorough fanatic—why don't he imitate Brown and do good by rushing to the gallows."[73] On 9 November, the *New York Daily Tribune*, while conceding that there were "some just and striking remarks" in the speech, nonetheless concluded it was filled with frequent "[s]neers at the Republicans" and disparaged "editors like those of *The Tribune* and *The Liberator*, who, while the lecturer was cultivating beans and killing woodchucks on the margin of Walden Pond, made a public opinion strong enough on Anti-Slavery grounds to tolerate a speech from him in defense of insurrection ... [and who thus] deserve better treatment than they receive from some of the upstart Abolitionists of the day."[74]

Stung by Thoreau's criticism, the *Liberator* somewhat disingenuously noted that the theme "awakened 'the hermit of Concord' from his usual state of philosophic indifference." In a short article, they commented that Thoreau bestowed "hearty praise upon the enterprise at Harpers Ferry, and as hearty dispraise upon the apathy and reserve shown in regard to it by ... the periodical press...."[75]

On 3 November, in what would be the final time, Thoreau repeated his speech in Worcester, Massachusetts. Thoreau's courageous and singular defense of Brown was not lost on Alcott, who noted in his journal the next day that "[Thoreau] has been the first to speak, and celebrate the hero's courage and magnanimity." Noting that Brown and Thoreau "have much in common," he alleged, "Thoreau has good right to speak fully his mind concerning Brown."[76] The young Edward Emerson would later reflect: "When the red morning began to dawn in Kansas and at Harpers Ferry, I saw ... [Henry] deeply moved, and though otherwise avoiding public meetings and organized civic action, come to the front, and moved to the core, speak among the foremost against oppression."[77]

The 4 November issue of the *Liberator*, which carried the review of Thoreau's speech, also carried extensive and seemingly expanded coverage of the Harpers Ferry affair. Almost as if in response to Thoreau's criticism of two nights before, the issue contained a reprinted article from the *Boston Atlas and Daily Bee* entitled "Harper's Ferry as a Success." The edition also included a speech by Governor Wise; James Redpath's letter defending Brown; a resolution of the Executive Committee of the American Anti-Slavery Society requesting observance of the day of Brown's execution; an article describing Brown "in bed" while the verdict was given; Brown's moving address to the court; and Lydia Maria Child's private note calling Brown "a brave old man."

Perhaps because of Thoreau's bravery, or maybe as a result of his own further reflection, Emerson revised his earlier perception of the raid. The importance of Emerson's conversion to Brown's cause cannot be overestimated. As one historian phrased it, while Thoreau was "eloquent about Brown," he "didn't come close to having Emerson's cultural clout."[78] On 26 October, in a letter to Sarah Forbes, Emerson wrote, "Captain Brown ... is a hero of romance, & seems to have made this fatal blunder only to bring out his virtues. I must hope for his escape to the last moment."[79] On 2 November, the day Brown was sentenced, Emerson was sufficiently aroused to lend his name, alongside that of Higginson, to a circular promoting Brown's defense fund. The circular, which was distributed throughout Boston, read:

BOSTON, Nov. 2, 1859

DEAR SIR:—

You are invited and urged to contribute and obtain contributions to aid in the defence of Capt. BROWN and his companions, on trial for their lives in Virginia. *Every moment is precious,* and whatever is done must be done now. The following gentlemen (with others who may be hereafter announced in the papers) will act a Committee to receive money and appropriate it to this purpose *only*.

The circular was signed "S.E. SEWALL, ESQ., S.G. HOWE, M.D., R.W. EMERSON, ESQ., REV. T.W. HIGGINSON."[80]

To one flyer Higginson appended a note which read: "An expense of about $1000 is already incurred for counsel. Mrs. Brown must also be aided to join her husband, & her two widowed daughters-in-law, aged 20 and 16, need help greatly."[81]

In the days following the raid, Lidian's friend Wendell Phillips, the famous abolitionist orator, urged Emerson to speak out in Brown's defense.[82] Nine days after Thoreau's Concord address, he did so. In a speech entitled "Courage," given at Tremont Temple in Boston and reported in the *Liberator*, Emerson posited the question "Why do we not say, in reference to the evil of the times, that we are Abolitionists of the most absolute abolition?—as every man must be...." Attacking those who would attack Brown, he said, "I think badly of cowardice," adding, "Fear is cowardly and mean, until at last we do not know virtue when we see it." Ruing a world turned "upside down," Emerson continued: "I wish we might have health enough to know virtue when we see it, and not cry with the fools, '*Madman!*' when a hero passes," a statement that was met with "[p]rolonged applause."[83]

In the speech, Emerson fearlessly confronted his fellow citizens of New England, saying "there is a 'Reign of Terror' also, in the North, and we have no right to boast, so long as love of trade, a preference of peace to justice, or the love of comsort [*sic*] at any cost, withholds men from vote and voice."[84] But nothing he had said to that point would equal the furor unleashed over his next remarks. Brown, he contended, was a "new saint, than whom none purer or more brave was ever led by love of man into conflict and death; a new saint, waiting yet his martyrdom; and who, if he shall suffer, will make the gallows glorious like the cross."[85] The line, supplied to Emerson by Mattie Griffith, a southern abolitionist, was received with "[p]rolonged and enthusiastic applause" by those present,[86] but was later widely condemned by pro-slavery forces as blasphemous. Nonetheless, it echoed earlier comparisons of Brown's gallows and Christ's cross by both Alcott and Thoreau.[87] Emerson's speech, like Thoreau's, showed great courage. Boston was not only full of strongly conservative businessmen but also "negro-hating and ruffianly element[s] of the Democracy," leading Edward Emerson to conclude that speaking out on behalf of Brown "had its dangers."[88]

On 9 November, Thoreau's campaign to save Brown took a more literal turn. Alcott recorded in his journal that "Thoreau calls again. He thinks someone from the North should see Gov. Wise, or write concerning Capt. Brown's character and motives, to influence the Governor in his favor." Alcott felt that "Thoreau is the man to write, or Emerson," but added, "there seems little or no hope of pleas for mercy."[89] In spite of Alcott's pessimism, Emerson did compose a letter to Governor Wise in his journal. Apparently, it was never mailed. In it, he refers to the public perception concerning Brown, saying, "I shall not insult you by referring to a public opinion changing every day, and which has softened every hour its first harsh judgment of him."[90] In the next several days, Thoreau would also continue his efforts on behalf of Brown. Traveling to Boston, he made a series of unsuccessful attempts to find a publisher willing to print "A Plea" to raise money for the Brown family. Alcott wrote Thoreau's friend Ricketson: "I wish the towns might become his auditors throughout the states and country."[91]

In Concord, excitement about the raid was "boiling over." Louisa May Alcott, in a letter to a friend, wrote, "We have a daily stampede for papers, & a nightly indignation meeting over the wickedness of our country, & the cowardice of the human race."[92] On 19 November, Thoreau and Sanborn dined with Alcott. Talk turned to Harpers Ferry, with Thoreau commenting "freely and enthusiastically about Brown." In what the *Spectator* might have referred to as a "violent diatribe," Thoreau soon digressed into a denunciation of "the Union, President, the States, and Virginia particularly."[93] Sanborn, for his part, suggested that Alcott go to Virginia and seek access to Brown and Governor Wise. While there, he could "ascertain whether Brown would accept a rescue from any company we might raise."[94] Still, such an outcome seemed unlikely. "A rescue of Brown is *possible*; but barely so; and he as yet refuses to be rescued. It would cost some lives, and might fail, at the best," Sanborn had written Theodore Parker several days before.[95]

As Brown's execution date approached, Emerson returned on 18 November to the lecture platform at the Tremont Temple in Boston with a lecture entitled "Speech at a Meeting to Aid John Brown's Family." An admission fee of 25 cents was charged and, "[a]lthough the weather was stormy and forbidding, the spacious Temple was thronged." John A. Andrew was chair of the event and read from John Brown's letter to Maria Child. He then introduced Emerson "in a highly complimentary and merited manner, with patriotic allusions to his town." Upon rising, Emerson "was greeted with the most enthusiastic and prolonged applause." Assuring his audience that he "share[d] the sympathy and the sorrow which has brought us together," he turned his attention to Brown, extolling Brown's virtues and tracing his roots from the Mayflower through the Revolution to the War of 1812. "He is a man to make friends wherever on earth courage and integrity are esteemed (Applause);—the rarest of heroes, a pure idealist, with no by-ends of his own," Emerson said.[96] After he finished his remarks and had left the hall, it was announced that "in addition to his excellent speech, [Emerson] had contributed the sum of $50 in behalf of the Brown family," a pronouncement which was greeted with "great applause."[97]

The successful lecture was subsequently published in Boston newspapers.[98] Sanborn, always a fan of Emerson, pronounced it "great" and "very enthusiastic" and concluded that "Mr. Emerson has a great admiration for Brown—and he has spoken bravely for him."[99] A week and a half later, Emerson noted in his accounts that Thoreau donated $10 to the relief effort.[100]

The remarks were not received with approbation in all quarters, however. The *Boston Post* complained that "the men who occupy seats of power in New England, the controlling men in the dominant party here, are bound hand and foot in the fetters prepared and riveted by the anti-slavery fanatics"; the *Post* called on "farmers, merchants, lawyers, doctors, all of every class and interest" to act "before it is too late." Specifically, the *Post* demanded, they must not allow "Wendell Phillips, Ralph Waldo Emerson, Rev. Mr. Manning and John A. Andrew ... to falsely assume to proclaim the sentiments of Boston in relation to recent deplorable events in Virginia." Prominent men did, in fact, speak out for the other side, pointing out unattractive incidents in the life of Brown and accusing him of "horse stealing and butchery."[101] John Brown, however, steadfastly continued to deny those allegations and in their allegiance, or naiveté, so did his followers.

Word of Brown's raid reached Maria Child in Medford where she was visiting a friend. Maria's niece, Mary Stearns, was living nearby and the women gathered to talk, much as Thoreau and Emerson were doing in Concord. Mary confided her plans to go to Charlestown and nurse Brown in prison. But before she could leave, word came that her husband, George Stearns, a friend of Higginson's and one of the Secret Six, was implicated in the Harpers Ferry affair. Shortly, Stearns would flee to Canada, and Child decided, given the circumstances, that it was she, rather than her niece, who was better

Eight. Literature's Version

suited to go to Brown's aid. On 26 October, she enclosed a letter to Brown along with a note to Governor Henry Wise asking the governor for permission to nurse his prisoner. To Wise, she disavowed any advance knowledge of Brown's plans, saying, "I and all my large circle of abolition acquaintances were taken by surprise when news came of Capt. Brown's recent attempt" and confessed "nor do I know of a single person who would have approved of it had they been apprised of his intention." Even so, she admitted to "a natural impulse of sympathy for the brave and suffering man." While referring to herself as a woman of "peace principles," she admitted that she "deeply regret[ted] the step that the old veteran has taken."[102]

Her letter to Brown was equally forthright. "Believing in peace principles, I cannot sympathize with the method you chose to advance the cause of freedom," she admonished. Nevertheless, she conceded, "I honor your generous intentions—I admire your courage, moral and physical. I reverence you for the humanity which tempered your zeal. I sympathize with you in your cruel bereavement, your sufferings, and your wrongs. In brief, I love you and bless you." Assuring Brown that hers was not the only sympathetic heart, she stated (perhaps overstated), "Thousands of hearts are throbbing with sympathy as warm as mine." Treading a fine line between adherence to her peace principles and support of Brown's violent act, she added, "May you be strengthened by the conviction that no honest man ever sheds blood for freedom in vain, however much he may be mistaken in his efforts."[103]

Once she had posted her letters, Maria began packing and collecting lint for bandages.[104] On 3 November, she received a reply from Governor Wise. In a letter chivalrous, if not warm, dated 29 October, he advised Maria that she was welcome to come and nurse the prisoner: "Why should you not be so allowed, Madam? Virginia and Massachusetts are involved in no civil war...." He then promised that her "mission being merciful and humane, will not only be allowed, but respected, if not welcomed." At the same time, he disingenuously warned, "A few unenlightened and inconsiderate persons, fanatical in their modes of thought and action, to maintain justice and right, might molest you, or be disposed to do so...." Still, he promised to protect her as best he could, adding, "I could not permit an insult even to woman in her walk of charity among us, though it be to one who whetted knives of butchery for our mothers, sisters, daughters and babes." Squarely placing the blame for Brown's attack on Maria and her abolitionist friends, he contended Brown's raid was "a natural consequence of your sympathy...."[105]

Maria wasted little time in formulating her response. She replied, "you inform me that I have a constitutional right to visit Virginia.... I was perfectly well aware that such was the *theory*...." But, she added, "I was also aware of what you omit to mention ... that the Constitution has, in reality, been completely and systematically nullified whenever it suited the convenience or the policy of the Slave Power." Further, she pointed out, the Constitution "for which you profess so much respect, has never proved any protection to ... black, brown , or yellow [citizens]; nor to any white citizen whom you even suspected of entertaining opinions opposite to your own...." In what would become Child's constant refrain, she affirmed Brown's intent while opposing his methods. Calling him an "old hero," she asserted he is "no criminal, but a martyr to righteous principles" in spite of the fact that his "methods [were] sanctioned by his own religious views, though not by mine." Comparing Wise to Brown, she insists, "*You* have threatened to trample on the Constitution, and break the Union, if a majority ... in these Confederated States dared to elect a President unfavorable to the extension of Slavery." Disavowing any blame for the raid, she placed it instead squarely on the slave-holding states: "You may believe it or not, Gov. Wise, but it is certainly the truth that, because slaveholders so recklessly sowed the wind in Kansas, they reaped a whirlwind at Harper's Ferry."[106]

John Brown also replied promptly to Maria's letter. While he much appreciated her offer of aid, he did not need nursing, he averred. Instead, he suggested that she help his struggling family in North Elba. "I have at home a wife and three young daughters, the youngest but little over five years old, the oldest nearly sixteen," he wrote. Asking Maria to come to their aid rather than his, he beseeched, "dear friend, would you not as soon contribute fifty cents now, and a like sum yearly, for the relief of those very poor and deeply afflicted persons?" Not only did Brown ask Child personally to contribute, but he sought her assistance in asking others to "join ... in giving a like amount...."[107] Brown, in requesting that Maria raise funds for his family, perhaps little understood how truly effective she was as a fund-raiser. That aspect aside, he had an ulterior motive for suggesting she remain in Massachusetts. He told his lawyer to keep all women away from his cell, fearing they might undermine his composure. Additionally, he had a second source of anxiety where Maria was concerned. He undoubtedly worried that he and his compatriots might be lynched should such a well-known abolitionist show up on the jail's doorstep.[108]

Shortly, word reached Maria that her correspondence with both Wise and Brown had been published in the *New York Tribune*. Wise, in a gesture which quite certainly he would ultimately come to regret, apparently submitted the letters for publication. On 10 November, Maria acknowledged as much, writing the *Tribune*'s editor: "I was much surprised to see my correspondence with Governor Wise published in your columns." Claiming that she was innocent of the publicity surrounding the letters, she stated, "As I have never given any person a copy, I presume you must have obtained it from Virginia." Her original intent, she reiterated, had nothing to do with publicity, but rather, was simply to go to Virginia and "nurse that brave and generous old man...."[109]

The publication of the correspondence between Child and Wise evoked considerable comment. The antislavery press widely reprinted the exchange. Maria received a barrage of letters both from admirers, many of whom enclosed money for Brown's family, and from detractors, who castigated Maria for her apparent disunionism. Emerson wrote saying that he cherished "to the last, hope for his [Brown's] life.'"[110]

On 4 November, Maria's pen was put to Brown's use once more. Directly above the *Liberator*'s review of Thoreau's *Plea* appeared a "private note" from Maria in which she wrote, "My thoughts are so much with Capt. John Brown, that I can scarcely take comfort in anything. I would expend all that I have to save his life!" While calling him a "Brave old man!" she repeated her oft-stated position that he was "sadly mistaken in his mode of operation."[111] Thus, with the publication of her correspondence with Wise, and this additional published statement, Maria joined Thoreau as one of the earliest of Brown's public defenders. Wendell Phillips would later speak of Maria's early defense of Brown, saying she did so at a time when "it yet hung in the balance whether the nation should acknowledge its prophet or crucify him...." It was at just this critical juncture that "she asked to share his prison...."[112]

Eight. Literature's Version

Child continued to deal with the influx of letters she received from all over the U.S. and Canada as a result of her published correspondence with Wise. She was so busy that she put off responding to a virulent letter which had arrived mid–November from Margaretta Mason, the wife of the Virginia senator. "I have been *so* overwhelmed with letters about John Brown, that I have been kept in a whirl," she wrote a friend. She confessed surprise at the ferocity prevalent in messages from the South. "You can hardly conceive of the violence and obscenity of those I receive from Virginia," she wrote. "I did not suppose that even Slavery could produce anything so foul." Maria also expressed bewilderment at the publicity surrounding her published correspondence with Wise, saying, "I cannot understand what I have done to deserve so much laudation on one side, and so much abuse on the other." Her intention, she affirmed, was nothing more than "to nurse the brave old man, when I supposed him to be alone, helpless and bleeding in prison." At the same time, Maria was shrewd enough to recognize a gift when she received it. Since the notoriety was thrust upon her, she would use her moment in the spotlight to ultimate advantage. "Gov. Wise, by publishing our correspondence, secured me a very large audience; and I siezed [*sic*] the opportunity to impress some powerful facts on their minds," she confessed.[113]

The events surrounding Brown's act both inspired and energized Maria. "A little while ago, I thought I was growing drowsy and old; but these stirring times make me strong as an eagle," she wrote.[114] To another friend she confided, "Recent events have renewed my youth and strength, and filled me with electricity, and one word of apology for slavery makes the sparks fly."[115]

Even as she raced to keep up with her voluminous correspondence, part of Maria's renewed energy would be spent in raising funds for the families of the Harpers Ferry conspirators.[116] On Christmas Day, she wrote S.E. Sewall: "You will see ... that I have requested the colored people, in Canada, to deposit their contributions with *you*." Explaining her rationale, she stated, "I think it would be well to make the *most* of their generous deed before the *public*, because ... it shows that the 'Fugitives from Injustice' can not only 'take care of themselves,' but of others also." She then suggested "A paragraph to that effect in the *Atlas & Bee* would do good to the public."[117]

Higginson, too, had his thoughts on Brown's conspirators, but he had quite a different sort of relief in mind. In spite of his long association with Brown, Higginson first learned of the events at Harpers Ferry indirectly. Upon walking into a newspaper shop shortly after the raid, he was astonished to hear someone say, "Old Osawatomie Brown has got himself into a tight place at last."[118] Higginson grabbed the morning paper and hastily read the story. His first reaction was remorse that he had not been with the old man, feeling that those who had given Brown resources should have been at his side. His second was surprise, both at the location and the scope of the raid. "I certainly had not that degree of faith in it which would have led me to abandon all else, and wait nearly a year and a half for the opportunity of fulfillment," Higginson declared, fearing that the "longer postponement had somewhat disturbed the delicate balance of the zealot's mind, and had made him, at the very outset, defy the whole power of the United States government, and that within easy reach of Washington."[119] But if the reverend's first reaction was stunned incredulity, his second was action.

As Higginson contemplated what his own course should be, he regarded his fellow conspirators' hasty treks to Canada with utter disdain: Sanborn had left almost immediately upon learning of the raid only to change course and return to Concord on 26 November. On the 25th both Stearns and Howe had followed Sanborn's trail to Canada. Gerrit Smith's fortuitously timed entry into the Utica Asylum for the insane on the 7th of November further grieved Higginson. Theodore Parker, then in Rome, held firm but from afar. With five of the Secret Six frightened or scattered, it fell to Higginson to help Brown. Fleeing "seemed to me undesirable.... [I]t rather looked as if, having befriended Brown's plans so far as we understood them, it was our duty to stand our ground...." As others hastily scrambled for the border, Higginson's "immediate impulse [was] to rescue Brown from prison."[120] Nothing, it seemed, could entice the manly Higginson to flee.

Like Thoreau and Child, Higginson understood the significance of Brown's potential martyrdom. He wrote his mother, saying, "I don't feel sure that [Brown's] acquittal or rescue would do half as much good as his being executed; so strong is the *personal* sympathy with him." Still, he was frustrated that "no way seems open for anything; there is (as far as one can say such a thing) *no* chance for forcible assistance, and next to none for stratagem." But even as he reassured his mother that "We have done what we could for him by sending counsel and in other ways that must be nameless," plans were fomenting for rescue.[121]

George H. Hoyt was dispatched from Boston to Harpers Ferry "ostensibly as counsel," but in reality he was sent to urge Brown to accept rescue plans which were already under consideration. On 28 October, Hoyt reported that Brown "positively refused his consent to any such plan."[122] Even so, Brown's northern supporters were unwilling to give up. That same day, Philadelphia abolitionist J.M. McKim wrote Higginson, saying, "I think that everything possible ... should be attempted. No stone should be left unturned. We rejoice to hear of the sympathy & active effort on the part of our friends in Worcester & other parts of Massachusetts."[123] But on 30 October, Hoyt again attempted to discourage talk of rescue: "*There is no chance* of ... [Brown's] ultimate escape; there is nothing but the most unmitigated failure, & the saddest consequences which it is possible to conjure, to ensue upon an attempt at *rescue*. The county all around is guarded by armed patrols & a large body of troops are constantly under arms. If you hear anything about such an attempt, for Heaven's sake do not *fail to restrain the enterprise.*"[124]

But even this cautionary advice did little to deter Higginson's zeal. While Brown was clearly not in the mood to be rescued, he had met his match in Higginson, who was not to be easily thwarted, even by Brown. "It occurred to me," Higginson maintained, "that his wife's presence would move him, if anything could, and that she might also be a valuable medium of communication, should he finally yield to the wishes of his friends." To that end, he struck out on 2 November for North Elba, New York, and, upon arrival, personally escorted Mrs. Brown directly to Boston, where funds were secured to send her on to Harpers Ferry.[125] Higginson was drawn to the quiet dignity of Brown's wife: "Dear Mrs. Brown—tall, erect, stately, simple, kindly, slow, sensible creature—won my heart pretty thoroughly before we got to Boston, and many people's there, for many visited her during the morning she was there, bringing money, shoes, gloves, handkerchiefs, kisses, and counsel."[126] En route, it was Higginson's sad duty to hand her the newspaper which reported her husband's death sentence, news Mrs. Brown received stoically. But, for all his efforts, Higginson's trip was in vain. Brown steadfastly refused to see his wife and she returned to North Elba from Baltimore on 8 November, for as all of Brown's supporters and family recognized, Brown was "as impregnable as Gibraltar when his mind was made up."[127]

On 5 November, Higginson wrote his mother, calling Harpers Ferry "the most formidable slave insurrection that has ever occurred," adding that even "through the confused and exaggerated accounts," it was apparent "that there are leaders of great capacity and skill behind it." He then asserted his belief that Brown and his men could "hold their own for a long time against all the force likely to be brought against them, and can at last retreat to the mountains and establish a Maroon colony there, like those in Jamaica and Guiana." Until such time, he confidently predicted, "the effect will be to frighten and weaken the slave power everywhere and discourage the slave trade."[128]

But even as rescue plans evolved, Higginson could not help but wonder whether he would be summoned to testify in the Brown affair. He felt "it rather due to the memory of Brown," maintaining "I could at least have made it plain that anything like slave insurrection, in the ordinary sense of the word, was remote from his thoughts, and that his plan was wholly different. He would have limited himself to advising a fugitive slave, if intercepted, to shoot down any one who attempted to arrest him," advice the radical Higginson felt "would have been given by every Abolitionist, unless a nonresistant."[129] Sanborn, for his part, continued to worry about capture and wrote Higginson on the 13th, advising that "a witness can only be released by a tumult." While that strategy seemed fine for Higginson, with his vigilant and boisterous antislavery neighbors, it seemed less than ideal to those elsewhere. "This may do very well in Worcester," Sanborn contended, "but is rather precarious in Boston...." Sanborn then asked, "Would your Worcester people go down to Boston to take Dr. Howe or Mr. Phillips out of the marshal's hands?" The problem, it seemed, was a little known law in which a witness could be arrested without previous summons if their testimony was deemed material. In another effort to manipulate public opinion, Sanborn urged Higginson to contact the press in an effort to make the contingencies of this law public: "Can you get some young (or old) lawyer to look it up and write articles about it for your city papers—I will try to get the *Springfield Republican* to do the same thing, and if possible, the Boston papers and the *Tribune* and ... the N. H. papers."[130] Such a frontal assault on the press would ostensibly pave the way for public support should any of the Six later be arrested.

But, even as uncertainty swirled concerning possible arrests, Higginson doggedly pursued plans for a rescue. The first to join him in taking action were John W. Le Barnes and Lysander Spooner. "Other clergymen might feel scruples about taking up arms when wearing the garb of the church and teaching the doctrines of the Prince of Peace, but Mr. Higginson had none," Brown biographer Oswald Villard explained.[131] The ingenious plot the three men concocted was shockingly bold and decidedly lacking in peace principles. Simply put, the plan was to kidnap Governor Wise of Virginia and hold him on board a vessel in the high seas, or in a secret location in the North, as hostage for the condemned Brown. The idea was Lysander Spooner's and first communicated to Higginson sometime before the middle of November. Higginson, who had part ownership in the vessel *Flirt* for aiding fugitive slaves by sea, was "not without sympathy for a maritime adventure."[132] An anonymous note in Higginson's papers proposed, "Why not *rescue* for a few days Gov. Wise...."[133] By 14 November, Higginson wondered, "Wd. it not be practicable for a party of men to go in a st[eam] boat to kidnap in the night ... & hold him as a hostage for the safety of—"[134] The next day, Le Barnes reported that the "idea has certainly the merit of audacity....."[135] In a missive signed "*Please burn* this," Spooner confirmed that he had found someone to locate "the men, a pilot, and a boat...."[136] But, it was Le Barnes who revealed what would ultimately turn out to be the fatal flaw in their plans: "I have *no* doubt that arrangements could be made—it is the *money* that is uncertain." After discussing the availability and cost of tugs, steamboats and gunboats, Le Barnes concluded, "The question is not, could the thing be 'got at' with money enough, but it is, is the money *ready*." As to the probable outcome of the plan, Le Barnes wrote, "My own impression is that *success* would be *brilliant—defeat* fatally inglorious." Then, considering the correspondence was addressed to Higginson, a minister, the letter took a startling turn: "H. suggests that Orsini? Bombs—which he says can be made in N.Y.—and hand grenades—would be effective in so frightening the soldier['s] chivalry that our object could be accomplished during the *panic*. Should hesitate about using anything so deadly, but an expedition ought to be thus provided in case of emergency. These things would doubtless be more formidable than cannon?"[137] Since Le Barnes had just so clearly advocated treason, it is not surprising that he closed his letter with "You will of course *burn* this immediately."[138] But for all its swashbuckling nature, the plan was destined to fail, not for lack of will, but for want of capital.

The group then turned their attention to an alternative plan involving a brazen overland attempt at rescue. On 22 November, it was reported that over one hundred Germans were ready to take their place alongside a rumored contingent of Ohioans under John Brown, Jr., to storm the Charlestown prison and rescue Brown. After freeing the prisoner, the group would make their escape on the backs of horses stolen from the cavalry.[139] On the 27th, LeBarnes wrote Higginson: "The men are ready and determined.... The *attack* to be made upon either Wednesday night, or *Friday*—at the *hour*.—The men are all daring and resolute. They are *confident*—strange as it may seem to us—of *success*. But they want *money*—$100 per man for expenses—.... Then the *survivors* must be [looked after] ... and ... the *families* of the *others* taken care of."[140]

But, by the end of November, clearly all hopes for any type of rescue were dashed. On the 28th Le Barnes cabled Higginson: "PROJECTS ABANDONED. SHALL LEAVE TOMORROW."[141] Sanborn wrote Higginson conceding failure, saying, "I suppose we must give up all hope of saving our old friend."[142] Higginson, finally convinced beyond a shadow of a doubt that rescue was futile, reluctantly acknowledged defeat. "I hv. taken some pains to sound & observe people on this point & hv. most unwillingly been compelled to abandon the hope of redeeming the honor of the Free States ... by the rescue of John Brown & his comrades. Virginia may be weak and cowardly but she has proven strong enough to defeat us," he wrote. In a final act of defiance, and in an effort no doubt designed to distance himself in his own mind from his less than manly colleagues, he signed the note "T.W. Higginson. There is no need of burning this."[143]

Higginson's grief over the failed rescue was compounded by his continued worry over the less than courageous acts of his fellow conspirators. On 14 November, Sanborn had written Theodore Parker: "Dr. H[owe] and Mr. Stearns of Medford have gone to Canada for a week or two. This is censured by Higginson, who wants all to stay and try the question, and if possible, raise a conflict between Massachusetts and the U.S."[144]

Eight. Literature's Version

Howe publicly issued a card in which he denied any preordained knowledge of John Brown's plans. In mid–November, in a letter composed, but apparently never sent, Higginson informed Howe, "I write to you under a sadness very rare for me," adding, "Soon after the affair at Harper's Ferry I said to you & Phillips & Sanborn ... that I thought it would be the extreme of baseness in us to *deny* complicity with Capt. Brown's general scheme." Higginson attempted, but failed, to soften his rebuke. "What am I, that I should judge you? But Gerrit Smith's insanity—& your letter—are to me the only two sad results of the whole affair," he contended.[145] Higginson expressed his feelings to Sanborn as well, plaintively asking, "Is there no such thing as *honor* among confederates?—Can yr. clear moral sense ... [justify] holding one's tongue ... to save ourselves fr. all share in even the reprobation of society when the nobler man whom we hv. pushed on? into danger is the scapegoat of that reprobation—& the gallows too?"[146]

Higginson's attempts to stoke Sanborn's courage had little effect. On the 19th Higginson received a letter in which Sanborn confided, "I have destroyed your letter as I do all letters which might be used against anyone," adding, "I cannot see the [Howe] matter as you do...."[147] By 25 December, Sanborn was even more direct, admonishing Higginson to "burn all my letters about these things."[148] Sanborn was not alone in fearing retribution. Anxiety was so high that Richard Josiah Hinton went so far as to suggest the men correspond in code: "Would it not be as well to write either in some cipher or with iodine—I have used numerals for the alphabet from 1 to 26 only commencing from the eight ... and occassionally [sic] leaving ... numerals & inserting letters so as to alter as circumstances may require."[149] But Higginson would not be cowed and pointedly ignored both Sanborn's entreaties to burn and Hinton's pleas to code their correspondence. Even so, in truth, their situation was precarious. An anonymous letter addressed to Higginson arrived from Alabama warning him to desist in efforts to procure counsel for Brown and announcing that if he were to try such "a little further South ... we will burn every mother's son of you...."[150] In spite of the threats both governmental and southern, on 11 January an unbowed Higginson forwarded a signed check dated 10 January in the amount of $300 to R.J. Hinton drawn on the Mechanics Bank of Worcester for continued support of a rescue.[151]

Nor was Higginson to be dissuaded from his continued charitable efforts on behalf of Brown's family. On 18 November a letter had arrived from Charles Slack urging Higginson to speak at Tremont Temple at a meeting to raise funds for Brown's family. "Please come to Boston, to-morrow, and speak in the evening," Slack implored Higginson, assuring him "all the proceeds to go to the family. High interest just now. Mr. Phillips, and all, desire yr. participancy. In haste, but truly, Chas. W. Slack."[152] Higginson did, in fact, appear in meetings in both Boston and Worcester, pleading for funds. While resources seemed frustratingly scarce for rescue, Higginson forwarded two letters from Mrs. Brown and her daughter Mrs. Thompson and marveled at the fact that "Money seems to be flowing for them from all directions...."[153] But, not all letters contained donations. "I have had some queer letters about them," he acknowledged, including "one from a man in Winchendon offering to adopt one of the daughters and teach her telegraphy."[154]

John Brown was profoundly grateful for Higginson's continued support of his family. On 22 November he wrote Higginson from prison expressing his "deep feelings of gratitude for your journey to visit & comfort my family as well as myself in different ways & at different times; since my imprisonment here. Truly you have proved yourself to be "a friend in need"; and *I feel* my many obligations for all your kind *attentions....*" Brown also thanked Higginson for sending $25 to his daughter along with "a bundle of papers," papers which no doubt reflected the changing public opinion surrounding the case. It was the last correspondence Higginson would ever receive from Brown, and Brown signed it "Yours for *God and the right*."[155] Higginson, for his part, was pleased with the financial contributions for Brown's family, and made particular note of the fact that "[t]he whole thing is having a tremendous influence on public sentiment."[156]

Yet even as Brown's reputation gradually began to be restored, his defenders faced yet another challenge to his character. In an attempt to save him, Brown's lawyers collected affidavits attesting to nine cases of insanity in his immediate family on the maternal side, including two of his own children and six first cousins.[157] This strategy might have saved Brown's life, but Brown's supporters realized it could yet destroy his reputation. Neither Brown's detractors nor his supporters approved of the defense. Governor Wise did not want Brown declared insane because he wanted to hang him. Emerson and Thoreau did not want him seen as demented because this would diminish his usefulness as an abolitionist martyr. Black supporters were infuriated at suggestions that someone wanting to overthrow slavery had to be crazy. In an unsent letter to Wise, Emerson defused the issue by admitting that Brown was "precisely what lawyers call crazy," but he undercut the admission by adding "[Brown] being governed by ideas, & not by external circumstance."[158] Thoreau's "A Plea" had been equally indignant on the subject. "Insane!" sputtered Thoreau. "A father and six sons, and one son-in-law, and several more men besides,—as many at least as twelve disciples,—all struck with insanity at once; while the sane tyrant holds ... his four millions of slaves."[159]

J. Sella Martin commented that Brown's "madness not only had a great deal of 'method' in it, but a great deal of philosophy and religion."[160] Reflecting these sentiments, a black man fumed, "The newspapers and able editors may talk as they will about the insanity of Capt. Brown, but to us there is something sacred in the madness of this old man."[161] An editorial in *Douglass' Monthly* echoed these concerns and posited the question whether heroism and insanity were synonymous. On the first page of the November 1859 issue, the *Douglass' Monthly* published an article entitled "Capt. Brown not Insane" in which it offered the following:

> One of the most painful incidents connected with the name of this old hero, is the attempt to prove him insane. Many journals have contributed to this effort from a friendly desire to shield the prisoner from Virginia's cowardly vengeance. This is a mistaken friendship, which seeks to rob him of his true character and dim the glory of his deeds, in order to save his life. Was there the faintest hope of assuring his release by this means, we would choke down our indignation and be silent. But a Virginia court would hang a crazy man without a moment's hesitation, if his insanity took the form of hatred of oppression....[162]

Child did not publicly enter the fray concerning the question of Brown's sanity. "Others may spend their time in debating whether John Brown did wrong, or not; whether he was sane, or not," she wrote, "[A]ll I know, or care to know, is that his example has stirred me up to consecrate myself with renewed earnestness to the righteous cause for which he died so bravely."¹⁶³ The question as a legal issue would be permanently put to rest when Brown refused the insanity plea, a refusal upheld by the court.¹⁶⁴

Whether Brown's defenders consciously attempted to address themes in concert, or whether they simply developed similar ideas and wording about Brown from their time spent together, or correspondence exchanged with one another, cannot be determined. However, the strategy was enormously effective as their perceptions about Brown as a Puritan, a sane, indeed a representative man and a martyr like Christ on the cross, gained a slow but steady foothold in the press and public mind.

Clearly Republican support for Brown was continuing to grow, in part as a result of the spirited defense by his articulate friends in the Northeast. On Friday, 11 November, the *Liberator* reprinted an article from the *Richmond Enquirer*, which quoted the *New York Journal of Commerce* as saying, "perhaps, the State of Virginia ... will exercise its mercy in the pardon of the prisoners." The *Enquirer* went on to express "surprise at such an intimation in a quarter distinguished as conservative and patriotic."¹⁶⁵ The Democratic *New York Herald* condemned "the leading journals of the Republican press which have ... exalt[ed] 'Old Brown' to the rank of a demi-god...." They further charged those same journalists with expressing "regret, not for what has been done [at Harpers Ferry], but that it has been done so badly...."¹⁶⁶ The *Valley Spirit* commented upon the efforts of the press to "create the impression that Brown ... has not had a fair trial."¹⁶⁷ A Virginia correspondent of the *Boston Courier* went so far as to lay blame directly on the transcendentalists, contending that the "whole mischief of these overt acts is distinctly traceable to ... the stupendous fallacy of the 'higher law.'"¹⁶⁸

Other periodicals also recognized the effectiveness of the campaign being waged on behalf of Brown by his literary friends. The *Staunton* (Virginia) *Spectator*, in an article reprinted from the *National Intelligencer*, called for "calmness and contempt" towards the "ultra editors and preachers in the North who fulminate violent diatribes," especially "certain leading politicians and fanatical literaturs [sic] who in no way express the sentiments of the mass of the Northern people."¹⁶⁹ In a departure from the earlier condemnation of Brown's scheme as "villainous," the *Boston Transcript* now proclaimed, "Whatever may be his guilt or folly, a man convicted under such circumstances, and, especially, a man *executed* after such a trial, will be the most terrible fruit that slavery has ever borne...." Such a verdict, the paper predicted, "will excite the execration of the whole civilized world."¹⁷⁰

Meanwhile, in the aftermath of the raid, the Virginia countryside, if not much of the slaveholding South, was "convulsed with fear and rage."¹⁷¹ At four o'clock Monday afternoon on the day of the raid, Mary Mauzy, a local resident, wrote her daughter:

> Oh my dear friend such a day as this. Heaven forbid that I should ever witness another.
> Last night a band of ruffians took possession of the town, took the keys of the armory and made Captive a great many of our Citizens. I cannot write the particulars for I am too Nervous. For such a sight as I have just beheld. Our men chased them in the river just below here and I saw them shot down like dogs. I saw one poor wrech [sic] rise above the water and some one strike him with a club he sank again and in a moment they dragged him out a Corpse. I do not know yet how many are shot but I shall never forget the sight. They just marched two wreches [sic] their Arms bound fast up to the jail. My dear husband shouldered his rifle and went to join our men May god protect him. Even while I write I hear the guns in the distance I heard they were fighting down the street. I cannot write any more I must wait and see what the end will be.¹⁷²

In the days following the raid, a pervasive unease continued to permeate the region. "[T]here was the fear—unspoken, or pooh-poohed at by the men who served as mouthpieces for our community—dark, boding, oppressive, and altogether hateful," a young Virginian woman confessed to her diary. "Rusty bolts were drawn and rusty fire-arms loaded. A watch was set where never before had eye or ear been lent to such a service. Peace, in short, had flown from the borders of Virginia."[173] With the fear, even natural events seemed imbued with special significance: "The great comet that flamed across the heavens was taken as a sign of approaching war. Strange celestial lights, which nightly illuminated the heavens for weeks with a lurid brazen glow ... filled ... minds with morbid dread."[174] In fact, a series of meteor showers coupled with an exceptionally bright single meteor (seen from Albany, NY, to Fredericksburg, VA) had danced through the skies.[175] Already uneasy citizens tended to view this astronomical anomaly with suspicion and fear. The tension was palpable, leading to at least one unfortunate incident in which a cow belonging to Mr. Ranson was mistakenly shot. Hearing the report, rumor spread that the northern army had arrived to rescue Brown.[176] "Vague rumors of a 'Yankee' invasion filled the air and emotional men and women were beside themselves with frantic excitement," claimed a local resident.[177] As historian Stephen B. Oates commented, "The raid of twenty-two men on one Virginia town had sent a spasm of uneasiness, resentment, and precautionary zeal from the Potomac to the Gulf."[178]

Further inciting foreboding in the local citizenry was a series of local fires. Unlike the meteor showers, in this case the connection to the Harpers Ferry raid appeared overt— three men who had been on the jury that convicted Brown suffered property loss by fire. Judge Lucas's haystack burned and a shot was fired near his window, leading the mayor of Charlestown to order the removal

Henry A. Wise, governor of Virginia at the time of the Harpers Ferry raid. The young Wise seemed increasingly unhinged by the events at the ferry, sensing conspiracy at every turn. He wrote Andrew Hunter: "Information from every quarter leads to the conviction that there is an organized plan to harass our whole slave-border at every point. Day is the very time to commit arson.... No light shines.... They come, one by one, two by two, in open day" (Library of Congress, Prints and Photographs Division).

of all strangers who were unable to give a proper accounting of their activities.[179] George Mauzy, a Harpers Ferry resident, wrote his daughter: "We are keeping nightly watch, all are vigilant, partys of 10 men out every night, quite a number of incendiary fires have taken place in this vicinity & County, such as stacks, barns & other out-buildings."[180]

The northern press was largely unsympathetic to the southern anxiety, ridiculing what it perceived as an overreaction to the raid. One newspaper recounted the story of a Harpers Ferry resident who, upon hearing a whippoorwill, thought it was the cry of a neighbor being attacked by abolitionists and stormed into town calling for citizens to arm themselves.[181] As to the raid in general, the *New York Evening Post* claimed that if such an event had happened in the North it would have been dealt with by the local police, whereas in the slaveholding South it required "the interposition of Governors, Presidents, marines, militias and mobs."[182] The black press joined in the barrage, with a black weekly insisting that Virginia would not have been frightened by 17 or 1,700 armed white men even if they were all John Browns. Rather, it was five black men "armed to the teeth, and the 500,000 black men in their midst, 'armed with a quarrel,' who caused the Virginians to shudder in fear."[183]

The governor of Virginia himself seemed increasingly unhinged by the attack, sensing conspiracy at every turn. On 6 November, Wise wrote Charlestown District Attorney Andrew Hunter:

> Mr. Robert Washington is a secret agent of the state Executive, employed to trace the threads of this Brown conspiracy, into other states. He visits Charlestown & Harpers Ferry to obtain clues to these threads. Let him have access to papers, names, prisoners & every where. Don't be seen with him, but indirectly & unobserved give him every facility to find out the means of detection.—
> Let no one else into this service.[184]

Ten days later, Wise received the following advice: "A Brother of 'Old Brown,' who has been sojourning at this place ... left ... this morning, to see Old Brown his brother. His name is Frederick Brown. He is a rank Abolitionist and will bear watching." The warning was signed "in haste."[185] That same day, Wise wrote Andrew Hunter:

> MY DEAR SIR,—Information from every quarter leads to the conviction that there is an organized plan to harass our whole slave-border at every point. *Day* is the *very* time to commit arson with the best chance agt detection. No light shines, nor smoke shows in daylight before the flame is off & up past putting out. The rascal too escapes best by day; he sees best whether he is not seen, and best how to avoid persons pursuing. I tell you those Devils are trained in all the Indian arts of predatory war. They come, *one by one, two by two,* in *open* day, and make you stare? that the thing be *attempted* as it was *done*.[186]

Wise concluded with a warning to "Watch Harper's Ferry people. Watch, I say, and I *thought* watch when there. Gerrit Smith is a stark madman, no doubt! Gods, what a moral, what a lesson. Whom the Gods wish to make mad they first set to setting others to destroying...."[187] While Hunter seemed less predisposed to panic than the governor, he did allow himself to contemplate tearing up the railroad tracks leading into town prior to the date of Brown's execution.[188]

By the 19th, Ed Gallaher wrote Andrew Hunter from New York:

PROCLAMATION!

IN pursuance of instructions from the Governor of Virginia, notice is hereby given to all whom it may concern,

That, as heretofore, particularly from now until after Friday next the 2nd of December, STRANGERS found within the County of Jefferson, and Counties adjacent, having no known and proper business here, and who cannot give a satisfactory account of themselves, will be at once arrested.

That on, and for a proper period before that day, stangers and especially parties, approaching under the pretext of being present at the execution of John Brown, whether by Railroad or otherwise, will be met by the Military and turned back or arrested without regard to the amount of force, that may be required to effect this, and during the said period and especially on the 2nd of December, the citizens of Jefferson and the surrounding country are *EMPHATICALLY* warned to remain at their homes armed and guard their own property.

Information received from reliable sources, clearly indicates that by so doing they will best consult their own interests.

No WOMEN or CHILDREN will be allowed to come near the place of execution.

WM. B. TALLIAFERRO, *Maj. Gen Com. troops,*
S BASSETT FRENCH, *Military Sec'y.*
THOMAS C. GREEN, *Mayor,*
ANDREW HUNTER, *Asst. Pros. Att'y.*
JAMES W. CAMPBELL, *Sheriff.*

November 28th, '59   Spirit Print

The governor of Virginia had this proclamation issued warning that strangers who could not account for their presence in Harpers Ferry would be arrested. Local citizens are told to "remain at their homes and guard their own property." In fact, a series of local fires caused great anxiety among the local citizenry and fostered legitimate questions about the extent of the conspiracy (Summit County Historical Association—Akron, Ohio).

> I have *good reasons* for believing that the abolition friends of John Brown, propose to make a [illeg.] in his favor.... The night previous to the hanging, a score or so of his friends are to destroy the gallows, in this way. The beams & posts of the scaffold are to be rendered (illeg.) useless by being *sawed* in such a manner as to insure its falling when the *officers ascend in it to arrange for the execution, & thereby cause confusion,*

delay, & probably danger to life and limb of those whose duty it will be to carry out the sentence.
   Wise suggests placing a guard to protect the scaffold and hoped in the process to assure the "probable capture of some of his friends...."

   Gallaher signed off, imploring, "*Secrecy in this is particularly essential to its success.*"[189]
   Meanwhile, "A Friend of Order" wrote Hunter, who forwarded it to Wise: "There are two persons in Masstts, and I think only two, who, if summoned as witnesses, can explain the whole of Brown's plot. Their names are Francis B. Sanborn of Concord & Rev. T.W. Higginson of Worcester, Mass. No time should be lost, as they may abscond...." The writer added, "I do not think they will, as they think you would not think it best to send for them."[190] On 26 November, Wise wrote Andrew Hunter with another plan:

> It has occurred to me that, on the day of execution, the stationing of a lookout sentinel — or half a dozen, for that matter — in the belfry of the "Episcopal Church," will serve a useful purpose. It affords a clear & extensive view, as you can readily understand, for many miles in all directions. It will do no harm & may prove useful in many respects. If they can be had, two or three good telescopes would prove an advantage in extending the range of view. Even on top of your House, the placing of a sentinel might be of good.[191]

   Virginia was certainly not in a mood to delay and did, in fact, move quickly to take control of the situation. Thus, a mere week after the raid, on 24 October, a feeble Brown, still recovering from his wounds, was charged with "'conspiring with Negroes to produce insurrection,' and murder in the first degree."[192] On 31 October, at 1:45 P.M., the case went to a jury. A slight forty-five minutes later, the jury returned with a verdict — guilty. A journalist described the scene in the courtroom:

> Not the slightest sound was heard in the vast crowd.... Not the slightest expression of elation or triumph was uttered from the hundreds present, who, a moment before, outside the court, joined in heaping threats and imprecations upon his head; nor was this strange silence interrupted during the whole of the time occupied by the forms of the Court. Old Brown himself said not even a word, but, as on previous days, turned to adjust his pallet, and then composedly stretched himself upon it.[193]

   Understandably, press interest in the trial and in Brown was enormous. The haste with which Virginia acted may have impressed her citizens, but the fact that Brown was arraigned while lying on a cot and that Stevens had to be carried into court deeply moved northern newspaper readers.[194] Recognizing this fact, Brown began giving interviews and writing stirring, compassionate letters, many of which found their way into print. Wendell Phillips commented: "Having taken possession of Harpers Ferry, [Brown] began to edit the *New York Tribune* and the *New York Herald* for the next three weeks."[195]
   There is little doubt that by mid–November there was changing public sentiment about Brown. Republican John A. Andrew, a future governor of Massachusetts, chaired a meeting to raise funds for Brown's family.[196] Sanborn, in a letter to Theodore Parker dated 14 November, exulted in the fact that "the feeling of sympathy with Brown is spreading fast over all the North, and will grow stronger if he is hanged...." Sanborn, no doubt, attributed this, in part, to the fact that "Phillips, Emerson and Thoreau have spoken unequivocally in his favor.... Phillips spoke in praise of Brown at Brooklyn two weeks ago; Thoreau at the Fraternity, Nov. 1st and Emerson Nov. 8th all using *unqualified*

A Porte Crayon rendering of John Brown's trial in Charlestown, Virginia, for treason and murder, 1859. Brown can be seen lying on his cot in the courtroom, an accurate portrayal that created sympathy for Brown among Northern newspaper readers (Historic Photo Collection, Harpers Ferry National Historic Park).

praise. Mrs. Child is to write B[rown]'s life,—so will James Redpath." Taking particular note of the reaction of women to the raid, he claimed, "[T]he *women* everywhere are on his side—the *failure* is a success,—it has done more for freedom than years of talk could...."[197] Like her male counterparts, Child, too, marveled at the changing public opinion about the raid, saying, "I rejoice to see indications that a ... [rededication to antislavery] is produced in a multitude of minds in all parts of the Free States."[198]

As Brown's execution date approached, his friends turned their attention from dreams of rescue to the practicality of memorializing their soon to be martyred friend. Thoreau called a meeting in the Concord Town Hall on 28 November to arrange a service to be held on 2 December, Brown's expected execution date. At the meeting, Thoreau, Lt. Governor Simon Brown (no relation), Emerson and John Shepard Keyes were selected to arrange the service. Thoreau approached this task with the same unswerving dedication with which he first defended Brown. Alcott noted in his journal, "Thoreau has taken a prominent part in this movement; and arranged for it chiefly."[199] Sanborn returned to Concord where plans were being made for a memorial service with "Mr. Thoreau being one of the principal persons interested."[200]

The next few days were extraordinarily busy ones for Thoreau. He had a broadside printed announcing the service. He found men to move a piano into the meeting hall.

Eight. Literature's Version

When he applied for permission to toll the town bell at the ascribed hour of the execution, not only was he denied, but he also was told that five hundred men had damned him for ever suggesting such a thing. Should he proceed with this plan, he was warned, a counter demonstration was planned with the firing of guns. Alcott calmed the angry Thoreau by suggesting that a quiet tone would more accurately reflect their sorrow.[201]

Throughout the week, planning continued for the service, with Alcott noting in his journal of 30 November, "We do not intend to have any speeches made on the occasion...."[202] Keyes felt that "all the speakers should be confined to reading other peoples [sic] writings, as there was too much danger of our giving way to treasonable utterances if we allowed ourselves to speak our own sentiments."[203] By 1 December, specific roles had been assigned the participants. Alcott would "read the Martyr Services, Thoreau selections from the poets, and Emerson from Brown's words. Sanborn has written a dirge, which will be sung; and Rev. Mr. Sears from Wayland, will offer prayer."[204] On the day of the service, only Thoreau diverged from the agreement, adding a few remarks of his own.[205] Sanborn's role in the service was also handled with care. He later recalled "an ode of mine was ... read; but so careful were my townsmen ... that I was described merely as a 'gentleman of Concord.'"[206]

Their caution was justified. The *Boston Post* the next day indicated that plans to toll the bell in Concord and to fly the flag upside down had "created considerable excitement among the conservative men of all parties, and measures were taken to prevent such proceedings." The article went on to mention that in the early morning hours of December 2, "an effigy, life size, of the 'old man Brown,' was discovered hanging on a large tree in front of the Town Hall." Attached to the "body" was Brown's "Last Will and Testament" with several behests. "To H.D. Thoreau, Esq." was left "my body and soul, he having eulogized my character and actions at Harpers Ferry above the Saints in Heaven...." A second behest to "Ralph Waldo Emerson" gave him "all my personal property, and my execution cap, which contains nearly all the brains I ever had."[207]

George Luther Stearns, who attended the memorial service, described a "very grave and serious" looking Emerson accompanied by his thoroughly annoyed wife, Lidian. "Are you not going to have the bells tolled?" she demanded. According to Stearns, it took some convincing for her to accept the fact that in light of the unrest "it would not be wise to attempt so much."[208] Thoreau read several selections from the poets, among them "The Soul's Errand," believed to have been written by Sir Walter Raleigh as he awaited execution. As Thoreau read the lines, "When I am dead,/Let not the day be writ,/*Nor bell be tolled.*/Love will remember it/When hate is cold," he gave special emphasis to the words "Nor bell be tolled" in pointed reference to the town's refusal to toll the bells at the service.[209]

Another of the poems Thoreau read at the service explains a great deal about how he came to view himself as a savior of Brown's reputation, and how consciously he undertook this role. Quoting Andrew Marvell, Thoreau read:

> When the sword glitters o'er the judge's head,
> And fear has coward churchmen silencèd,
> Then is the poet's time, 'tis then he draws,
> And single fights forsaken virtue's cause;
> He, when the wheel of empire whirleth back,

And though the world's disjointed axle crack,
Sings still of ancient rights and better times,
Seeks suffering good, arraigns successful crimes.[210]

Alcott afterwards deemed the services "affecting" and characterized by "modesty, simplicity, and earnestness; worthy alike of the occasion and of the man," and noted that Thoreau was "highly pleased" with the proceedings.[211]

Maria Child also turned her attention to helping plan a memorial service for Brown. Working alongside William Lloyd Garrison, she helped arrange a program to take place at Boston's Faneuil Hall on 2 December. As the impending execution date neared, she vacillated between hope that Brown might be rescued and fear that he would be lynched. "Whichever way events turn, the results will be of vast importance," she contended. Like Thoreau, she implicitly recognized the significance of Brown to the abolitionist cause be he dead or alive. "Whether he lives or dies, he has struck a blow at slavery, from the effects of which it will never recover," she predicted.[212] Emerson wrote Child saying "I have hopes for his brave life. He is one for whom miracles wait."[213]

In Boston, when the date of the execution arrived, rather than attend the large gathering she had helped to plan, Maria chose instead to attend an all day prayer meeting at an African American church. Sitting at the Twelfth Baptist Church alongside those whose rights she had so long championed, she felt a kinship, with "nothing to jar upon the tender sadness" of her feelings. Here, no one would "question the old hero's claims to reverence, or to doubt his sanity of mind."[214] Speakers at the service included Leonard A. Grimes, an ex-slave and the church's minister, and Charles Lenox Remond.[215] During the service a former slave beseeched, "'since it has pleased thee to take away our Moses, oh! Lord God! raise us up a Joshua.' To which, Maria noted, the congregation responded with a loud 'Amen!'"[216]

The black community throughout Massachusetts responded to the day of Brown's execution with great dismay. In Worcester, where bells tolled from 10 A.M. to noon, blacks, wearing crepe in mourning, elected not to work from 11:00 A.M. to 3:00 P.M. in honor of their fallen hero. Instead, they attended a meeting held by the Anti-Slavery and Temperance Society of the Colored Citizens of Worcester, during which they expressed sympathy not only for Brown's family, but also for the families of his black conspirators.[217] In a New Bedford resolution, blacks declared Brown the greatest man of the nineteenth century, while in Lowell, a large bell was rung by a black man as it was pulled through the streets on a cart.[218]

The day was also marked in black communities throughout the country. "No event of a similar nature for many years had produced a more marked sensation," reported the *Weekly Anglo-African*, adding that on the 2 December execution day, "Most of the colored men closed their places of business, and many wore crape on their arms, rosettes in mourning...."[219] A Detroit church endorsed a statement honoring Brown as "the first disinterested martyr who, upon the true Christian principles of his Divine Lord and Master, has freely delivered up his life for the liberty of our race in this country. Therefore will we ever venerate his character, and regard him as our temporal leader whose name shall never die."[220] In Philadelphia, the day was noted by prayer meetings.

Throughout Ohio, blacks and whites stood together at services honoring Brown. Charles Langston spoke in a Cleveland hall draped in black to a crowd of 1,400 mourners.

At the center of the stage stood a large portrait of John Brown encased in a wreath. To the left of the picture were the words "JOHN BROWN, the Hero of 1859" and to the right, "He being dead, yet speaketh."[221] In his remarks, Langston said, "I find in Capt. John Brown, the hero of Harper's Ferry, a lover of mankind—not of any particular class or color, but of all men." He further claimed, "He is the only American citizen who has lived fully up to the Declaration of Independence."[222] In Rockford, from a liberty pole draped in mourning where the flag flew at half mast, this statement was taken: "When our citizens are hanged for attempting to carry out the principles of the Declaration of Independence, and the freedom of speech at the Capitol of the Republic is suppressed, it is meet that the people should mourn."[223]

On the day following the execution, Higginson also helped to memorialize Brown at a meeting in Worcester. To an audience containing nine other ministers, an unrepentant Higginson said, "Virginia acts; Massachusetts talks. If ever a man despised words when deeds were needed that man was John Brown." He then reminded his listeners that "John Brown is now beyond our reach; but the oppressed for whom he died still live."[224]

In Virginia, the day of Brown's execution had dawned clear and sunny. Murat Halstead, reporting for *The New York Times*, described the scene for northern readers:

> The sun shown brightly and the picture presented to the eye was really splendid. As each company arrived it took its allotted position. On the easterly side were the cadets, with their right wing flanked by a detachment of men with howitzers, on the northeast the Richmond Greys; on the south Company F, of Richmond; on the north the Winchester Continentals, and to preserve order in the crowd the Alexandria Riflemen and Capt. Gibson's Rockingham Company were stationed at the entrance gait and on the outskirts. At eleven o'clock the procession came in sight and at once all conversation and noise ceased. A dead stillness reigned over the field and the tramp of the approaching troops alone broke the silence.[225]

The solemnity and pageantry of the scene were also commented upon by the local citizenry. Elijah Avey described "Continentals ... dressed in buckskin suits of the days of 1776, and the other companies in equally as picturesque raiment."[226] Security was extraordinary, he noted: "[O]rders were given for no citizens to be on the streets within four blocks of the jail" in the days leading up to the hanging. On the execution date itself, "No stranger was allowed in the city and no citizen within the enclosure surrounding the scaffold."[227] George Mauzy, a local resident, wrote to his daughter:

> There is an immense concourse of military at Charlestown, not less than 2000 men are quartered there, the Courthouse, all the churches & all the Lawyers offices are occupied. We have upwards of 300 regulars & 75 or 80 Montgomery Guards. These men were all sent here by the Sec. of War & Gov. Wise to prevent a rescue of Brown & his party by northern infidels and fanatics: of which they boasted loudly, but their courage must have oozed out of their finger ends, as none made their appearance.[228]

Yet, while Virginia no doubt felt her extraordinary precautions justified, the huge contingent of military presence and the accompanying majesty once again elevated Brown's importance in the minds of friends and foes alike. Among those watching the proceedings was John Wilkes Booth of the 1st Virginia regiment out of Richmond, who viewed Brown and abolitionists like him as "the only *traitors* in the land."[229] Soon, Booth would assume his own ignominious role on the nation's stage.

In spite of the best efforts of both Governor Wise and the state of Virginia, public sentiment in the wake of the execution only swelled for Brown. A minister from Dover, New Hampshire, borrowed an image from Emerson and said of Brown, "The gallows from which he ascends into Heaven, *will be in our politics*, what the cross is in our religion.... To be hanged in Virginia, is like being crucified in Jerusalem...." In Wisconsin, the *Milwaukee Free Democrat* announced, "John Brown is CRUCIFIED as the representative of an idea," and continued by referencing Emerson: "The gallows of John Brown ... will be glorified ... like the cross, and so it will, because the gallows of John Brown, as the cross, is used to persecute ideas, or *great principles of enduring benefit* and necessity to humanity."[230] Several days after the execution, Governor Wise, in a speech to the Virginia legislature, commented on the public relations campaign that he appeared to be losing. "It is not to be denied that we have many sound and sincere friends in the non-slaveholding States," he maintained. Yet, he bemoaned the fact that "the conservative elements are passive, whilst the fanatical are active; and the former is fast diminishing, whilst the latter is increasing in numbers and force."[231]

In Concord, on the day after the services, Thoreau was given a singular opportunity to perform one last service for his hero. Francis Merriam, one of Brown's conspirators who had successfully escaped capture in Harpers Ferry by fleeing to Canada, turned up unexpectedly on Sanborn's doorstep. Two weeks before, the young man "in a state of painful excitement" had knocked on Howe's door in Montreal seeking aid.[232] An appalled Howe had sent him away and then proceeded to check out of his hotel that same day. Stearns, for his part, also had declined to help the disoriented fugitive. The young man then showed up at Sanborn's home in Concord where he hoped to "raise another expedition against the slave-holders." Sanborn was not at all happy to see him. Fearing his own involvement with Brown would be revealed, he borrowed a horse and covered wagon from Emerson and asked Thoreau's help in getting Merriam on the next train to Canada.[233] Sanborn, concerned Thoreau might be called to testify at the Senate hearings on the raid, introduced Merriam only as "Mr. Lockwood."[234] Thoreau, presumably, did not know who Sanborn's visitor was, but realized enough not to ask too many questions. In the horse and wagon borrowed from Emerson, Thoreau drove the addled Merriam to the South Acton train station and put him on a train. On the way, the highly excited fugitive, "being weak in body and almost distracted in mind," jumped out of the wagon. Sanborn would later claim, "What measures [Thoreau] took to get his passenger in again he never told me, but I suspect some judicious force was used...."[235] Thoreau, by aiding the escaped fugitive, would become what one historian described as "an accessory after the fact of Harpers Ferry."[236]

Higginson, for his part, also had a hand in the Merriam affair; however, unlike Sanborn, Howe or Stearns, he volunteered his home in Worcester to shelter the distraught young man. On 6 December, Merriam's grandfather, Francis Jackson, declined Higginson's offer: "I had a word with you about my grandson's residing in Worcester, where the numerous friends would be willing & glad to protect him; but upon reflection, his friends here decide against it; mainly because his mind is so wrought up, & over excited about the scenes of Harpers Ferry; among friends, he dwells upon it continually, & with increasing ardor; We therefore advise him to go out of the Country...."[237]

On 4 December, two days after Brown's execution, Emerson delivered a lecture entitled "Morals" at the Parker Fraternity. Lydia Maria Child was in attendance and later wrote Mrs. Mason, the wife of the Virginia senator, that "Emerson, the Plato of America, leaves the scholastic seclusion he loves so well, and, disliking noise with all his poetic soul, bravely takes his stand among the trumpeters."[238]

Child also continued her activities on behalf of Brown's family. True to her word, she solicited funds for the families of the Harpers Ferry conspirators. It was not a difficult job, she claimed, as most people offered to help even before she asked. She contemplated a biography of Brown, but when she became aware that James Redpath, a friend of Thoreau's, was undertaking the task, she demurred, instead "yield[ing] all her material for Mr. Redpath's use."[239] Maria then focused her attention on responding to Margaretta Mason's letter. As she did so, little could she have realized the impact her response would make.

No sooner had the fervor from her correspondence with Wise begun to abate than Child had received an outraged, somewhat hysterical, letter from Mrs. Mason, the wife of Senator Mason of Virginia. Writing on 11 November 1859, Mason scathingly attacked Maria in a startling pronouncement which Higginson would wryly observe came "very near swearing, for a lady."[240] "Do you read your Bible, Mrs. Child?" Mason wrote. "If you do, read there, 'Woe unto you, hypocrites,' and take to yourself with two-fold damnation that terrible sentence...." Fuming, Mason charged, "*You* would soothe with sisterly and motherly care the hoary-headed murderer of Harper's Ferry!" Mrs. Mason was appalled that Maria would support a man who would wish upon southern women "their husbands and fathers murdered, their children butchered, the ground strewed with the brains of their babes." As to slaves, Mrs. Mason wrote, "Have *you* ever watched the last, lingering illness of a consumptive.... Do *you* soften the pangs of maternity in those around you.... Do *you* grieve with those *near* you.... Did *you* ever sit up until the 'wee hours' to complete a dress for a motherless child?"[241]

Having seemingly dispatched Maria for her misplaced sympathies, she then turned her attention to literary matters, saying, "[N]o Southerner ought, after your letter to Governor Wise and to Brown, to read a line of your composition, or to touch a magazine which bears your name...."[242] Years later, Higginson would claim, "To begin with double-dyed future torments, and come gradually to the climax of 'Stop my paper,' admits of no other explanation than that Mrs. Mason had dabbled in literature herself, and knew how to pierce the soul of a sister in the trade."[243]

After a brief apology for her delay in writing, Maria responded to Mrs. Mason, saying, "I have no disposition to retort upon you the 'two-fold damnation,' to which you consign me. On the contrary, I sincerely wish you well, both in this world and the next." Leaving the judgment of Brown to "him who knoweth the secrets of all hearts," Maria insisted that "[m]en, however great they may be, are of small consequence in comparison with principles; and the principle for which John Brown died is the question at issue between us."[244] In response to the question "Do you read your Bible Mrs. Child?" Maria left little doubt of her familiarity with the sacred book. She responded by quoting eighteen of the abolitionists' favorite texts regarding slavery.

As she had done so effectively in her *Appeal*, Child next chose to discuss the abuses of slavery as documented in southern sources, including newspapers, court testimony and conversations with fugitive slaves. Beginning her discussion with runaway slave advertisements, she pointed out that runaways were often described as having "'straight, light hair, blue eyes and clear complexion.'" This was impossible, she maintained, unless "their fathers, grandfathers, and great-grandfathers had been white men." Having thus concluded, she added, "The sale of one's own children, brothers, or sisters, has an ugly aspect to those who are unaccustomed to it...."[245] Quoting from the *North Carolina Standard* (Raleigh), she cited an ad placed by a Mr. Micajah Ricks: "Runaway, a negro woman and her two children. A few days before she went off, I burned her with a hot iron on the left side of her face. I tried to make the letter 'M.'" This ad was not exceptional, Maria maintained, saying that she might have quoted from "hundreds of such advertisements, offering rewards for runaways, 'dead or alive' ... with 'ears cut off,' 'jaws broken,' 'scarred by rifle-balls,' &c."[246]

In the most searing indictment of her response, Maria turned her attention to the "personal questions you ask me," to which she replied in the name of "all the women of New England": "It would be extremely difficult to find any woman in our villages who does *not* sew for the poor, and watch with the sick.... We pay our domestics generous wages, with which they can purchase as many Christmas gowns as they please; a process far better for their characters, as well as our own, than to receive their clothing as a charity, after being deprived of just payment for their labor."[247]

But the line for which many would long remember Maria's articulate response involved Mason's charge that northern women did not help those in the pangs of maternity. Maria retorted, "I have never known an instance where the 'pangs of maternity' did not meet with requisite assistance; and here at the North, after we have helped the mothers, *we do not sell the babies.*"[248]

In a final, parting thrust, Maria turned to Mason's admonishment that no Southerner should read her work, responding that she had "nothing to lose in that quarter," having labored for twenty-seven years for the slave and having long ago lost her appeal to southern readers. Maria contended that many of the greatest minds in America opposed slavery and insinuated that she would take her stand alongside the likes of Emerson. In point of truth, concluded Maria, "[T]he whole civilized world proclaims Slavery an outlaw, and the best intellect of the age is active in hunting it down."[249] After reading her articulate response, few impartial observers would exclude Maria herself from that category.

Because Mason's letter had been sent to the Virginia press, Maria sent a copy of her letter to the *New York Tribune*, asking Horace Greeley to run her reply.[250] Having thus disposed of Mrs. Mason, she turned her attention to the "*next* fatal Friday," which would bring about a series of hangings of Brown's accomplices.[251] "The 16th of December was more painful to me than the 2d," she maintained. "Those other victims were young, and wanted to live; and they had not so many manifestations of sympathy to sustain them as their grand old leader had."[252] On 19 December, she once again wrote a prisoner of Virginia. This time the recipient of her attention would be Aaron D. Stevens as he sat in a Charlestown prison awaiting execution. As she had done previously with Brown, Maria assured him both of her personal support and the broader support of "thousands and thousands of hearts in the Free States [who] are earnestly praying for you...."

True to Brown's request, she inquired whether he had "wife, or children, or mother, for whom you wish us to do anything; and whether those who have gone left families

Eight. Literature's Version

that need assistance; especially the *colored* men." She was particularly interested in the colored conspirators, whom she saw as "Poor victims of their generous zeal for their persecuted and downtrodden race!" If he chose to answer, Maria suggested he address his letter to "Mrs. Spring" because "My name might perhaps be the occasion of stopping the letter; for though I am by nature very averse to conflict with my fellow beings, God has given me the strength of ten, wherever questions of oppression are concerned."[253]

As Christmas approached, Maria continued to respond to the huge volume of mail which had been directed her way as a result of her published correspondence with Wise and Mason. Saying she was "overwhelmed with letters," she persisted in replying to as many as she could. "I have answered twenty three letters, since this week came in; all, but two, about John Brown," she wrote.[254] By January, she would claim, "I have been *so* overwhelmed with letters, in these exciting times. Last week, I answered 43, and still a pile remains." Maria viewed the attention as an opportunity and she was determined to take full advantage of it, saying, "It gives me a grand chance to do mischief, and I do it with all diligence."[255]

With the start of the new year, Maria's correspondence with Wise and Mason was published in pamphlet form. To everyone's amazement, the *Correspondence between Lydia Maria Child and Gov. Wise and Mrs. Mason of Virginia* achieved a circulation of 300,000 copies in an era when a typical best seller might run to 8,000. The pamphlet provided by far the largest contemporary readership of Child's career, producing a "wider circulation than anything she ever wrote."[256] Samuel May claimed that Maria's letter to Mason was "copied by hundreds of thousands, and was doubtless one of the efficient agencies that prepared the mind of the North for the final great crisis."[257] Higginson would later pronounce it "one of the best things she ever wrote."[258] For her part, Child looked upon this publication as the most noteworthy of all her antislavery efforts.[259]

To no one's surprise, however, the pamphlet was not well received in the southern states. Maria received, in the words of Higginson, "many private letters from the slave States, mostly anonymous, and often grossly insulting."[260] The published letters, while commanding an "immense circulation all over the free states ... were blazoned by all manner of anathemas in the Southern papers."[261] In an effort to discredit Maria, the southern press began circulating the story that she had a child in Mississippi whom she did not support. Maria denied the story, and the woman in question, while from Massachusetts, was found to be named Childs, not Child.[262]

But even as she publicly defended Brown at every turn, privately Maria continued to harbor reservations about Brown's methods. In January of 1860, she wrote Maria Chapman, saying, "I *can't* explain ... [how] ... any man in his senses could have undertaken such an enterprise."[263] Still, she steadfastly reiterated her support: "We cannot help reverencing the *man* while we disapprove of his *measures....*" In what may be a statement of how she ultimately reconciled the violence of Brown's act with her peace principles, she wrote, "I must be true to the principles of *Freedom*, as well as of *peace.*"[264] Yet, she continued to rail against slavery: "I think from this time till I die, I shall stop firing only long enough to load my guns"[265]

Following Brown's execution, Higginson, too, turned his attention to Brown's compatriots awaiting execution in Charlestown, but again he had quite a different sort of relief in mind. Another daring rescue plot was forming. Higginson now threw himself into rescue plans to save Albert Hazlett and Aaron D. Stevens, the former of whom he had met in Kansas.[266] James Redpath, a Scottish journalist who had been with Brown in Kansas, wrote Higginson warning him that he was being watched and urging him to be careful in matters concerning written correspondence.[267] But, as was his wont, Higginson refused to succumb to fear. On 13 December, R.J. Hinton wrote Higginson: "Something ought to be done.... Count me in for one—Stephens & Haslett *must be* saved."[268] By February, in consultation with Mrs. Brown, Higginson transferred funds designated for relief for the Brown family, for use in the rescue of his associates. Thayer and Eldridge, two Boston publishers, were also involved in fundraising for this purpose. At a meeting in their office, Higginson met Walt Whitman, who was there on literary business.[269] It is safe to say that with thoughts of conspiracy paramount, Higginson did not take the time to apprise Whitman of his opinion of his poetry.

Once again it would be left to Higginson, Hinton and Le Barnes to formulate a rescue strategy. Hinton returned to Kansas, with funds provided by Higginson and Le Barnes, to enlist the aid of Captain James Montgomery "and eight or ten tried and trusty men." Higginson planned to rendezvous with the men in Harrisburg, Pennsylvania, while Le Barnes recruited German Americans from New York.[270] On 17 February, Higginson checked into the United States Hotel in Harrisburg under the alias Charles P. Carter and carefully assessed the rescue plan before him:

> The enterprise would involve traversing fifty miles of mountain country by night, at the rate of about ten miles each night, carrying arms, ammunition, blankets, and a week's rations, with the frequent necessity of camping without fire in February, and with the certainty of detection in case of snow. It would include crossing the Potomac, possibly at a point where there was neither a bridge nor a ford. It would culminate in an attack on a building with a wall fourteen feet high, with two sentinels outside and twenty-five inside: with a certainty of raising the town in the process, and then, if successful, with the need of retreating, perhaps with wounded men and probably by daylight.[271]

In spite of the overwhelming odds against the endeavor, Montgomery and his comrade Soulé traveled to Charlestown to check out the terrain in question. Once there, Soulé pretended to be intoxicated, an adept performance which landed him in a jail cell near the prisoners. Under the "guise of a jovial, half-drunken Irishman," he learned in hasty communications with Hazlett and Stevens that they considered rescue quite hopeless. Further, the men were concerned that any escape attempt would put Avis, the jailer, at risk. Like Brown, both men greatly appreciated their kind treatment at the hands of Avis and neither wished him harm.[272] The prisoners' strong sentiments in this regard, coupled with a series of heavy snowfalls, convinced Montgomery of the impracticality of the attempt and thus "the bold scheme of rescuing the two doomed men was reluctantly abandoned."[273] Montgomery returned to the waiting Higginson in Harrisburg and pronounced the rescue "absolutely hopeless." A disappointed Higginson returned to Worcester, where he entitled his next journal entry "Recalled to Life," a clue to how desperate he believed the enterprise to be.[274]

Once Higginson had resigned himself to the deaths of the prisoners, he wrote Stevens on 12 March 1860, sounding less like a revolutionary and more like a minister: "Death is only a step in life and there is no more reason why we should fear to go from one world into another than from one room into another.... The world where John Brown is cannot be a bad one to live in.... My wife would have been willing that I should risk my life to save yours had that been possible."[275]

In an October 1860 journal entry Higginson reflected on the unrealized rescue plot: "Last year at this time I was worn and restless with inability to do anything for John Brown. Not that I grudged him his happy death—but it seemed terrible to yield him to Virginia. The effort to rescue Stevens and Hazlett—undertaken on my sole responsibility—restored my self-respect." Higginson noted with some satisfaction that the plan "did not fail like the Burns rescue through the timidity of others—but simply through the impracticability of the thing." He went on to say, "I think it was a disappointment to me not to be summoned to testify before the [Senate] committee, nor do I know why I was passed over.... Certainly I should have told them all I knew...." [276]

Unlike Emerson, Thoreau, Higginson, or Child, Frederick Douglass would wait until the end of January before he was comfortable enough to mention John Brown in a public address. In an Edinburgh lecture entitled "John Brown and the Slaveholders' Insurrection," he called Brown a "martyr" and a "brave, heroic, and Christian man" who had sought to free a people held in bondage.[277] In March, he was more philosophical and less emotional than usual when he shared a platform with radical antislavery leader George Thompson. Thompson vehemently attacked America, and Douglass responded with a "learned analysis of the American Constitution," citing articles and sections to make his point, while taking care to steer clear of the inflammatory John Brown.[278] One cannot ascertain how long Douglass might have stayed in England giving speeches in a dispassionate and philosophic vein had not word reached him of the death of his beloved daughter, Anna. On 13 March 1860 he immediately began the long, circuitous journey back to New York.

Douglass returned home to a country with decidedly different views on Brown and the events at Harpers Ferry than the one he left. Even though testimony given in the January Senate hearings clearly implicated him, the mood to pursue accomplices (with the potential of creating more martyrs in the process) had dimmed considerably.[279] Charles W. Chesnutt, in an 1899 biography of Douglass, contended, "So rapid had been the course of events since [Douglass's] departure that the excitement over the ... raid had subsided."[280] Frederic May Holland, writing in 1891, also commented on the "great change in public opinion" by the time of his return. With the John Brown song now ringing throughout northern streets, and the election of a Republican president not far in the future, "no notice of [Douglass's return] was taken ... by ... Wise."[281]

While Douglass was undoubtedly relieved by this change in circumstance, Brown's Concord friends were about to experience one last tumultuous repercussion from their friendship with Brown. On the quiet, moonlit evening of April 3, Thoreau was awakened to screams coming from across the street, at the home of Sanborn. Deputy marshals had come to issue a subpoena for Sanborn to appear in Washington to give testimony regarding the Brown affair. Pretending to ask for charity, they gained entrance to the house and once inside announced Sanborn's arrest. Sanborn was dragged down the steps screaming "Murder!" while his sister grabbed a marshal by his beard and struck at the horses.[282] Anne Whiting, one of Concord's most fervent abolitionists, responded by jumping into the carriage and "spreading her crinoline ... [thereby] preventing the forcible entry of Sanborn into the vehicle."[283] Townsend Scudder further credited Miss

In April of 1860, federal marshals came to Concord in an attempt to arrest Sanborn. Hearing his cries of "Murder!" Concord residents rushed to his defense. The marshals then "found it convenient to leave town as fast as their horses would take them, pursued by stones and other missiles" hurled by Sanborn's "pupils and neighbors." Emerson would credit the women of the town for the successful rescue. This drawing appeared in *Harper's Weekly* in 1860 (courtesy Concord Free Public Library).

Whiting with "belabor[ing] the horses with a broom so that their plunging would hinder the abductors."[284] Ellen Emerson marveled at how "The men hurt her and scratched her and tore her dress trying to get her out, but she stayed in and hindered them a long time."[285] Colonel Whiting, Anne's seventy-year-old father, joined the fray, beating the marshals with his cane.[286] Meanwhile, the handcuffed Sanborn, "in thin slippers and cotton stockings," commenced "waving frantically his manacles and calling for help and rescue."[287] Soon someone pulled the fire alarm and hundreds of people, Thoreau among them, rushed into the streets to find Sanborn kicking and screaming and refusing to be loaded into the marshal's wagon. According to Sanborn's account, Emerson also arrived, demanding, "By what right do you hold this man?"[288] Judge Hoar quickly issued a writ of habeas corpus, effectively freeing Sanborn. The marshals and their company then "found it convenient to leave town as fast as their horses would take them, pursued by stones and other missiles" hurled by Sanborn's "pupils and neighbors."[289] Mary Brooks wrote a friend of her neighbors' heroism: "You never saw a more resolute set of people. One word from one they considered wise, and those wretches would have been torn to pieces in a moment. One of the officers told the Deputy Sheriff that he had been in all kinds of mobs and in all kinds of danger, but he never felt in such fear before...."[290] The *Boston Herald* reported that the marshals' carriage was "somewhat demolished in the melee."[291]

In truth, not only the marshals but the townspeople were unnerved as well. Fearing the marshals might return, someone gave Sanborn a revolver and urged him to stay with friends. Thoreau then spent the night at Sanborn's in order to protect his sister.[292] But for all the excitement, Thoreau's understated journal account reads simply, "Lodged at Sanborn's last night after his *rescue*, he being away."[293] Once the furor had subsided, it was discovered that Concord citizen Rufus Hosmer "had fallen dead of heart disease in the tumult," making him the sole casualty of the episode.[294] It seems Hosmer had often commented that he wouldn't live "to see Sanborn carried away from Concord" and apparently the "unfortunate man ... did not."[295]

The following day, a throng of people gathered in Boston with the intention of rescuing Sanborn as he attended a hearing to determine whether or not the Supreme Court of Massachusetts would rule in his favor. Among Sanborn's defenders in the crowd was Walt Whitman. Happily, the court declared that the arrest was "without warrant of law, and Mr. Sanborn returned to Concord a hero to his townspeople."[296] Whitman's services would not be needed. Meanwhile, in Concord, the townspeople anxiously gathered at the railroad station to await the arrival of the cars. When word came that Sanborn had been released, "[A] shout rent the air that might have shook the rafters of the depot." A number of the women present "waved their handkerchiefs" as a "cannon ... belched forth its thunder." In short, "for a spontaneous demonstration it was about as stirring an affair as could have been desired...."[297]

That evening at 8:00 P.M., a triumphant Sanborn arrived in Concord to share the speaker's platform with Thoreau, Emerson, Higginson and Alcott. In a town whose population was estimated to be only 2,500, the enthusiastic crowd of both men and women was 500 strong. The evening belonged largely to the women who had proven themselves "almighty strong in this 'second Concord fight.'" Both Sanborn's sister and Anne Whiting were received with "unbounded enthusiasm."[298] Keyes arrived home to discover "Concord stirred to its depths, with reporters ... of all kinds, and more foolish stories in circulation of attacks, and captures, than could be imagined...."[299]

At the speaker's platform, Sanborn opined that the decision of the Massachusetts court to free him "agreed with the sentiments of two-thirds of the people" of the state.[300] In a speech covered by the Boston papers, Thoreau seized the moment to decry the "mean and sneaking method" used to ensnare Sanborn and suggested it was a mistake that someone didn't arrest the marshals themselves. Upon hearing the fire bell ring, Thoreau initially thought it a fire and it was—the "hottest fire he ever witnessed in Concord." Complaining that some said the incident was freely settled according to the law, Thoreau said, "No. The Concord people didn't ring the fire alarm bells according to law—they didn't cheer according to law—they didn't groan according to law—(loud applause)—and as he didn't talk according to law, he thought he would stop and give way to some other speaker."[301]

Emerson, "well known all over the Union for his eccentricities, and at the same time for the warmth of his heart," also addressed the meeting and was "received with great tokens of approbation." Calling the women who had saved Sanborn "heroic," Emerson declared that it was they who "by their prompt and devoted exertions" prevented Sanborn's arrest.[302] Higginson also took the stage and called for "an effective military organization ... [in Concord] to carry out the principles of resistance to the United States laws." Citing the Butman incident, he asserted the need for a "military organization to resist such arrests in future."[303]

As the meeting drew to a close, "[I]t was announced that Sanborn would be arrested on charges of assaulting federal officers," a legal trick allowing the Massachusetts courts to maintain jurisdiction over him. To prevent the marshals from attempting another arrest, Sanborn spent the following few nights at the homes of various friends, including Thoreau.[304] That spring, Higginson joined a group of bodyguards in Concord determined to protect Sanborn from further attempts at arrest.[305]

For his part, Thoreau would address the John Brown issue publicly for a final time in a speech he sent with friends to be delivered at memorial services for Brown on 4 July 1860 in North Elba, New York. In his remarks, he commented upon the "meteor-like" career of Brown and marveled at the fact that "Years were not required for a revolution of public opinion; days, nay hours, produced marked changes in this case." In a glowing tribute to Brown, he continued: "He has liberated many thousands of slaves, both North and South. They seem to have known nothing about living or dying for a principle. They all called him crazy then; who calls him crazy now?"[306] The speech was published in the *Liberator* on 27 July 1860. Richard Hinton read Thoreau's remarks, prefacing them with the following: "Mr. Thoreau's voice was the first which broke the disgraceful silence or hushed the senseless babble with which the grandest deed of our time was met."[307]

Later that year, Douglass and Sanborn addressed a gathering on 3 December in Boston's Tremont Temple. Sanborn was about to take the platform when "some well-dressed men who wished to break up the meeting" insisted that their man speak in opposition to Brown. Douglass, on the platform, handed the man a glass of water saying, "If thine enemy thirst, give him drink."[308] His resolve to be temperate evaporated, however, when one man attempted to forcibly take away his chair, and another called out racial slurs from the audience. At that final indignity, Douglass, pointing at the man, cried, "If I were a slave-driver, and had hold of that man ... I would let more daylight through his skin than ever got there before." With this exchange, men rushed forward and grabbed chairs, and the furniture ended up "all thrown in a heap" at the rear of the stage.[309]

Emerson, too, would encounter conflict at the podium, at a speech before the Massachusetts Anti-Slavery Society at Tremont Temple on 24 January 1861. Maria Child was in attendance and described the gathering. "Such yelling, screeching, stamping, and bellowing I never heard," she wrote, adding, "It was a full realization of the old phrase, 'All hell broke loose.'"[310] Emerson, as he attempted to speak, was "interrupted with all kinds of insults." Choosing to ignore the commotion, Emerson, after attempting a few words, stood quietly on the platform, in the words of Higginson "undisturbed."[311] Higginson was also in the auditorium, leading a band of "sixty armed sympathizers protecting the speaker." After dodging both pillows and verbal volleys on the speaker's platform, Emerson and Phillips withdrew. Higginson, however, determined that he would speak. He would speak, he said, for a cause more basic than abolition. That day, he would advocate for "the right of white men in Massachusetts to be heard in Boston."[312]

Eight. Literature's Version

On 8 December 1859, John Brown was laid to his final rest in North Elba, New York. Wendell Phillips' eulogy paid tribute to Brown and marveled at the changing tide of public opinion:

> How vast the change in men's hearts! Insurrection was a harsh, horrid word to millions a month ago. John Brown went a whole generation beyond it, claiming the right for white men to help the slave to freedom by arms. And now men run up and down, not disputing his principle, but trying to frame excuses for Virginia's hanging of so pure, honest, high-hearted, and heroic a man. Virginia stands at the bar of the civilized world on trial.[313]

Few today would doubt that John Brown's actions at Harpers Ferry, coupled with the strong defense mounted in the press by his literary friends, further divided an already agitated public. Many believe that the raid and the subsequent publicity surrounding it contributed to the Republicans' win in the national election, the South's secession from the Union, and ultimately to the advent of the Civil War. Frederick Douglass maintained, "If John Brown did not end the war that ended slavery, he did at least begin the war that ended slavery."[314] Sanborn, in his *Recollections of Seventy Years*, wrote glowingly of John Brown and Abraham Lincoln, saying, "[O]ne began and the other completed the forcible freeing of 4,000,000 slaves in the United States."[315] At Brown's burial, Phillips called him a "[m]arvellous old man," and predicted, "He has abolished slavery in Virginia," adding "History will date Virginia Emancipation from Harpers Ferry." Borrowing an image from Thoreau he intoned "[Brown's] words,—they are stronger even than his rifles. These crushed a State. Those have changed the thoughts of millions, and will yet crush slavery."[316]

And so it was that Brown, with the help of his literary friends Emerson, Thoreau, Douglass, Child and Higginson, may indeed have ultimately succeeded in striking a deathblow to slavery in the United States of America.

Nine

Epilogue

The legacy of Emerson, Thoreau, Douglass, Child, Higginson and others who sought to restore John Brown's reputation was profound and long lasting. For his part, Brown, before he died, had the satisfaction of knowing "that an estate, as well as a reputation, had been retrieved from his ruin."[1] He may not have fully understood, however, the legacy his friends had assured him. Near the second anniversary of Brown's death, Julia Ward Howe wrote the "Battle Hymn of the Republic." In the song, she borrowed an image from Thoreau and Emerson and compared Brown's death to Jesus' death on the cross. The line "As He died to make men holy, let us die to make men free" was taken directly from the well-known "John Brown's Body," sung by Union soldiers throughout the Civil War.[2] By the war's end, the song would be performed in the halls of Congress, and, like earlier efforts to enshrine Brown, it would take its place in American culture.[3]

In 1860, Thoreau, Emerson, Child and Higginson provided material for one of the first biographies of Brown, *The Public Life of Capt. John Brown*, by James Redpath, a mutual friend of Thoreau and Brown. The work, painting Brown as a hero and martyr, was dedicated to "Wendell Phillips, Ralph Waldo Emerson, and Henry D. Thoreau, Defenders of the Faithful, who, when the mob shouted, 'Madman!' Said, 'Saint!'"[4] For seventy years, biographers would follow Redpath's lead and extol the virtues of Brown. In the introduction to Robert Penn Warren's 1929 biography of Brown, C. Vann Woodward wrote, "With very few exceptions the twenty or more books about John Brown [prior to this one] ... were devoted in some degree to the making or the perpetuation of [Brown's] name as a hero and a martyr."[5] W.E.B. Du Bois proclaimed in his complimentary 1909 biography that "the memory of John Brown stands to-day as a mighty warning to his country."[6]

The cast of players in the verbal assault on Harpers Ferry never publicly wavered in their support of Brown. Emerson, who lived through another generation, remained strongly committed to social reform. Through his Saturday Club he served the interests of the North by the issuance of a number of broadsides. In February of 1861, at the annual school festival in Concord, Louisa May Alcott attempted to share a song she had written which paid tribute to John Brown. When some of the "old fogies" in the audience objected to the verse about Brown, Emerson rose, took the paper from her hand and said, "No, no, that is the best. It must be sung, & not only sung but read. *I* will read it." And he proceeded to do so, much to the delight and amazement of the Alcotts.[7] Louisa May marveled, "when the great man of the town says 'Do it,' the thing is done."[8] Emerson mentioned Brown publicly only once again. In 1865, Concord commemorated the death of Abraham Lincoln. Emerson spoke at the service and compared John Brown's remarks to the court with Lincoln's Gettysburg address, thereafter linking the two men

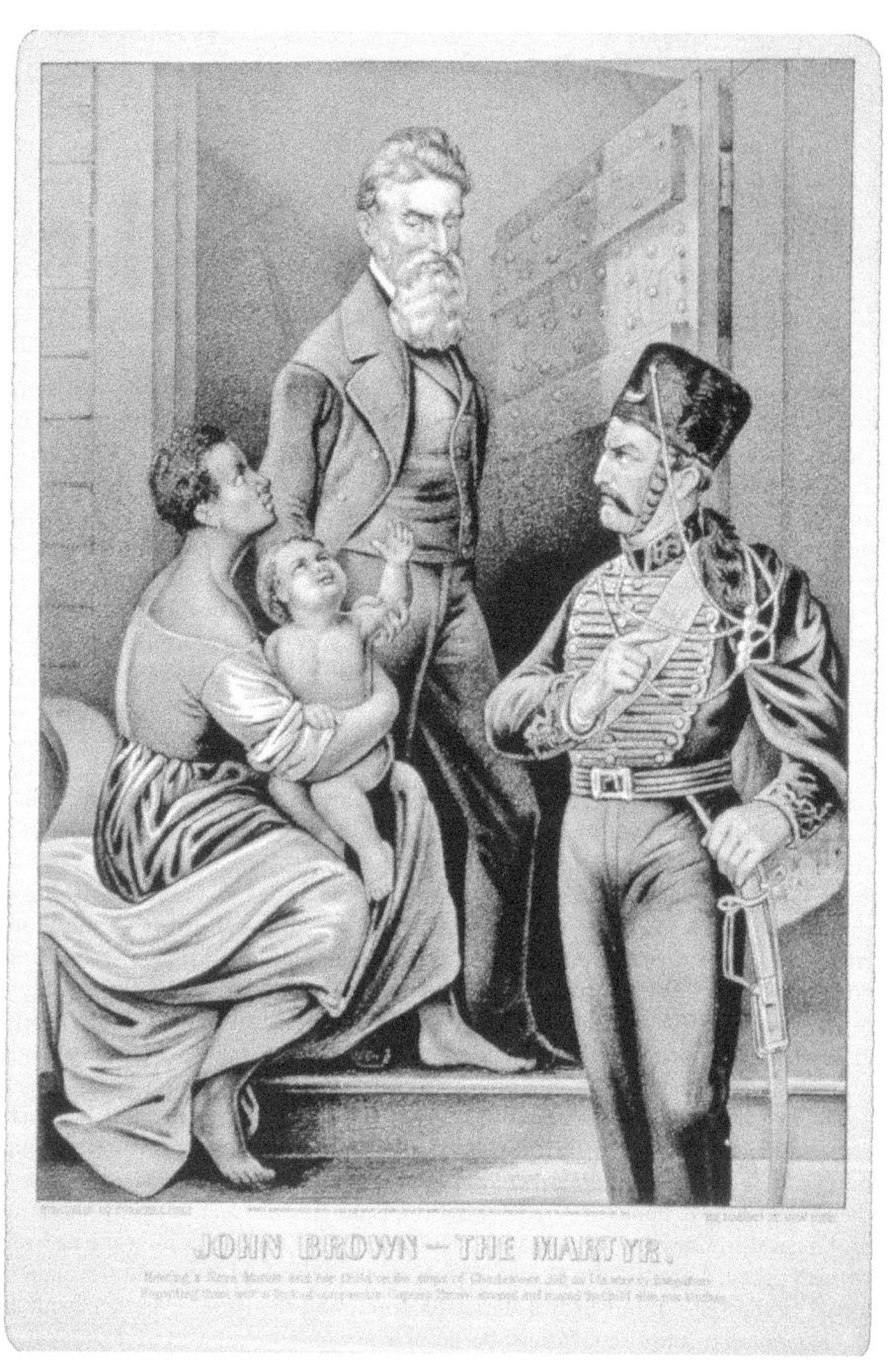

In 1870, Currier & Ives published this lithograph entitled Brown—The Martyr. Although the story of Brown kissing a black baby on the jailhouse steps is apocryphal, it had gained widespread traction since appearing in the press and was widely believed as factual. Lydia Maria Child joined the many who commented upon the moment, writing a poem about the event (Library of Congress, Prints and Photographs Division).

Nine. Epilogue

This portrait of Ralph Waldo Emerson was published circa 1906. Emerson's stature in later years is evidenced by the fact that, by the time of his death in 1882, four presidents had heard him speak: Rutherford B. Hayes, Martin Van Buren, Abraham Lincoln and James Garfield (Library of Congress, Prints and Photographs Division).

in the minds of Brown supporters.[9] By the time of Emerson's death in 1882, four presidents, either before or after they were in office, had heard him speak, including Rutherford B. Hayes, Martin Van Buren, Abraham Lincoln and James Garfield.[10]

For her part, Lidian Emerson, ever the agitator, refused to allow her son to enlist in the Civil War so long as preservation of the union was the official reason for the fighting. Ellen, consoling her unhappy brother, wrote "[Mother] says when emancipation is proclaimed you may [fight], and she believes she takes the truly patriotic ground."[11] In 1868 Lidian served as one of Concord's representatives to the American Anti-Slavery Society helping to collect clothing for poor blacks. Her efforts on behalf of the disadvantaged reached full circle in 1873 when she expressed concern at the treatment of the Modoc Indians, much as she had spoken for the Cherokees nearly a half century before.[12]

Frederick Douglass, his sterling reputation restored, became one of the best-selling authors of his time, and, like Emerson, lived to be the guest of presidents. One of very few Americans ever to publish three autobiographies, in 1881 he would tell a more complete story of his interactions with Brown in the *Life and Times of Frederick Douglass*. During the Civil War he helped recruit African American soldiers for black regiments led by Thomas Wentworth Higginson and Robert Gould Shaw. His stirring recruitment speeches would often include a break into song, more often than not "John Brown's Body."[13] His two sons, Lewis and Charles, would both fight in, and survive, the Civil War, incorporating in their personal struggle against slavery the violence their father so often shunned.[14]

Eventually, Douglass journeyed to Harpers Ferry, where on 20 May 1881 he delivered an address at Storer College. He shared the platform with Andrew Hunter, the Charlestown District Attorney who had prosecuted John Brown. In his remarks, Douglass finally, and thoroughly, put to rest any lingering doubts about his feelings concerning Brown, paying "a just debt long due, to vindicate in some degree a great historical

Frederick Douglass achieved great prominence by the time of his death. One of very few Americans ever to publish three autobiographies in his lifetime, in 1881 he would tell a more complete version of his interactions with Brown in *The Life and Times of Frederick Douglass*. This portrait of an older Douglass was published sometime between 1865 and 1880 (Library of Congress, Prints and Photographs Division).

character [John Brown] ... one with whom I was myself well acquainted, and whose friendship and confidence it was my good fortune to share...." Comparing himself to Brown, he conceded, "His zeal in the cause of my race was far greater than mine—it was as the burning sun to my taper light—mine was bounded by time, his stretched away to the boundless shores of eternity," adding "I could live for the slave, but he could die for him." Of Brown's enemies, Douglass opined, "They could kill him, but they could not answer him"[15] Upon conclusion of the speech, Hunter rose, shook Douglass's hand and invited him to visit Charlestown, the scene of Brown's execution. "That such an address could be delivered at such a place, at such a time, is strikingly significant, and illustrates the rapid, vast and wonderful changes through which the American people have been passing since 1859," concluded the editor who would later publish the address. Proceeds from the sale of the speech in pamphlet form would go towards the establishment of a John Brown professorship at the college whose student body was comprised largely of "colored youth."[16]

Upon Douglass's death, his obituaries, like so many previous articles about him, stubbornly continued to mention his "intellectual ... ability" and the "genius hidden in the negro race," as if it was surprising to find these attributes in a black man.[17] Child perhaps paid a more fitting tribute to Douglass in *The Freedmen's Book* (1865) by incorporating his words as a model for the freed slaves.[18] She distributed the work to blacks, with proceeds designated to help educate freedmen and their children.[19] In an 1880 remembrance, she cited Douglass as one who "loomed above the horizon" in the early antislavery crusade, because having been a slave he "knew whereof he affirmed."[20]

Lydia Maria Child, for the remainder of her life, continued to work tirelessly and courageously for the slave. Twice more Child encountered violence in response to her antislavery efforts. Later that winter (1860), a crowd gathered outside an abolitionist assembly hurling threats toward the speaker, Wendell Phillips. Samuel Gridley Howe later described the meeting's end, as Phillips exited the building surrounded by Maria on one side and Mrs. Chapman on the other. The women calmly walked him out the door and through the mob to safety.[21] In mid–December, Child was "'tumbled up and down' by 'one burly rioter.'"[22] Maria grabbed the man's collar and then focused on a fellow mutineer nearby whom she lectured on his inappropriate behavior, not leaving until she had attained from him a promise to redeem his ways.[23]

In 1860 Child wrote and then distributed at her own expense fifteen hundred copies of her emancipation tract, *The Right Way the Safe Way*, to persons in the South.[24] After others had declined, she undertook to help fugitive slave Harriet Jacobs edit *Incidents in the Life of a Slave Girl* (1861), a powerful slave narrative still widely read today. In an apparent, and much written about, contradiction, she advised Jacobs to delete a chapter about John Brown, saying it does "not naturally come into your story."[25] Instead, as Bruce Mills has suggested, Maria most likely urged Jacobs to channel her thoughts about rebellion into a section on Nat Turner, thereby commenting indirectly on the times, much as Maria herself had been forced to do so often throughout her career.[26]

Child's practical, less literary pursuits on behalf of the slaves continued as well. She knitted for the army, but "only for Kansas troops [because] they have vowed a vow unto the Lord that no fugitive shall ever be surrendered in their camps."[27] She lobbied tirelessly for black suffrage, education and job training, and supported the reallocation of slaveholders' assets to the poor.[28] In 1870, Higginson reminisced about the early days of the abolitionist movement: "'Mrs. Child describes her collaring and pulling away a man who was shaking his fist in Mr. Phillips's face at Music Hall mob—and her surprise when he tumbled down.' When Jonas H. French said, 'This is no place for women,' she answered, 'They are needed here to teach civilization to men.'"[29]

Upon Child's death in 1880, John Greenleaf Whittier paid tribute to his friend of many years. Quoting from Hebrews, he said of Maria, "'Many daughters have done virtuously, but thou excellest them all.'"[30] Higginson also rendered homage to Child, saying that reading her *Letters from New York* resulted in his desire "to put myself on more equal terms with that vast army of hand-workers who were ignorant of much that I knew, yet could do much that I could not."[31] But, Maria herself would perhaps have preferred the tribute from a black correspondent to the *Liberator* who suggested she had earned a place next to John Brown in the hierarchy of white patrons in his people's estimation.[32] Speaking at her funeral, Wendell Phillips also linked Brown with Child saying, "She was among the first to welcome John Brown."[33]

Higginson, for his part, continued to display the physical courage that so distinguished

In 1870, L. Prang & Co. published this lithograph containing the portraits of seven eminent women involved in the suffrage and women's rights movement. Included are (clockwise from bottom) Lydia Maria Child, Susan B. Anthony, Grace Greenwood, Lucretia Mott, Elizabeth Cady Stanton, Mary Livermore, and Anna E. Dickinson in the center (Library of Congress, Prints and Photographs Division).

him in the Brown affair, as he fought in the war to save the very Union that he had "worked quite industriously for ... fifteen years to destroy."[34] Surprising almost no one, his initial response to the onset of the conflict was a plan to gather Montgomery and the Kansas recruits and raise a company for John Brown, Jr. Such a company, he believed, would divert attention from the nation's vulnerable capital. He wrote his mother: "I want at least to get the *name* of John Brown rumored on the border and then the whole party may come back and go to bed—they will frighten Virginia into fits all the same."[35] He enlisted Howe's help in raising funds and procured a letter of introduction from Governor Andrew, which he then presented to the governor of Pennsylvania. Andrew had reservations, but said of Higginson, "He is a man capable of facing great perils, of gallant and ardent spirit, and one whose plans I would not endorse in blank or in advance. You may find on enquiry that he proposes some scheme not only courageous, but wise."[36]

Once it became apparent that the South would not be easily cowed, and that his guerilla raiders would not, in fact, be the salvation of Washington, Higginson changed course. Given the opportunity to lead white soldiers, he chose, instead, to fight alongside blacks, reveling in his position as commander of the first black regiment:

> Here is ... a position of great importance; as many persons have said, the first man who organizes and commands a successful black regiment will perform the most important Service in the history of the war.... To say that I would rather do it than anything else in the world is to say little; it is such a masterpiece of felicitous opportunity that all casualties of life or death appear trivial in connexion with it.[37]

The Rev. A.W. Jackson, one of his officers, later credited Higginson with the success of the regiment, echoing Douglass's words: "He met a Slave; he made him a Man."[38] Higginson himself reflected, "Till the blacks were armed, there was no guaranty of their freedom. It was their demeanor under arms that shamed the nation into recognizing them as men."[39] Years later, he confided that his army service was "partial expiation" for what he continued to view as his and the Six's "abandonment" of Brown.[40] In 1870, he described his experience leading the troops in a book entitled *Army Life in a Black Regiment*. The book is still in print today.

In matters of literary criticism, Higginson, the man whose skills as a critic seemed to many so woefully ineffectual, redeemed himself somewhat with his appraisal of both Emerson and Thoreau. On 20 February 1863, he wrote Ralph Waldo Emerson from Camp Saxton: "I thought it might be pleasant for you to know that your [Boston] Hymn was read aloud to this regiment during the services last Sunday...."[41] Not only did Higginson admire Emerson, but he stood quite apart from contemporary critics who found Thoreau's literary accomplishments lacking. In an effort to encourage Thoreau's family to publish Henry's journals, Higginson personally traveled to Concord to approach the formidable Judge Hoar. Before he finished his plea, Hoar interrupted him: "'But you have left unsettled the preliminary question, why should any one care to have Thoreau's journals put in print?'" Recognizing the futility of his request, Higginson was forced to abandon the project as "hopeless."[42] After the war, he did, however, publish "sympathetic reviews" of two of Thoreau's lesser known works, *The Maine Woods* and *Cape Cod*.[43]

To the end of his life Higginson remained a staunch champion of not only Thoreau's writing but of his politics as well. "Thoreau died at forty-four, without having achieved fame or fortune," he wrote. "It is common to speak of his life as a failure; but to me it seems, with all its drawbacks, to have been a great and eminent success."[44] Higginson challenged Lowell's assessment of Thoreau as aloof from the important matters of his day. "Lowell says that Thoreau 'looked with utter contempt on the august drama of destiny, of which his country was the scene, and on which the curtain had already risen;' but was it Thoreau, or Lowell," Higginson asked, "who found a voice when the curtain fell, after the first act of that drama, upon the scaffold of John Brown?"[45] In 1905, nearly half a century after the raid, Higginson continued to marvel at Thoreau's defense of Brown, declaring that Henry had "ranged himself on the side of John Brown as placidly as if he were going for huckleberries."[46]

Higginson also turned his pen to Brown's aid. In the February and May 1860 issues of the *Atlantic Monthly* he contributed pieces entitled "The Maroons of Jamaica" and "The Maroons of Surinam" about successful slave uprisings, of the ilk Brown had attempted, thus suggesting by inference that Brown's plans were, in fact, not impractical.[47] He urged Fields to publish his essay on the Denmark Vesey slave insurrection of 1822, saying, "These times are particularly seasonable for that."[48] Unlike Redpath, he refused to write of John Brown directly, adamantly refusing to make money from the death of his friend.

For many years, not only Higginson, but also Sanborn and Stearns independently made annual pilgrimages to the graveside of John Brown to pay their respects. With the death of Stearns, Sanborn asked James Redpath to accompany him. Redpath, for want of time, declined. The man whose credentials included authorship of the first highly influential biography of Brown had turned to another money-making venture—helping Jefferson Davis write *A Short History of the Confederate States of America*. The book would stand in opposition to nearly everything Brown believed.[49]

Over the years, Higginson continued his solitary visits to Brown's grave in the Adirondacks, where, according to Edward Renehan, he would "kick up the leaves above the grave, stand silent, and meditate on who John Brown was, what his story meant, and how history would treat them all."[50] Several years before he died, Higginson wrote a friend, saying, "We did what we did. In the end, we were trying to do right. And I believe, in the greatest measure, we *did* do right." Nevertheless, Higginson forever regretted the death of Brown: "A counter-proposal to his Harpers Ferry scheme should have been made: something that would have both attracted and protected Brown," he contended. "In retrospect, I think the bombing of a few fine southern buildings, or a few famous southern men, with notes crediting the blasts to some choice northern abolitionist group, would have done the job."[51]

Despite repeated requests from his coconspirators to burn correspondence, Higginson steadfastly refused, instead carefully preserving all correspondence surrounding the raid and donating it to the Boston Public Library where it remains for use by scholars a century and a half later. And lest someone not locate it there, one can find nineteen pages of typewritten copies of many of these same letters at the Massachusetts Historical Society—donated by Thomas W. Higginson on 9 June 1887.

Fifty years after the raid, on 17 October 1909, Higginson and other surviving members of the Secret Six gathered to share their stories with Katherine Mayo, a reporter assisting Oswald Villard in the preparation of his upcoming biography of Brown. Higginson at first had been disinclined to participate. "'Why do you want to know of *us*?' he wrote in response to Mayo's initial request for an interview. 'Did any historian ever bother to write down the name of the man who bought the donkey on which Christ rode into Jerusalem?'"[52] Ultimately he was persuaded by Sanborn, who urged, "My book about Brown was the biography for our generation. We need a biography for the new generation, a biography for the next thirty years.'"[53] In the finished work, Oswald Villard paid

Nine. Epilogue

tribute to Higginson, saying "Of the men who ... knew most about John Brown's plans and principally aided him,—Sanborn, Howe, Stearns, Gerrit Smith, Parker and Higginson,—the Boston and Worcester clergymen alone stand out as being entirely ready to take the consequences, whatever they might be."[54] In regard to Brown, Higginson chose his own epitaph, saying he wanted to be remembered as "[T]he only one of John Brown's friends and advisers who was not frightened by the silly threats of Hugh Forbes into desiring that year's delay which ruined the enterprise"[55] Upon his death in 1911, in a final tribute to a man who gave so much of his life to the cause of antislavery, Higginson's coffin was borne to the altar by a group of young Negro soldiers.[56]

As for Hugh Forbes, Congress was interested in interviewing the man who seemingly had so much to say about the raid on the ferry. "In conducting the inquiry, the committee deemed it a matter of importance to have the testimony of Forbes. It appeared, however, that not long after the explosion at Harper's Ferry, Forbes left the country, and the committee were not able to procure his attendance before them."[57]

This photograph of Higginson is dated 24 October 1905. Higginson lived until 9 May 1911. Upon his death, his body was carried to the altar by a young group of black soldiers (Boston Public Library/Rare Books Department—courtesy the Trustees).

Anthony Burns and Thomas Sims, the fugitive slaves whom Higginson had hoped to forcibly liberate, were both subsequently freed through abolitionists' efforts. Several months after the failed rescue attempt, Burns wrote Richard Henry Dana, his Boston attorney, saying, "They tole my oner to not let you all have me but I am for sale. And if you all my friends will please to haelp your friend this much I will Bee to you all A friend all my days."[58] A year after his return to slavery, Burns was, in fact, purchased by Boston philanthropists and given funds to attend Oberlin College, where he studied to become a Baptist minister.[59]

Thomas Sims was also the beneficiary of abolitionist fund-raising efforts. Lydia Maria Child worked tirelessly and successfully to solicit donations for the purchase of Sims, who had been returned to his master from Boston in 1852. Resolved that since, "Massachusetts had sent him into slavery, Massachusetts should bring him back," she set out to raise $1,800 from specifically "*pro-slavery*" sources for this purpose. "A large sum for an abolitionist to get out of pro-slavery purses! But I got it! I got it! I got it!" she wrote.[60]

EPILOGUE

John Brown's Fort survived the ravages of the Civil War. In this photograph circa 1889–1892 one can barely make out the writing on the White Hall Tavern to the right advertising "Oysters and Lunches." Buildings in the area advertised on their exteriors to attract tourists who came in by train to see the scene of John Brown's raid. Two such visitors were Thomas Wentworth Higginson and his new bride, Mary Thacher, who honeymooned in the area (Historic Photo Collection, Harpers Ferry National Historic Park).

Many years after his attempted capture by federal marshals, Franklin Sanborn would experience one further brush with the law when he was fined $50 for "failure to have his premises connected with the town sewer." Serving as his own counsel, Sanborn told those present that he had been arrested only once before in his life, in connection with the John Brown episode. He reminded the court that he was represented in that endeavor by the late J.S. Keyes, "father of the justice who imposed the fine yesterday." It is unknown whether his reference to Brown or the senior Keyes helped his case or reduced his fine.[61]

The aftermath of the raid not only affected the men and women involved in it, but the locations that would forever be associated with it. The effect of the war upon Harpers Ferry was disastrous. Because of its strategic location, the town changed hands on a number of occasions throughout the conflict. In February of 1862, a Union soldier described the village: "The appearance of ruin by war and fire was awful. Charred ruins were all that remain of the splendid public works, arsenals, workshops and railroads, stores, hotels, and dwelling houses all mingled in one common destruction." Only John Brown's

Engine House remained, "like a monument which no Rebel hands were permitted to demolish."[62]

Early in the conflict, Governor Henry Wise himself conspired to capture the federal arsenal at Harpers Ferry, when he worked with the Virginia military to seize the facility for use by the state of Virginia.[63] After the war, Wise returned home to find his plantation converted into a missionary school for freedmen and their children. Each school day began with song—a rousing rendition of "John Brown's Body," perhaps led by one of the teachers, a daughter of Brown. It would be 1868 before he regained possession of his Virginia home.

In another twist of fate, Harpers Ferry became part of the only successful secession of the Civil War, when it voted 196 to 1 to join the newly formed state of West Virginia. Although fraud was charged in the election, the Supreme Court would let the balloting stand. On 20 June 1863, West Virginia became a state and took with it the disputed areas, including Harpers Ferry.[64]

Not long after the war, the town became a tourist attraction, which it remains to this day. In the 1890s, John Speer wrote, "So enthusiastically did the mass of peop[l]e sustain Brown, that railroad trains sometimes stopped at Harpers Ferry to let them sing: 'John Brown's body lies a mouldering in the grave/But his soul goes marching on'"[65] One such visitor was the widowed Thomas Wentworth Higginson, who honeymooned in Harpers Ferry with his second wife, Mary Thacher. During their visit, he traveled to the prison in Charlestown where Brown, Hazlett and Stevens lay captive so many years before. Upon gazing at the high, seemingly unassailable wall, he was convinced that Montgomery's decision not to attempt a rescue was the correct one.[66]

Faneuil Hall, the site of six 19th century antislavery fairs, would for many years proudly display a bust of Daniel Webster.[67] It would be the last decade of the 20th century, however, before a statue of Frederick Douglass would join the author of the Fugitive Slave Law at the podium. A bust of Brown would also find a home—at the Boston Athenaeum, which had once retracted Maria Child's library privileges upon publication of her *Appeal*.[68]

On 15 June 1860, the Mason Report was published. The minority report of Congress's official inquiry into the Harpers Ferry affair came to an astonishing conclusion:

> Although some of the testimony tends to show that some abolitionists have at times contributed money to what is occasionally called practical abolitionism—that is, in aiding the escape of slaves—and may have placed too implicit confidence in John Brown ... there is no evidence to show, or cause to believe, they had any complicity with this conspiracy, or any suspicion of its existence or design, before its explosion.... There was no evidence tending to show that there ever was any conspiracy or design, by any one, to rescue John Brown or his associates from prison in Virginia.[69]

The majority report concurred: "It does not appear that ... contributions were made with actual knowledge of the use for which they were designed by Brown, although it does appear that money was freely contributed by those styling themselves friends of this man Brown ... without inquiry as to the way in which the money would be used...."[70] With this publication in late spring of 1860, Brown's friends were publicly exonerated of all complicity in his actions. The panel was chaired by Senator Mason, husband of Margaretta Mason, Lydia Maria Child's irate correspondent.

Few in America were more anxious for the Emancipation Proclamation to come into being than were Brown's literary supporters. Child, never one to "sit on [her] hands and wait," wrote Lincoln, urging him to act in freeing the slaves: "It may seem a violation of propriety for a woman to address the Chief Magistrate of the nation at a crisis so momentous as this," she began, "[but] surely an American woman of the nineteenth century need not apologize for pleading with the rulers of her country in behalf of the poor, the wronged, the cruelly oppressed." Pointedly, she added, "I would respectfully ask how much longer the nation is to wait, paying, meanwhile $2,000,000 a day, and sending thousands of its best and bravest to be stabbed, shot, and hanged by the rebels, whose property they are employed to guard."[71]

On 1 January 1863, Lincoln issued the long-awaited Emancipation Proclamation—the first step in the process that would eventually free the country's slaves. Brown's literary supporters celebrated the historic occasion. During festivities at the Music Hall Emerson read his "Boston Hymn," in which God's voice declares,

> I break your bonds and masterships,
> And I unchain the slave:
> Free be his heart and hand henceforth,
> As wind and wandering wave.[72]

At Tremont Temple, Frederick Douglass led a crowd in the singing of "Blow Ye the Trumpets Blow," Brown's favorite hymn. The jubilation continued into the evening when Emerson, Bronson and Louisa May Alcott, Franklin Sanborn, Julia Ward Howe, Wendell Phillips and William Lloyd Garrison gathered at the home of Maria Child's nephew-in-law, George Stearns. They came to pay tribute to John Brown, honoring one who, in their estimation, helped to bring about the end of slavery[73]

Higginson was not present for the festivities, remaining instead at Camp Saxton, where the proclamation was read to his troops. Upon hearing the words, the black soldiers spontaneously began to sing "My Country 'Tis of Thee." With tears in his eyes, Higginson accepted the colors of the regiment, saying, "It seemed the choked voice of a race at last unloosed."[74]

Of the cast of characters in the verbal assault on Harpers Ferry, only Thoreau did not live to see the liberation of the slaves. Increasingly weakened from consumption, he seemed to withdraw from the events of this world, perhaps in preparation for the next. Nonetheless, friends continued to call. Emerson and Higginson came, as did Sam Staples, who had jailed Thoreau for nonpayment of taxes. Staples reported to Emerson that he "never saw a man dying with so much pleasure and peace."[75] Ellery Channing visited and contended that whenever John Brown's name was mentioned, Thoreau's pulse would accelerate and his hands clench involuntarily, so moved was he by Brown's fate.[76] In the final days, Sanborn stopped by and confessed the true identity of "Mr. Lockwood." Thoreau admitted to Sanborn that he suspected as much and the two shared a laugh as Thoreau recounted his adventures attempting to corral the frantic Harpers Ferry fugitive onto the train. Bronson Alcott, who had stood by Higginson on the courthouse steps, returned for a final visit on the day before Thoreau's death. Upon leaving, he stooped and kissed Thoreau's forehead. "'It was affecting,' said Channing, 'to see this venerable man kissing his brow, when the damps and sweat of death lay upon it, even if Henry knew it not. It seemed to me an extreme unction, in which a friend was the best priest.'"[77]

Nine. Epilogue

This photographic print was published circa 1879. It shows a bearded Henry Thoreau in his later years. Thoreau's beard was not an imitation of Brown's, but rather was a futile attempt to protect his throat from the ravages of the consumption which ultimately took his life on 6 May 1862 (Library of Congress, Prints and Photographs Division).

Although Thoreau lived to see the start of the Civil War, he died shortly thereafter. At Emerson's insistence, a public funeral was held at the First Parish Church in Concord. While some who knew Henry felt he would not have approved, they deferred to Emerson, whose "sorrow was so great he wanted all the world to mourn with him."[78] The service itself was patterned after the one Thoreau had designed for John Brown less than two years before, with Bronson Alcott reading selections from Henry's works and Ellery Channing penning stanzas to be sung.[79] Emerson gave the eulogy, in which he praised Thoreau's courageous defense of Brown, saying, "Before the first friendly word had been spoken for Captain John Brown, [Thoreau] sent notices to most houses in Concord, that he ... would speak."[80]

Shortly after the raid, Brown's daughters journeyed to Concord, where they enrolled in Sanborn's school in February 1860 and lived for a time with the Emersons. They also linked Thoreau to Brown, confiding in Alcott that Thoreau reminded them of their father. And legend has it, in a gesture which perhaps only Thoreau or Brown would have recognized as deeply symbolic, the Brown family, in recognition of his assistance, presented Thoreau with a huge knife that had once belonged to his hero, Captain John Brown.[81]

—

In one of history's ironies, time has distanced Brown's ghost from the spirits of his literary supporters. Over the last century and a half, the verbal assault on Harpers Ferry, as executed by a small group of American writers, has for many years all but disappeared from the public consciousness. Today, Emerson is best remembered as the father of American literary transcendentalism, while Higginson calls to mind not Brown, but Emily Dickinson. Douglass's autobiographical *Narrative* is taught in high schools throughout the country, enshrining him as the courageous slave who confronted the cruel overseer,

Mr. Covey. Annually, at Thanksgiving, we make passing notice of Child's children's verse "Over the River and Through the Woods," although other, more literary admirers will credit her as editor of Harriet Jacobs' *Incidents in the Life of a Slave Girl*. And in a final irony of the raid, Thoreau is remembered less for his association with the violent Brown than for *Civil Disobedience*, a treatise often cited as an inspiration for the peaceful protests of Mahatma Gandhi and the Rev. Dr. Martin Luther King, Jr.

And yet, to a person, these writers would be stunned at this turn of events. For in the fall of 1859 and the winter of 1860, at that time and in that place, they turned their pens with an unparalleled intensity to an almost impossible task, the resurrection of Brown. For a few brief months, "When the sword glitter[ed] o'er the judges head/And fear ha[d] coward churchmen silenced," they rose as a chorus to defend Brown, deftly separating man from means and motive from method. It was the poet's time.

But for all their efforts, were Brown's literary supporters successful in *their* raid on Harpers Ferry, a volley waged not with pikes or broadswords but with words and images? One might ask Thoreau, who perhaps foresaw more clearly than his fellow writers the implications of, and possibilities within, their creation of a martyred Brown. On 22 October 1859, a mere three days after John Brown's ostensibly failed raid on the engine house, Thoreau perhaps spoke for them all when he predicted of the events at Harpers Ferry:

> I foresee the time when the painter will paint that scene, the poet will sing it, the historian record it, and, with the Landing of the Pilgrims and the Declaration of Independence, it will be the ornament of some future national gallery, when the present form of slavery shall be no more. We shall then be at liberty to weep for John Brown. Then and not till then we will take our revenge.[82]

TIMELINE

1800	John Brown is born.
1802	Lydia Maria Francis (Child) is born.
1803	Ralph Waldo Emerson is born.
1817	Henry David Thoreau is born in Concord, Massachusetts.
1818	Frederick Douglass is born.
1823	Thomas Wentworth Storrow Higginson is born in Cambridge on the street "down which the provincial troops marched to the Battle of Bunker Hill."
1824	Child's *Hobomok*, a startling tale of miscegenation is published in May.
	Child publishes *Evenings in New England* in which she reveals some of her earliest thoughts on the slavery question.
1826	Child begins editing first children's magazine in the United States, *The Juvenile Miscellany*.
1828	Child marries lawyer David Lee Child, whose various enterprises, ensuing lawsuits and charitable causes will leave the couple penniless.
1829	Child publishes *The Frugal Housewife*, the first cost saving book of household hints written solely for American women.
1831	William Lloyd Garrison's *Liberator* goes to press, saved by a $54 subscription contribution from James Forten, a black abolitionist.
1833	Child's controversial *Appeal in Behalf of That Class of Americans Called Africans* appears in August and "startles the country."
1834	Child forced to give up editorship of *Juvenile Miscellany* as a result of unfavorable public response to *Appeal*. Undaunted, she publishes a second antislavery book, *The Oasis*.
1835	Child and a group of women escort British abolitionist George Thompson from an antislavery address in Boston amidst threats of violence.
1835	William Ellery Channing in *Slavery* condemns the practice.
	Ralph Waldo Emerson marries Lidian Jackson and moves to Concord, Massachusetts.
1837	Child and two-hundred like-minded women come together in New York to establish the "first Anti-Slavery Convention of American Women."
	Emerson publicly addresses slavery question for the first time at an address in Second Church in Concord.
1838	Frederick Douglass escapes from slavery, settles in New Bedford, Massachusetts.
	Emerson delivers his "Appeal on Behalf of the Cherokees" address in Concord, considered a significant step in his reform consciousness (April 22).
	Emerson expresses outrage at forced relocation of Cherokees in a letter to United States President Martin Van Buren (April 23).
1840	Thoreau writes unpublished piece "The Service," discussing the relationship of the individual to society.
1841	Higginson graduates from Harvard at fourteen, the youngest in his class.
	Child and husband, David, accept editorship of the *National Anti-Slavery Standard*. The majority of the responsibility will fall to Maria, while David tends to his failing beet business.

	Douglass delivers first antislavery remarks at a black church in New Bedford and is approached to become an antislavery lecturer.
1841	Douglass is asked to leave his first-class seat on the Eastern Railroad and is forcibly removed. He returns a week later and is again evicted, but this time holds the seat so firmly it is ripped from the floor.
1842	Subscriptions to the *National Anti-Slavery Standard* double from previous year, since Child's assumed leadership.
	Douglass speaks at annual meeting of New England (Anti-Slavery) Society.
1843	Thoreau's "Paradise to Be Regained" reiterates view that reform comes from individual change and that political systems limit individual freedom.
1844	Nathaniel P. Rodgers, editor of the *Herald of Freedom*, responds to Thoreau's earlier, positive review, saying Thoreau must be a "German" to take "notice of the most odious and despised publication of the time."
	Emerson's friends, the Hoars, travel to South Carolina, from which they must flee for their safety. On December 17, Emerson sends letter to *New York Daily Tribune* praising their courage and articulating circumstances surrounding their departure.
1845	Emerson delivers speech, "Address on the Emancipation of the Negroes in the British West Indies," at invitation of Concord Women's Anti-Slavery Society. The speech is generally considered to mark his entrance into the abolitionist movement (August 1).
	Emerson and Thoreau forcefully defend abolitionist Wendell Phillips' right to speak at Concord Lyceum. *Thoreau* sends anonymous but forceful letter to *Liberator* defending Phillips (March 28).
	Emerson delivers his second major antislavery address in Waltham, Massachusetts, at the anniversary of West Indian Emancipation (August).
	The *Narrative of the Life of* Frederick Douglass is published by the American Anti-Slavery Society in May 1845. By fall, it has sold 5,000 copies at 50 cents each. The *National Anti-Slavery Standard* reviews Douglass's *Narrative*, saying, "It is the story of the life of a man of great intellectual power."
1846	Thoreau spends his famous night in jail for nonpayment of taxes as a protest of the Mexican war (July).
	Bronson Alcott, friend and neighbor of both Emerson and Thoreau, harbors a fugitive slave in his home (December).
1848	Thoreau delivers a lecture entitled "The Relation of the Individual to the State" in response to neighbors' questions about his night in jail. The lecture will later be published as *Civil Disobedience* (January 26).
	Higginson becomes active in politics, championing the Free Soil party.
	Higginson preaches his "Man Shall Not Live by Bread Alone" sermon castigating church members for their antislavery views and their lukewarm reception of Frederick Douglass (November 30). Less than a week later, Higginson finds himself defending the choice of Emerson as speaker at the Newburyport lyceum.
1849	Higginson and wife, Mary, journey to Concord and meet Thoreau.
1850	Passage of Fugitive Slave Law, which mandates that fugitive slaves be returned to their owners, even from the free states (September 18). Emerson calls the law "a filthy enactment," while Higginson urges "Disobey it."
1851	Fugitive slave Shadrach is arrested in Boston under auspices of the Fugitive Slave Law. Higginson joins the vigilance committee. Emerson provides letter of protest dated March 18.
	Fugitive slave Thomas Sims is arrested in Boston. Higginson plans an unsuccessful rescue (April).
	Emerson delivers his first Fugitive Slave Law speech, "Address to the Citizens of Concord" (May 3).

	Emerson campaigns for Free Soil candidate John G. Palfrey, who goes on to lose the election but carries Concord by sixty-eight votes (May).
1852	Higginson accepts call to be minister at Free Church in Worcester, Massachusetts
	Douglass delivers the most famous antislavery speech of his life, entitled "What to the Slave Is the Fourth of July?" (July 5).
	Emerson contributes funds to Boston Vigilance Committee (November).
1853	Douglass publishes a novella, *The Heroic Slave*, whose hero is the preeminent figure in a violent slave uprising.
1854	Emerson delivers his second Fugitive Slave Law speech at the New York Tabernacle on the fourth anniversary of Webster's speech endorsing the Compromise of 1850 (March 7).
	Douglass delivers an address entitled "We Are in the Midst of a Moral Revolution" to a large audience at the Broadway Tabernacle in New York (May 10).
	Fugitive slave Anthony Burns is arrested in Boston (May 25). Higginson batters down courthouse door in an attempt at rescue.
	Higginson preaches sermon entitled "Massachusetts in Mourning," saying, "I am grateful for every additional gun and saber that forces the truth deeper into our hearts" (June 4).
	Emerson crafts new antislavery address in response and delivers it in Boston on 25 January 1855 and then in Worcester, New York, Philadelphia, Syracuse and elsewhere.
	Douglass, in his *Frederick Douglass Paper*, describes Kansas as a "hell-bent scheme for extending human bondage" and encourages emigrants be "sent out to possess the goodly land" (April 14).
	Kansas-Nebraska Act opens possibility that new territories could become slave states (May 25).
	Waldo and Lidian Emerson attend public protest in Concord over return of fugitive slave Anthony Burns (July).
	Thoreau delivers an address entitled "Slavery in Massachusetts" in which he utters the now-famous line, "My thoughts are murder to the State, and involuntarily go plotting against her" (July 4).
	Brown, with son Oliver and son-in-law Henry Thompson, joins sons Owen, Frederick, Salmon, Jason and John, Jr., in Kansas (October 6).
	Higginson helps rescue Boston policeman, Asa Butman, from angry mob in Worcester (October 29).
1855	John Brown, Jr., in lengthy letter to Douglass confides fear that a free Kansas would mean freedom for whites only (August).
1856	Senator Charles Sumner is beaten by southern congressman Preston Brooks, an event which galvanizes Thoreau, Emerson, Child, Higginson and Brown (May 19).
	Brown and sons drag five men from homes at Pottawatomie in the night and kill them (May 24).
	Emerson donates $50 to the Free State Cause (June).
	Frederick Brown killed by pro-slavery forces at Osawatomie (August 30).
	Higginson leaves for Kansas as an agent of the National Kansas Committee in a trip that will be chronicled by letters to the *New York Tribune* and later in a pamphlet entitled "A Ride Through Kansas" (September).
	Emerson speaks at Kansas relief meeting in Cambridge, urging his audience to "give largely, lavishly" towards the purchase of Sharp's rifles (September).
	Child writes *The Kansas Emigrants*, a piece serialized in the *New York Tribune* (November) and sews garments for Free State settlers.
1857	Brown speaks in Concord in March and Emerson and Thoreau meet him for the first time. Emerson gives $50, Thoreau's father gives $10, and Sanborn gives $100. Thoreau, annoyed because Brown will not outline his plans for the money, contributes only a "trifle" (March 12).

	Brown attacks and defeats two dozen Missourians on the Missouri-Kansas border (June 2).
1858	Higginson receives his first letter from John Brown (February 2) and responds on February 8: "I am always ready to invest money in treason, but at present have none to invest."
	Brown finalizes plans for Harpers Ferry, writing constitution while visiting Frederick Douglass. He also writes supporters, including Higginson, whom he tells he is involved in "By far the most *important* undertaking of my whole life" (February).
1859	Brown returns to Concord and gives lecture in town hall. Emerson, Thoreau and Sanborn are present (May 8).
	Higginson chafes at delay in Brown's enterprise as a result of Hugh Forbes's threats of exposure (June 1).
	Sanborn writes Higginson that "Brown has set out on his expedition" (June 4).
	Douglass and Shields Green meet with Brown at quarry in Chambersburg, Pennsylvania. Green agrees to accompany Brown on the raid, Douglass does not, a claim that is later disputed (Fall).
October 16	John Brown and twenty-one followers seize the federal arsenal at Harpers Ferry.
	Sanborn leaves for Canada October 18.
	Stearns and Howe leave for Canada October 25.
	Gerrit Smith checks into Utica Asylum for the Insane November 7.
	Douglass leaves for Canada.
	Higginson stands firm in Worcester, writing Sanborn, "Is there no such thing as *honor* among confederates?"
	Brown, feeble and still recovering from his wounds, is charged with "conspiring with Negroes to produce insurrection" and murder in the first degree (October 24).
	Child writes Brown and Wise asking permission to nurse the prisoner. To Brown, she says, "Believing in peace principles I cannot sympathize with the method you chose to advance the cause of freedom" (October 26).
	Higginson helps secure counsel for Brown, but attorney George H. Hoyt is also charged with determining Brown's position on rescue. He reports that Brown "positively refused his consent to any such plan" (October 28).
	An aroused Thoreau delivers his speech "The Character of John Brown, Now in the Clutches of the Slaveholder" to neighbors in Concord, Massachusetts (October 30).
	At 1:45 P.M., the Brown case goes to a Virginia jury. A scant forty-five minutes later, the jury returns a guilty verdict (October 31).
	Douglass writes supporters from "Canada West," saying, "I have always been more distinguished for running than fighting" (October 31).
	Higginson leaves for New York to recruit Mrs. Brown in efforts to persuade her husband to accept a rescue (November 2).
	John Brown sentenced to death in a Virginia courtroom (November 2).
	Emerson and Higginson lend their names to a flyer to raise money for Brown family (November 2).
	Thoreau delivers his "Plea for Captain John Brown" in Boston to a packed auditorium and challenges the press "Do yourselves the honor to recognize him."
	Child receives reply from Governor Wise advising she was welcome to come nurse Brown in prison, although warning, "A few unenlightened and inconsiderate persons, fanatical in their modes of thought and action ... might molest you...." (November 3). Child responds to Wise: "You inform me that I have a constitutional right to visit Virginia.... I was perfectly well aware that such was the *theory*."
	Child's note appears in *Liberator* above review of Thoreau's *Plea* in which she

refers to Brown as a "Brave old man!" (November 4). All of Boston's major newspapers carry reports of Thoreau's *Plea*, while the *Liberator*, as if in response to Thoreau's demand, carries extensively expanded coverage of the affair.

Governor Wise appoints a special prosecutor to indict Douglass (November 6).

Emerson delivers speech entitled "Courage," in which he unleashes a furor by describing Brown as a "new saint ... who, if he shall suffer, will make the gallows glorious like the cross." The statement will be widely condemned as blasphemous by pro-slavery forces (November 8).

Child writes the editor of the *Tribune*, claiming surprise that her correspondence with Wise appeared in the paper: "As I have never given any person a copy, I presume you must have obtained it from Virginia" (November 10).

Margaretta Mason, wife of Senator Mason of Virginia, scathingly attacks Child in a letter saying, "Do you read your Bible, Mrs. Child? If you do, read there, 'Woe unto you, hypocrites,' and take to yourself with twofold damnation," a pronouncement Higginson declares came "very near to swearing for a lady" (November 11).

Higginson, with Le Barnes and Spooner, plans to kidnap Wise and hold him in exchange for Brown (mid–November).

Douglass defends his decision to go to Europe, saying, "At the present moment Slavery seems to have gained an advantage." Black abolitionist J. Sella Martin chastises Douglass for "writing from the broad latitude of Canada West" (November).

Governor Wise of Virginia writes United States President Buchanan saying he had made a requisition to Michigan for "delivery up of the person of Frederick Douglass, supposed now to be in Michigan, charged with murder, robbery, and inciting servile insurrection" (November 13).

Emerson takes to the platform at Tremont Temple in Boston with a lecture entitled "Speech at a Meeting to Aid Brown's Family." Speaking to a full house, he calls upon those present to be "abolitionists of the most absolute abolition." He also donates $50 to Brown's family (November 18).

Thoreau and Sanborn dine with Alcott. Sanborn urges Alcott to go to Virginia and seek access to Brown and Wise. While there, he could "ascertain whether Brown would accept a rescue from any company we might raise" (November 19).

Le Barnes writes Higginson of a second rescue plan—this one an overland, direct attack on the prison—saying, "The men are ready and determined" (November 27).

Higginson concedes rescue is impossible. Sanborn writes, "I guess we must give up all hope of saving our old friend" (November 28).

Thoreau calls meeting in Concord Town Hall to arrange memorial service for Brown. Emerson is present (November 28).

John Brown is executed December 2. In the early morning hours, a lifesize effigy of Brown is hung in front of the Concord Town Hall with "behests" to Emerson and Thoreau attached to the "body" (December 2).

At Brown's memorial service in Concord, Thoreau and Emerson take part (December 2).

Child eschews a large memorial service she helped plan at Faneuil Hall, opting instead to spend the day at a prayer meeting in an African American Church (December 2).

Blacks in Worcester elect not to work from 11:00 A.M. to 3:00 P.M. on the day of Brown's execution in support of their fallen hero (December 2).

In Virginia, Brown is hanged, guarded by "Continentals ... dressed in buckskin suits of the days of 1776 [with] other companies in equally picturesque raiment." Among those witnessing the execution were Robert E. Lee and John Wilkes Booth (December 2).

One of the Harpers Ferry conspirators, Francis Merriam, shows up on Sanborn's doorstep. Sanborn borrows a wagon from Emerson and Thoreau drives Merriam to the train station, thus becoming what one historian calls "an accessory after the fact of Harpers Ferry" (December 3).

Child attends lecture by Emerson entitled "Morals" at the Parker Fraternity and writes Mrs. Mason that "Emerson ... leaves the scholastic seclusion he loves so well, and disliking noise with all his poetic soul, bravely takes his stand among the trumpeteers" (December 4).

Frederick Douglass shares a speaker's platform in England with old abolitionist friends. In an address "remarkably optimistic," he doesn't utter a word about John Brown (December 7).

Higginson plans rescue for Brown's accomplices Hazlett and Stevens (December 13).

Four of Brown's raiders hanged (Copeland, Green, Coppoc and Cook) (December 16).

Child responds to Mrs. Mason's letter. In answer to Mason's question as to whether women in the North "soften[ed] the pangs of maternity" in those around them, Child retorted, "I have never known an instance where the 'pangs of maternity' did not meet with requisite assistance, and here at the North, after we have helped the mothers, *we do not sell the babies*" (December 17).

Governor Wise receives thunderous applause in a speech to medical students in Richmond when he vows, "Oh if I had had one good ... well-armed steamer [Douglass] should have been taken ... with very particular instructions not to hang him before I had the privilege of seeing him well hung" (December 21).

1860   Emerson speaks in Salem to raise money for Brown's family (January 6).

Child's correspondence with Wise and Mason is published in pamphlet form, achieving a circulation of 300,000 copies in an era where a typical best-selling book might run to 8,000. The pamphlet, provides, by far, the largest readership of Child's career (January).

Douglass mentions Brown in an Edinburgh lecture entitled "John Brown and the Slaveholders' Insurrection," calling him a "martyr" and a "brave, heroic and Christian man" (end of January).

Thoreau, Emerson, Child and Higginson provide material for James Redpath's *The Public Life of Captain John Brown*. The work, painting Brown as a hero and martyr, is dedicated to Thoreau, Emerson and Wendell Phillips.

Albert Hazlett and Arron Dwight Stevens go to trial for acts at Harpers Ferry (February 2).

Upon the death of his beloved daughter, Anna, Douglass begins journey back to New York, returning home to a country with "decidedly different views on Brown than the one he left" (March 13).

Albert Hazlett and Aaron Dwight are executed for their part in the raid in spite of Higginson's plans for rescue (March 16).

United States marshals attempt to arrest Sanborn. He is saved from arrest by Concord citizens, among them Thoreau and Emerson (April 3).

Thoreau sends remarks for Brown's eulogy in an essay entitled "The Last Days of John Brown," commenting on the fact that "Years were not required for a revolution of public opinion; day, nay hours, produced marked changes in this case.... They all called him crazy then; who calls him crazy now?" The speech was published in the *Liberator* on July 27.

1861   Emerson attempts to speak at Massachusetts Anti-Slavery Society gathering at Tremont Temple but is drowned out by the crowd. Child is in attendance and

	said, "It was a full realization of the old phrase 'All hell broke loose'" (January 24).
	Confederate artillery open fire on the federal fort in Sumter, South Carolina (April 12).
1862	Thoreau dies on May 6.
	Higginson takes command of the first black regiment of the Civil War.
1863	President Lincoln issues the Emancipation Proclamation June 1, freeing the slaves of the Confederate states.
1866	Four years after Thoreau's death, "Civil Disobedience" is published.
1880	Lydia Maria Child dies on July 7.
1881	Ralph Waldo Emerson dies on April 27.
1895	Frederick Douglass dies on February 20.
1911	Thomas Wentworth Higginson dies on May 9.

Chapter Notes

Chapter One

1. United States Senate, "Mason Report: Select Committee on the Events at Harper's Ferry, Virginia" (1860), in *Mass Violence in America: Invasion at Harper's Ferry* (New York: Arno, 1969) 6.
2. Osborne P. Anderson, *A Voice from Harpers Ferry* (1861; repr., Freeport, NY: Books for Libraries Press, 1972), 28–29.
3. Jeffrey Rossbach, *Ambivalent Conspirators: John Brown, the Secret Six, and a Theory of Slave Violence* (Philadelphia: University of Pennsylvania Press, 1982), 215.
4. Thomas Featherstonhaugh, *John Brown's Men: The Lives of Those Killed at Harper's Ferry* (Harrisburg, PA: Harrisburg Publishing, 1899), 8.
5. Anderson, *Voice*, 32.
6. Ibid.
7. Oswald Garrison Villard, *John Brown, 1800–1859: A Biography Fifty Years After* (1910; repr., New York: Knopf, 1943), 430; Anderson, *Voice from Harpers Ferry*, 33.
8. Anderson, *Voice*, 33.
9. Ibid., 34.
10. Ibid., 34–35.
11. Ibid., 35.
12. Villard, *John Brown*, 431–32.
13. United States Senate, "Journal of the Select Committee into the Invasion of the United States Armory at Harper's Ferry," in *Mass Violence in America: Invasion at Harper's Ferry*, 36th Cong., 1st sess., ed. Robert M. Fogelson and Richard E. Rubenstein (1860; New York: Arno, 1969), 34.
14. United States, "Mason Report," 4–5.
15. Quoted in Villard, *John Brown*, 433.
16. Ibid., 434.
17. Joseph Barry, *The Strange Story of Harper's Ferry* (1903; repr., Shepherdstown, WV: Woman's Club of Harpers Ferry District, 1969), 50.
18. George Mauzy, Letter to "Mr. and Mrs. James H. Burton," 3 December 1859, ed. David T. Gilbert, 2 June 2005, Harpers Ferry National Historical Park, www.nps.gov/hafe/historyculture/the-mauzy-letters.htm (accessed 1 September 2008).
19. Anderson, *Voice*, 36.
20. Quoted in United States, Dept. of Interior, *John Brown's Raid* (Washington: GPO, 1974), 27.
21. Anderson, *Voice*, 37.
22. Edward J. Renehan, Jr., *The Secret Six: The True Tale of the Men Who Conspired with John Brown* (New York: Crown, 1995), 199–200.
23. Anderson, *Voice*, 39–40.
24. Joseph Barry, *Strange Story*, 81–82.
25. Benjamin Quarles, *Allies for Freedom: Blacks and John Brown* (New York: Oxford University Press, 1974), 96.
26. Renehan, *The Secret Six*, 202.
27. United States, *John Brown's Raid*, 35; Barry, 53.
28. United States, *John Brown's Raid*, 35.
29. Quoted in Featherstonhaugh, 9.
30. United States, *John Brown's Raid*, 37.
31. Anderson, *Voice*, 43.
32. Quarles, *Allies*, 97.
33. United States, *John Brown's Raid*, 39.
34. Quarles, *Allies*, 97.
35. United States, *John Brown's Raid*, 43–44.
36. Qtd. in Villard, *John Brown*, 453.
37. Ibid.
38. United States, "Mason Report," 7, 40.
39. Henry David Thoreau, *A Plea for Captain John Brown: The Major Essays of Henry David Thoreau*, ed. Richard Dillman (1860; Albany: Whitston, 2001), 101.

Chapter Two

1. John Brown, Letter to Henry L. Stearns, 15 July 1857, in *John Brown: The Making of a Revolutionary*, by Louis Ruchames (New York: Grossett, 1971), 46.
2. United States, Dept. of Interior, *John Brown's Raid* (Washington: GPO, 1974), 5.
3. David S. Reynolds, *John Brown: Abolitionist* (New York: Knopf, 2005), 40.
4. Frederick Douglass, "An Address by Frederick Douglass at the Fourteenth Anniversary of Storer College, Harpers Ferry, West Virginia, May 30, 1881" (Dover, NH: Morning Star, 1881), 19.
5. Stephen Oates, *Our Fiery Trial: Abraham Lincoln, John Brown, and the Civil War* (Amherst: University of Massachusetts Press, 1979), 9.
6. Qtd. in Benjamin Quarles, *Black Abolitionists* (London: Oxford University Press, 1969), 236.
7. John Brown, Letter to "Father," 10 January 1849, in *John Brown: The Making of a Revolutionary*, by Louis Ruchames (New York: Grossett and Dunlap, 1971), 75.
8. William S. McFeely, *Frederick Douglass* (New York: Norton, 1991), 186.
9. Sam'l Lawrence, Letter to Charles Hovey, 30 October 1874, ts., John Brown Papers, 1 (Massachusetts Historical Society, Boston).
10. United States, *John Brown's Raid*, 6.
11. McFeely, *Frederick Douglass*, 186.

12. Qtd. in Thomas Wentworth Higginson, *Contemporaries* (Boston: Houghton Mifflin, 1899), 242.
13. Lawrence, letter, 2.
14. John Brown, Jr., *John Brown of Asawatomie—A History Not an Apology,* 1883, A35 Folder 6, Franklin Benjamin Sanborn Papers Series II, ms, 1, Concord Free Public Library, Concord.
15. John Brown, Letter to Ruth and Henry Thompson, 30 September 1854, in *John Brown: The Making of a Revolutionary,* by Louis Ruchames (New York: Grossett, 1971), 94.
16. Brown, Jr., *John Brown,* 4–5.
17. Qtd. in Brown, Jr., *John Brown,* 5.
18. Brown, Jr., *John Brown,* 7–9.
19. Louis Ruchames, *John Brown: The Making of a Revolutionary* (New York: Grossett and Dunlap 1971), 95.
20. Ibid., 30.
21. Qtd. in Ruchames, *John Brown,* 30.
22. Qtd. in Villard, *John Brown,* 151–53.
23. Ibid., 154.
24. Villard, *John Brown,* 160.
25. Qtd. in Villard, *John Brown,* 161.
26. Villard, *John Brown,* 161.
27. Ibid., 163–64.
28. Qtd. in Villard, *John Brown,* 165.
29. Brown, Jr., *John Brown,* 16–17.
30. As Reynolds notes, "The historical record indicates that the proslavery side committed most acts of violence. Of the fifty-two who died in the Kansas slavery battles of 1855 to 1858, almost 75 percent were Free State settlers. Of the thirty-six Free State casualties, twenty-eight were murders; the remaining eight occurred during battle. In contrast only eight on the proslavery side were murdered. Among the rest, five died in battle, two were killed accidentally by their own violence, and one was shot when he disturbed a Free State meeting" (163).
31. Mahala Doyle, Letter to Amos A. Lawrence, 26 May 1885, ms, John Brown Collection, 1–2, Massachusetts Historical Society, Boston.
32. Brown, Jr., *John Brown,* 20–21.
33. Ruchames, *John Brown,* 33.
34. United States, *John Brown's Raid,* 6.
35. Carlos Baker, *Emerson among the Eccentrics: A Group Portrait* (New York: Viking, 1996), 380.
36. Benjamin Quarles, *Allies for Freedom: Blacks and John Brown* (New York: Oxford University Press, 1974), 33.
37. Quarles, *Allies,* 35.
38. John Brown, Letter to "Dear Wife and Children Every One," 7 September 1856, Personal papers, folder 1.17, John Brown Papers, microfilm MS 1425, 2, Kansas State Historical Society.
39. Ruchames, *John Brown,* 34.
40. John Brown, "Old Brown's Farewell to the Plymouth Rocks, Bunker Hill Monuments, Charter Oaks, and Uncle Tom's Cabbins [sic]," April 1857, Personal papers, folder 1.22, John Brown's Papers, microfilm MS 1245, 1, Kansas State Historical Society.
41. Brown, "Old Brown's Farewell," 1, Boston Public Library, Boston.
42. Renehan, *The Secret Six,* 117.
43. Ruchames, *John Brown,* 35.
44. Quarles, *Allies,* 61; James Redpath, *The Public Life of Capt. John Brown* (Boston: Thayer and Eldridge, 1860), 239.
45. Oates, *Trial,* 10.
46. Ruchames, *John Brown,* 35.
47. Thomas Featherstonhaugh, *John Brown's Men: The Lives of Those Killed at Harper's Ferry* (Harrisburg, PA: Harrisburg Publishing, 1899), 6.
48. Qtd. in Featherstonhaugh, *John Brown's Men,* 7.
49. Featherstonhaugh, *John Brown's Men,* 6–7.
50. United States, *John Brown's Raid* 23.
51. Ibid.

Chapter Three

1. Qtd. in Edward Waldo Emerson, *Emerson in Concord: A Memoir Written for the "Social Circle" in Concord* (Boston: Houghton Mifflin; Cambridge: Riverside, 1888), 83.
2. Qtd. in William Lloyd Garrison, *The Letters of William Lloyd Garrison 1850–1860,* ed. Louis Ruchames, 6 vol. (Cambridge: Harvard University Press, 1975), 3, note on 10.
3. Thomas Wentworth Higginson, *Contemporaries* (Boston: Houghton Mifflin, 1899), 330–31.
4. Ibid., 331.
5. Ralph Waldo Emerson, *The Journals and Miscellaneous Notebooks of Ralph Waldo Emerson,* ed. Merton Sealts, 13 vols. (Cambridge: Harvard University Press, 1965), 9: 120.
6. Qtd. in Len Gougeon, *Virtue's Hero: Emerson, Antislavery, and Reform* (Athens: University of Georgia Press, 1990), 24.
7. Gougeon, *Virtue's Hero,* 24.
8. William Ellery Channing, *Slavery* (Boston: James Munroe, 1835), 1.
9. Ralph Waldo Emerson, *Journals and Miscellaneous Notebooks* 5: 150.
10. Channing, *Slavery,* 128.
11. Qtd. in Gougeon, *Virtue's Hero,* 42.
12. Samuel J. May, "Antislavery Conflict," in *Some Recollections of Our Antislavery Conflict* (1869; repr., New York: Arno, 1968), 129.
13. Qtd. in Gougeon, *Virtue's Hero,* 4.
14. Sallee Fox Engstrom, *The Infinitude of the Private Man: Emerson's Presence in Western New York, 1851–1861* (New York: Lang, 1997), 7.
15. Len Gougeon, "Abolition, the Emersons and 1837," *The New England Quarterly* 54.3 (1981): 351.
16. Len Gougeon, "Historical Background," *Emerson's Antislavery Writings* (New Haven: Yale University Press, 1995), xiii.
17. Qtd. in Annie Russell Marble, *Thoreau His Home, Friends and Books* (1902; repr., New York: AMS, 1969), 18–19.
18. Ibid., 18.
19. T.W. Higginson, *Contemporaries* 13.
20. Ralph Waldo Emerson, *Journals and Miscellaneous Notebooks* 5: 505.
21. Gougeon, "Abolition," 348–49.
22. R.W. Emerson, *Journals* 5: 32.
23. Qtd. in Edward Emerson, *Emerson in Concord,* 74.
24. T.W. Higginson, *Contemporaries,* 9.
25. Qtd. in Engstrom, *Infinitude,* 26.
26. R.W. Emerson, *Journals and Miscellaneous Notebooks* 12: 152; 5: 437.
27. Lidian Jackson Emerson, "To Sophia Brown," 9 September 1837, in *The Selected Letters of Lidian Jackson*

Notes—Chapter Three

Emerson, ed. Delores Bird Carpenter (Columbia: University of Missouri Press, 1987), 61.

28. Delores Bird Carpenter, introduction, in *The Selected Letters of Lidian Jackson Emerson*, by Lidian Jackson Emerson (Columbia: University of Missouri Press, 1987), xvi; Sandra Harbert Petrulionis, "'Swelling That Great Tide of Humanity': The Concord, Massachusetts, Female Anti-Slavery Society," *New England Quarterly* 74, no. 3 (2001): 404.
29. R.W. Emerson, *Journals* 5: 15.
30. Ibid., 5: 437.
31. Qtd. in Gougeon, "Historical Background," xvi.
32. Ibid., xvi-xvii.
33. Gougeon, "Abolition," 345.
34. Qtd. in Gougeon, "Historical Background," xvii.
35. Qtd. in Edward Emerson, *Emerson in Concord* 85.
36. Carpenter, introduction, *Selected Letters*, xvii.
37. Lidian Jackson Emerson, "To Lucy Jackson Brown," 23 Apr. 1838, *The Selected Letters of Lidian Jackson Emerson*, ed. Delores Bird Carpenter (Columbia: University of Missouri Press, 1987), 74.
38. R.W. Emerson, *Journals* 5: 479.
39. Engstrom, *Infinitude*, 28.
40. Lidian Emerson, "To Lucy Jackson Brown" [June 1838], 76.
41. Len Gougeon, "Emerson and Abolition: The Silent Years, 1837–1844," *American Literature* 54.4 (1982): 569.
42. Edward Emerson, *Emerson in Concord*, 87.
43. John Carlos Rowe, *At Emerson's Tomb: The Politics of Classic American Literature* (New York: Columbia University Press, 1997), 18.
44. R.W. Emerson, *Journals* 8: 185.
45. Engstrom, *Infinitude*, 50.
46. Petrulionis, "Swelling," 387.
47. Qtd. in Petrulionis, "Swelling," 389.
48. Gougeon, "Historical Background," xxiii.
49. Ralph Waldo Emerson, *The Complete Works of Ralph Waldo Emerson, Essays*, 2d series, vol. 3, ed. Edward Waldo Emerson (Boston: Houghton Mifflin, 1903–1904), 265, 267, 353.
50. Rowe, 25; Petrulionis, "Swelling," 395.
51. Qtd. in Wendell P. Glick, "Thoreau and the 'Herald of Freedom,'" *The New England Quarterly* 22, no. 2 (1949): 201.
52. Engstrom, *Infinitude*, 30.
53. Rowe, *Emerson's Tomb*, 21.
54. Ralph Waldo Emerson, "Address on the Emancipation of the Negroes in the British West Indies," *Emerson's Antislavery Writings*, ed. Len Gougeon and Joel Myerson (New Haven: Yale University Press, 1995), 9–10.
55. Gougeon, "Historical Background," xxx.
56. Ralph Waldo Emerson, "My Dear Friend," 31 December 1844, in *The Correspondence of Emerson and Carlyle*, ed. Joseph Slater (New York: Columbia University Press, 1964), 373.
57. Ralph Waldo Emerson, "To John Greenleaf Whittier," 13 September 1844, in *The Letters of Ralph Waldo Emerson*, ed. Ralph L. Rusk, 6 vols. (New York: Columbia University Press, 1939), 3: 261.
58. E. Emerson, *Emerson in Concord*, 76.
59. R.W. Emerson, *Journals* 9: 173.
60. Gougeon, "Historical Background," xxxi.
61. Gougeon, "Virtue's Hero," 16.
62. Engstrom, *Infinitude*, 32.
63. Wesley T. Mott, "Emerson and the New Bedford Affair in Boston Newspapers," *Emerson Society Papers* 3, no. 1 (1992): 3.
64. Ibid., note no. 4.
65. Gougeon, "Historical Background," xx.
66. Ibid., xxxii–xxxv.
67. Qtd. in Walter Harding, *The Days of Henry Thoreau: A Biography* (Princeton: Princeton University Press, 1992), 205.
68. Ralph Waldo Emerson, *Journals of Ralph Waldo Emerson*, ed. Edward Waldo Emerson and Waldo Emerson Forbes, 10 vols. (Boston: Houghton Mifflin, 1903–1914), 7:221.
69. Ibid., 9:447.
70. Qtd. in Harding, *The Days of Henry Thoreau: A Biography* (Princeton: Princeton University Press, 1992), 205–06.
71. Walter Harding, *The Days*, 206.
72. R.W. Emerson, *Journals* 9: 445.
73. Francis B. Dedmond, "A Fugitive Emerson Letter," *The American Transcendental Quarterly* 41 (1979): 15.
74. Qtd. in Dedmond, "A Fugitive," 15.
75. Petrulionis, "Swelling," 401.
76. Benjamin Quarles, *The Negro in the Making of America* (New York: Simon, 1964), 107.
77. R.W. Emerson, *Journals* 11: 412.
78. Rowe, *Emerson's Tomb*, 30.
79. Ralph Waldo Emerson, "Address to the Citizens of Concord," in *Emerson's Antislavery Writings*, ed. Len Gougeon and Joel Myerson (New Haven: Yale University Press, 1995), 53.
80. E. Emerson, *Emerson in Concord*, 78.
81. Ralph Waldo Emerson, "The Fugitive Slave Law," in *Emerson's Antislavery Writings*, ed. Len Gougeon and Joel Myerson (New Haven: Yale University Press, 1995), 78.
82. E. Emerson, *Emerson in Concord*, 77.
83. Qtd. in Robert D. Richardson, Jr., *Emerson: The Mind on Fire* (Berkeley: University of California Press, 1995), 498.
84. Engstrom, *Infinitude*, 34.
85. Qtd. in Mary Kupiec Cayton, "The Making of an American Prophet," in *Ralph Waldo Emerson: A Collection of Critical Essays*, ed. Lawrence Buell (Englewood Cliffs: Prentice Hall, 1993), 97.
86. Frank Preston Stearns, "From Sketches from Concord and Appledore (1895)," in *Emerson in His Own Time*, ed. Ronald A. Bosco and Joel Myerson (Iowa City: University of Iowa Press, 2003), 207.
87. Qtd. in Stearns, "Sketches," 207–208.
88. Qtd. in Thomas Wentworth Higginson, "The American Lecture System," *Living Age*, fourth series, vol. 9, April-June 1868 (Boston: Littell and Gay), 636.
89. Engstrom, *Infinitude*, 3.
90. Robert D. Richardson, Jr., *Emerson: The Mind on Fire* (Berkeley: University of California Press, 1995), 498.
91. Petrulionis, "Swelling," 408.
92. R.W. Emerson, "Fugitive Slave Law," 77–88.
93. Richardson, *Emerson*, 498.
94. Petrulionis, "Swelling," 408.
95. Ralph Waldo Emerson, "To William Emerson," 17 January 1855, in *The Letters of Ralph Waldo Emerson*, ed. Ralph L. Rusk, 6 vols. (New York: Columbia University Press, 1939), 4:484–485.
96. Richardson, *Emerson*, 527
97. Ralph Waldo Emerson, "To William Emerson," 2 June 1856, in *The Letters of Ralph Waldo Emerson*, vol. 5: 22–23.

98. Gougeon, "Historical Background," xlvi.
99. Franklin Benjamin Sanborn, *Recollections of Seventy Years*, vol. 1 (1909; repr., Detroit: Gale, 1967), 105.
100. Carlos Baker, *Emerson among the Eccentrics: A Group Portrait* (New York: Viking, 1996), 379.
101. Emerson, "Kansas Relief Meeting," in *Emerson's Antislavery Writings*, ed. Len Gougeon and Joel Myerson (New Haven: Yale University Press, 1995), 112.
102. Baker, *Emerson*, 380.
103. Ralph Waldo Emerson, *Journals of Ralph Waldo Emerson*, ed. Edward Waldo Emerson and Waldo Emerson Forbes, 10 vols. (Boston: Houghton Mifflin, 1912), 9: 81.
104. Baker, *Emerson*, 380–381.
105. Qtd. in Julia Ward Howe, *Reminiscences, 1819–1899* (1899; repr., New York: Negro University Press, 1969), 435.
106. Baker, *Emerson*, 383.
107. Bronson Alcott, *The Journals of Bronson Alcott*, vol. 2, ed. Odell S. Shepard (1938; repr., Port Washington, NY: Kennikat, 1966), 315–16.
108. Ralph Waldo Emerson, *The Selected Letters of Ralph Waldo Emerson*, ed. Joel Myerson (New York: Norton, 1992), 397.

Chapter Four

1. Qtd. in Henry Seidel Canby, *Thoreau* (Boston: Beacon, 1939), 383.
2. Henry David Thoreau, "To Harrison Blake," 26 September 1855, 1906, in *The Writings of Henry David Thoreau*, ed. F.B. Sanborn (New York: AMS, 1968), 260.
3. Petrulionis, "Swelling," 397.
4. Harding, *Days*, 201.
5. Franklin Benjamin Sanborn, "Mrs. Mary Merrick Brooks and the Anti-Slavery Movement," *Thoreau, Sanborn, John Brown and Slavery*, ed. Kenneth Walter Cameron (Hartford: Transcendental, 2000), 16.
6. Petrulionis, "Swelling," 396.
7. Henry David Thoreau, *Walden, or Life in the Woods* (Boston: Ticknor and Fields, 1854), 165, 154.
8. Walter Harding, "Thoreau's Reputation," in *The Cambridge Companion to Henry David Thoreau*, ed. Joel Myerson (New York: Cambridge University Press, 1995), 3.
9. Henry David Thoreau, "The Last Days of John Brown," 1860, in *The Major Essays of Henry David Thoreau*, ed. Richard Dillman (Albany: Whitston, 2001), 107.
10. Michael Meyer, "Thoreau and Black Emigration," *American Literature* 53.3 (1981): 390, 380.
11. Qtd. in Len Gougeon, "Thoreau and Reform," in *The Cambridge Companion to Henry David Thoreau*, ed. Joel Myerson (New York: Cambridge University Press, 1995), 197.
12. Thoreau, *Walden*, 348.
13. Richard Dillman, "Thoreau's Achievements as an Essayist," in *The Major Essays of Henry David Thoreau*, by Henry David Thoreau (Albany: Whitston, 2001), 8.
14. Gougeon, "Thoreau," 199.
15. Qtd. in Wendell Glick, "Thoreau and the 'Herald of Freedom,'" *The New England Quarterly* 22.2 (1949), 199–200.
16. "Concord Stirred by the Spirit of Liberty," letter from H.M., *Liberator* (26), 16 February 1844, p. 3.
17. Kenneth Walter Cameron, *Thoreau, Sanborn, John Brown and Slavery* (Hartford: Transcendental, 2000), 8.
18. "Concord Stirred," *Liberator* (26), p. 3.
19. Cameron, *Thoreau*, 8.
20. Qtd. in "Concord Stirred" *Liberator* (26), p. 3.
21. Gougeon, "Thoreau," 200.
22. "Wendell Phillips before the Concord Lyceum," *Liberator* [Boston], 28 March 1845, p. 3.
23. Ibid.
24. Ibid.
25. Qtd. in Marble, *Thoreau*, 16.
26. Thoreau, *Walden*, 152.
27. Dillman, "Achievements," 9.
28. Harding, *The Days*, 199–204.
29. Harding, "Thoreau's Reputation," 2.
30. Henry David Thoreau, "Civil Disobedience," 1849, in *The Major Essays of Henry David Thoreau*, ed. Richard Dillman (New York: Whitston, 2001), 48–49.
31. Ibid., 50, 55.
32. Nancy L. Rosenblum, introduction, *Thoreau: Political Writings*, by Henry David Thoreau, ed. Nancy L. Rosenblum (Cambridge: Cambridge University Press, 1996), xxvi.
33. Henry David Thoreau, "Journal," in *The Writings of Henry David Thoreau*, ed. Bradford Torrey, vol. 2 (Boston: Houghton Mifflin, 1906), 175–76.
34. Ibid., 178–79.
35. Ibid., 181–82.
36. Canby, *Thoreau*, 386.
37. Henry David Thoreau, "Slavery in Massachusetts," in *The Major Essays of Henry David Thoreau*, ed. Richard Dillman (New York: Whitston, 2001), 80.
38. Dillman, "Thoreau's Achievements," 11.
39. Thoreau, "Slavery," 77, 79, 73.
40. Ibid., 80.
41. Ibid., 74–75.
42. Harding, *The Days*, 346.
43. Ibid.
44. Gougeon, "Thoreau," 205.
45. Franklin Benjamin Sanborn, *Recollections of Seventy Years*, vol. 1 (1909; repr., Detroit: Gale, 1967), 103.
46. Thoreau, "Journal," *The Writings*, vol. 12, 437.
47. Ibid.
48. Michael Meyer, "Thoreau's Rescue of John Brown from History," in *Studies in the American Renaissance*, ed. Joel Myerson (Boston: Twayne, 1980), 303.
49. Paul Finkelman, preface, *His Soul Goes Marching On: Responses to John Brown and the Harpers Ferry Raid*, ed. Paul Finkelman (Charlottesville: University Press of Virginia, 1995), 6.
50. Meyer, "Thoreau's Rescue," 303.
51. Harding, *The Days*, 416.
52. Alcott, *Journals*, vol. 2: 316.
53. Ibid.
54. Ibid.
55. Ibid., 317.
56. Bertram Wyatt-Brown, "'A Volcano beneath a Mountain of Snow': John Brown and the Problem of Interpretation," in *His Soul Goes Marching On: Responses to John Brown and the Harpers Ferry Raid*, ed. Paul

Finkelman (Charlottesville: University Press of Virginia, 1995), 22–23.
57. Thoreau, "Last Days," 107.

Chapter Five

1. C. Peter Ripley, introduction, *The Black Abolitionist Papers*, ed. C. Peter Ripley, vol. 3 (Chapel Hill: University of North Carolina Press, 1991), 35.
2. Daniel C. Littlefield, "Blacks, John Brown and a Theory of Manhood," in *His Soul Goes Marching On: Responses to John Brown and the Harpers Ferry Raid*, ed. Paul Finkelman (Charlottesville: University Press of Virginia, 1995), 72.
3. William Lloyd Garrison. "To Our Free Colored Brethren," *Liberator* [Boston], 1 January 1831, p. 3.
4. Quarles, *Black Abolitionists*, 19–20.
5. Qtd. in Ripley, introduction, *Papers* 3: 9.
6. Ripley, introduction, *Papers* 3: 20.
7. T.W. Higginson, *Contemporaries*, 337.
8. May, "Antislavery Conflict," 129.
9. Qtd. in John W. Blassingame, introduction to vol. 1, in *The Frederick Douglass Papers*, by Frederick Douglass (New Haven: Yale University Press, 1999), xxvii–xxviii.
10. Qtd. in Ripley, introduction, *Papers* 3: 20.
11. Ripley, introduction, *Papers* 3: 18.
12. Ripley, introduction, *Papers* 3: 29; William S. McFeely, *Frederick Douglass* (New York: Norton, 1991), 83, 85.
13. Qtd. in McFeely, *Frederick Douglass*, 88–89.
14. Quarles, *Black Abolitionists*, 63.
15. Qtd. in Quarles, *Black Abolitionists*, 63.
16. Qtd. in Ripley, *Papers* 3: 29–30.
17. Qtd. in Quarles, *Black Abolitionists*, 63.
18. Blassingame, *Frederick Douglass Papers*, xxiv.
19. Qtd. in Sandra Thomas, "From Slave to Abolitionist Editor," in *Frederick Douglass* (2001), http://www.history.rochester,edu/class/douglass/part2.html.
20. William F. Andrews, introduction, *The Oxford Frederick Douglass Reader*, ed. William F. Andrews (New York: Oxford University Press, 1996), 21.
21. Ripley, introduction, *Papers* 3: 32.
22. Blassingame, introduction, *Frederick Douglass Papers*, xviii.
23. Qtd. in Blassingame, introduction, *Frederick Douglass Papers*, xxxiv–xxxv.
24. Qtd. in Rowe, *Emerson's Tomb*, 105.
25. Benjamin Quarles, *Black Mosaic: Essays in Afro-American History and Historiography* (Amherst: University of Massachusetts Press, 1988), 71.
26. Qtd. in Benjamin Quarles, *Allies for Freedom: Blacks and John Brown* (New York: Oxford University Press, 1974), 63.
27. Quarles, *Allies*, 64.
28. John Brown, Jr., "Letter from John Brown, Jr.," *Frederick Douglass Paper*, 25 December 1851.
29. Qtd. in Quarles, *Allies*, 27, 63–64.
30. Frederick Douglass, *Narrative of the Life of Frederick Douglass, an American Slave, Written By Himself*, 1845, in *The Oxford Frederick Douglass Reader*, ed. William L. Andrews (New York: Oxford University Press, 1996), 68–69.
31. Raymond Hedin, "Probable Readers, Possible Stories: The Limits of Nineteenth-Century Black Narrative," in *Readers in History: Nineteenth-Century American Literature and the Contexts of Response*, ed. James L. Machor (Baltimore: Johns Hopkins University Press, 1993), 204.
32. Frederick Douglass, "The Colonization Revival," in *The Frederick Douglass Papers*, ed. John W. Blassingame and John R. McKivigan, vol. 2 (New Haven: Yale University Press, 1992), 216–17.
33. Frederick Douglass, "What to the Slave Is the Fourth of July?" (1852), in *The Oxford Frederick Douglass Reader*, ed. William L. Andrews (New York: Oxford University Press, 1996), 111–13.
34. McFeely, *Frederick Douglass*, 189.
35. Frederick Douglass, "We Are in the Midst of a Moral Revolution," in *The Frederick Douglass Papers*, ed. John W. Blassingame and John R. McKivigan, vol. 2 (New Haven: Yale University Press, 1992), 482.
36. Qtd. in McFeely, *Frederick Douglass*, 189.
37. James H. Cook, "Fighting with Breath, Not Blows: Frederick Douglass and Antislavery Violence," in *Antislavery Violence: Sectional, Racial, and Cultural Conflict in Antebellum America*, ed. John R. McKivigan and Stanley Harrold (Knoxville: University of Tennessee Press, 1999), 131.
38. Qtd. in Cook, "Fighting," 132.
39. Cook, "Fighting," 131, 135.
40. Frederick Douglass, *The Life and Times of Frederick Douglass* (1892), in *The Oxford Frederick Douglass Reader*, ed. William L. Andrews (New York: Oxford University Press, 1996), 238–39.
41. Qtd. in David S. Reynolds, *John Brown Abolitionist: The Man Who Killed Slavery, Sparked the Civil War, and Seeded Civil Rights*, (New York: Knopf, 2005), 103.
42. Reynolds, *John Brown*, 103.
43. Qtd. in Edward J. Renehan, Jr., *The Secret Six: The True Tale of the Men Who Conspired with John Brown* (New York: Crown, 1995), 24.
44. Quarles, *Black Abolitionists*, 237–238.
45. McFeely, *Frederick Douglass*, 186.
46. Quarles, *Black Abolitionists*, 235.
47. Douglass, *Life and Times*, 233, 232.
48. James M. Gregory, *Frederick Douglass the Orator* (1893; repr., Springfield, MA: Willey, 1907), 35, 234.
49. Douglass, *Life and Times*, 230–232.
50. Reynolds, *John Brown*, 103.
51. Douglass, *Life and Times*, 231–232.
52. Ibid., 234.
53. Qtd. in Littlefield, "Blacks," 77.
54. Quarles, *Black Abolitionists*, 237.
55. Qtd. in Quarles, *Allies*, 29.
56. [A Free State Settler], "Letter from Kansas," in *Frederick Douglass Paper*, 4 July 1856, p. 4.
57. Qtd. in Quarles, *Allies*, 30.
58. Ibid., 34.
59. Ibid., 35–36.
60. Douglass, *Life and Times*, 246.
61. Qtd. in Cook, "Fighting," 141.
62. Quarles, *Allies*, 67.
63. Ibid., 38–39.
64. Frederic May Holland, *Frederick Douglass: The Colored Orator* (1891; Greenwood: Negro University Press, 1970), 267; Douglass, *Life and Times*, 246.
65. Douglass, *Life and Times*, 247.
66. Quarles, *Allies*, 39–40.
67. Douglass, *Life and Times*, 247–48.

68. Quarles, *Allies,* 77.
69. Douglass, *Life and Times,* 249–50.

Chapter Six

1. Carolyn Karcher, introduction to part three, *A Lydia Maria Child Reader* (Durham: Duke University Press, 1997), 141.
2. Karcher, *Reader,* 2.
3. Ibid., 4–5.
4. John G. Whittier, introduction, *Letters of Lydia Maria Child* (1883; repr., New York: Arno and *The New York Times,* 1969), v.
5. Karcher, *Reader,* 7.
6. Deborah Pickman Clifford, *Crusader for Freedom: A Life of Lydia Maria Child* (Boston: Beacon, 1992), 40.
7. T.W. Higginson, *Contemporaries,* 114.
8. Clifford, *Crusader,* 40.
9. Ibid., 42–43.
10. Qtd. in Clifford, *Crusader,* 44.
11. Clifford, *Crusader,* 44–45.
12. Qtd. in T.W. Higginson, *Contemporaries,* 117.
13. Qtd. in Clifford, *Crusader,* 56.
14. Karcher, *Reader,* 135.
15. Clifford, *Crusader,* 80.
16. Karcher, *Reader,* 136.
17. Ibid., 13.
18. Ibid., 12.
19. T.W. Higginson, *Contemporaries,* 117; Clifford, *Crusader,* 78.
20. T.W. Higginson, *Contemporaries,* 119.
21. Whittier, *Letters,* vii.
22. Lydia Maria Child, "Jumbo and Zairee," in *A Lydia Maria Child Reader,* ed. Carolyn L. Karcher (Durham: Duke University Press, 1997), 159.
23. Clifford, *Crusader,* 96.
24. Karcher, *Reader,* 138.
25. Ibid., 137–38.
26. Qtd. in Petrulionis, "Swelling," 385.
27. Petrulionis, "Swelling," 385.
28. Qtd. in T.W. Higginson, *Contemporaries,* 140.
29. Whittier, *Letters,* viii.
30. Qtd. in Karcher, *Reader,* 14.
31. Whittier, *Letters,* ix.
32. T.W. Higginson, *Contemporaries,* 121.
33. Lydia Maria Child, *An Appeal on Behalf of That Class of Americans Called Africans* (Boston: Allen and Ticknor, 1833), 138, 155.
34. Child, *Appeal,* 220.
35. Ibid., 147, 152.
36. Ibid., 232.
37. Samuel J. May, "Mrs. L. Maria Child," in *Some Recollections of Our Antislavery Conflict* (1869; repr., New York: Arno, 1968), 98.
38. Qtd. in T.W. Higginson, *Contemporaries,* 121.
39. May, "Mrs. L. Maria Child," 98.
40. Whittier, *Letters,* ix.
41. Wendell Phillips, appendix, "Remarks of Wendell Phillips at the Funeral of Lydia Maria Child, October 23, 1880," in *Letters of Lydia Maria Child* (1883; repr., New York: Arno and *The New York Times,* 1969), 264.
42. Whittier, *Letters,* ix.
43. Harriet Martineau, *The Martyr Age of the United States* (1839; repr. New York: Arno and *The New York Times,* 1969), 15.
44. May, "Mrs. L. Maria Child," 100.
45. Phillips, "Remarks," 264.
46. Clifford, *Crusader,* 103–04.
47. Qtd. in Karcher, *Reader,* 14–15.
48. Child, preface, *Appeal* 3: 1.
49. Whittier, *Letters,* ix.
50. Clifford, *Crusader,* 106.
51. May, "Mrs. L. Maria Child," 100.
52. Lydia Maria Child, "By Mrs. Child," *Liberator,* 19 October 1833, p. 168.
53. Karcher, *Reader,* 14.
54. [Rev. Mr.] Ludlow, "Annual Meeting of the State Society," *Liberator,* 5 November 1836, p. 178.
55. Thomas Wentworth Higginson, *Cheerful Yesterdays* (Boston: Houghton Mifflin, 1898), 77; Lydia Maria Child, "To Charles Sumner," 7 July 1856, in *Lydia Maria Child Selected Letters, 1817–1880,* ed. Milton Meltzer and Patricia G. Holland (Amherst: University of Massachusetts Press, 1982), 286.
56. Lydia Maria Child, "Reminiscences of Dr. Channing," in *Letters of Lydia Maria Child* (1883; repr., New York: Arno and *The New York Times,* 1969), 48.
57. Child, "Reminiscences" 48.
58. Ibid.
59. Clifford, *Crusader,* 103.
60. Martineau, *Martyr,* 16.
61. Lydia Maria Child, *The Oasis* (Boston: Benjamin C. Bacon, 1834), 3.
62. Lydia Maria Child, *The Oasis* (Boston: Benjamin C. Bacon, 1834), vii.
63. Lydia Maria Child, "Letters from New-York, No. 33," in *A Lydia Maria Child Reader,* ed. Carolyn L. Karcher (Durham: Duke University Press, 1997), 233–35.
64. Clifford, *Crusader,* 118.
65. Child, "Letters from New-York," 231.
66. Lydia Maria Child, "To Mrs. Ellis Gray Loring," 15 August 1835, in *Letters of Lydia Maria Child* (1833; repr., New York: Arno and *The New York Times,* 1969), 15.
67. Child, "Letters from New-York," 231–32.
68. Martineau, *Martyr,* 15.
69. Lydia Maria Child, "To Rev. Convers Francis," 25 September 1835, in *Letters of Lydia Maria Child* (1833; repr., New York: Arno and *The New York Times,* 1969), 17.
70. Child, Mrs. [Lydia Maria], *Philothea: A Romance* (Boston: Otis, Broaders, 1836), vi-vii.
71. Child, L. Maria, *Philothea: A Grecian Romance* (New York: C.S. Francis, 1848), 7.
72. Edgar Allan Poe, "Philothea," *Southern Literary Messenger* 2 (September 1836): 662.
73. Qtd. in T.W. Higginson, *Contemporaries,* 125.
74. Child, "To Rev. Convers Francis," 25 October 1836, in *Letters of Lydia Maria Child* (1883; repr., New York: Arno and *The New York Times,* 1969), 21.
75. Lydia Maria Child, "To E. Carpenter," 4 September 1836, in *Letters of Lydia Maria Child* (1883; repr., New York: Arno and *The New York Times,* 1969), 20.
76. Clifford, *Crusader,* 126–27.
77. Qtd. in Child, "To E. Carpenter," 4 September 1836, in *Letters of Lydia Maria Child* (1883; repr., New York: Arno and *The New York Times,* 1969), 21.
78. Lydia Maria Child, "To Lydia (Bigelow) Child," 19 October 1836, in *Lydia Maria Child: Selected Letters, 1817–1880,* ed. Milton Meltzer and Patricia G. Holland (Amherst: University of Massachusetts Press, 1982), 54–55.

79. Clifford, *Crusader*, 128–29.
80. Dorothy Sterling, *Turning the World Upside Down: The Anti-Slavery Convention of American Women, May 9–12, 1837* (New York: Feminist, 1987), 3.
81. Qtd. in Sterling, *Turning the World*, 4.
82. Ibid., 11.
83. Ibid., 12.
84. Ibid., 23.
85. Ibid., 24.
86. Ibid., 25.
87. Ibid.
88. Sterling, *Turning the World*, 4.
89. Qtd. in Clifford, *Crusader*, 135.
90. D. Lee Child, "David Lee Child to Angelina Grimke," 12 February 1838, in *Letters of Theodore Dwight Weld, Angelina Grimke Weld and Sarah Grimke, 1822–1844*, ed. Gilbert H. Barnes and Dwight L. Dumond, vol. 2 (1934; repr., New York: Da Capo, 1970), 544.
91. Qtd. in Petrulionis, "Swelling," 390.
92. Petrulionis, "Swelling," 393.
93. Lydia Maria Child, "To Angelina (Grimke) Weld," 2 October 1838, in *Lydia Maria Child Selected Letters, 1817–1880*, ed. Milton Meltzer and Patricia G. Holland (Amherst: University of Massachusetts Press, 1982), 92.
94. Lydia Maria Child, "To Rev. Convers Francis," 22 December 1838, in *Letters of Lydia Maria Child* (1883; repr., New York: Arno and *The New York Times*, 1969), 34.
95. Clifford, *Crusader*, 144.
96. Ibid., 145.
97. Ibid., 155–56.
98. T.W. Higginson, *Contemporaries*, 126.
99. Karcher, *Reader*, 139–40.
100. Clifford, *Crusader*, 160–61.
101. May, "Mrs. L. Maria Child," 100–01.
102. Qtd. in Clifford, *Crusader*, 164.
103. Ibid., 167.
104. Clifford, *Crusader*, 168.
105. Karcher, *Reader*, 3.
106. Clifford, *Crusader*, 180.
107. T.W. Higginson, *Contemporaries*, 130.
108. Child, "To Ellis Gray Loring," 21 February 1843, in *Lydia Maria Child: Selected Letters 1817–1880*, ed. Milton Meltzer and Patricia G. Holland (Amherst: University of Massachusetts Press, 1982), 189.
109. Child, "To Miss Lucy Osgood," 11 May 1856, in *Letters of Lydia Maria Child* (1883; repr., New York: Arno and *The New York Times*, 1969), 77.
110. Edgar Allen Poe, "The Literati of New York City," *Godey's Lady's Book*, September 1846, 129–30.
111. Lydia Maria Child, *Isaac T. Hopper: A True Life* (Boston: John P. Jewett, 1853), vi.
112. Ibid., vi-vii.
113. Child, "To Prof. Convers Francis," 14 July 1848, in *Letters of Lydia Maria Child* (1883; repr., New York: Arno and *The New York Times*, 1969), 65.
114. Qtd. in Clifford, *Crusader*, 223.
115. Ibid., 212.
116. Lydia Maria Child, "To Charles Sumner," 7 July 1856, in *Selected Letters 1817–1880*, ed. Milton Meltzer and Patricia G. Holland (Amherst: University of Massachusetts Press, 1982), 283.
117. Ibid., 285.
118. Lydia Maria Child, "To Lucy and Mary Osgood," 9 July 1856, in *Selected Letters 1817–1880*, ed. Milton Meltzer and Patricia G. Holland (Amherst: University of Massachusetts Press, 1982), 287.
119. Lydia Maria Child, "To Mrs. S.B. Shaw," [no date] 1856, in *Letters of Lydia Maria Child* (1883; repr., New York: Arno and *The New York Times*, 1969), 78.
120. Child, "To Miss Lucy Osgood," 9 July 1856, in *Letters*, 80.
121. Child, "To Lucy and Mary Osgood," 20 July 1856, in *Selected Letters*, 289.
122. Child, "To Sarah Shaw," 3 August 1856, in *Selected Letters*, 290–91.
123. Child, "To Mrs. Ellis Gray Loring," 26 October 1856, in *Letters*, 82.
124. Child, "To David Lee Child," 27 October 1856, in *Letters*, 82–83.
125. Ibid., 83–84.
126. T.W. Higginson, *Contemporaries*, 132.
127. Qtd. in Clifford, *Crusader*, 229.

Chapter Seven

1. Thomas Wentworth Higginson, "Emily Dickinson," *Magnificent Activist*, ed. Howard N. Meyer (New York: Da Capo, 2000), 555.
2. Thomas Wentworth Higginson, *Cheerful Yesterdays* (Boston: Houghton Mifflin, 1898), 230.
3. Thomas Wentworth Higginson, *Part of a Man's Life* (Boston: Houghton Mifflin, 1905), 164.
4. T.W. Higginson, *Magnificent Activist*, 321.
5. Qtd. in Edward J. Renehan, Jr., *The Secret Six: The True Tale of the Men Who Conspired with John Brown* (New York: Crown, 1995), 64–65.
6. Anna Mary Wells, *Dear Preceptor: The Life of Thomas Wentworth Higginson* (Boston: Houghton Mifflin, 1963), 1.
7. T.W. Higginson, *Cheerful*, 138.
8. Ibid., 3–4.
9. Wells, *Dear Preceptor*, 9, 11.
10. T.W. Higginson, *Cheerful*, 42.
11. T.W. Higginson, *Cheerful*, 67; Qtd. in Tilden G. Edelstein, *Strange Enthusiasm: A Life of Thomas Wentworth Higginson* (New Haven: Yale University Press, 1968), 38.
12. T.W. Higginson, *Cheerful*, 95, 92.
13. Edelstein, *Strange Enthusiasm*, 52.
14. T.W. Higginson, *Cheerful*, 126.
15. Ibid.
16. Qtd. in Mary Thacher Higginson, *Thomas Wentworth Higginson: The Story of His Life* (1914; Port Washington, NY: Kennikat, 1971), 76.
17. T.W. Higginson, *Cheerful*, 47.
18. Ralph Waldo Emerson, "My Dear Friend" [Thomas Carlyle]," 30 October 1840, in *The Correspondence of Emerson and Carlyle*, ed. Joseph Slater (New York: Columbia University Press, 1964), 283–84.
19. T.W. Higginson, *Cheerful*, 77.
20. Ibid., 100, 103–104, 102.
21. T.W. Higginson, "Review of *Letters from New-York*," *Present* 1 (1843): 45.
22. T.W. Higginson, *Cheerful*, 114.
23. Wells, *Dear Preceptor*, 51.
24. Qtd. in Mary Higginson, *Thomas*, 82.
25. T.W. Higginson, *Cheerful*, 120.
26. Qtd. in Wells, *Dear Preceptor*, 53.
27. Edelstein, *Strange Enthusiasm*, 68; Qtd. in John A. Pollard, *John Greenleaf Whittier: Friend of Man* (Boston: Houghton Mifflin, 1949), 152–53.

28. Edelstein, *Strange Enthusiasm*, 73–74.
29. T.W. Higginson, *Cheerful*, 125–26.
30. Edelstein, *Strange Enthusiasm*, 74.
31. T.W. Higginson, *Cheerful*, 127.
32. Ibid, 119.
33. Qtd. in Mary Higginson, *Thomas*, 96.
34. Edelstein, *Strange Enthusiasm*, 83.
35. Qtd. in Edelstein, *Strange Enthusiasm*, 86.
36. Wells, *Dear Preceptor*, 64–65.
37. Thomas Wentworth Higginson, "T.W.H. to J.G. Whittier," 3 August 1848, in *Whittier Correspondence from the Oak Knoll Collections, 1830–1892,* ed. John Albree (Salem, MA: Essex Book and Print Club, 1911), 105–06.
38. Edelstein, *Strange Enthusiasm*, 85.
39. T.W. Higginson, *Cheerful*, 128; Edelstein, *Strange Enthusiasm*, 85.
40. Edelstein, *Strange Enthusiasm*, 86.
41. Ibid., 87.
42. Thomas Wentworth Higginson, *Man Shall Not Live by Bread Alone: A Thanksgiving Sermon Preached in Newburyport, November 30, 1848,* (Boston: Crosby and Nichols, 1848), 5 (Massachusetts Historical Society, Boston).
43. Higginson, *Man Shall Not,* 9.
44. Ibid., 9–10.
45. Ibid., 10.
46. Ibid., 10–11.
47. Wells, *Dear Preceptor,* 65; Edelstein, *Strange Enthusiasm,* 90.
48. Qtd. in Edelstein, *Strange Enthusiasm,* 90.
49. Ibid.
50. Ibid.
51. Ralph Waldo Emerson, *The Heart of Emerson's Journals,* ed. Bliss Perry (New York: Dover, 1958), 241.
52. Wells, *Dear Preceptor,* 66.
53. Thomas Wentworth Higginson, *Part of a Man's Life* (Boston: Houghton Mifflin, 1905), 94–95.
54. Qtd. in Edelstein, *Strange Enthusiasm,* 95–96.
55. Qtd. in Mary Higginson, *Thomas,* 98.
56. Mary Higginson, *Thomas,* 122.
57. Henry David Thoreau, "Journal," in *The Writings of Henry David Thoreau,* vol. 5, ed. Bradford Torrey (Boston: Houghton Mifflin, 1906), 459.
58. Edelstein, *Strange Enthusiasm,* 97.
59. Qtd. in Wells, *Dear Preceptor,* 66.
60. Qtd. in Edelstein, *Strange Enthusiasm,* 93–94.
61. Qtd. in Mary Higginson, *Thomas,* 93.
62. Qtd. in Wells, *Dear Preceptor,* 69.
63. Qtd. in Mary Higginson, *Thomas,* 92.
64. Mary Higginson, *Thomas,* 92.
65. Higginson, *Cheerful,* 129.
66. Ibid., 130.
67. Qtd. in Mary Higginson, *Thomas,* 104.
68. Thomas Wentworth Higginson, *Mr. Higginson's Address to the Voters of the Third Congressional District of Massachusetts* (Lowell, MA: C.L. Knapp, 1850), 6 (pamphlet, Boston Public Library Rare Books and Manuscripts, Boston).
69. Qtd. in Mary Higginson, *Thomas,* 111–12.
70. Qtd. in Edelstein, *Strange Enthusiasm,* 105–06.
71. Edelstein, *Strange Enthusiasm,* 110.
72. Julia Ward Howe, *Reminiscences, 1819–1899* (1899; repr., New York: Negro University Press, 1969), 165.
73. Higginson, *Cheerful,* 137–38.
74. Qtd. in Edelstein, *Strange Enthusiasm,* 110.
75. Edelstein, *Strange Enthusiasm,* 110.
76. T.W. Higginson, *Cheerful* 139.
77. Qtd. in T.W. Higginson, *Cheerful,* 139.
78. Qtd. in Edelstein, *Strange Enthusiasm,* 115.
79. T.W. Higginson, *Cheerful,* 139.
80. T.W. Higginson, *Cheerful,* 141; Edelstein, *Strange Enthusiasm,* 114.
81. T.W. Higginson, *Cheerful,* 141–42.
82. Ibid., 142.
83. Qtd. in Edelstein, *Strange Enthusiasm,* 114.
84. T.W. Higginson, *Cheerful,* 142–43.
85. Ibid., 143.
86. Thomas Wentworth Higginson, "Burns Case Narrative," incomplete ms., Ms. B.1.22 (105), Boston Public Library Rare Books and Manuscripts, Boston, 2.
87. Higginson, *Cheerful,* 144.
88. Thomas Wentworth Higginson, *Burns Case,* 1–2, Boston: Boston Public Library.
89. Mary Higginson, *Thomas,* 103.
90. Irving J. Bartlett, *Wendell Phillips: Brahmin Radical* (Boston: Beacon, 1961), 157.
91. T.W. Higginson, *Cheerful,* 131.
92. Ibid., 145.
93. Qtd. in Wells, *Dear Preceptor,* 114.
94. T.W. Higginson, *Cheerful,* 131.
95. Wells, *Dear Preceptor,* 79–80.
96. T.W. Higginson, *Cheerful,* 181.
97. Thomas Wentworth Higginson, *Letters and Journals of Thomas Wentworth Higginson, 1846–1906,* ed. Mary Thacher Higginson (Boston: Houghton Mifflin, 1921), 33–34.
98. T.W. Higginson, *Cheerful,* 181.
99. Qtd. in Mary Higginson, *Thomas,* 129.
100. Henry David Thoreau, *The Writings of Henry David Thoreau: Journal,* vol. 3, ed. Bradford Torrey (Boston: Houghton Mifflin, 1906), 213.
101. Wells, *Strange Enthusiasm,* 77.
102. T.W. Higginson, *Cheerful,* 193–94.
103. Ibid., 146.
104. Qtd. in Mary Higginson, *Thomas,* 124.
105. *The Boston Slave Riot and Trial of Anthony Burns* (Boston: Fetridge, 1854).
106. Ibid., 7.
107. Qtd. in Mary Higginson, *Thomas,* 142.
108. A. Bronson Alcott, 1854, Journals and Diaries of Amos Bronson Alcott, vol. 34, ms. 47 (Houghton Library, Cambridge).
109. T.W. Higginson, "Burns Case Narrative," 3.
110. T.W. Higginson, *Cheerful,* 148.
111. Ibid., 148–49.
112. "Murderers, Thieves, and Blacklegs Employed by Marshal Freeman!!" [1854] broadside, Massachusetts Historical Society, Boston, 1.
113. T.W. Higginson, "Burns Case Narrative," 4.
114. T.W. Higginson, *Cheerful,* 149–50.
115. Ibid., 150.
116. T.W. Higginson, "Burns Case Narrative," 4; Edelstein, *Strange Enthusiasm,* 156.
117. T.W. Higginson, *Cheerful,* 151.
118. T.W. Higginson, "Burns Case Narrative," 4.
119. T.W. Higginson, *Cheerful,* 150, 152.
120. *Boston Slave Riot,* 8
121. Ibid., 9–10.
122. T.W. Higginson, *Cheerful,* 152–53.
123. *Boston Slave Riot,* 10.
124. Edelstein, *Strange Enthusiasm,* 158–59.
125. *Boston Slave Riot,* 11–12.
126. T.W. Higginson, *Cheerful,* 153–54.

Notes—Chapter Seven

127. Thomas Wentworth Higginson, Letter to "Dear Brother," 30 May 1854, ts. Burns Collection, 1, Massachusetts Historical Society, Boston.
128. *Boston Slave Riot*, 10.
129. T.W. Higginson, *Cheerful*, 154.
130. Ibid.
131. Ibid., 155.
132. *Boston Slave Riot*, 11.
133. T.W. Higginson, *Cheerful*, 158.
134. *Boston Slave Riot*, 11.
135. Ibid., 13.
136. Ibid., 17.
137. *Boston Slave Riot*, n. 86.
138. Ibid., 17.
139. Edelstein, *Strange Enthusiasm*, 161.
140. *Boston Slave Riot*, 85.
141. Samuel Gridley Howe, "To Horace Mann," 18 June 1854, in *Letters and Journals of Samuel Gridley Howe*, ed. Laura E. Richards, vol. 2 (1909; repr., New York: AMS, 1973), 270.
142. *Boston Slave Riot*, 86.
143. Edelstein, *Strange Enthusiasm*, 159–60.
144. Thomas Wentworth Higginson, Letter to "Dearest Mother," May 29, 1856, ms., Ms.B.1.22 (7), 3, Boston Public Library Rare Books and Manuscripts, Boston.
145. Thomas Wentworth Higginson, Letter to "Dearest Mother," 29 May 1854, ms., Thomas Wentworth Higginson Papers, 1–3, Ms.B.1.22 (7), Boston Public Library Rare Books and Manuscripts, Boston.
146. Thomas Wentworth Higginson, Letter to Richard Henry Dana, 29 May 1854, ms., Dana Family Papers, April-May 1854), 1–2, Massachusetts Historical Society, Boston.
147. Qtd. in Edelstein, *Strange Enthusiasm*, 159.
148. Thomas Wentworth Higginson, Letter to "Dear Brother," 30 May 1854, ts. Burns Collection, 1, Massachusetts Historical Society, Boston.
149. T.W. Higginson, Letter to "Dear Brother," 30 May 1854, ts., Burns Collection, 1, Massachusetts Historical Society, Boston.
150. Qtd. in Mary Higginson, *Thomas*, 144.
151. T.W. Higginson, *Cheerful*, 155.
152. Thomas Wentworth Higginson, Letter to "Darling Mother," 31 May [1854] 10 P.M., ms., Ms.B.1.22(16), Thomas Wentworth Higginson Papers, 2–3, Boston Public Library Rare Books and Manuscripts. Boston.
153. Qtd. in Mary Higginson, *Thomas*, 146.
154. Thomas Wentworth Higginson, Letter to "Dearest Mother," 11 A.M., [1854], ms., Ms.B.1.22 (28), Thomas Wentworth Higginson Papers, 1, Boston Public Library Rare Books and Manuscripts, Boston.
155. Thomas Wentworth Higginson, Letter to "Dearest Mother," 1 June [1854], ms., Ms.B.1.22 (19), Thomas Wentworth Higginson Papers, 1, Boston Public Library Rare Books and Manuscripts, Boston.
156. Mary Higginson, *Thomas*, 147.
157. Edelstein, *Strange Enthusiasm*, 161.
158. Louisa Storrow Higginson, Letter to "Dear Son" [Thomas Wentworth Higginson], 1 June 1854, ms., Ms.B.1.22 (17), 1, Boston Public Library Rare Books and Manuscripts, Boston.
159. Qtd. in Edelstein, *Strange Enthusiasm*, 160.
160. Thomas Wentworth Higginson, *Massachusetts in Mourning: A Sermon Preached in Worcester on Sunday, June 4, 1854 by Thomas Wentworth Higginson* (Boston: James Munroe, 1854), 3–15.
161. Ibid., 12–13.
162. Ibid., 14–15.
163. [Louisa Storrow] Higginson, Letter to T.W.H, 9 June 1854, ms., Ms.B.1.22 (32), 1, Boston Public Library Rare Books and Manuscripts, Boston.
164. Renehan, *The Secret Six*, 73.
165. Qtd. in Edelstein, *Strange Enthusiasm*, 164.
166. T.W. Higginson, Telegram to L. Higginson. 10 June 1854, 1, Boston Public Library Rare Books and Manuscripts, Boston.
167. Thomas Wentworth Higginson, Letter to "Dear Mrs. Chapman," 30 November 1854, 1, ms., Ms.A.9.2.28, Boston Public Library Rare Books and Manuscripts, Boston.
168. Thomas Wentworth Higginson, "Attempted Rescue of Burns," *Liberator*, 24 August 1855, p. 134.
169. Qtd. in Mary Higginson, *Thomas*, 148.
170. T.W. Higginson, note, *Cheerful*, 155.
171. Wells, *Dear Preceptor*, 89.
172. Thomas Wentworth Higginson, Letter to "Darling Mother," 31 May [1854] 10 P.M., ms., Ms.B.1.22(16), Thomas Wentworth Higginson Papers, 3 Boston Public Library Rare Books and Manuscripts, Boston.
173. T.W. Higginson, *Cheerful*, 162.
174. Qtd. in Edelstein, *Strange Enthusiasm*, 167; qtd. in Renehan, *The Secret Six*, 73.
175. Edelstein, *Strange Enthusiasm*, 167.
176. Renehan, *Strange Enthusiasm*, 73–74; T.W. Higginson, *Cheerful*, 162–65.
177. T.W. Higginson, *Cheerful*, 163–65.
178. T.W. Higginson, Letter to "Dear Mrs. Chapman," 30 November 1854, ms., Ms.A.9.2.28p34, 2, Boston Public Library Rare Books and Manuscripts, Boston.
179. Qtd. in Mary Higginson, *Thomas*, 150.
180. T.W. Higginson, *Cheerful*, 160.
181. "Celebration of W.I. Emancipation at Abington, August First, 1854," *Liberator* [Boston], 11 August 1854, p. 126.
182. Edelstein, *Strange Enthusiasm*, 172–73.
183. Wells, *Dear Preceptor*, 90.
184. Qtd. in Mary Higginson, *Thomas*, 132, 134.
185. T.W. Higginson, *Cheerful*, 197–99.
186. Ibid., 199–205.
187. Ibid., 210–211.
188. Ibid., 209.
189. Ibid., 235.
190. Qtd. in Mary Higginson, *Thomas*, 172–73.
191. Ibid., 179–80.
192. T.W. Higginson, *Cheerful*, 214.
193. Qtd. in Mary Higginson, *Thomas*, 180–81.
194. T.W. Higginson, *Cheerful*, 237.
195. Ibid., 215–16.
196. Ibid., 215.
197. Ibid., 207–08.
198. John Brown, Letter to Rev. T.W. Higginson, 2 February 1858, ms., Ms.E.5.1 pt. 1 p 4, Thomas Wentworth Higginson Papers, 1, Boston Public Library Rare Books and Manuscripts, Boston.
199. T.W. Higginson, Letter to N. Hawkins [John Brown], 8 February 1858, ms., Ms.E.5.1 pt. 1 p. 5, Thomas Wentworth Higginson Papers, 1, Boston Public Library Rare Books and Manuscripts, Boston.
200. John Brown, Letter to Rev. T.W. Higginson, 12 February 1858, ms., Ms.E.5.1 pt. 1 p 7, Thomas Wentworth Higginson Papers, Boston Public Library Rare Books and Manuscripts, Boston 1.
201. Ibid.

202. John Brown, Letter to Rev. T.W. Higginson, 4 Mar 1858, ms., Thomas Wentworth Higginson Papers, 1 (Boston Public Library Rare Books and Manuscripts, Boston).
203. T.W. Higginson, *Cheerful*, 219–20.
204. Ibid., 220–21.
205. F[ranklin] B[enjamin] Sanborn, Letter to "Dear Friend" [T.W.H.] 8 March 1858, ms., Ms.E.5.1. pt. 1 p 11, Thomas Wentworth Higginson Papers, 1, Boston Public Library Rare Books and Manuscripts, Boston.
206. Geo[rge] L. Stearns, Letter to Rev. T.W. Higginson, 1 April 1858, ms., Ms.E.5.1 pt. 1 p 14, Thomas Wentworth Higginson Papers, 1, Boston Public Library Rare Books and Manuscripts, Boston.
207. John Brown, Letter to "My Dear Sir" [T.W.H.], 14 May 1858, ms., Ms.E.5.1 pt. 1 p. 26, Thomas Wentworth Higginson Papers, 1, Boston Public Library Rare Books and Manuscripts, Boston.
208. John Brown, Letter to Rev. Thomas Wentworth Higginson, 14 May 1858, ts., John Brown Collection, 1, Massachusetts Historical Society, Boston.
209. Wells, *Dear Preceptor*, 104–06.
210. T.W. Higginson, *Cheerful*, 221.
211. Ibid., 221.
212. Thomas Wentworth Higginson, Letter to John Brown, 18 May 1858, ms., Ms.E.5.1 pt. 1 p.29, Thomas Wentworth Higginson Papers, 1, Boston Public Library Rare Books and Manuscripts, Boston.
213. Thomas Wentworth Higginson, Letter to Jason Brown, 7 May 1858, ms., Ms.E.5.1 pt. 1 p. 18, Thomas Wentworth Higginson Papers, 1–2, Boston Public Library Rare Books and Manuscripts, Boston.
214. Thomas Wentworth Higginson, Letter to John Brown, 18 May 1858, 1.
215. Thomas Wentworth Higginson, Letter to Theodore Parker, 18 May 1858, ms., Ms.E.5.1 pt. 1 p. 28, Thomas Wentworth Higginson Papers, 1–3, Boston Public Library Rare Books and Manuscripts, Boston.
216. Higginson, *Cheerful*, 222.
217. Thomas Wentworth Higginson, Letter to Unnamed, 1 June 1858, ms., Thomas Wentworth Higginson Papers, 1–2, Boston Public Library Rare Books and Manuscripts.
218. John Brown, Letter to T.W. Higginson, 13–16 September 1858, ts., John Brown Collection, 1–2, Massachusetts Historical Society, Boston.
219. Thomas Wentworth Higginson, Letter to John Brown, 1 May 1859, ms., Ms.E.5.1. p. 1 p. 51, Thomas Wentworth Higginson Papers, 1–2, Boston Public Library Rare Books and Manuscripts.
220. Mary Higginson, *Thomas*, 192–93.
221. Qtd. in Villard, *John Brown*, 303.
222. Thomas Wentworth Higginson, Letter to John Brown, 29 October 1858, ms., Thomas Wentworth Higginson Papers, 1–2, Boston Public Library Rare Books and Manuscripts, Boston.
223. T.W. Higginson, *Cheerful*, 222.
224. F.B. Sanborn, Letter to T.W. Higginson, 4 June 1859, ms., Ms.E.5.1.pt. 1 p. 54, Thomas Wentworth Higginson Papers, 1, Boston Public Library Rare Books and Manuscripts.
225. T.W. Higginson, *Cheerful*, 223.
226. F.B. Sanborn, Letter to "Dear Friend" [T.W. Higginson], 6 October 1859, ms., Ms.E.5.1. p. 60, Thomas Wentworth Higginson Papers, 1, Boston Public Library Rare Books and Manuscripts, Boston.
227. Villard, *John Brown*, 529.

Chapter Eight

1. "Servile Insurrection," *New York Times,* 18 October 1859, p. 1.
2. Qtd. in John Edward Byrne, "The News from Harpers Ferry: The Press as Lens and Prism for John Brown's Raid," PhD. diss., George Washington University, 1987, 123.
3. "News of the Day," *New York Times,* 19 October 1859, p. 4; qtd. in Byrne, "The News from Harpers Ferry," 124, 126.
4. Qtd. in Byrne, "The News from Harpers Ferry," 128.
5. "The Harper's Ferry Rebellion," *New York Times,* 20 October 1859, p. 1.
6. Qtd. in Byrne, "The News from Harpers Ferry," 135.
7. Ibid., 147–48.
8. "The 'Irrepressible Conflict,'" *Nashville Tennessee Republican Banner and Nashville Whig* [opposition], 25 October 1859, Furman Secession Era Editorials Project, http://history.furman.edu/benson/docs/jbmenu.htm.
9. "The Virginia Insurrection," *Liberator* [Boston], 21 October 1859, p. 2.
10. No title, *Indianapolis (IN) Locomotive* [Democratic], 22 October 1859, Furman Secession Era Editorials Project: "John Brown's Raid on Harper's Ferry" (October–December 1859), http://history.furman.edu/benson/docs/jbmenu/htm.
11. "The Harper's Ferry Insurrection," *Charleston (SC) Mercury,* 19 October 1859, Furman Secession Era Editorials Project: "The Insurrection," *Charleston (SC) Mercury,* 21 October 1859, http://history.furman.edu/benson/docs/jbmenu.htm.
12. "The Cloud in the Distance," *Cincinnati Enquirer,* 19 October 1859, p. 1., Furman Secession Era Editorials Project: "John Brown's Raid on Harper's Ferry" (October–December 1859), http://history.furman.edu/benson/docs/jbmenu.htm.
13. "The True Policy," *Chicago Press and Tribune* [Republican], 22 October 1859, p. 2, Furman Secession Era Editorials Project, http://history.furman.edu/benson/docs/jbmenu.htm.
14. "Who's to Blame?" *Liberator* [Boston], 11 November 1859, p. 1.
15. Qtd. in Stephen B. Oates, *Our Fiery Trial: Abraham Lincoln, John Brown, and the Civil War Era* (Amherst: University of Massachusetts Press, 1979), 19–20.
16. Frederick Douglass, "John Brown's Raid on Harpers Ferry," in *Frederick Douglass: The Narrative and Selected Writings,* ed. Michael Meyer (New York: Modern Library, 1984), 197.
17. Qtd. in Benjamin Quarles, *Allies for Freedom: Blacks and John Brown* (New York: Oxford University Press, 1974), 114.
18. "The Examination of Brown's Dwelling—Northern Abolitionists Apparently Implicated," *New York Times,* 20 October 1859, p. 1.
19. Qtd. in William S. McFeely, *Frederick Douglass* (New York: Norton, 1991), 198.
20. Douglass, "John Brown's Raid," 197, 198.
21. David S. Reynolds, *John Brown: Abolitionist* (New York: Knopf, 2005), 359.
22. Douglass, "John Brown's Raid," 199.
23. Ibid., 198.
24. McFeely, *Frederick Douglass,* 199.
25. Henry Wise, Letter to "Dear Sir," 6 November

1859, ms., John Brown Collection, 3, Massachusetts Historical Society, Boston.
26. Qtd. in Quarles, *Allies,* 115.
27. Qtd. in Douglass, "John Brown's Raid," 200.
28. Letter from Frederick Douglass, 31 October 1859, *Douglass' Monthly* (November 1859): 163.
29. Ibid.
30. James H. Cook, "Fighting with Breath, Not Blows: Frederick Douglass and Antislavery Violence," in *Antislavery Violence: Sectional, Racial, and Cultural Conflict in Antebellum America,* ed. John R. McKivigan and Stanley Harrold (Knoxville: University of Tennessee Press, 1999), 146–47.
31. Qtd. in McFeely, *Frederick Douglass,* 202.
32. "Fred. Douglass and Harper's Ferry," *Chambersburg (PA) Valley Spirit,* 16 November 1859, p. 4.
33. Qtd. in Quarles, *Allies,* 117–18.
34. Charles H. Langston, "Charles H. Langston," *Blacks on John Brown,* ed. Benjamin Quarles (Urbana: University of Illinois Press, 1972), 12.
35. Frederick Douglass, "To My American Readers and Friends," *Douglass Monthly* (November 1859): 162.
36. Ibid.
37. Ibid.
38. Frederick Douglass, Letter to Maria Webb, November 30, 1859, in *Admiration* and *Ambivalence: Frederick Douglass and John Brown* (New York: Gilder Lehman Institute of American History, 2005), 8.
39. McFeely, *Frederick Douglass,* 203.
40. Qtd. in Frederic May Holland, *Frederick Douglass: The Colored Orator* (1891; repr., New York: Haskell, 1969), 276.
41. Walter Harding, *The Days of Henry Thoreau: A Biography* (Princeton: Princeton University Press, 1992), 416.
42. Carlos Baker, *Emerson among the Eccentrics: A Group Portrait* (New York: Viking, 1996), 385.
43. Ralph Waldo Emerson, Letter To William Emerson, 23 October 1859, in *The Letters of Ralph Waldo Emerson,* ed. Ralph L. Rusk, vol. 5 (New York: Columbia University Press, 1939), 178.
44. Baker, *Emerson,* 384.
45. Franklin Benjamin Sanborn, Letter to "Dear Friend" [Theodore Parker], 22 October 1859, ms., Folder 43: 1, 3, 5, Concord Free Public Library, Concord, MA.
46. Franklin Benjamin Sanborn, *Recollections of Seventy Years,* vol. 1 (1909; repr., Detroit: Gale, 1967), 196.
47. Franklin Benjamin Sanborn, Letter to "Dear Friend" [T.W.H.], 10 November 1859, ms., 1, Boston Public Library Rare Books and Manuscripts, Boston.
48. "Backing Out," *Liberator* (28), October 1859, p. 1.
49. Henry David Thoreau, "Journal," in *The Writings of Henry D. Thoreau,* ed. Bradford Torrey, vol. 12 (Boston: Houghton Mifflin, 1906), 435.
50. George W. Cooke, "The Two Thoreaus," in *Thoreau as Seen by His Contemporaries,* ed. Walter Harding (New York: Dover, 1989), 84.
51. Ralph Waldo Emerson, "Thoreau," in *Walden and Resistance to Civil Government,* ed. William Rossi (New York: Norton, 1992), 324.
52. Richard Dillman, "Thoreau's Achievements as an Essayist," in *The Major Essays of Henry David Thoreau,* by Henry David Thoreau (Albany: Whitston, 2001), 12.
53. Qtd. in Harding, *The Days,* 417.
54. Bronson Alcott, *The Journals of Bronson Alcott,* ed. Odell S. Shepard, vol. 2 (1938; repr., Port Washington, NY: Kennikat, 1966), 320.
55. Bronson Alcott, *The Letters of A. Bronson Alcott,* ed. Richard L. Hernstadt (Ames: Iowa State University Press, 1969), 306.
56. Minot Pratt, Letter to Mrs. Minot Pratt, October 30, 1859, in *Thoreau as Seen by His Contemporaries,* ed. Walter Harding (New York: Dover, 1989), 158.
57. Cooke, "The Two Thoreaus," 84.
58. Franklin Benjamin Sanborn, "The Personality of Thoreau," in *Thoreau as Seen by His Contemporaries,* ed. Walter Harding (New York: Dover, 1989), 99.
59. Walter Harding, "Thoreau's Reputation," *The Cambridge Companion to Henry David Thoreau,* ed. Joel Myerson (Cambridge: Cambridge University Press, 1995), 4.
60. Henry David Thoreau, "To Harrison Blake," 31 October 1859, in *Familiar Letters of Henry David Thoreau,* ed. F.B. Sanborn (Boston: Houghton Mifflin, 1894), 413.
61. Qtd. in McFeely, *Frederick Douglass,* 202.
62. Ralph Waldo Emerson, Letter to [Charles] Slack, 31 October 1859 (Worcester: American Antiquarian Society), 1–3.
63. Henry David Thoreau, Letter to Charles W. Slack, 1 November 1859 (Worcester: American Antiquarian Society), 1.
64. C.K.W., "Fifth Fraternity Lecture," *Liberator* [Boston], 4 November 1859, p. 2.
65. Qtd. in A. Bronson Alcott, 1859 Journal, vol. 34, 605, Journals and Diaries of Amos Bronson Alcott, ms., Houghton Library, Cambridge.
66. Frederick Douglass, Letter to C.W. Slack, Esqr., 28 October 1859 (Worcester: American Antiquarian Society), 1.
67. Qtd. in A. Bronson Alcott, 1859 Journal, vol. 34, 605, Journals and Diaries of Amos Bronson Alcott, ms., Houghton Library, Cambridge.
68. Henry David Thoreau, "A Plea for Captain John Brown" (1860), in *The Major Essays of Henry David Thoreau,* ed. Richard Dillman (Albany: Whitston, 2001), 101.
69. Henry Seidel Canby, *Thoreau* (Boston: Beacon, 1939), 391, 393.
70. Thoreau, "A Plea," 90–92.
71. C.K.W., "Fifth Fraternity Lecture," *Liberator,* 4 November 1859 [Boston], p. 174; qtd. in Alcott, Journals and Miscellaneous Notebooks, 606.
72. Harding, *The Days,* 419.
73. Qtd. in Michael Meyer, "Thoreau's Rescue of John Brown from History," in *Studies in the American Renaissance,* ed. Joel Myerson (Boston: Twayne, 1980), 309.
74. Qtd. in Harding, *The Days,* 419.
75. "Fifth Fraternity Lecture," 2.
76. A. Bronson Alcott, 1859 Journal, vol. 34, Journals and Diaries of Amos Bronson Alcott, ms., 613, Houghton Library, Cambridge.
77. Edward Waldo Emerson, *Henry Thoreau as Remembered by a Young Friend* (Mineola, NY: Dover, 1999), 13.
78. Reynolds, *John Brown,* 364.
79. Ralph Waldo Emerson, Letter to Sarah Swain Forbes, 26 October 1859, *The Letters of Ralph Waldo Emerson,* ed. Ralph L. Rusk, vol. 5 (New York: Columbia University Press, 1939), 179–180.
80. John A. Andrew, "List of Contributors to Defense of John Brown," November 2–8, 1859, E187MSS, ms., 1, Massachusetts Historical Society, Boston.

81. Thomas Wentworth Higginson, Circular with Personal Note by T.W.H., 2 November 1859, Ms E 5.1 pt. 1 p 71, 1, Boston Public Library Rare Books and Manuscripts.
82. Bertram Wyatt-Brown, "'A Volcano beneath a Mountain of Snow': John Brown and the Problem of Interpretation," in *His Soul Goes Marching On: Responses to John Brown and the Harpers Ferry Raid*, ed. Paul Finkelman (Charlottesville: University Press of Virginia, 1995), 31.
83. "Emerson on Courage," *Liberator* [Boston, 18 November 1859, p. 1.
84. Ibid.
85. Ibid.
86. Ibid.
87. Baker, *Emerson*, 386.
88. Qtd. in Gougeon, *Virtue's Hero*, 242.
89. Alcott, *Journals*, vol. 2, 321.
90. Ralph Waldo Emerson, *Journals of Ralph Waldo Emerson*, ed. Edward Waldo Emerson and Waldo Emerson Forbes, 10 vols. (Boston: Houghton Mifflin, 1913), 4: 248.
91. A. Bronson Alcott, Letter to Daniel Ricketson, 6 November 1859, in *The Letters of A. Bronson Alcott*, ed. Richard L. Herrnstadt (Ames: Iowa State University Press, 1969), 306.
92. Louisa May Alcott, Letter to Alfred Whitman, 8 November [1859], in *The Selected Letters of Louisa May Alcott*, ed. Joel Myerson and Daniel Shealy (Athens: University of Georgia Press, 1995), 49.
93. A. Bronson Alcott, 1859 Journal, vol. 34, of Amos Bronson Alcott, ms., 633, Houghton Library, Cambridge.
94. Alcott, *Journals*, vol. 2, 321–22.
95. Franklin Benjamin Sanborn, Letter to Theodore Parker, 14 November 1859, ms., 1, Franklin Benjamin Sanborn Papers, Concord Free Public Library, Concord.
96. Qtd. in Alcott, 1859 Journal, vol. 34, Journals and Diaries of Amos Bronson Alcott, ms., 635–636.
97. A. Bronson Alcott, 1859 Journal, vol. 34, Journals and Diaries of Amos Bronson Alcott, ms., 636.
98. Dillman, "Thoreau's Achievements," 13.
99. Qtd. in Gougeon, *Virtue's Hero*, 246.
100. Gougeon, *Virtue's Hero*, 245.
101. Qtd. in Gougeon, *Virtue's Hero*, 245–246.
102. Lydia Maria Child, Letter to Gov. Wise, 26 October 1859, in *Correspondence between Lydia Maria Child and Gov. Wise and Mrs. Mason, of Virginia* (Boston: American Anti-Slavery Society, 1860), 3.
103. Lydia Maria Child, "Mrs. Child to John Brown," 26 October 1859, in *Correspondence between Lydia Maria Child and Gov. Wise and Mrs. Mason, of Virginia* (Boston: American Anti-Slavery Society, 1860), 14.
104. Deborah Pickman Clifford, *Crusader for Freedom: A Life of Lydia Maria Child* (Boston: Beacon, 1992), 239.
105. Henry A. Wise, "Reply of Gov. Wise," 29 October 1859, in *Correspondence between Lydia Maria Child and Gov. Wise and Mrs. Mason, of Virginia* (Boston: American Anti-Slavery Society, 1860), 4–5.
106. Lydia Maria Child, "Mrs. Child to Gov. Wise [undated]," in *Correspondence between Lydia Maria Child and Gov. Wise and Mrs. Mason, of Virginia* (Boston: American Anti-Slavery Society, 1860), 6–7, 12.
107. John Brown, "Reply of John Brown," [undated], in *Correspondence between Lydia Maria Child and Gov. Wise and Mrs. Mason, of Virginia* (Boston: American Anti-Slavery Society, 1860), 15–16.
108. Clifford, *Crusader*, 239.
109. Lydia Maria Child, "Explanatory Letter," 10 November 1859, in *Correspondence between Lydia Maria Child and Gov. Wise and Mrs. Mason, of Virginia* (Boston: American Anti-Slavery Society, 1860), 13.
110. Qtd. in Clifford, *Crusader*, 240.
111. Lydia Maria Child, "Private Note," *Liberator* [Boston], 4 November 1859, p. 2.
112. Wendell Phillips, appendix, "Remarks of Wendell Phillips at the Funeral of Lydia Maria Child, October 23, 1880," in *Letters of Lydia Maria Child* (1883; New York: Arno and *The New York Times*, 1969), 267.
113. Lydia Maria Child, Letter to "Dear Friend" [unnamed—Anne Warren Weston (?)], 28 November 1859, ms., Ms.A.5.1 no. 79, 1–4, Boston Pub. Library Rare Books and Manuscripts, Boston.
114. Ibid., 4.
115. Lydia Maria Child, "To Mrs. S.M. Parsons," December 1859, in *Letters of Lydia Maria Child* (1883; repr., New York: Arno and *The New York Times*, 1969), 137.
116. Carolyn Karcher, introduction to *A Lydia Maria Child Reader*, ed. Karcher (Durham: Duke University Press, 1997), 17.
117. Lydia Maria Child, Letter to S.E. Sewall, 25 December 1859, ms., Robie-Sewall Collection Folder 1855–1861, 1, Massachusetts Historical Society, Boston.
118. Thomas Wentworth Higginson, *Cheerful*, 223.
119. Ibid., 223.
120. Ibid., 224, 226.
121. Thomas Wentworth Higginson, "Dearest Mother," 27 October 1859, in *Letters and Journals of Thomas Wentworth Higginson, 1846–1906*, ed. Mary Thacher Higginson (Boston: Houghton Mifflin, 1921), 85.
122. Qtd. in Villard, *John Brown*, 512.
123. J.M. McKim, Letter to "Dear Sir" [T.W.H.], 28 October 1859, ms., Ms.E.5.1 pt. 1 p. 69:2, Boston Public Library Rare Books and Manuscripts, Boston.
124. Qtd. in Villard, *John Brown*, 512.
125. T.W. Higginson, *Cheerful*, 226.
126. T.W. Higginson, "Dearest Mother," 5 November 1859, in *Letters*, 87.
127. Villard, *John Brown*, 513; T.W. Higginson, *Cheerful*, 228.
128. T.W. Higginson, "Dearest Mother," 5 November 1859, in *Letters* 87.
129. T.W. Higginson, *Cheerful*, 225–226.
130. Franklin Benjamin Sanborn, Letter to "Dear Friend" [T.W.H.], 13 November 1859, ms., Ms. E.5.1.pt. 1p.89, 2–4 (Boston Public Library Rare Books and Manuscripts, Boston).
131. Villard, *John Brown*, 511.
132. Ibid.
133. Anonymous Note, Thomas Wentworth Higginson Papers, ms., Ms.E.5.1.pt.1p.111, 1 (Boston Public Library Rare Books and Manuscripts, Boston).
134. Thomas Wentworth Higginson, note dated November 14 appended to Letter from J.W. Le Barnes to "Dr. Sir" [T.W.H.], 15 November 1859, ms., Ms.E.5.1.pt. 1p.95, 1 (Boston Public Library Rare Books and Manuscripts, Boston).
135. J.W. Le Barnes, Letter to "Dr. Sir" [T.W.H.], 15 November 1859, ms., Ms.E.5.1.pt.1 p. 95, 1 (Boston Public Library Rare Books and Manuscripts, Boston).

Notes—Chapter Eight

136. Lysander Spooner, Letter to Dear Sir" [T.W.H.], 20 November [1859], ms., Ms.E.5.1 pt. 1 p.110, 1, Boston Public Library Rare Books and Manuscripts, Boston.

137. J.W. Le Barnes, Letter to Dear Sir [T.W.H.], 22 November 1859, ms., Ms.E.5.1.pt.2p118, 1–8, Boston Public Library Rare Books and Manuscripts, Boston.

138. J.W. Le Barnes, Letter to "Dear Sir" [T.W.H.], 1–8.

139. Villard, *John Brown*, 516–17.

140. J.W. Le Barnes, Letter to Dr. Sir [T.W.H.], 27 November 1859, ms., Ms.E.5.1pt.2p.123, 1, Boston Public Library Rare Books and Manuscripts, Boston.

141. J.W. Le Barnes, Cable to Rev. T.W. Higginson, 28 November 1859, ms, Ms.E.5.1pt.2p124, 1, Boston Public Library Rare Books and Manuscripts, Boston.

142. F.B. Sanborn, Letter to "Dear Friend" [T.W.H.], 28 November 1859, ms., Ms.E.5.1 pt. 2 p. 126, 1, Boston Public Library Rare Books and Manuscripts, Boston.

143. T.W. Higginson, Letter to "Dear Sir" [unnamed Lysander Spooner], 28 November 1859, ms., Ms.A.8.1p. 27, 3, Boston Public Library Rare Books and Manuscripts, Boston.

144. Franklin Benjamin Sanborn, Letter to Theodore Parker, 14 November 1859, ms., 2, Concord Free Public Library, Concord.

145. Thomas Wentworth Higginson, Letter to Dr. S.G. Howe [not sent], 15 November 1859, ms., Ms.E.5.1pt.1p.96, 1, Boston Public Library Rare Books and Manuscripts, Boston.

146. T.W. Higginson, Letter to "Dear Friend" [F.B.S.], 17 November 1859, ms., Ms.E.5.1pt.1p.108, 1–2, Boston Public Library Rare Books and Manuscripts, Boston.

147. F.B. Sanborn, Letter to "Dear Friend" [T.W.H.], 19 November 1859, ms., Ms.E.5.1pt1p 108, 1, Boston Public Library Rare Books and Manuscripts, Boston.

148. F.B. Sanborn, Letter to T.W. Higginson, 25 December 1859, ms., 3, Boston Public Library Rare Books and Manuscripts.

149. R[ichard] J[osiah] Hinton, Letter to "Dear Sir" [T.W.H.], 27 December 1859, ms., Ms.E.5.1pt.2p.150, 2, Boston Public Library Rare Books and Manuscripts, Boston.

150. Anonymous, Letter to Rev. T.W. Higginson, 1 November 1859, ms., Ms.E.5.1 pt.1p.111, 3, Boston Public Library Rare Books and Manuscripts.

151. Thomas Wentworth Higginson, Check dated 11 January 1860, ms., Ms.E.5.1 pt. 2 p. 155 (in folder with Le Barnes letter dated 11 January 1860), 1, Boston Public Library Rare Books and Manuscripts, Boston.

152. C.W. Slack, Letter to "Dear Mr. Higginson," 18 November 1859, ms., Ms.E.5.1 pt. 1 p. 107, 1, Boston Public Library Rare Books and Manuscripts, Boston.

153. T.W. Higginson, Letter to "Unnamed," 22 November 1859, in *Letters* 87–88.

154. Ibid., 88.

155. John Brown, Letter to Rev. T.W. Higginson, 22 November 1859, ms., 1, Boston Public Library Rare Books and Manuscripts, Boston.

156. T.W. Higginson, Letter to "His Mother"], 22 November 1859, in *Letters* 88.

157. Robert Penn Warren, *John Brown: The Making of a Martyr* (1929; repr., Nashville: Sanders, 1993), 418.

158. Emerson, *Journals of Ralph Waldo Emerson* 4:334.

159. Thoreau, "A Plea," 93.

160. J. Sella Martin, "Great Meeting in Boston: Speech of Rev. J.S. Martin," *Liberator* [Boston], 9 December 1859, p. 194.

161. Qtd. in Daniel C. Littlefield, "Blacks, John Brown, and a Theory of Manhood," in *His Soul Goes Marching On: Responses to John Brown and the Harpers Ferry Raid*, ed. Paul Finkelman (Charlottesville: University Press of Virginia, 1995), 80.

162. *Douglass' Monthly* (November 1859): 1.

163. L. Maria Child, Letter to "Dear Friend" [unnamed], 22 December 1859, ms., Ms.A.5.1.no. 82, 1, Boston Public Library Rare Books and Manuscripts, Boston.

164. Quarles, *Allies,* 119.

165. "Article from Richmond Enquirer," *Liberator* [Boston], 11 November 1859, p. 1.

166. "Alarming Condition of the Country—Probable Triumph of Black Republican Revolution," *Liberator* [Boston], 11 November 1859, p. 1.

167. "Black-Republican Sympathy," *Chambersburg (PA) Valley Spirit,* 16 November 1859, p. 1.

168. "Va. Correspondent of Boston Courier," *Liberator* [Boston], 11 November 1859, p. 1.

169. "Northern Sentiment," *Staunton (VA) Spectator,* 22 November 1859, p. 2.

170. Qtd. in Villard, *John Brown,* 481.

171. Elijah Avey, *The Capture and Execution of John Brown: A Tale of Martyrdom* (Elgin, IL: Brethren Publishing House, 1906), 69.

172. M.E. Maury, "Letter to Eugenia Burton," 17 October 1859, ed. David T. Gilbert, 2 June 2005, Harpers Ferry National Historical Park, www.nps.gov/archive/hafe/mauzy.htm (accessed September 1, 2008).

173. C.C. Harrison, "A Virginia Girl in the First Year of the War," Electronic Text Center, ed. David Seaman (2002), Alderman Library, University of Virginia 14 Mar 2008, http://etext.Libraryvirginia.edu (accessed 14 March 2008).

174. Avey, *The Capture,* 31.

175. Reynolds, *John Brown, Abolitionist,* 383.

176. Avey, *The Capture,* 31.

177. Ibid., 12.

178. Qtd. in Oates, *To Purge This Land with Blood: A Biography of John Brown* (New York: Harper, 1970), 321.

179. Villard, *John Brown,* 520.

180. George Mauzy, Letter to Mr. and Mrs. James H. Burton, 3 December 1859, ed. David T. Gilbert, 2 June 2005, Harpers Ferry National Historical Park, www.nps.gov/archive/hafe/mauzy.htm (accessed 1 September 2008).

181. Quarles, *Allies,* 106.

182. Ibid.

183. Qtd. in Quarles, *Allies,* 106–107.

184. Henry A. Wise, Letter to Andrew Hunter, Esq., 6 November 1859, ms., 1, Massachusetts Historical Society, Boston.

185. John W. Merritt [illegible], To "His Exy Gov. Wise," 16 November 1859, ms., John Brown Collection, 1, Massachusetts Historical Society, Boston.

186. Qtd. in Villard, *John Brown,* 521.

187. Ibid., 522.

188. Ibid.

189. Ed Gallaher, Letter to Andrew Hunter, Esq., 19 November 1859, ms., John Brown Collection, 1–2, Massachusetts Historical Society, Boston.

190. "A Friend" [unnamed], Letter to Gov. Wise, October 1859, ms., John Brown Collection, 1, Massachusetts Historical Society, Boston.

191. Henry Wise, Letter to Andrew Hunter, Esq., 26 November 1859, ms., John Brown Collection, 1, Massachusetts Historical Society, Boston.
192. Qtd. in Quarles, *Allies*, 109.
193. Qtd. in Dept. of Interior, *John Brown's Raid* (Washington: GPO, 1974), 53.
194. Villard, *John Brown*, 479.
195. Qtd. in Quarles, *Allies*, 111.
196. Paul Finkelman, "Manufacturing Martyrdom: The Antislavery Response to John Brown's Raid," in *His Soul Goes Marching On: Responses to John Brown and the Harpers Ferry Raid*, ed. Paul Finkelman (Charlottesville: University Press of Virginia, 1995), 42.
197. Sanborn, Letter to Theodore Parker, 14 November 1859, ms., Franklin Benjamin Sanford Papers, 1–4, Concord Free Public Library, Concord.
198. Lydia Maria Child, Letter to "Dear Friend" [unnamed], 22 December 1859, ms., Ms.A.5.1 no.82, 1–2, Boston Public Library Rare Books and Manuscripts, Boston.
199. A. Bronson Alcott, 1859, vol. 34, Journals and Diaries of Amos Bronson Alcott, ms., 643.
200. F.B. Sanborn, Letter to "Dear Friend" [T.W.H.], 28 November 1859, ms., Ms.E.5.1pt. 2 p.126, 2, Boston Public Library Rare Books and Manuscripts, Boston.
201. Harding, *The Days*, 420–21.
202. A. Bronson Alcott, 1859, vol. 34, Journals and Diaries of Amos Bronson Alcott, ms., 645.
203. John Shepard Keyes, Autobiography, ms., A45, John Shephard Keyes Papers, 167, Concord Free Public Library, Concord.
204. A. Bronson Alcott, 1859, vol. 34, Journals and Diaries of Amos Bronson Alcott, ms., 649–650.
205. Keyes, Autobiography, 168.
206. Franklin Benjamin Sanborn, *Recollections of Seventy Years*, vol. 1 (1909; repr., Detroit: Gale, 1967), 203.
207. Qtd. in Gougeon, *Virtue's Hero*, 248.
208. Frank Preston Stearns, *The Life and Public Services of George Luther Stearns* (1907; repr. New York: Arno and *The New York Times*, 1969), 198.
209. Annie Russell Marble, *Thoreau: His Home, Friends and Books* (1902; repr. New York: AMS, 1969), 169.
210. Henry David Thoreau, "After the Death of John Brown" (1860) in *The Major Essays of Henry David Thoreau*, ed. Richard Dillman (Albany: Whitston, 2001), 110.
211. A. Bronson Alcott, 1859, vol. 34, Journals and Diaries of Amos Bronson Alcott, ms., 653, 661.
212. Lydia Maria Child, Letter to "Dear Friend" [unnamed—Anne Warren Weston (?)], 28 November 1859, ms. A.5.1.no.79, 4, Boston Public Library Rare Books and Manuscripts, Boston.
213. Qtd. in Lydia Maria Child, Letter to "Dear Friend" [unnamed—Anne Warren Weston (?)], 28 November 1859, ms., Ms.A.5.1 no. 79, 3, Boston Public Library Rare Books and Manuscripts, Boston.
214. Lydia Maria Child, "To Mrs. S.M. Parsons," [undated—December] 1859, in *Letters of Lydia Maria Child*, (1883; New York: Arno and *The New York Times*, 1969), 137–38; *Allies* 126.
215. Quarles, *Allies* 126.
216. Child, Letter to Mrs. S.M. Parsons, [undated—December] 1859, in *Letters*, 138.
217. Quarles, *Allies*, 126; David S. Reynolds, *John Brown Abolitionist: The Man Who Killed Slavery, Sparked the Civil War, and Seeded Civil Rights* (New York: Knopf, 2005), 406.

218. Qtd. in Benjamin Quarles, *Black Abolitionists* (Oxford: Oxford University Press, 1969), 244; Reynolds, *John Brown*, 406.
219. Qtd. in Littlefield, "Blacks," 67.
220. Qtd. in Reynolds, *John Brown*, 408.
221. *A Tribute of Respect, Commemorative of the Worth and Sacrifice of John Brown of Ossawatomie Published for the Benefit of the Widows and Families of the Revolutionists of Harper's Ferry* (1859), 5, Boston Public Library Rare Books and Manuscripts, Cleveland.
222. Ibid., 18.
223. Ibid., 1.
224. Qtd. in Tilden G. Edelstein, *Strange Enthusiasm: A Life of Thomas Wentworth Higginson* (New Haven: Yale University Press, 1968), 231.
225. Murat Halstead, "The Execution of Capt. Brown in *The New York Tribune* 3 December 1859," in *History of John Brown's Raid on Harper's Ferry Sunday, October 16, 1859 as Published in the NY Tribune and NY Times who had Reporters on the Ground* (Des Moines: Watters-Talbott Printing, 1895), 9.
226. Avey, *The Capture*, 32.
227. Ibid., 37.
228. George Mauzy, Letter to Mr. and Mrs. James H. Burton, 3 December 1859, ed. David T. Gilbert, 2 June 2005, M.E. Maury, 17 October 1859, ms., Harpers Ferry National Historical Park, www.nps.gov/archive/hafe/mauzy.htm (accessed 1 September 2008).
229. Oates, *To Purge*, 352.
230. Qtd. in Reynolds, *John Brown*, 406–407.
231. Qtd. in A. Bronson Alcott, 1859, vol. 34, Journals and Diaries of Amos Bronson Alcott, ms., 654.
232. Qtd. in Edward J. Renehan, Jr., *The Secret Six: The True Tale of the Men Who Conspired with John Brown* (New York: Crown, 1995), 231.
233. Franklin Benjamin Sanborn, "Henry David Thoreau," in *Thoreau as Seen by His Contemporaries*, ed. Walter Harding (New York: Dover, 1960), 53–54.
234. Ibid., 54.
235. Ibid.
236. John R. McKivigan, "His Soul Goes Marching On: The Story of John Brown's Followers after the Harpers Ferry Raid," in *Antislavery Violence: Sectional, Racial, and Cultural Conflict in Antebellum America*, ed. John R. McKivigan and Stanley Harrold (Knoxville: University of Tennessee Press, 1999), 280.
237. Francis Jackson, Letter to T.W. Higginson, 6 December 1859, ms., 1, Boston Public Library Rare Books and Manuscripts, Boston.
238. Lydia Maria Child, "Reply of Mrs. Child [to Mrs. Mason],"in *Correspondence between Lydia Maria Child and Gov. Wise and Mrs. Mason, of Virginia* (Boston: American Anti-Slavery Society, 1860), 27.
239. Qtd. in A. Bronson Alcott, 1859, vol. 34, Journals and Diaries of Amos Bronson Alcott, ms., 655.
240. Thomas Wentworth Higginson, *Contemporaries* (Boston: Houghton Mifflin, 1899), 134.
241. M.J.C. Mason, "Letter of Mrs. Mason," 11 November 1859, in *Correspondence between Lydia Maria Child and Gov. Wise and Mrs. Mason, of Virginia* (Boston: American Anti-Slavery Society, 1860), 16–17.
242. Mason, "Letter," 17.
243. T.W. Higginson, *Contemporaries* 134.
244. Child, "Reply of Mrs. Child," 18.
245. Ibid., 20.
246. Ibid., 22.
247. Ibid., 26.

Notes—Chapter Eight

248. Ibid., 26.
249. Ibid., 27–28.
250. Clifford, *Crusader,* 242.
251. Lydia Maria Child, Letter to "Dear Friend" [S.E. Sewall], 13 December 1859, ms., Robie-Sewall Collection, Folder 1855–1861, 1, Massachusetts Historical Society, Boston.
252. Lydia Maria Child, Letter to S.M. Parsons, [undated] 1859, in *Letters of Lydia Maria Child,* 138.
253. Lydia Maria Child, Letter to Aaron D. Stevens, 19 December 1859, ts., Stevens Family Papers, 1770–1911, Folder December 18–23, 1859, 1 (Massachusetts Historical Society, Boston).
254. Lydia Maria Child, Letter to "Dear Friend" [unnamed], 22 December 1859, ms., Ms.A.5.1. no. 82, 2, Boston Public Library Rare Books and Manuscripts, Boston.
255. Lydia Maria Child, Letter to Marianne Silsbee, 12 January 1860, ms., Letters to Marianne Silsbee, 1847–1880, Miscellaneous mss., C Box 4 Folder 7, 1 (American Antiquarian Society, Worcester).
256. Thomas Wentworth Higginson, *Contemporaries,* 135.
257. Samuel J. May, "Mrs. L. Maria Child," in *Some Recollections of Our Antislavery Conflict* (1869; repr., New York: Arno, 1968), 100.
258. T.W. Higginson, *Contemporaries,* 135.
259. Clifford, *Crusader,* 244.
260. T.W. Higginson, *Contemporaries,* 135.
261. Lydia Maria Child, Letter to S.J. May, 29 September 1867, in *Lydia Maria Child Selected Letters, 1817–1880,* ed. Milton Meltzer and Patricia G. Holland (Amherst: University of Massachusetts Press, 1982), 474.
262. Clifford, *Crusader,* 244.
263. Lydia Maria Child, Letter to "Dear Friend" [Maria Chapman], 15 January 1860, ms., 1–2, Boston Public Library Rare Books and Manuscripts, Boston.
264. Qtd. in Clifford, *Crusader,* 245.
265. Lydia Maria Child, Letter to "Dear Friend," 11 January 1860, ms., 3, Boston Public Library Rare Books and Manuscripts, Boston.
266. T.W. Higginson, *Cheerful,* 229.
267. Mary Higginson, *Thomas,* 196–197.
268. R[ichard] J[osiah] Hinton, Letter to "Dear Sir" [T.W.H.], 13 December 1859, ms., Ms.E.5.1 pt. 2 p. 136, 1, Boston Public Library Rare Books and Manuscripts, Boston.
269. T.W. Higginson, *Cheerful,* 231.
270. Ibid., 231–232.
271. Ibid., 232.
272. Ibid., 233–234.
273. Mary Higginson, *Thomas,* 198.
274. T.W. Higginson, *Cheerful,* 234.
275. Qtd. in Mary Higginson, *Thomas,* 199.
276. Ibid., 199–200.
277. Qtd. in McFeely, *Frederick Douglass,* 203–204.
278. Ibid., 204.
279. Ibid., 207–208.
280. Charles W. Chesnutt, *Frederick Douglass* (Boston: Small, Maynard, 1899), 88–89.
281. Holland, *Frederick Douglass,* 277.
282. Qtd. in A. Bronson Alcott, 1859, vol. 34, Journals and Diaries of Amos Bronson Alcott, ms., 130.
283. Ibid., 123.
284. Townsend Scudder, *Concord: American Town* (Boston: Little, Brown, 1947), 224.
285. Ellen Tucker Emerson, "Dear Agnes," 4 April 1860, *The Letters of Ellen Tucker Emerson,* vol. 1, ed. Edith E. W. Gregg (Kent, OH: Kent State University Press, 1982), 213.
286. Qtd. in A. Bronson Alcott, 1859, vol. 34, Journals and Diaries of Amos Bronson Alcott, ms., 130.
287. Qtd. in A. Bronson Alcott, 1859, vol. 34, Journals and Diaries of Amos Bronson Alcott, ms., 130; Keyes, Autobiography, 168–169.
288. Qtd. in A. Bronson Alcott, 1859, vol. 34, Journals and Diaries of Amos Bronson Alcott, ms., 130.
289. "A Concord Arrest in 1860," *The Middlesex Patriot* 2, no. 15 [Concord, MA] (29 March 1901): C. Pam 29, Item 33, 1, Concord: Concord Free Public Library.
290. Mary Brooks, Letter to "Dear Mrs. Chapman," 9 April 1860, ms., 1, Boston Public Library Rare Books and Manuscripts, Boston.
291. "The Last Concord Fight," 5 April 1860, *Boston Herald,* Collection of newspaper clippings relating to F.B. Sanborn, 1860–1973, C. Pam 29 Item 71, Concord Free Public Library.
292. Harding, *The Days,* 423–424.
293. Henry David Thoreau, "Journal," in *The Writings of Henry David Thoreau,* ed. Bradford Torrey, vol. 13 (Boston: Houghton Mifflin, 1906), 241.
294. Keyes, Autobiography, 169.
295. Qtd. in A. Bronson Alcott, 1859, vol. 34, Journals and Diaries of Amos Bronson Alcott, ms., 122.
296. Villard, *John Brown,* 534.
297. Qtd. in A. Bronson Alcott, 1859, vol. 34, Journals and Diaries of Amos Bronson Alcott, ms., 122.
298. Ibid., 123.
299. Keyes, Autobiography, 170.
300. Qtd. in Jeffrey Rossback, *Ambivalent Conspirators: John Brown, the Secret Six, and a Theory of Slave Violence* (Philadelphia: University of Pennsylvania Press, 1982), 264.
301. Qtd. in A. Bronson Alcott, 1859, vol. 34, Journals and Diaries of Amos Bronson Alcott, ms., 123.
302. Ibid., 122.
303. Ibid.
304. Harding, *The Days,* 425.
305. Tilden Edelstein, *Strange Enthusiasm: A Life of Thomas Wentworth Higginson* (New Haven: Yale University Press, 1968), 237.
306. Henry David Thoreau, "The Last Days of John Brown" (1860), in *The Major Essays of Henry David Thoreau,* ed. Richard Dillman (Albany: Whitston, 2001), 103, 106.
307. Qtd. in Harding, *The Days,* 425.
308. Qtd. in Holland, *Frederick Douglass,* 281.
309. Qtd. in McFeely, *Frederick Douglass,* 209.
310. Lydia Maria Child, Letter to Mrs. S.B. Shaw, [undated] 1861, in *Letters of Lydia Maria Child* 148.
311. Qtd. in Mary Higginson, *Thomas,* 201.
312. Edelstein, *Strange Enthusiasm,* 241–242.
313. Wendell Phillips, "Burial of John Brown," in *Speeches, Lectures, and Letters* (1884; New York: Negro University Press, 1968), 291.
314. Frederick Douglass, "An Address by Frederick Douglass at the Fourteenth Anniversary of Storer College, Harpers Ferry, West Virginia, May 30, 1881 (Dover, NH: Morning Star, 1881), 28.
315. Sanborn, *Recollections,* 252.
316. Wendell Phillips, "Burial of John Brown," 289, 290, 293.

Chapter Nine

1. Robert Penn Warren, *John Brown: The Making of a Martyr* (1929; repr., Nashville: J.S. Sanders, 1993), 430.
2. Carlos Baker, *Emerson among the Eccentrics: A Group Portrait* (New York: Viking, 1996), 386.
3. Lydia Maria Child, Letter to Miss Eliza Scudder, [undated] 1864, in *Letters of Lydia Maria Child* (1883; New York: Arno and *The New York Times*, 1969), 180.
4. James Redpath, *The Public Life of Capt. John Brown* (Boston: Thayer and Eldridge, 1860), 1.
5. C. Vann Woodward, introduction, *John Brown: The Making of a Martyr*, by Robert Penn Warren (1929; repr., Nashville: Sanders, 1993), xi.
6. W.E.B. DuBois, *John Brown*, (1909; Armonk, NY: Sharpe, 1997), 196.
7. Louisa May Alcott, Letter to Anna Alcott Pratt, 18[?] March 1861, in *The Selected Letters of Louisa May Alcott*, ed. Joel Myerson and Daniel Shealy (Athens: University of Georgia Press, 1995), 62–63.
8. Louisa May Alcott, *The Journals of Louisa May Alcott*, ed. Joel Myerson and Daniel Shealy (Athens: University of Georgia Press, 1997), 104.
9. Gilman M. Ostrander, "Emerson, Thoreau, and John Brown," *The Mississippi Valley Historical Review* 39, no. 4, (March 1953): 726.
10. Sallee Fox Engstrom, *The Infinitude of the Private Man: Emerson's Presence in Western New York, 1851–1861* (New York: Lang, 1997), 34.
11. Qtd. in Delores Bird Carpenter, introduction, *The Selected Letters of Lidian Jackson Emerson*, by Lidian Jackson Emerson (Columbia: University of Missouri Press, 1987), xvi–xvii.
12. Sandra Harbert Petrulionis, "Swelling That Great Tide of Humanity: The Concord, Massachusetts, Female Anti-Slavery Society," *The New England Quarterly* 74, no. 3 (2001): 417.
13. David W. Blight, *Admiration and Ambivalence: Frederick Douglass and John Brown* (New York: Gilder Lehrman Institute of American History, 2005), 7.
14. Questions persist about exactly what Douglass promised Brown at Chambersburg prior to the raid, leaving us to forever wonder what was actually agreed upon at the quarry. Four months prior to the raid, on 17 June 1859, raider Jeremiah G. Anderson maintained the following: "Douglass is to be one of us. Brown's daughter, Annie Brown Adams, asserted that both her father and Kagi, upon their return from Chambersburg, claimed Douglass had promised to follow Brown 'even unto death.' After the raid, conspirator John E. Cook declared from his jail cell that Douglass failed to provide promised men and weapons for the venture. Brown himself never publicly disavowed Douglass, but Mrs. Thomas Russell, upon returning from a visit to Brown in his cell, reported to Massachusetts friends that Brown "had no fondness for Fred Douglass." Another who questioned Douglass' account was Alfred Webb, the son of Irish abolitionists, who had known Douglass from his trips abroad, and in 1907 wondered "to what extent Frederick Douglass's recollections were correct as to the degree of his definite advice to Brown against the raid" (quoted in Quarles, *Allies*, 78). Yet, Alex R. Boteler, a local congressman and eyewitness to the raid, claimed to have seen a list Brown had compiled of "reliable" and "nonreliable" recruits with the name Frederick Douglass topping the latter column, suggesting that perhaps Douglass had not, in fact, fully committed to the project (Quarles, *Allies* 78–79). John Brown, Jr., would assert that neither Kagi nor his father ever wrote a word about the gathering in Chambersburg, adding that his brother Owen, a participant at the ferry, had never heard his father mention the disputed meeting. The final word, therefore, is perhaps left to John, Jr., who said, "It may be that the mist will never be cleared away respecting this actor in the drama" (qtd. in Quarles, *Allies* 79). And to this day that seems to be the closest truth one can assert.
15. Frederick Douglass, "Did John Brown Fail?: An Address Delivered in Harpers Ferry, West Virginia, on 30 May 1881," in *The Frederick Douglass Papers*, ed. John W. Blassingame and John R. McKivigan, vol. 5 (New Haven: Yale University Press, 1992), 8, 12, 23.
16. Introduction, Frederick Douglass, "Did John Brown Fail?" 1.
17. "Death of Frederick Douglass, *Chicago Tribune* 22 February 1895," in *In Memoriam: Frederick Douglass* (1897; Freeport, NY: Books for Libraries, 1971), 297; "Frederick Douglass, *New York Independent]* 28 February 1895," in *In Memoriam: Frederick Douglass*, 307.
18. Lydia Maria Child, *The Freedmen's Book* (Boston: Ticknor and Fields, 1865).
19. Bruce Mills, "Lydia Maria Child and the Endings to Harriet Jacobs's *Incidents in the Life of a Slave Girl*," *American Literature* 64.2 (1992), 265; Lydia Maria Child, Letter to Rev. Samuel J. May, January, 1866, in *Letters of Lydia Maria Child* (1883; New York: Arno and *The New York Times*, 1969), 192.
20. Lydia Maria Child, Letter to Theodore D. Weld, 10 July 1880, in *Letters of Lydia Maria Child* (1883: New York: Arno and *The New York Times*, 1969), 259.
21. Clifford, *Crusader*, 249–250.
22. Qtd. in Clifford, *Crusader*, 250.
23. Clifford, *Crusader*, 250.
24. Thomas Wentworth Higginson, *Contemporaries* (Boston: Houghton Mifflin, 1899), 136.
25. Qtd. in Mills, "Endings," 255.
26. Mills, "Endings," 257.
27. Lydia Maria Child, Letter to John G. Whittier, 21 January 1862, in *Letters of Lydia Maria Child* (1883; repr., New York: Arno and *The New York Times*, 1969), 161.
28. Carolyn Karcher, introduction, *A Lydia Maria Child Reader*, ed. Karcher. (Durham: Duke University Press, 1997), 18.
29. Thomas Wentworth Higginson, *Letters and Journals of Thomas Wentworth Higginson, 1846–1906*, ed. Mary Thacher Higginson (Boston: Houghton Mifflin, 1921), 82.
30. John Greenleaf Whittier, introduction, *Letters of Lydia Maria Child* (1883; repr., New York: Arno and *The New York Times*, 1969), xxv.
31. Thomas Wentworth Higginson, *Cheerful Yesterdays* (Boston: Houghton Mifflin, 1898), 77.
32. Karcher, introduction, *A Lydia Maria Child Reader*, 1.
33. Wendell Phillips, appendix, "Remarks of Wendell Phillips at the Funeral of Lydia Maria Child, October 23, 1880," in *Letters of Lydia Maria Child*, (1883; repr., New York: Arno and *The New York Times*, 1969), 267.
34. Anna Mary Wells, *Dear Preceptor: The Life of Thomas Wentworth Higginson* (Boston: Houghton Mifflin, 1963), 50.
35. Qtd. in Mary Thacher Higginson, *Thomas Wentworth Higginson: The Story of His Life* (Port Washington, NY: Kennikat, 1971), 204.

Notes—Chapter Nine

36. Qtd. in Mary Thacher Higginson, *Thomas,* 204.
37. Ibid., 215.
38. Ibid., 217.
39. Thomas Wentworth Higginson, *Army Life in a Black Regiment* (1869; New York: Norton, 1984), 206.
40. Edward J. Renehan, Jr., *The Secret Six: The True Tale of the Men Who Conspired with John Brown* (New York: Crown, 1995), 5.
41. Thomas Wentworth Higginson, Letter to Ralph Waldo Emerson, 20 February 1863, in *The Complete Civil War Journal and Selected Letters of Thomas Wentworth Higginson,* ed. Christopher Looby (Chicago: University of Chicago Press, 2000), 262.
42. T.W. Higginson, *Cheerful,* 170.
43. Tilden G. Edelstein, *Strange Enthusiasm: A Life of Thomas Wentworth Higginson* (New Haven: Yale University Press, 1968), 357–58.
44. Thomas Wentworth Higginson, "Thoreau," in *Short Studies of American Authors* (1880; Norwood, PA: Norwood, 1978), 30.
45. Thomas Wentworth Higginson, "Thoreau," 23–24.
46. Thomas Wentworth Higginson, *Part of a Man's Life* (Boston: Houghton Mifflin, 1905), 16.
47. Wells, *Dear Preceptor,* 117.
48. Qtd. in Edelstein, *Strange Enthusiasm,* 242.
49. Renehan, *The Secret Six,* 273, 221.
50. Ibid., 273.
51. Qtd. in Renehan, *The Secret Six,* 273.
52. Renehan, *The Secret Six,* 5.
53. Qtd. in Renehan, *The Secret Six,* 5.
54. Oswald Garrison Villard, *John Brown 1800–1859: A Biography Fifty Years After* (1910; New York: Knopf, 1943), 529.
55. Mary Thacher Higginson, *Thomas,* 400.
56. Ibid., 400.
57. United States, "The Mason Report," in *Mass Violence in America: Invasion at Harpers Ferry,* ed. Robert M. Fogelson and Richard E. Rubenstein (New York: Arno and *The New York Times,* 1969), 3.
58. Anthony Burns, Letter to Richard Henry Dana, 30 August 1857, ms., Dana Family Papers, Box 15, PD12103, 1, Massachusetts Historical Society, Boston.
59. Wells, *Dear Preceptor,* 90.
60. Lydia Maria Child, Letter to Mrs. S.B. Shaw, [undated] 1860, in *Letters of Lydia Maria Child* (1883; New York: Arno and *The New York Times,* 1969), 144–145.
61. "Frank Sanborn, Concord Sage, Appeals Fine," 17 Nov [undated], Collection of Newspaper Clippings Related to F.B. Sanborn, 1860–1973, Concord Free Public Library, Concord, MA.
62. Qtd. in United States, Dept. of Interior, *John Brown's Raid* (Washington: GPO, 1974), 61.
63. Zoe Trodd and John Stauffer, eds., *Meteor of War: The John Brown Story* (Maplecrest, NY: Brandywine, 2004), 257–258.

64. David T. Gilbert, *A Walker's Guide to Harpers Ferry West Virginia,* 1983 (Harpers Ferry: Harpers Ferry Historical Association, 2003), 49.
65. John Speer, "John Brown: John Speer's Note Referring to, Omitted from His Annual Address before the Society," 18 January 1898, Personal papers, folder 3.09, John Brown Papers, microfilm MS 1246, Kansas State Historical Society.
66. Mary Thacher Higginson, *Thomas,* 200.
67. Benjamin Quarles, *Black Mosaic: Essays in Afro-American History and Historiography* (Amherst: University of Massachusetts Press, 1988), 75–76.
68. David S. Reynolds, *John Brown Abolitionist: The Man Who Killed Slavery, Sparked the Civil War, and Seeded Civil Rights* (New York: Knopf, 2005), 6.
69. United States, "Views of the Minority to the Mason Report," in *Mass Violence in America: Invasion at Harpers Ferry,* ed. Robert M. Fogelson and Richard E. Rubenstein (New York: Arno and *The New York Times,* 1969), 23.
70. United States, "The Mason Report," in *Mass Violence in America: Invasion at Harpers Ferry,* ed. Robert M. Fogelson and Richard E. Rubenstein (New York: Arno and *The New York Times,* 1969), 7–8.
71. Lydia Maria Child, "Mrs. L. Maria Child to the President of the United States," in *A Lydia Maria Child Reader,* ed. Carolyn L. Karcher (Durham: Duke University Press, 1997), 254.
72. Thomas Wentworth Higginson, Letter to Ralph Waldo Emerson, 20 February 1863, in *The Complete Civil War Journal and Selected Letters of Thomas Wentworth Higginson,* ed. Christopher Looby (Chicago: University of Chicago Press, 2000), 262, note.
73. David S. Reynolds, *John Brown Abolitionist,* 3–6.
74. Qtd. in Edelstein, *Strange Enthusiasm,* 261.
75. Edward Waldo Emerson, *Henry Thoreau as Remembered by a Young Friend* (Mineola, NY: Dover, 1999), 49.
76. Walter Harding, *The Days of Henry Thoreau: A Biography* (Princeton, Princeton University Press, 1992), 426
77. Qtd. in Harding, *The Days,* 465.
78. Louisa May Alcott, Letter to Sophia Foord, 11 May 1862, in *The Selected Letters of Louisa May Alcott,* eds. Joel Myerson and Daniel Shealy (Athens: University of Georgia Press, 1995), 74.
79. Louisa May Alcott, Letter to Sophia Foord, 11 May 1862, 75.
80. Ralph Waldo Emerson, "Thoreau," *Walden and Resistance to Civil Government,* ed. William Rossi (New York: Norton, 1992), 323–324.
81. Harding, *The Days,* 422–423.
82. Henry David Thoreau, "Journal," in *The Writings of Henry David Thoreau,* ed. Bradford Torrey, vol. 12 (Boston: Houghton Mifflin, 1906), 421.

Bibliography

"Alarming Condition of the Country—Probable Triumph of Black Republican Revolution." *Liberator* [Boston], 11 November 1859, p. 1.

Alcott, Bronson. Journals and Diaries of Amos Bronson Alcott. Amos Bronson Alcott Papers. Vol. 24 [MS Am 1130.12 (34)]; Vol. 29 [MS Am 1130.12 (29)]. Houghton Library, Harvard University, Cambridge, MA. By permission of the Houghton Library, Harvard University.

———. *The Journals of Bronson Alcott.* 1938. Edited by Odell S. Shepard. Vol. 2. Port Washington, NY: Kennikat, 1966.

———. "To Daniel Ricketson." 6 November 1859. In *The Letters of A. Bronson Alcott*, ed. Richard L. Herrnstadt. Ames: Iowa State University Press, 1969.

Alcott, Louisa May. *The Journals of Louisa May Alcott.* Edited by Joel Myerson and Daniel Shealy. Athens: University of Georgia Press, 1997.

———. *The Selected Letters of Louisa May Alcott.* Edited by Joel Myerson and Daniel Shealy. Athens: University of Georgia Press, 1995.

Anderson, Osborne P. *A Voice from Harpers Ferry.* 1861. Reprint, Freeport, NY: Books for Libraries, 1972.

Andrew, John A. *List of Contributors to Defense of John Brown.* 2–8 November 1859. Special Collections, Massachusetts Historical Society, Boston.

Andrews, William F. Introduction. *Narrative of the Life of Frederick Douglass.* In *The Oxford Frederick Douglass Reader.* Edited by William F. Andrews. New York: Oxford University Press, 1996.

———. Introduction. *The Oxford Frederick Douglass Reader.* Edited by William F. Andrews. New York: Oxford University Press, 1996.

Anonymous. Letter to T.W. Higginson. 1 November 1859. Boston Public Library Rare Books and Manuscripts, Boston. 1–3. Boston Public Library/Rare Books Department. Courtesy of the Trustees.

Anonymous. Note. Ms.E.5.1.pt.1p.111. Thomas Wentworth Higginson Papers. Boston Public Library Rare Books and Manuscripts, Boston. 1. Boston Public Library/Rare Books Department. Courtesy of the Trustees.

"Article from *Richmond Enquirer.*" *Liberator* [Boston], 11 November 1859, p. 1.

Avey, Elijah. *The Capture and Execution of John Brown: A Tale of Martyrdom.* Elgin, IL: Brethren, 1906.

"Backing Out." *Liberator* [Boston], 28 October 1859, p. 1.

Baker, Carlos. *Emerson among the Eccentrics: A Group Portrait.* New York: Viking, 1996.

Barry, Joseph. *The Strange Story of Harper's Ferry.* 1903. Reprint, Shepherdstown, WV: Woman's Club of Harpers Ferry District, 1969.

Bartlett, Irving H. *Wendell Phillips: Brahmin Radical.* Boston: Beacon, 1961.

"Black-Republican Sympathy." *Chambersburg (PA) Valley Spirit*, 16 November 1859, p. 1.

Blassingame, John W., ed. Introduction to vol. 1. In *The Frederick Douglass Papers*, by Frederick Douglass. Eds. John Blassingame, John R. McKivigan, and Peter P. Hinks. New Haven: Yale University Press, 1999.

Blight, David W. *Admiration & Ambivalence: Frederick Douglass and John Brown.* New York: Gilder Lehrman, 2005.

The Boston Slave Riot and Trial of Anthony Burns: Report of the Faneuil Hall Meeting; The Murder of Bachelder; Theodore Parker's Lesson for the Day; Speeches of Counsel on Both Sides, Corrected by Themselves; Verbatim Report of Judge Loring's Decision; And, A Detailed Account of the Embarkation. Boston: Fetridge, 1854.

Brooks, Mary. Letter to "Dear Mrs. Chapman." 9 April 1860. Ms.A.9.2.30 p.39. Boston Public Library Rare Books and Manuscripts, Boston. 1–4. Boston Public Library/Rare Books Department. Courtesy of the Trustees.

Brown, John. *John Brown: The Making of a Revolutionary.* Edited by Louis Ruchames. New York: Grossett, 1971.

———. Letter to "Dear Wife and Children Every

One." 7 September 1856. Personal papers, folder 1.17, John Brown Papers, microfilm MS 1245. Kansas State Historical Society.

———. Letter to Rev. T.W. Higginson. 2 February 1858. Ms.E.5.1 pt. 1 p. 4. Thomas Wentworth Higginson Papers. Boston Public Library Rare Books and Manuscripts, Boston. 1. Boston Public Library/Rare Books Department. Courtesy of the Trustees.

———. Letter to Rev. T.W. Higginson. 12 February 1858. Ms.E.5.1.pt.1 p.7. Thomas Wentworth Higginson Papers. Boston Public Library Rare Books and Manuscripts, Boston. 1. Boston Public Library/Rare Books Department. Courtesy of the Trustees.

———. Letter to Rev. T.W. Higginson. 4 March 1858. Thomas Wentworth Higginson Papers. Boston Public Library Rare Books and Manuscripts, Boston. 1. Boston Public Library/Rare Books Department. Courtesy of the Trustees.

———. Letter to Rev. T.W.H. 14 May 1858. ts. John Brown Collection. Massachusetts Historical Society, Boston. 1–2. Courtesy of the Massachusetts Historical Society.

———. Letter to T.W.H. 14 May 1858. Ms.E.5.1 pt. 1 p. 26. Thomas Wentworth Higginson Papers. Boston Public Library Rare Books and Manuscripts, Boston. 1. Boston Public Library/Rare Books Department. Courtesy of the Trustees.

———. Letter to T.W. Higginson. 13–16 September 1858. ts. John Brown Collection. Massachusetts Historical Society, Boston. 1–2. Boston Public Library/Rare Books Department. Courtesy of the Trustees.

———. Letter to Rev. T.W. Higginson. 22 November 1859. Ms.E.5.1 p. 117. Boston Public Library Rare Books and Manuscripts, Boston. 1. Boston Public Library/Rare Books Department. Courtesy of the Trustees.

———. *The Life and Letters of John Brown: Liberator of Kansas, and Martyr of Virginia*. 1885. Edited by F.B. Sanborn. New York: Negro University Press, 1969.

———. Old Brown's Farewell to the Plymouth Rocks, Bunker Hill Monuments, Charter Oaks, and Uncle Tom's Cabbins [*sic*]. April 1857. Personal papers, folder 1.22, John Brown Papers, microfilm MS 1245. Kansas State Historical Society.

———. "Reply of John Brown." *Correspondence between Lydia Maria Child and Gov. Wise and Mrs. Mason, of Virginia*. Boston: American Anti-Slavery Society, 1860.

Brown, John, Jr. *John Brown of Asawatomie—A History Not an Apology*. 1883. A35 Folder 6. Franklin Benjamin Sanborn Papers Series II 1845–1901. Concord Free Public Library, Concord, MA. Courtesy Concord Free Public Library.

———. Letter from John Brown, Jr., Frederick Douglass Papers. 25 December 1851.

Burns, Anthony. Letter to Richard Henry Dana. 23 August 1854. Dana Family Papers, Massachusetts Historical Society, Boston. 1. Courtesy of the Massachusetts Historical Society.

———. Letter to Richard Henry Dana. 30 August 1857. Dana Family Papers, Massachusetts Historical Society, Boston. 1. Courtesy of the Massachusetts Historical Society.

Byrne, John Edward. "The News from Harpers Ferry: The Press as Lens and Prism for John Brown's Raid." PhD. diss., George Washington University, 1987.

C.K.W. "Fifth Fraternity Lecture." *Liberator* [Boston], 4 November 1859, p. 174.

Cameron, Kenneth Walter. *Thoreau, Sanborn, John Brown and Slavery*. Hartford: Transcendental, 2000.

Canby, Henry Seidel. *Thoreau*. Boston: Beacon, 1939.

Carpenter, Delores Bird. Introduction. In *The Selected Letters of Lidian Jackson Emerson*, by Lidian Jackson Emerson. Columbia: University of Missouri Press, 1987.

Cayton, Mary Kupiec. "The Making of an American Prophet: Emerson, His Audiences, and the Rise of the Culture Industry in Nineteenth-Century America." In *Ralph Waldo Emerson: A Collection of Critical Essays*, ed. Lawrence Buell. Englewood Cliffs: Prentice-Hall, 1993.

"Celebration of W.I. Emancipation at Abington, August First, 1854." *Liberator* [Boston], 11 August 1854, p. 126.

Channing, William E. *Slavery*. Boston: James Munroe, 1835.

Chesnutt, Charles W. *Frederick Douglass*. Boston: Small, Maynard, 1899.

Child, D. Lee. To Angelina Grimke. 12 February 1838. In *Letters of Theodore Dwight Weld, Angelina Grimke Weld and Sarah Grimke, 1822–1844*. 1934. Vol. 2, ed. Gilbert H. Barnes and Dwight L. Dumond. Reprint, New York: Da Capo, 1970.

Child, Lydia Maria. *An Appeal in Favor of That Class of Americans Called Africans*. 1836. Reprint, New York: Arno & *The New York Times*, 1968.

Child, Mrs. [Lydia Maria]. *An Appeal in Favor of That Class of Americans Called Africans*. New York: Allen and Ticknor, 1833.

———. "By Mrs. Child." *Liberator* [Boston], 19 October 1833, p. 168.

_____. "Explanatory Letter." 10 November 1859. *Correspondence between Lydia Maria Child and Gov. Wise and Mrs. Mason, of Virginia.* Boston: American Anti-Slavery Society, 1860.

_____. *The Freedmen's Book.* Boston: Ticknor and Fields, 1865.

_____. "Jumbo and Zairee." In *A Lydia Maria Child Reader*, ed. Carolyn L. Karcher. Durham: Duke University Press, 1997.

_____. Letter to "Dear Friend." 11 January 1860. Boston Public Library Rare Books and Manuscripts, Boston. 1–4. Boston Public Library/Rare Books Department. Courtesy of the Trustees.

_____. Letter to "Dear Friend" [Maria Chapman]. 15 January 1860. Boston Public Library Rare Books and Manuscripts, Boston. 1–2. Boston Public Library/Rare Books Department. Courtesy of the Trustees.

_____. Letter to "Dear Friend" [S.E. Sewall]. 13 December 1859. Robie-Sewall Family Papers, Massachusetts Historical Society, Boston. 1–2. Courtesy of the Massachusetts Historical Society.

_____. Letter to "Dear Friend" [unnamed—Anne Warren Weston (?)]. 28 November 1859. Ms.A.5.1. no. 79. Boston Public Library Rare Books and Manuscripts, Boston. 1–4. Boston Public Library/Rare Books Department. Courtesy of the Trustees.

_____. Letter to "Dear Friend" [unnamed]. 22 December 1859. Ms.A.5.1 no. 82. Boston Public Library Rare Books and Manuscripts, Boston. 1–4. Boston Public Library/Rare Books Department. Courtesy of the Trustees.

_____. "Letter to Gov. Wise." 26 October 1859. *Correspondence between Lydia Maria Child and Gov. Wise and Mrs. Mason of Virginia.* Boston: American Anti-Slavery Society, 1860.

_____. Letter to Marianne Silsbee. 12 January 1860. Letters to Marianne Silsbee, 1847–1880. Miscellaneous Mss. C Box 4, Folder 7. Worcester: American Antiquarian Society.

_____. Letter to Mr. [Aaron] Stevens. 19 December 1859. ts. Stevens Family Papers, Massachusetts Historical Society, Boston. 1–4.

_____. Letter to S.E. Sewall. 25 December 1859. Robie-Sewall Family Papers, Massachusetts Historical Society, Boston. 1–2. Courtesy of the Massachusetts Historical Society.

_____. "Letters from New-York, No. 33." In *A Lydia Maria Child Reader*, ed. Carolyn L. Karcher. Durham: Duke University Press, 1997.

_____. *Letters of Lydia Maria Child.* 1883. New York: Arno & *The New York Times*, 1969.

_____. *Lydia Maria Child Selected Letters, 1817–1880.* Edited by Milton Meltzer and Patricia G. Holland. Amherst: University of Massachusetts Press, 1982.

_____. "Mrs. Child to Gov. Wise [undated]." *Correspondence between Lydia Maria Child and Gov. Wise and Mrs. Mason, of Virginia.* Boston: American Anti-Slavery Society, 1860.

_____. "Mrs. Child to John Brown." 26 October 1859. *Correspondence between Lydia Maria Child and Gov. Wise and Mrs. Mason, of Virginia.* Boston: American Anti-Slavery Society, 1860.

_____. "Mrs. L. Maria Child to the President of the United States." In *A Lydia Maria Child Reader*, ed. Carolyn L. Karcher. Durham: Duke University Press, 1997.

_____. *The Oasis.* Boston: Benjamin C. Bacon, 1834.

_____. *Isaac T. Hopper: A True Life.* Boston: John P. Jewett, 1853.

_____. *The Oasis.* Boston: Benjamin C. Bacon, 1834.

_____. *Philothea: A Grecian Romance.* New York: C.S. Francis, 1848.

_____. *Philothea: A Romance.* Boston: Otis, Broaders, 1836.

_____. "Private Note." *Liberator* [Boston], 4 November 1859, p. 2.

_____. "To Prof. Convers Francis." 14 July 1848. In *Letters of Lydia Maria Child.* 1883. Reprint, New York: Arno & *The New York Times*, 1969.

_____. "Reminiscences of Dr. Channing by Mrs. Child, Written after His Death and Published in His Memoirs." In *Letters of Lydia Maria Child.* 1883. Reprint, New York: Arno & *The New York Times*, 1969.

_____. "Reply of Mrs. Child [to Mrs. Mason]." *Correspondence between Lydia Maria Child and Gov. Wise and Mrs. Mason, of Virginia.* Boston: American Anti-Slavery Society, 1860.

Clifford, Deborah Pickman. *Crusader for Freedom: A Life of Lydia Maria Child.* Boston: Beacon, 1992.

"The Cloud in the Distance." *Cincinnati Enquirer*, 19 October 1859. Furman Secession Era Editorials Project. John Brown's Raid on Harper's Ferry (October–December 1859), http://history.furman.edu/benson/docs/jbmenu.htm.

Coalition of Publishers for Employment. *Turning the World Upside Down: The Anti-Slavery Convention of American Women May 9–12, 1837.* New York: Feminist, 1987.

"A Concord Arrest in 1860." *The Middlesex Patriot* 2, no. 15 (29 March 1901). C. Pam 29, Item 33. Concord Free Public Library, Concord. 1.

Cook, James H. "Fighting with Breath, Not Blows:

Frederick Douglass and Antislavery Violence." In *Antislavery Violence: Sectional, Racial, and Cultural Conflict in Antebellum America*, ed. John R. McKivigan and Stanley Harrold. Knoxville: University of Tennessee Press, 1999.

Cooke, George W. "The Two Thoreaus." In *Thoreau as Seen by His Contemporaries*, ed. Walter Harding. New York: Dover, 1989.

Dana, Richard Henry. *The Journal of Richard Henry Dana, Jr.* Vol. 2. Edited by Robert F. Lucid. Cambridge, MA: Belknap Press of Harvard University Press, 1968.

"Death of Frederick Douglass, *Chicago Tribune*, 22 February 1895." In *In Memoriam: Frederick Douglass*. 1897. Reprint, Freeport, NY: Books for Libraries, 1971.

Dedmond, Francis B. "A Fugitive Emerson Letter." In *The American Transcendental Quarterly: A Journal of New England Writers* 41(1979): 13–16.

Dillman, Richard. "Thoreau's Achievements as an Essayist." In *The Major Essays of Henry David Thoreau*, by Henry David Thoreau. Albany: Whitston, 2001.

Douglass, Frederick. "An Address by Frederick Douglass at the Fourteenth Anniversary of Storer College, Harpers Ferry, West Virginia, May 30, 1881." Dover, NH: Morning Star, 1881.

———. "Capt. Brown Not Insane." *Douglass' Monthly*. (November 1859): 1.

———. "The Colonization Revival." In *The Frederick Douglass Papers*, ed. John W. Blassingame and John R. McKivigan. Vol. 2. New Haven: Yale University Press, 1992.

———. "Did John Brown Fail?: An Address Delivered in Harpers Ferry, West Virginia, on 30 May 1881." In *The Frederick Douglass Papers*, ed. John W. Blassingame and John R. McKivigan. Vol. 5. New Haven: Yale University Press, 1992.

———. "John Brown's Raid on Harpers Ferry." In *Frederick Douglass: The Narrative and Selected Writings*, ed. Michael Meyer. New York: Modern Library, 1984.

———. "Letter from Frederick Douglass." *Liberator* [Boston], 11 November 1859, p. 1.

———. "Letter from Frederick Douglass." 31 October 1859. *Douglass' Monthly* (November 1859): 163.

———. Letter to C.W. Slack, Esqr. 28 October [1859]. American Antiquarian Society, Worcester. 1.

———. *The Life and Times of Frederick Douglass*. 1892. In *The Oxford Frederick Douglass Reader*, ed. William L. Andrews. New York: Oxford University Press, 1996.

———. *Narrative of the Life of Frederick Douglass, an American Slave, Written by Himself*. 1845. In *The Oxford Frederick Douglass Reader*, ed. William L. Andrews. New York: Oxford University Press, 1996.

———. "To Maria Webb." November 30, 1859. *Admiration & Ambivalence: Frederick Douglass and John Brown*. New York: Gilder Lehrman, 2005.

———. "To My American Readers and Friends." *Douglass' Monthly* (November 1859): 162–163.

———. "We Are in the Midst of a Moral Revolution." In *The Frederick Douglass Papers*, ed. John W. Blassingame and John R. McKivigan. Vol. 2. New Haven: Yale University Press, 1992.

———. "What to the Slave Is the Fourth of July?" 1852. In *The Oxford Frederick Douglass Reader*, ed. William L. Andrews. New York: Oxford University Press, 1996.

Doyle, Mahala. Letter to Amos A. Lawrence. 26 May 1885. John Brown Collection, Massachusetts Historical Society, Boston. 1–2. Courtesy of the Massachusetts Historical Society.

Du Bois, W.E.B. *John Brown*. 1909. Reprint, New York: Sharpe, 1997.

Edelstein, Tilden G. *Strange Enthusiasm: A Life of Thomas Wentworth Higginson*. New Haven: Yale University Press, 1968.

Emerson, Edward Waldo. *Emerson in Concord: A Memoir Written for the "Social Circle" in Concord, Massachusetts*. Boston: Houghton Mifflin; Cambridge: Riverside, 1888.

———. *Henry Thoreau as Remembered by a Young Friend*. Mineola, NY: Dover, 1999.

Emerson, Ellen Tucker. "To Dear Agnes." 4 April 1860. In *The Letters of Ellen Tucker Emerson*, ed. Edith E.W. Gregg. Vol. 1. Kent, OH: Kent State University Press, 1982.

Emerson, Lidian Jackson. *The Selected Letters of Lidian Jackson Emerson*. Edited by Delores Bird Carpenter. Columbia: University of Missouri Press, 1987.

Emerson, Ralph Waldo. "Address on the Emancipation of the Negroes in the British West Indies." In *Emerson's Antislavery Writings*, ed. Len Gougeon and Joel Myerson. New Haven: Yale University Press, 1995.

———. "Address to the Citizens of Concord." In *Emerson's Antislavery Writings*, ed. Len Gougeon and Joel Myerson. New Haven: Yale University Press, 1995.

———. *The Complete Works of Ralph Waldo Emerson*. Essays. 2d Series. Edited by Edward Waldo Emerson. Vol. 3. Boston: Houghton Mifflin, 1903–1904.

———. *The Correspondence of Emerson and Car-*

lyle. Edited by Joseph Slater. New York: Columbia University Press, 1964.

———. "The Fugitive Slave Law." In *Emerson's Antislavery Writings*, ed. Len Gougeon and Joel Myerson. New Haven: Yale University Press, 1995.

———. *The Heart of Emerson's Journals*. Edited by Bliss Perry. New York: Dover, 1958.

———. *The Journals and Miscellaneous Notebooks of Ralph Waldo Emerson*. Edited by Merton Sealts. 16 vols. Cambridge: Belknap-Harvard University Press, 1960–1982.

———. *Journals of Ralph Waldo Emerson*. Edited by Edward Waldo Emerson and Waldo Emerson Forbes. 10 vols. Boston: Houghton Mifflin, 1909–1914.

———. "Kansas Relief Meeting." (10 September 1856.) In *Emerson's Antislavery Writings*, ed. Len Gougeon and Joel Myerson. New Haven: Yale University Press, 1995.

———. Letter to Mr. [Charles] Slack. (31 October [1859].) Worcester: American Antiquarian Society, 1859. 1–3.

———. *The Letters of Ralph Waldo Emerson*. Edited by Ralph L. Rusk. 6 vols. New York: Columbia University Press, 1939.

———. *The Selected Letters of Ralph Waldo Emerson*. Edited by Joel Myerson. New York: Columbia University Press, 1997.

———. "Thoreau." *Walden and Resistance to Civil Government*. Edited by William Rossi. New York: Norton, 1992. Engstrom, Sallee Fox. *The Infinitude of the Private Man: Emerson's Presence in Western New York, 1851–1861*. New York: Lang, 1997.

"Emerson on Courage." *Liberator* [Boston], 18 November 1859, p. 1.

"The Examination of Brown's Dwelling—Northern Abolitionists Apparently Implicated." *New York Times*, 20 October 1859, p. 1.

Featherstonhaugh, Thomas. *John Brown's Men: The Lives of Those Killed at Harper's Ferry*. Harrisburg, PA: Harrisburg Publishing, 1899.

"Fifth Fraternity Lecture." *Liberator* [Boston], 4 November 1859, p. 2.

Finkelman, Paul. "Manufacturing Martyrdom: The Antislavery Response to John Brown's Raid." In *His Soul Goes Marching On: Reponses to John Brown and the Harpers Ferry Raid*, ed. Paul Finkelman. Charlottesville: University Press of Virginia, 1995.

———. Preface. *His Soul Goes Marching On: Responses to John Brown and the Harpers Ferry Raid*. Edited by Paul Finkelman. Charlottesville: University Press of Virginia, 1995.

"Frank Sanborn, Concord Sage, Appeals Fine." 17 November [undated], Newspaper Clippings Relating to F.B. Sanborn, 1860–1973. C PAM 29, Item 71, Concord Free Public Library, Concord, MA: 1.

"Fred. Douglass and Harper's Ferry." *Chambersburg (PA) Valley Spirit*, 16 November 1859, p. 4.

"Frederick Douglass, Independent [New York], 28 February 1895." In *In Memoriam: Frederick Douglass*. 1897. Reprint, Freeport, NY: Books for Libraries, 1971.

"A Free State Settler." *Frederick Douglass Paper*. 4 July 1856: 4.

A Friend [unnamed]. Letter to Gov. Wise. October 1859. John Brown Collection. Massachusetts Historical Society, Boston. 1. Courtesy of the Massachusetts Historical Society.

Gallaher, Ed. Letter to Andrew Hunter, Esq. 19 November 1859. John Brown Collection. Massachusetts Historical Society, Boston. 1–2. Courtesy of the Massachusetts Historical Society.

Garrison, William Lloyd. *The Letters of William Lloyd Garrison, 1850–1860*. Edited by Louis Ruchames. Vol. 4. Cambridge: Belknap Press of Harvard University Press, 1975.

———. "To Our Free Colored Brethren." *Liberator* [Boston], 1 January 1831, p. 3.

Gilbert, David T. *A Walker's Guide to Harpers Ferry West Virginia*. 1983. Reprint, Harpers Ferry: Harpers Ferry Historical Association, 2003.

Glick, Wendell P. "Thoreau and the 'Herald of Freedom.'" *The New England Quarterly* 22, no. 2 (1949): 193–204.

Gougeon, Len. "Abolition, the Emersons and 1837." *The New England Quarterly* 54, no. 3 (1981): 345–364.

———. "Emerson and Abolition: The Silent Years, 1837–1844." *American Literature* 54, no. 4 (1982): 560–575.

———. Historical Background. *Emerson's Antislavery Writings*. Edited by Len Gougeon and Joel Myerson. New Haven: Yale University Press, 1995.

———. "Thoreau and Reform." *The Cambridge Companion to Henry David Thoreau*. Edited by Joel Myerson. New York: Cambridge University Press, 1995.

———. *Virtue's Hero: Emerson, Antislavery, and Reform*. Athens: University of Georgia Press, 1990.

Gregory, James M. *Frederick Douglass the Orator*. 1893. Reprint, Springfield, MA: Willey, 1907.

H.M. Letter. "Concord Stirred by the Spirit of Liberty." *Liberator* 26, no. 3 (16 February 1844).

Halstead, Murat. "The Execution of Capt. Brown, in *The New York Tribune*, 3 December 1859." In

History of John Brown's Raid on Harper's Ferry, Sunday, October 16, 1859, as Published in the NY Tribune and NY Times, Who Had Reporters on the Ground. Des Moines: Watters-Talbott Printing, 1895.

Harding, Walter. *The Days of Henry Thoreau: A Biography.* Princeton: Princeton University Press, 1992.

———. "Thoreau's Reputation." In *The Cambridge Companion to Henry David Thoreau*, ed. Joel Myerson. Cambridge: Cambridge University Press, 1995.

"The Harper's Ferry Insurrection." *Charleston (SC) Mercury*, 19 October 1859. Furman Era Editorials Project. http://history.furman.edu/benson/docs/jbmenu.htm.

"The Harper's Ferry Rebellion." *New York Times*, 20 October 1859, p. 1.

Harrison, C.C. "A Virginia Girl in the First Year of the War." Electronic Text Center. Edited by David Seaman. 2002. Alderman Library, University of Virginia. http://etext.libraryvirginia.edu/modeng/modengH.browse.html (accessed 14 March 2008).

Hedin, Raymond. "Probable Readers, Possible Stories: The Limits of Nineteenth-Century Black Narrative." In *Readers in History: Nineteenth-Century American Literature and the Contexts of Response*, ed. James L. Machor. Baltimore: Johns Hopkins University Press, 1993.

Higginson, [Laura Storrow]. Letter to "Dear Son" [Thomas Wentworth Higginson]. 1 June 1854. Ms.B.1.22(17). Boston Public Library Rare Books and Manuscripts, Boston. 1–3. Boston Public Library/Rare Books Department. Courtesy of the Trustees.

———. Letter to T.W.H. 9 June 1854. Boston Public Library Rare Books and Manuscripts, Boston. 1–2. Boston Public Library/Rare Books Department. Courtesy of the Trustees.

Higginson, Mary Thacher. *Thomas Wentworth Higginson: The Story of His Life.* 1914. Port Washington, NY: Kennikat, 1971.

Higginson, Thomas Wentworth. "The American Lecture System." In *Living Age*. Fourth series, vol. 9. April–June 1868. Boston: Littell and Gay.

———. *Army Life in a Black Regiment.* 1869. Reprint, New York: Norton, 1984.

———. "Attempted Rescue of Burns." *Liberator* [Boston], 24 Aug. 1855, p. 134.

———. Burns Case Narrative. Incomplete ms. Boston Public Library Rare Books and Manuscripts, Boston. 1–4. Boston Public Library/Rare Books Department. Courtesy of the Trustees.

———. Check dated 11 January 1860. Ms.E.5.1 pt. 2 p. 155 (in folder with Le Barnes letter dated 11 January 1860). Boston Public Library Rare Books and Manuscripts, Boston. 1. Boston Public Library/Rare Books Department. Courtesy of the Trustees.

———. *Cheerful Yesterdays.* Boston: Houghton Mifflin, 1898.

———. *Circular with Personal Note by TWH.* 2 November 1859. Ms.E 5.1 pt. 1 p 71. Boston Public Library Rare Books and Manuscripts. 1. Boston Public Library/Rare Books Department. Courtesy of the Trustees.

———. *Contemporaries.* Boston: Houghton Mifflin, 1899.

———. "Emily Dickinson." In *Magnificent Activist*, ed. Howard N. Meyer. New York: Da Capo, 2000.

———. Letter to "Darling Mother." 31 May [1854] 10 P.M. Ms.B.1.22 (16). Boston Public Library Rare Books and Manuscripts, Boston. 1–4. Boston Public Library/Rare Books Department. Courtesy of the Trustees.

———. Letter to "Dear Brother." 30 May 1854. ts. Dana Family Papers, Massachusetts Historical Society. Boston. 1. Courtesy of the Massachusetts Historical Society.

———. Letter to "Dear Friend." [F.B. Sanborn]. 17 November 1859. Ms.E.5.1pt.1p.108. Boston Public Library Rare Books and Manuscripts. 1–2. Boston Public Library/Rare Books Department. Courtesy of the Trustees.

———. Letter to "Dear Mrs. Chapman." 30 November 1854. Ms.A. 9.2.28 p. 34. Boston Public Library Rare Books and Manuscripts, Boston. 1–4. Boston Public Library/Rare Books Department. Courtesy of the Trustees.

———. Letter to "Dear Sir" [unnamed—Lysander Spooner]. 28 November 1859. Ms.A.8.1p.27. Boston Public Library Rare Books and Manuscripts, Boston. 1–3. Boston Public Library/Rare Books Department. Courtesy of the Trustees.

———. Letter to "Dearest Mother." 29 May 1854. Ms.B.1.22 (7). Boston Public Library Rare Books and Manuscripts, Boston. 1–6. Boston Public Library/Rare Books Department. Courtesy of the Trustees.

———. Letter to "Dearest Mother." 1 June [1854]. Ms.B.1.22 (19). Boston Public Library Rare Books and Manuscripts, Boston. 1–3. Boston Public Library/Rare Books Department. Courtesy of the Trustees.

———. Letter to Dearest Mother. 11 A.M. (n.d.) Ms.B.122 (28). Boston Public Library Rare Books and Manuscripts, Boston. 1–2. Boston Public Library/Rare Books Department. Courtesy of the Trustees.

_____. Letter to Dr. S.G. Howe [not sent]. 15 November 1859. Ms.E.5.1 pt. 1. p. 96. Boston Public Library Rare Books and Manuscripts. 4. Boston Public Library/Rare Books Department. Courtesy of the Trustees.

_____. Letter to Jason Brown. 7 May 1858. Ms.E.5.1. pt. 1 p. 18. Thomas Wentworth Higginson Papers. Boston Public Library Rare Books and Manuscripts, Boston. 1–2. Boston Public Library/Rare Books Department. Courtesy of the Trustees.

_____. Letter to John Brown. 18 May 1858. Ms.E.5.1. pt. 1 p. 29. Thomas Wentworth Higginson Papers. Boston Public Library Rare Books and Manuscripts, Boston. 1. Boston Public Library/Rare Books Department. Courtesy of the Trustees.

_____. Letter to John Brown. 29 October 1858. Thomas Wentworth Higginson Papers. Boston Public Library Rare Books and Manuscripts, Boston. 1–2. Boston Public Library/Rare Books Department. Courtesy of the Trustees.

_____. Letter to John Brown. 1 May 1859. Ms.E.5.1pt.1.p.51. Thomas Wentworth Higginson Papers. Boston Public Library Rare Books and Manuscripts, Boston. 1–2. Boston Public Library/Rare Books Department. Courtesy of the Trustees.

_____. Letter to N. Hawkins [John Brown]. 8 February 1858. Ms.E.5.1.pt.1p.5. Thomas Wentworth Higginson Papers. Boston Public Library Rare Books and Manuscripts, Boston. 1. Boston Public Library/Rare Books Department. Courtesy of the Trustees.

_____. Letter to Richard Henry Dana. 29 May 1854. Dana Family Papers. Massachusetts Historical Society, Boston. 1–2. Courtesy of the Massachusetts Historical Society.

_____. Letter to Theodore Parker. 18 May 1858. Ms.E.5.1pt. 1 p. 28. Thomas Wentworth Higginson Papers. Boston Public Library Rare Books and Manuscripts, Boston. 1–3. Boston Public Library/Rare Books Department. Courtesy of the Trustees.

_____. Letter to [Unnamed]. 1 June 1858. Thomas Wentworth Higginson Papers. Boston Public Library Rare Books and Manuscripts, Boston. 1–2. Boston Public Library/Rare Books Department. Courtesy of the Trustees.

_____. *Letters and Journals of Thomas Wentworth Higginson, 1846–1906*. Edited by Mary Thacher Higginson. Boston: Houghton Mifflin, 1921.

_____. "Lydia Maria Child." In *Contemporaries*. Boston: Houghton Mifflin, 1899.

_____. *The Magnificent Activist: The Writings of Thomas Wentworth Higginson (1823–1911)*. Edited by Howard N. Meyer. New York: Da Capo, 2000.

_____. *Man Shall Not Live by Bread Alone: A Thanksgiving Sermon Preached in Newburyport, November 30, 1848*. 2nd ed. Boston: Crosby and Nichols, 1848.

_____. *Massachusetts in Mourning: A Sermon Preached in Worcester on Sunday, June 4, 1854, by Thomas Wentworth Higginson*. Boston: James Munroe, 1854.

_____. *Mr. Higginson's Address to the Voters of the Third Congressional District of Massachusetts*. Lowell, MA: C.L. Knapp, 1850. Boston Public Library Rare Books and Manuscripts, Boston. Boston Public Library/Rare Books Department. Courtesy of the Trustees.

_____. Note dated November 14 appended to letter from J.W. Le Barnes to "Dr. Sir" [T.W.H.]. 15 November 1859. Ms.E.5.1.pt.1p.95. Boston Public Library Rare Books and Manuscripts, Boston. 1. Boston Public Library/Rare Books Department. Courtesy of the Trustees.

_____. *Part of a Man's Life*. Boston: Houghton Mifflin, 1905.

_____. "Review of *Letters from New-York*." *Present* Vol. 1 (1843).

_____. Telegram to L. Higginson. 10 June 1854. Boston Public Library Rare Books and Manuscripts, Boston. 1. Boston Public Library/Rare Books Department. Courtesy of the Trustees.

_____. "Thoreau." In *Short Studies of American Authors*. 1880. Reprint, Norwood, PA: Norwood, 1978.

_____. "To Ralph Waldo Emerson." 20 February 1863. In *The Complete Civil War Journal and Selected Letters of Thomas Wentworth Higginson*, ed, Christopher Looby. Chicago: University of Chicago Press, 2000.

_____. "T.W.H. to J.G. Whittier." 3 August 1848. In *Whittier Correspondence from the Oak Knoll Collections, 1830–1892*, ed. John Albree. Salem, MA: Essex Book and Print Club, 1911.

Hinton, R[ichard] J[osiah]. Letter to "Dear Sir" [T.W.H.]. 13 December 1859. Ms.E.5.1.pt.2p. 136. Boston Public Library Rare Books and Manuscripts, Boston. 1–2. Boston Public Library/Rare Books Department. Courtesy of the Trustees.

_____. Letter to "Dear Sir" [T.W.H.]. 27 December 1859. Ms.E.5.1.pt.2p.150. Boston Public Library Rare Books and Manuscripts, Boston. 1–3. Boston Public Library/Rare Books Department. Courtesy of the Trustees.

Holland, Frederic May. *Frederick Douglass: The Colored Orator*. Rev. ed. 1891. Reprint, New York: Haskell, 1969.

Howe, Julia Ward. *Reminiscences, 1819–1899.* 1899. Reprint, New York: Negro University Press, 1969.

Howe, Samuel Gridley. "To Horace Mann." June 18, 1854. In *Letters and Journals of Samuel Gridley Howe,* ed. Laura E. Richards. Vol. 2. 1909. Reprint, New York: AMS, 1973.

In Memoriam: Frederick Douglass. 1897. Freeport, NY: Books for Libraries, 1971.

Indianapolis Locomotive [Democratic], 22 October 1859. Furman Secession Era Editorials Project. "John Brown's Raid on Harper's Ferry." (October-December 1859). http://history.furman.edu/benson/docs/jbmenu/htm.

"The Insurrection." *Charleston (SC) Mercury,* 21 October 1859. Furman Secession Era Editorials Project. http://history.furman.edu/benson/docs/jbmenu.htm.

"The 'Irrepressible Conflict.'" *Nashville Tennessee Banner and Nashville Whig* [opposition], 25 October 1859. Furman Secession Era Editorials Project. http:// history.furman.edu/benson/docs/jbmenu.htm.

Jackson, Francis. Letter to T.W. Higginson. 6 December 1859. Boston Public Library Rare Books and Manuscripts, Boston. 1. Boston Public Library/Rare Books Department. Courtesy of the Trustees.

Karcher, Carolyn, editor. *A Lydia Maria Child Reader.* Durham, N.C.: Duke University Press, 1997.

Keyes, John Shepard. Autobiography. ms. A45, 167. John Shepard Keyes Papers. Concord: Concord Free Public Library. Courtesy Concord Free Public Library.

Langston, Charles H. "Charles H. Langston." In *Blacks on John Brown,* ed. Benjamin Quarles. Urbana: University of Illinois Press, 1972.

"The Last Concord Fight," *Boston Herald,* 5 April 1860, p. 1. CFPL C. PAM 29 Item 71. Clippings Related to F.B. Sanborn, 1860–1973.

Lawrence, Sam'l. Letter to Charles Hovey. 30 October 1874. ts. John Brown Papers. Massachusetts Historical Society, Boston.

Le Barnes, J.W. Cable to Rev. T.W. Higginson. 28 November 1859. Ms.E.5.1.pt.2p124. Boston Public Library Rare Books and Manuscripts, Boston. 1. Boston Public Library/Rare Books Department. Courtesy of the Trustees.

———. Letter to "Dr. Sir" [T.W.H.]. 15 November 1859. Ms.E.5.1.pt.1 p.95. Boston Public Library Rare Books and Manuscripts, Boston. 1–3. Boston Public Library/Rare Books Department. Courtesy of the Trustees.

———. Letter to "Dr. Sir" [T.W.H.]. 22 November 1859. Ms.E.5.1.pt.2p.118. Boston Public Library Rare Books and Manuscripts, Boston. 1–8. Boston Public Library/Rare Books Department. Courtesy of the Trustees.

———. Letter to Dear Sir [T.W.H.]. 27 November 1859. Ms.E.5.1pt.2p.123. Boston Public Library Rare Books and Manuscripts, Boston. 1–2. Boston Public Library/Rare Books Department. Courtesy of the Trustees.

"Letter from Kansas." *Frederick Douglass Paper,* 4 July 1856, p. 4.

Littlefield, Daniel C. "Blacks, John Brown, and a Theory of Manhood." In *His Soul Goes Marching On: Responses to John Brown and the Harpers Ferry Raid,* ed. Paul Finkelman. Charlottesville: University Press of Virginia, 1995.

Ludlow, Rev. Mr. "Annual Meeting of the State Society." *Liberator* 5 (November 1836): 178.

Magdol, Edward. *The Antislavery Rank and File: A Social Profile of the Abolitionist's Constituency.* New York: Greenwood, 1986.

Marble, Annie Russell. *Thoreau: His Home, Friends and Books.* 1902. Reprint, New York: AMS, 1969.

Martin, J.S. "Speech of Rev. J.S. Martin." In *Blacks on John Brown,* ed. Benjamin Quarles. Urbana: University of Illinois Press, 1972.

Martineau, Harriet. *The Martyr Age of the United States.* 1839. Reprint, New York: Arno & The New York Times, 1969.

Mason, M.J.C. "Letter of Mrs. Mason." 11 November 1859. In *Correspondence between Lydia Maria Child and Gov. Wise and Mrs. Mason, of Virginia.* Boston: American Anti-Slavery Society, 1860.

Mauzy, George. "Letter to Mr. & Mrs. James Burton." 3 December 1859. Edited by David T. Gilbert. 2 June 2005. Harpers Ferry National Historical Park. 1 September 2008. www.nps.gov/archive/hafe/mauzy.htm.

Mauzy, M.E. "Letter to Eugenia Burton." 17 October 1859. Edited by David T. Gilbert. 2 June 2005. Harpers Ferry National Historical Park. 1 September 2008. www.nps.gov/archive/hafe/mauzy.htm.

May, Samuel J. "Antislavery Conflict." *Some Recollections of Our Antislavery Conflict.* 1869. Reprint, Boston: Fields, Osgood; New York: Arno, 1968.

———. "Mrs. L. Maria Child." In *Some Recollections of Our Antislavery Conflict.* 1869. Reprint, Boston: Fields, Osgood; New York: Arno, 1968.

McFeely, William S. *Frederick Douglass.* New York: Norton, 1991.

McKim, J.M. Letter to "Dear Sir" [T.W.H.]. 28 October 1859. Ms.E.5.1 pt. 1 p. 69. Boston Public Library Rare Books and Manuscripts,

Boston. 1–4. Boston Public Library/Rare Books Department. Courtesy of the Trustees.

McKivigan, John R. "His Soul Goes Marching On: The Story of John Brown's Followers after the Harpers Ferry Raid." In *Antislavery Violence: Sectional, Racial, and Cultural Conflict in Antebellum America*, ed. John R. McKivigan and Stanley Harrold. Knoxville: University of Tennessee Press, 1999.

Merritt, John W. [illegible]. Letter to "His Exy Gov. Wise." 16 November 1859. John Brown Collection, Massachusetts Historical Society, Boston. 1. Courtesy of the Massachusetts Historical Society.

Meyer, Michael. "Thoreau and Black Emigration." *American Literature* 53, no. 3 (1981): 380–396.

_____. "Thoreau's Rescue of John Brown from History." In *Studies in the American Renaissance*. Edited by Joel Myerson. Boston: Twayne, 1980.

Mills, Bruce. "Lydia Maria Child and the Endings to Harriet Jacobs's *Incidents in the Life of a Slave Girl*." *American Literature* 64, no. 2 (1992): 255–72.

Mott, Wesley T. "Emerson and the New Bedford Affair in Boston Newspapers." *Emerson Society Papers*. 3, no. 1 (1992): 3–4.

"Murderers, Thieves, and Blacklegs Employed by Marshal Freeman!!" [1854] broadside, Massachusetts Historical Society, Boston. 1.

Nevins, Allan. *The Emergence of Lincoln*. Vol. 2. New York: Scribner's, 1950.

"News of the Day." *New York Times*, 19 October 1859, p. 4.

"Northern Sentiment." *Staunton (VA) Spectator*, 22 November 1859, p. 2.

Oates, Stephen B. *Our Fiery Trial: Abraham Lincoln, John Brown, and the Civil War Era*. Amherst: University of Massachusetts Press, 1979.

_____. *To Purge This Land with Blood: A Biography of John Brown*. New York: Harper, 1970.

Ostrander, Gilman M. "Emerson, Thoreau, and John Brown." In *The Mississippi Valley Historical Review* 39, no. 4 (1953): 713–26.

Petrulionis, Sandra Harbert. "Swelling That Great Tide of Humanity." (The Concord, Massachusetts, Female Anti-Slavery Society) *The New England Quarterly* 74, no. 3 (2001): 385–418.

Phillips, Wendell. Appendix. "Remarks of Wendell Phillips at the Funeral of Lydia Maria Child, October 23, 1880." In *Letters of Lydia Maria Child*. 1883. Reprint, New York: Arno & The New York Times, 1969.

_____. "Burial of John Brown." In *Speeches, Lectures, and Letters*. 1884. Reprint, New York: Negro University Press, 1968.

Poe, Edgar Allan. "The Literati of New York City." In *Godey's Lady's Book*, September 1846.

_____. "Review of *Philothea*." *Southern Literary Messenger* 2 (September 1836): 662.

Pollard, John A. *John Greenleaf Whittier: Friend of Man*. Boston: Houghton Mifflin, 1949.

Pratt, Minot. "To Mrs. Minot Pratt." October 30, 1859. In *Thoreau as Seen by His Contemporaries*, ed. Walter Harding. New York: Dover, 1989.

Quarles, Benjamin. *Allies for Freedom: Blacks and John Brown*. New York: Oxford University Press, 1974.

_____. *Black Abolitionists*. London: Oxford University Press, 1969.

_____. *Black Mosaic: Essays in Afro-American History and Historiography*. Amherst: University of Massachusetts Press, 1988.

_____. *The Negro in the Making of America*. New York: Simon, 1964.

Redpath, James. *The Public Life of Capt. John Brown*. Boston: Thayer and Eldridge, 1860.

Renehan, Edward J., Jr. *The Secret Six: The True Tale of the Men Who Conspired with John Brown*. New York: Crown, 1995.

Reynolds, David S. *John Brown Abolitionist: The Man Who Killed Slavery, Sparked the Civil War, and Seeded Civil Rights*. New York: Knopf, 2005.

Richardson, Robert D., Jr. *Emerson: The Mind on Fire*. Berkeley: University of California Press, 1995.

Ripley, C. Peter. Introduction. *The Black Abolitionist Papers*. Edited by C. Peter Ripley. Vol. 3. Chapel Hill: University of North Carolina Press, 1991.

Rosenblum, Nancy L. Introduction. *Thoreau: Political Writings*, by Henry David Thoreau. Edited by Rosenblum. Cambridge: Cambridge University Press, 1996.

Rossbach, Jeffrey. *Ambivalent Conspirators: John Brown, The Secret Six, and a Theory of Slave Violence*. Philadelphia: University of Pennsylvania Press, 1982.

Rowe, John Carlos. *At Emerson's Tomb: The Politics of Classic American Literature*. New York: Columbia University Press, 1997.

Ruchames, Louis. Introduction. *John Brown: The Making of a Revolutionary*. New York: Grossett, 1971.

Sanborn, F.B. "Henry David Thoreau." In *Thoreau As Seen by His Contemporaries*, ed. Walter Harding. New York: Dover, 1960.

_____. Letter to Theodore Parker. 14 November

1859. Franklin Benjamin Sanborn Papers, Concord Free Public Library, Concord, MA. 1–4. Courtesy Concord Free Public Library.

———. Letter to "Dear Friend" [Theodore Parker]. 22 October 1859. Folder 43. Correspondent: Theodore Parker, Concord Free Public Library, Concord, MA. 1–7. Courtesy Concord Free Public Library.

———. Letter to Dear Friend [T.W.H.]. 8 Mar 1858. Ms.E.5.1 pt. 1 p. 11. Thomas Wentworth Higginson Papers. Boston Public Library Rare Books and Manuscripts, Boston. 1–2. Boston Public Library/Rare Books Department. Courtesy of the Trustees.

———. Letter to "Dear Friend" [T.W.H.]. 4 June 1859. ms. Ms.E.5.1 pt. 1 p. 54. Thomas Wentworth Higginson Papers. Boston Public Library Rare Books and Manuscripts, Boston. 1. Boston Public Library/Rare Books Department. Courtesy of the Trustees.

———. Letter to "Dear Friend" [T.W.H.]. 10 November 1859. Boston Public Library Rare Books and Manuscripts, Boston. 1–3. Boston Public Library/Rare Books Department. Courtesy of the Trustees.

———. Letter to "Dear Friend" [T.W.H.]. 13 November 1859. Ms.E.5.1pt.1p.89. Boston Public Library Rare Books and Manuscripts, Boston. 1–4. Boston Public Library/Rare Books Department. Courtesy of the Trustees.

———. Letter to Dear Friend [T.W.H.]. 19 November 1859. Ms.E.5.1pt.1p.108, Boston Public Library Rare Books and Manuscripts, Boston. 1–3. Boston Public Library/Rare Books Department. Courtesy of the Trustees.

———. Letter to "Dear Friend" [T.W. Higginson]. 6 October 1859. Ms.E.5.1 p. 60. Thomas Wentworth Higginson Papers, Boston Public Library Rare Books and Manuscripts, Boston. 1. Boston Public Library/Rare Books Department. Courtesy of the Trustees.

———. Letter to Dear Friend [T.W.H.]. 28 November 1859. ms. Ms.E.5.1.pt.2p. 126. Boston Public Library Rare Books and Manuscripts, Boston. 1–4. Boston Public Library/Rare Books Department. Courtesy of the Trustees.

———. Letter to T.W. Higginson. 25 December 1859. Boston Public Library Rare Books and Manuscripts, Boston. 1–3. Boston Public Library/Rare Books Department. Courtesy of the Trustees.

———. "Mrs. Mary Merrick Brooks and the Anti-Slavery Movement." In *Thoreau, Sanborn, John Brown and Slavery*, ed. Kenneth Walter Cameron. Hartford: Transcendental, 2000.

———. "The Personality of Thoreau." In *Thoreau as Seen by His Contemporaries*, ed. Walter Harding. New York: Dover, 1989.

———. *Recollections of Seventy Years*. 1909. Vol. 1. Reprint, Detroit: Gale, 1967.

Scudder, Townsend. *Concord: American Town*. Boston: Little, 1947.

"Servile Insurrection." *New York Times*, 18 October 1859, p. 1.

Sheridan, Richard. "Charles Henry Langston and the African American Struggle in Kansas." *Kansas History* 22 (1999–2000): 271.

Slack, .W. Letter to "Dear Mr. Higginson." 18 November 1859. Ms.E.5.1 pt. 1 p. 107. 1. Boston Public Library Rare Books and Manuscripts, Boston.

Speer, John. "John Brown: John Speer's Note Referring to, Omitted from His Annual Address before the Society." 18 January 1898. Personal papers, folder 3.09. John Brown Papers, microfilm MS 1246. Kansas State Historical Society.

Spooner, Lysander. Letter to "Dear Sir" [T.W.H.]. 20 November [1859]. Ms.E.5.1pt.1p.110. Boston Public Library Rare Books and Manuscripts, Boston. 1–2. Boston Public Library/Rare Books Department. Courtesy of the Trustees.

Stearns, Frank Preston. "From Sketches from Concord and Appledore (1895)." In *Emerson in His Own Time*, ed. Ronald A. Bosco and Joel Myerson. Iowa City: University of Iowa Press, 2003.

———. *The Life and Public Services of George Luther Stearns*. Edited by James M. McPherson and William Loren Katz. 1907. Reprint, New York: Arno & *The New York Times*, 1969.

Stearns, Geo[rge] L[uther]. Letter to Rev. T.W. Higginson. 1 Apr 1858. Ms.E.5.1 pt. 1 p. 14. Boston Public Library Rare Books and Manuscripts, Boston. 1. Boston Public Library/Rare Books Department. Courtesy of the Trustees.

Sterling, Dorothy. Introduction. *Turning the World Upside Down: The Anti-Slavery Convention of American Women, May 9–12, 1837*. New York: Feminist, 1987.

Thomas, Sandra. "From Slave to Abolitionist Editor." In *Frederick Douglass*. 2001. http://www.history.rochester.edu/class/douglass/part2.html.

Thoreau, Henry David. "After the Death of John Brown." 1860. In *The Major Essays of Henry David Thoreau*, ed. Richard Dillman. Albany: Whitston, 2001.

———. "Civil Disobedience." 1849. In *The Major Essays of Henry David Thoreau*, ed. Richard Dillman. New York: Whitston, 2001.

———. "Journal." In *The Writings of Henry D.*

Thoreau, ed. Bradford Torrey. 12 Vols. Boston: Houghton Mifflin, 1906.

———. "The Last Days of John Brown." 1860. In *The Major Essays of Henry David Thoreau*, ed. Richard Dillman. Albany: Whitston, 2001.

———. Letter to Mr. Charles W. Slack. 1 November 1859. American Antiquarian Society, Worcester. 1.

———. "Paradise to Be Regained." In *The Major Essays of Henry David Thoreau*, ed. Richard Dillman. New York: Whitston, 2001.

———. "A Plea for Captain John Brown." 1860. In *The Major Essays of Henry David Thoreau*, ed. Richard Dillman. Albany: Whitston, 2001.

———. "Slavery in Massachusetts." 1854. In *The Major Essays of Henry David Thoreau*, ed. Richard Dillman. New York: Whitston, 2001.

——— "To Harrison Blake." 26 September 1855. In *The Writings of Henry David Thoreau*. Vol. 6: Familiar Letters. Edited by F.B. Sanborn. 1906. Reprint, New York: AMS, 1968.

———. "To Harrison Blake." 31 October 1859. In *Familiar Letters of Henry David Thoreau*, ed. F.B. Sanborn. Boston: Houghton Mifflin, 1894.

———. *Walden; or, Life in the Woods*. Boston: Ticknor, 1854.

——— [Unsigned]. "Wendell Phillips before the Concord Lyceum." *Liberator* [Boston], 28 March 1845, p. 3.

A Tribute of Respect, Commemorative of the Worth and Sacrifice of John Brown of Ossawatomie Published for the Benefit of the Widows and Families of the Revolutionists of Harper's Ferry. 1859. Boston Public Library Rare Books and Manuscripts, Boston. 1, 5. Boston Public Library/Rare Books Department. Courtesy of the Trustees.

Trodd, Zoe, and John Stauffer, eds. *Meteor of War: The John Brown Story*. Maplecrest, NY: Brandywine, 2004.

"The True Policy." *Chicago Press and Tribune* [Republican], 22 October 1859. Furman Secession Era Editorials Project. http://history.furman.edu/benson/docs/jbmenu/htm.

United States. Cong. Senate. "Journal of the Select Committee into the Invasion of the United States Armory at Harpers Ferry." In *Mass Violence in America: Invasion at Harper's Ferry*, ed. Robert M. Fogelson and Richard E. Rubenstein. 36th Cong., 1st sess. 1860. New York: Arno, 1969.

———. ———. ———. Select Committee on the Harper's Ferry Invasion. "Report of the Select Committee of the Senate Appointed to Inquire into the Late Invasion and Seizure of the Public Property at Harper's Ferry." Submitted to 36th Cong., 1st sess. 1860, by J.M. Mason, committee chairman. Reprinted as "The Mason Report" in *Mass Violence in America: Invasion at Harper's Ferry*, ed. Robert M. Fogelson and Richard E. Rubenstein. New York: Arno & New York Times, 1969.

———. ———. ———. "Views of the Minority to the Mason Report." In *Mass Violence in America: Invasion at Harper's Ferry*, ed. Robert M. Fogelson and Richard E. Rubenstein. 36th Cong., 1st sess. 1860. New York: Arno, 1969.

———. Dept. of Interior. *John Brown's Raid*. Washington: GPO, 1974.

Villard, Oswald Garrison. *John Brown 1800–1859: A Biography Fifty Years After*. 1910. Reprint, New York: Knopf, 1943.

"Va. Correspondent of *Boston Courier*." *Liberator* [Boston], 11 November 1859, p. 1.

"The Virginia Insurrection." *Liberator* [Boston], 21 October 1859, p. 2.

Warren, Robert Penn. *John Brown: The Making of a Martyr*. 1929. Reprint, Nashville: Sanders, 1993.

Wells, Anna Mary. *Dear Preceptor: The Life of Thomas Wentworth Higginson*. Boston: Houghton, 1963.

"Wendell Phillips before the Concord Lyceum." *Liberator* [Boston], 28 March 1845, p.3.

Whittier, John G. Introduction. *Letters of Lydia Maria Child*. 1883. Reprint, New York: Arno & The New York Times, 1969.

"Who's to Blame?" *Liberator* [Boston], 11 November 1859: 1.

Wise, Henry A. Letter to Andrew Hunter, Esq. 6 November 1859. John Brown Collection, Massachusetts Historical Society, Boston. 1. Courtesy of the Massachusetts Historical Society.

———. Letter to Andrew Hunter, Esq. 26 November 1859. John Brown Collection. Massachusetts Historical Society, Boston. 1–2. Courtesy of the Massachusetts Historical Society.

———. Letter to "My Dear Sir." 6 November 1859. John Brown Collection. Massachusetts Historical Society, Boston. 1–3. Courtesy of the Massachusetts Historical Society.

———. "Reply of Gov. Wise." 29 October 1859. In *Correspondence between Lydia Maria Child and Gov. Wise and Mrs. Mason, of Virginia*. Boston: American Anti-Slavery Society, 1860.

Woodward, C. Vann. Introduction. *John Brown: The Making of a Martyr*. 1929. Reprint, Nashville: Sanders, 1993.

Wyatt-Brown, Bertram. "'A Volcano beneath a Mountain of Snow': John Brown and the Problem of Interpretation." In *His Soul Goes Marching On: Responses to John Brown and the Harpers Ferry Raid*, ed. Paul Finkelman. Charlottesville: University Press of Virginia, 1995.

INDEX

Abolitionists 14, 19, 29, 31–33, 35–40, 42, 44, 46–47, 52–55, 66, 68, 70–71, 90, 92, 99, 102, 104, 111–112, 116, 118–119, 121, 123–124, 126–127, 130, 133, 138, 148, 155, 158, 159, 161; *see also* Black Abolitionists
Adams, Pres. John Quincy 37
"Address on the Emancipation of the Negroes in the British West Indies" [1844] (Emerson) 34–35
"Address to the Slaves of the United States of America" (Garnet) 58
Aesthetic Papers 46
Alcott, Amos Bronson 36, 37, 40, 50, 51, 91, 92, 95, 116, 118, 120–122, 136–138, 147, 162, 163
Alcott, Louisa May 5, 73, 76, 121, 151, 162
Allstadt, John 13, 16
American and Foreign Anti-Slavery Reporter 55
American Anti-Slavery Society (AASS) 55, 67, 76, 120, 153
Anderson, Jeremiah 17, 18
Anderson, Osborne 4, 13
Andrew, Gov. John A. 122, 135, 157
Anglo-African 114
Anti-slavery 5, 21, 32, 36, 38–40, 42, 44, 45, 52–57, 64, 66, 69–81, 83–85, 87, 88, 91, 100–102, 104, 112, 114, 119, 122, 124, 136, 143, 145, 155, 159, 161
Anti-Slavery Almanac 55
Anti-Slavery and Temperance Society of the Colored Citizens of Worcester 138
Appeal (David Walker) 58, 68
Appeal in Behalf of That Class of Americans Called Africans 68–71, 77, 83, 141, 161
"Appeal on Behalf of the Cherokees" (Emerson) 33
Army Life in a Black Regiment (Higginson) 157
Atlantic Monthly 90, 158

Auld, Thomas 56
Autumnal Leaves 80
Aves, Thompson 73
Avey, Elijah 139
Avis, John 144

Baltimore & Ohio 13
Baltimore Republican 111
Batchelder, James 94–95, 97–98, 100
Bearse, Captain 92–93
Benét, Stephen Vincent 1
Black Abolitionists 53, 55, 58, 59, 61, 63, 71, 74, 81, 83, 84, 86, 114–116, 133, 138
Black Jack, Battle of 40
Blake, Harrison Gray Otis (H.G.O.) 91, 92, 118
Booth, John Wilkes 139
Boston Artillery 95
Boston Athenaeum 66, 69, 161
Boston Atlas and Daily Bee 119, 120, 125
Boston Courier 131
Boston Daily Journal 111, 119
Boston Evening Transcript 111, 131
Boston Female Anti-Slavery Society (BFASS) 74
Boston Herald 47, 86, 112, 147
"Boston Hymn" (Emerson) 162
Boston Post 79, 122, 137
Boston Transcript 111, 131
Boston Traveler 119
Boston Vigilance Committee 39, 92
Broadsides 48, 93, 96, 134
Brooks, Mary 146
Brooks, Congressman Preston 22, 50, 70, 78
Brown, Frederick 21, 22, 24, 133
Brown, Jason 21–23, 25, 106
Brown, John 1–5, 11–14, 16–25, 29, 40, 42, 43, 49–52, 56, 58–63, 70, 80, 91, 103–133, 135–145, 148, 149, 151, 153–171
Brown, John, Jr. 21, 22, 23, 25, 56, 60, 128, 156
Brown, Lucy Jackson 33

Brown, Mrs. Mary 62, 120, 124, 126, 129, 144
Brown, Oliver 12, 18, 21, 22, 24
Brown, Owen 11, 21–23, 25
Brown, Salmon 21, 22, 24
Brown, Theophilus 91
Brown, Watson 11, 16, 18, 60
Brown, William Wells 85
Buchanan, Pres. James 14, 25, 79, 113
Buffum, Arnold 30
Burleigh, Charles 29
Burns, Anthony 7, 39, 47, 49, 88, 92, 94, 95, 97, 99, 102, 145, 159
Butman, Asa 100, 101, 148

Cambridge, MA 38, 39, 82, 89
Canby, Henry 47, 119
Cape Cod (Thoreau) 157
Carlyle, Thomas 83
Chambersburg, PA 62, 114
Channing, (William) Ellery 91
Channing, Dr. William Ellery 29, 30, 32
Chapman, Maria Weston 101, 143, 155
"The Character of John Brown, now in the clutches of the slaveholder" (Thoreau) 118
Charlestown, WV 14, 122, 128, 132, 139, 142–144, 153, 154, 161
Cherokees 33, 65, 153
Chesnutt, Charles W. 145
Chicago Press and Tribune 112
Child, David Lee 64–66, 71–73, 75, 76, 79, 80
Child, Lydia Maria 2, 3, 5, 6, 63–80, 81, 82, 120, 122–126, 130, 136, 138, 141–143, 145, 148, 149, 151, 155, 159, 161, 162, 164–171; correspondence with Gov. Wise 124, 125
Cincinnati Enquirer 112
"Civil Disobedience" 42, 46, 47, 164
Civil War 1, 2, 78, 79, 149, 151, 153, 161, 163
Clarke, James Freeman 85

Index

"The Clergy and Reform" (Higginson) 83
Cleveland Plain Dealer 115
Clifford, Deborah 64, 73
Collins, John A. 54, 57
Commercial Gazette 73
Commonwealth 47, 90
Compromise of 1850 38, 88
Conant, Mary 64
Concord Female Anti-Slavery Society 32, 35, 42
Concord Freeman 31, 34
Concord Lyceum 36, 44–46
Concord, MA 4, 5, 7, 25, 31–34, 36, 38–43, 45, 46, 50, 51, 73, 87, 91, 102, 106, 116–118, 122, 126, 135–137, 140, 145, 147, 148, 153, 157, 163
Cook, John E. 11, 18, 114
Copeland, John 12, 17
Coppoc, Barclay 11
Coppoc, Edwin 14, 16
Correspondence Between Lydia Maria Child and Gov. Wise and Mrs. Mason of Virginia 143
"Courage" (Emerson) 121
Covey, Edward 52, 56, 164

Dana, Richard Henry, Jr. 97, 159
Davis, Jefferson 158
Delaney, Martin R. 58
Devens, U.S. Marshal Charles 88–89
The Dial 83, 87
Dickens, Charles 79
Dickinson, Emily 70, 81, 90, 163
Douglass, Anna 145
Douglass, Charles 153
Douglass, Frederick 2, 3, 5, 6, 19, 20, 25, 36, 39, 45, 52–62, 76, 80–82, 85, 86, 104, 112–116, 118, 119, 145, 148, 149, 151, 153–155, 157, 161–163, 165–171
Douglass, Lewis 153
Douglass' Monthly 114, 115, 130
Doyle, Drury 22
Doyle, John 22
Doyle, Mahala 22
Doyle, William 22
Dred Scott 3
Drew, Thomas 98
Du Bois, W.E.B. 151
Dunbar, Louisa 42

Ellis, Charles Mayo 90
Emancipation Proclamation 162
Emancipator 55
Emerson, Charles 31, 36
Emerson, Edward 33, 36, 38, 118, 120, 121

Emerson, Ellen 91, 146, 153
Emerson, Lidian Jackson 31–34, 39, 42, 91, 121, 137, 153
Emerson, Mary Moody 29
Emerson, Ralph Waldo 2–6, 25, 29–44, 47, 49, 50, 52, 59, 63, 65, 66, 70, 72, 75–77, 81–84, 86–88, 91, 116–118, 120–122, 124, 130, 135–138, 140–142, 145–149, 151, 153, 157, 162, 163, 165–171
Emerson, William (Emerson's brother) 39, 116
Emerson, the Rev. William (Emerson's father) 29
Essex County Anti-Slavery Society 84
Essex County Free Soil Convention 85
Evenings in New England (Child) 65, 66

Faneuil Hall 37, 54, 56, 92, 93, 138, 161
Fields, James 158
First Parish Church [Concord] 44, 163
The First Settlers of New England (Child) 65
Forbes, Col. Hugh 25, 62, 106, 107, 159
Forbes, Sarah 120
Forten, James 53, 71
Framingham, MA 47, 49
Francis, Convers 63, 64, 72, 73, 75, 77, 78, 83
Frederick Douglass' Paper 56, 60
Frederick Herald [Maryland] 112
Free Church [Worcester] 91, 98
Free Soil 23, 85, 90
Free State 24, 39, 60, 79, 103, 104
The Freedmen's Book (Child) 155
Fremont, John 79
The Frugal Housewife (Child) 63, 65, 70, 75, 82
Fugitive Slave Law 3, 29, 38, 46, 47, 57, 60, 88, 98, 99, 101, 161
Fugitive Slave Law Speech [1851] (Emerson) 38–39
Fugitive Slave Law Speech [1854] (Emerson) 39
Fugitive Slaves 37, 38, 42, 46, 49, 54–56, 73, 88–90, 92, 93, 95, 105, 127, 142

Gallaher, Ed 133
Gandhi, Mahatma 46, 164
Garfield, Pres. James 153
Garnet, the Rev. Henry Highland 58, 59, 61

Garrison, William Lloyd 3, 31, 47, 52–54, 57, 66–68, 75, 80, 89, 109, 112, 138, 162
Gault House Saloon 18
Geary, Gov. John W. 24
Gloucester, the Rev. James 62
Gougeon, Len 5, 36
Greeley, Horace 36, 142
Green, Lt. Israel 18
Green, Shields 14, 62
Griffith, Mattie 121
Grimes, the Rev. Leonard A. 90, 138
Grimke, Angelina 32
Grimke, Sarah 32

Haiti 65
Hale, Edward Everett 69
Hale, S.J. 73
Halstead, Murat 139
Harding, Walter 4, 42, 49
Harpers Ferry 1, 3, 4, 11–14, 19, 21, 25, 50, 51, 61–63, 80, 104, 106, 108–112, 114–116, 120–122, 124–127, 129, 131–133, 135, 137, 139–141, 145, 149, 151, 153, 158–164
Harpers Ferry National Park 1
Harris, James 22
Harvard University 30, 38, 63, 82, 83
Hawes, Charlotte 65
Hawthorne, Nathaniel 35
Hayden, Lewis 89, 93, 100
Hayes, Pres. Rutherford B. 153
Hazlett, Albert 144, 145, 161
Hedin, Raymond 56
Herald of Freedom 43–44
"Heroism" (Emerson) 33
Higginson, Louisa Storrow 98, 99, 126
Higginson, Mary Channing 84, 85, 87, 88, 102
Higginson, Mary Thacher 161
Higginson, Thomas Wentworth 2, 3, 5, 6, 20, 29, 39, 42, 53, 64, 65, 70, 75, 80, 81–108, 117, 118, 120, 125–130, 135, 139–141, 143–145, 147–149, 151, 153, 155–159, 161–163, 165–171
Hildreth, Richard 54
Hinton, Richard Josiah 129, 144, 148
Hoar, Judge Ebeneezer Rockwood 40, 146, 157
Hoar, Elizabeth 36
Hoar, Judge Samuel 34, 36
Hobomok 63, 64, 67
Holland, Frederic May 145
Hopper, Isaac T. 55
Hosmer, Rufus 147
Howe, Julia Ward 40, 88, 151, 162

Index

Howe, Dr. Samuel Gridley 89, 92, 93, 97, 104–106, 108, 120, 126–129, 140, 155, 157, 159
Hoyt, George H. 126
Huffmaster, Mrs. 25
Hughes, Langston 115
Hunter, Andrew (Charlestown D.A.) 113, 133, 135, 153, 154

Incidents in the Life of a Slave Girl (Jacobs) 155, 164
Isaac T. Hopper: A True Life (Child) 77

Jackson, the Rev. A.W. 157
Jackson, Francis 95, 140
Jackson, Lidian *see* Emerson, Lidian Jackson
Jacobs, Harriet 155, 164
"John Brown and the Slaveholders' Insurrection" (Douglass) 145
"John Brown's Body" 151, 153, 161
Jumbo and Zairee (Child) 66
The Juvenile Miscellany (Child) 65, 69, 70, 82

Kagi, John 12, 14, 16, 17, 62
Kansas 3, 14, 20, 21, 25, 39, 40, 49–51, 57, 59, 60, 78–80, 102–104, 107–111, 120, 124, 144, 155, 156
"The Kansas Emigrants" (Child) 79
Kansas-Nebraska Act 20
Kemp, Walter 16
Kennedy, Pres. John F. 1
Kennedy, Sen. Ted 1
Kennedy Farmhouse 5, 13, 25
Keyes, John Shepard 136, 137, 147
King, Martin Luther, Jr. 46, 164

Langston, Charles H. 58, 115, 138, 139
Lawrence, Samuel 20
Lawrence, K[ansas] T[erritory] 21, 40, 102
League of Gileadites 60
Leary, Lewis Sherrard 13, 14, 17
Leaves of Grass (Whitman) 81
Le Barnes, John W. 127, 128, 144
Lee, Colonel Robert E. 16
Leeman, William 16, 17
Letters from New York (Child) 63, 76, 77, 83, 155
Liberator 3, 31, 33, 36, 44, 45, 47, 49, 53, 55, 68, 70, 89, 101, 111, 112, 117, 119–121, 131, 148, 155
Liberty Bell 55

Life and Times of Frederick Douglass (Douglass) 57, 59, 153
Lincoln, Abraham 149, 151, 153, 162
Locomotive (Indianapolis) 112
Loguen, the Rev. Jermain W. 58–59
Loring, Lucy 79
Lovejoy, Elijah 29, 32, 33
Lowell, James Russell 41, 157
Lyceum, Concord *see* Concord Lyceum

The Maine Woods (Thoreau) 157
"Man Shall Not Live by Bread Alone" (Higginson) 85–86
Martin, J. Sella 114, 115, 130
Martineau, Harriet 69, 71
Martinsburg, WV 14
Martinsburg Journal 1
Marvell, Andrew 137
Mason, Sen. James Murray (Va.) 141, 161
Mason, Margaretta 5, 125, 141–143, 161
Mason Report 161
Massachusetts Anti-Slavery Society 36, 54, 103, 148
"Massachusetts in Mourning" (Higginson) 98
Massachusetts Journal 65
Massachusetts State Kansas Committee 104, 107
Mauzy, George 14, 133, 139
Mauzy, Mary 131
May, Samuel Joseph 30, 53, 68, 76, 114, 143
McKim, J.M. 126
Memoirs of Archy Moore (Hildreth) 54
Mercury [Charleston, SC] 112
Merriam, Francis J. 11, 18, 108, 140
Mexican War 36, 37, 45
Meyer, Michael 43, 50
Milwaukee Free Democrat 140
Missouri 23, 25, 60, 103
Montgomery, Capt. James 144, 156, 161
"Morals" (Emerson) 141
The Mother's Book (Child) 66, 70
Mott, Lucretia 76

Narrative of James Williams 54
Narrative of the Life of Frederick Douglass (Douglass) 52, 55, 56, 163
National Anti-Slavery Standard 49, 55, 63, 75, 76
National Intelligencer 131
Nature (Emerson) 30, 72

New Bedford, MA 36, 45, 52–54, 95, 138
New Bedford Lyceum 36
New England Anti-Slavery Society 66
New Orleans Bulletin 112
New York Commercial Advertiser 74
New York Courier 111
New York Daily Tribune 36, 49, 79, 102, 111, 119, 124, 127, 135, 142
New York Herald 131, 135
New York Journal of Commerce 131
New York Post 111, 133
New York Times 111, 113, 139
New York Tribune 49, 111
Newburyport, MA 84–87, 90–91
Newburyport Union 90
Newby, Dangerfield 14
North American Review 64, 67
North Carolina Standard [Raleigh] 142
North Elba, NY 19, 124, 127, 148, 149
North Star 56, 58, 60

The Oasis (Child) 69, 71
Oates, Stephen B. 4, 132
Osawatomie 24, 56
Osgood, Lucy 78
Osgood, Mary 78

Palfrey, Dr. John G. 39, 77
"Paradise to be Regained" (Thoreau) 43
Parker, Theodore 40, 85, 88, 92, 94, 98, 100, 104–107, 116, 122, 126, 128, 135, 159
Peabody, Elizabeth 46
Philadelphia Evening Bulletin 112
Philadelphia Freeman 76
Phillips, Wendell 7, 31–33, 36, 43–45, 69, 92, 93, 95, 121, 122, 124, 127, 129, 135, 148, 149, 151, 155, 162
Philothea 72–73, 77
Pierce, Pres. Franklin 79
"A Plea for Captain John Brown" (Thoreau) 46, 119, 130
Poe, Edgar Allan 73, 77
Polk, Pres. James K. 84
Pottawatomie, K[ansas] T[erritory] 21–23, 40, 50, 59, 60, 104
Pratt, Minot 118
"Pray Without Ceasing" (Emerson) 30
"The Present Age" (Emerson) 31

INDEX

The Press 20, 47, 49, 50, 55, 111, 112, 116, 117, 119, 120, 124, 127, 131, 133, 135, 142; *see* specific newspapers by title
The Progress of Religious Ideas Through Successive Ages (Child) 77
Pro-slavery 21, 22, 23, 36, 39
The Public Life of Capt. John Brown (Redpath) 151

Recollections of Seventy Years (Sanborn) 149
Redpath, James 3, 120, 136, 141, 143, 151, 158
"The Relation of the Individual to the State" (Thoreau) 46
Remond, Charles Lenox 138
The Republican Banner and Nashville Whig 111
"Resistance to Civil Government" 46; *see also* "Civil Disobedience" (Thoreau)
Rhodes, James Ford 21
Rice, Mary 42
Richmond Enquirer 112, 131
Ricketson, Daniel 118, 121
A Ride Through Kansas (Higginson) 102
The Right Way, the Safe Way 155
Ripley, the Rev. Ezra 29
Rochester, NY 25, 38, 39, 56, 59, 60, 104, 113, 114, 116
Rochester Democrat and American 114
Rogers, Nathaniel P. 43–44, 75
Ross, Chief John 65

Salem Lyceum 31
Sanborn, Franklin Benjamin 3, 36, 40, 42, 49–51, 91, 104–108, 116–118, 121, 122, 126–129, 135–137, 140, 145–149, 158–160, 162–163
Scudder, Townsend 145
Secret Six 106, 126, 127, 157
Sedgwick, Catherine 69
"The Service" (Thoreau) 43
Sewall, S.E. 120, 125
Shadrach [Fred Wilkins] 88–89
Shaw, Robert Gould 153
Shaw, Sarah 78, 79
Shepherd, Haywood 13
A Short History of the Confederate States (Davis) 158
Sims, Thomas 37, 46, 49, 88–90, 159
Slack, Charles 118, 129
Slavery 1, 2, 19, 21, 25, 31, 32, 33–35, 37, 39, 40, 43–47, 51, 52, 54–60, 63, 65, 66, 68, 70, 73–79, 84–86, 88–90, 92, 93, 97–99, 101, 103, 112, 114, 115, 123–125, 127, 130, 131, 138, 141–143, 148, 149, 158, 159, 162, 164
Slavery (W. E. Channing) 29, 70
"Slavery in Massachusetts" (Thoreau) 47, 49, 119
Smith, Gerritt 19, 105–106, 108, 126, 129, 133, 159
Smith, Isaac *see* Brown, John
Smith, Stephen 58, 61
Soule 144
Spectator [Staunton, VA] 121, 131
"Speech at a Meeting to Aid Brown's Family" (Emerson) 122
Spooner, Lysander 127–128
Springfield Republican 119, 127
Staples, Sam 45, 46, 162
Starry, Dr. John D. 17
Staunton [Virginia] *Spectator* 121, 131
Stearns, Frank Preston 38
Stearns, George Luther 50, 80, 103–108, 122, 126, 128, 137, 140, 158, 159, 162
Stearns, Mary 122
Stevens, Aaron D. 13, 17, 135, 142, 144, 145, 161
Stewart, Maj. Gen. George H. 14
Still, William 58, 61
Storer College 153
Storrow, Thomas 82
Stowe, Harriet Beecher 63
Stowell, Martin 92–94, 98, 101
Stuart, Lt. J.E.B. 16
Sumner, Sen. Charles 22, 36, 50, 70, 77–79, 102

Tales of Oppression 55, 77
Taylor, Stewart 11
Taylor, Pres. Zachary 85
Texas 36, 45
Thomas, Thomas 58
Thompson, Dauphin 18
Thompson, George 71, 72, 145
Thompson, William Henry 12, 16, 17, 21, 22, 24, 102
Thoreau, Cynthia 42, 91
Thoreau, Helen 42, 44, 45, 91
Thoreau, Henry David 2–6, 18, 25, 36, 37, 40, 42–52, 59, 66, 73, 75, 76, 81–83, 87, 90, 91, 102, 116–122, 124, 126, 130, 135–138, 140, 141, 145–149, 151, 157, 158, 162–171; night in jail 37, 45
Thoreau, Jane 42
Thoreau, Maria 42, 45
Thoreau, Sophia 42, 44
Ticknor, George 64
Tidd, Charles 11, 13
Timeline 165–171
"To My American Readers and Friends" (Douglass) 115

Town and Country Club 88
Townsley, James 22
Transcendentalism 34, 37, 42, 63, 72, 83, 163
Turner, Nat 68, 115, 155

Underground Railroad 31, 55, 57–58, 62, 99
Unitarians 2, 3, 29, 30, 40, 70, 75, 81, 84, 85, 100

Valley Spirit [Chambersburg, PA] 114, 131
Van Buren, Pres. Martin 33, 153
Vesey, Denmark 158
Vigilance Committee [Boston] 89
Villard, Oswald 4, 127, 158

Wager House Bar 18
Walden 4, 45
Walden Pond 4, 42, 43, 50, 119
Walker, David 58, 68
Waltham, MA 37, 39
War in Mexico *see* Mexican War
Warren, Robert Penn 151
Washington, Col. Lewis W. 13, 14, 16, 18
Watkins, William J. 115
"We Are in the Midst of a Moral Revolution" (Douglass) 57
Webb, Maria 116
Webster, Sen. Daniel 31, 38, 39, 161
A Week on the Concord and Merrimac Rivers (Thoreau) 87
Weekly Anglo-African 138
Weiner, Theodore 22
"What to the Slave Is the Fourth of July?" (Douglass) 56
Whipple, William 54
Whiting, Anne 145–147
Whiting, Colonel 146
Whitman, Walt 81, 144, 147
Whittier, John Greenleaf 35, 66, 69, 84, 85, 155
Wilkins, Fred (Shadrach) 88
Wilkinson, Allen 22
Wise, Gov. Henry A. 14, 113, 116, 120–125, 127, 130, 133, 135, 139–141, 143, 145, 161
Woman's Anti-Slavery Convention [1837] 74
Worcester, MA 60, 91, 92, 97, 100–102, 106, 108, 118, 120, 126, 127, 129, 135, 138–140, 144, 159
Worcester [MA] *Spy* 99

Yeoman's Gazette 31

www.ingramcontent.com/pod-product-compliance
Ingram Content Group UK Ltd.
Pitfield, Milton Keynes, MK11 3LW, UK
UKHW050526150426
5217IPUK00026B/1822